Contemporary Portugal

Contemporary Portugal.

The Revolution and Its Antecedents

EDITED BY LAWRENCE S. GRAHAM
AND HARRY M. MAKLER

FOREWORD BY JUAN J. LINZ

University of Texas Press, Austin and London

Publication of this book was assisted by
Fundação Calouste Gulbenkian of Lisbon, Portugal

Library of Congress Cataloging in Publication Data

Main entry under title:

Contemporary Portugal.

Includes bibliographical references.
1. Portugal—History—1910–1974. 2. Portugal—History—
1974– I. Graham, Lawrence S. II. Makler, Harry M., 1935–
DP680.C594   946.9′04   78-11213
ISBN 0-292-71047-X
ISBN 0-292-71048-8 pbk.

Contents

Foreword

Social scientists and even historians of contemporary Europe have shown a consistent bias in focusing their attention on the great nations, neglecting the smaller countries. Only recently the project on the smaller European democracies initiated by Hans Daalder, Robert Dahl, Stein Rokkan, and Val Lorwin has tried to correct that imbalance. Now the reader has in hand a book that tries to do the same for one of the smaller nondemocratic countries of southern Europe, which fortunately has now become one of the smaller democracies. Our image of nondemocratic polities in Europe has been shaped by the vast and thorough literature on Nazi Germany, the not so vast or impressive but still important work on fascist Italy, and some research on Franco's Spain. Portugal was left largely to more or less competent journalistic accounts, generally favorable to Salazar, or to voices of the opposition to the Estado Novo. This work and other writings of the authors represented in it are a first step to include Portugal in comparative research on themes central to the understanding of European and world politics. Comparative social science is confronted with the difficulty that the number of cases of micropolitical and social phenomena is limited, but that limited universe is even further reduced by our neglect of phenomena that can be conceptualized in the same generalized terms and middle-range theories. We shall not make progress in understanding issues like totalitarianism and authoritarianism, the role of fascist movements, the nature of corporatism and bureaucratic authoritarianism, the importance of cultural tradition versus diffusion in the success of political ideologies, the role of the military in nondemocratic regimes and their crises, the transition from induced mass apathy to mass mobilization, or the emergence of party systems, to mention just a few, until we study them in a larger number of countries, including the smaller countries of Europe. A solid empirical and monographic research on a larger number of countries will allow the generalists and the theorists to avoid the pitfall of building their efforts on a single central and well-studied case, for example, fascist Italy, rather than considering Italy to be one more case with its distinctive characteristics. Certainly, the debate on corporatism in this volume is an important contribution to a theme of significance not only to the study of Portugal. It should also be noted that a number of the scholars represented in this debate have worked on Latin American politics. This is no accident and reflects the need to consider southern Europe, particularly the countries of the Iberian peninsula, in a broader framework.

Portugal is one more instance of a pattern of social and economic development common to the periphery of advanced industrial or post-industrial societies—a pattern that extends across a variety of political systems from Bulgaria through the south of Europe and even across the Atlantic to the shores of Acapulco. All those countries share the advantage of being close to the richer industrial countries that consume their products, particularly those of their agriculture and increasingly those of their industries. Almost all of them have benefited from the possibility of sending their surplus labor to work abroad and from the remittances of those new proletarians in the advanced countries. Their geographic location and climate have attracted millions of tourists and with them the development of a tertiary sector that has allowed them to compensate for the weakness of their balance of payments. In addition, their relatively modern infrastructure, compared to most of the third world, and their periods of political stability, achieved by coercion or consensus, have attracted foreign investors and accelerated indigenous economic development. Those changes have had different incidence from country to country in both time and intensity—maximum in Italy, less so and later in Portugal—but in all of them have altered fundamentally the social structure, most concretely reducing the absolute and relative weight of the population active in agriculture. The gigantic changes in rural society, the disruption of peasant life, and the transfer of men and women from rural settings to growing metropoles and to the labor market in central and western Europe, or in the case of Mexico to the American Southwest, raise the questions of central interest to anthropologists on the one side and sociologists on the other and have far-reaching political implications. All those changes have their positive side but no one studying them can ignore the human costs, the social discontinuities that go with them, and the other consequences that are not always positive for social stability. It is natural that the issues connected with the theory of *dependencia* formulated in the context of Latin American societies should also enter the intellectual discourse about southern European countries.

The impact of decolonization on both the society and the national consciousness has been central to the history of western Europe since Spain lost its colonies in the nineteenth century. Let us not forget that Spanish liberalism found some of its most active supporters in the first half of the nineteenth century among officers unwilling to fight for the overseas empire (the Riego *pronunciamiento* in 1820) and among those returning from the hopeless struggle to retain it (the Ayacuchos and Espartero). Exaggerating the analogy, we could say that the Spanish bourgeois revolution in the nineteenth century was carried largely by military men in an era of decolonization, just as the Movimento das Fôrças Armadas was in 1974 the carrier of a socialist revolution—two revolutions that in many respects went beyond what the social structure of those countries would have produced without that externally created crisis. The problem of reintegration into the society of expellees after defeat has been a recurrent phenomenon since the Greeks left Turkey after World War I. Germans and Finns had to move westward after World War II, Algerians returned to France, and now overseas Portuguese have to be integrated in Portuguese society. The success or failure of that process is important to the stability of the receiving country, and certainly the historical economic context of the return of the Angolans has not been the most favorable.

Democracy has been far from stable in western Europe, and the transition from constitutional monarchy to democracy, often a discontinuous process as in the case of Germany, in southern Europe has been marked by even greater discontinuity even when it was initiated as early as or earlier than in other west European countries. After all, nazism lasted only twelve years while nondemocratic rule in Italy, Portugal, and Spain lasted several decades and Greece intermittently suffered nondemocratic rule in the twentieth century. Southern European countries provide unique examples of early and accelerated political modernization in socially and, particularly, economically underdeveloped societies and, perhaps as a result, of the breakdown of "democracies in the making." In this they contrast with other countries, such as Imperial Germany, whose industrialization went ahead of political change. Being "democracies in the making" has characterized southern European nations, and with it totalitarian and authoritarian periods and therefore a discontinuity in their political development. We need to know much more about the crises of democracies, the periods of authoritarian rule, the transitions to new democratic regimes, and the legacies left by the political past to understand the present and the future. It is in this area that this volume makes important contributions.

Fortunately, American scholarship, even when slowly and with insufficient means, has developed an interest in southern Europe. The organizations and institutions mentioned in the Acknowledgments, particularly the Council for European Studies with its workshops and conferences, the Concilium for International and Area Studies here at Yale, the University of New Hampshire, and the Gulbenkian Foundation on the other side of the Atlantic, had helped to create a nucleus of scholars before the Portuguese Revolution spurned an unfortunately somewhat flashy interest in Portugal. It is our hope that these scholars, now integrated into the Conference Group on Modern Portugal, will continue their activities coordinated with the Committee on Southern Europe COSE that is trying to bring together scholars from both sides of the Atlantic—a common effort to study and understand this part of Europe, so long neglected. Let us not forget that more Europeans live in Portugal than in any of the Scandinavian countries or even Austria or Switzerland. In fact, the population of Italy, Spain, Portugal, and Greece in 1975 added up to almost 110 million people, while the Benelux countries, Sweden, Austria, and Switzerland, the largest of the smaller European democracies, only contained 45.9 million people. The GNP of Italy, Spain, Portugal, and Greece in 1975 at market prices in U.S. dollars was $290,110 million with an average per capita income of $2,641, while the absolute GNP of the smaller European countries just mentioned was almost the same, $299,490 million. But the difference in population meant that per capita income in the latter was $6,776. Southern Europe is the home of a large number of people: one out of every five Europeans outside the Soviet Union and more than one out of every four in non-Communist Europe. Politicians probably more than scholars are aware of the importance of the southern European votes in the new Europe. All of us should be conscious that the political stability in this part of the world, which in turn is dependent on continuous social and economic progress and the capacity to overcome the cleavages created by political conflict and a difficult past, is central to the future of Europe. Dramatizing things, let us imagine the impact of a Pinochet in any southern European country on the consciousness of western Europe, on the stability of other European democracies. Certainly, knowledge and understanding of southern European societies and politics might not be decisive in preventing serious crises but they can help to prevent them and to deal with them intelligently. My hope is that this work and future work by scholars in the area and by Americans interested in it will increase our pool of knowledge, understanding, and love for millions of Europeans confronted with difficult problems that other parts of Europe faced or solved earlier. Let us hope that this work will represent only a first step in a continuing and every day more intense effort of the scholarly community.

Juan J. Linz
Pelatiah Perit Professor of
Political and Social Science
Yale University

Acknowledgments

This volume, which is devoted to bringing to the attention of the academic community and the interested public the political and social dynamics of modern Portugal, is very much the result of collective endeavors extending across numerous years. First and foremost, those who have contributed the most to organizing and sustaining the Conference Group on Modern Portugal, Douglas L. Wheeler and Joyce F. Riegelhaupt, warrant acknowledgment. Juan J. Linz has continually encouraged the group and has inspired and guided many of the authors who appear in this volume. Yet none of this could have been accomplished were it not for the sustained support of the Fundação Calouste Gulbenkian in Lisbon. Not only did the Foundation generously support the meetings of the Conference Group at which the majority of these papers were presented but also, once again through the good offices of José Blanco, it has come to our assistance by making this book possible through the granting of a subsidy to the University of Texas Press. The Council for European Studies, the Canada Council, and the Interuniversity Centre for European Studies (Montreal) also generously contributed to the meetings of the Conference Group. No less importantly, mention should be made of the Universities of New Hampshire, Texas (Austin), Toronto, Wisconsin, and Yale which subsidized and graciously hosted our meetings. At Texas three people have been instrumental in the preparation of this book: William P. Glade, Director of the Institute of Latin American Studies (who made the resources and facilities of the Institute available to facilitate manuscript preparation); Mary Esther Bailey of the Institute (who did so much of the typing and retyping of the individual chapters, not to mention enlisting other secretarial assistance and coordinating communication among the editors and authors between May 1976 and February 1978—the time period over which this book was in preparation); and Barbara L. Burnham, Social Science Editor at the University of Texas Press (who gave us encouraging personal support and professional cooperation during the manuscript's final stages). At Toronto, David L. Raby (history department); Harold

Nelson, Director of the International Studies Programme; and Enid D'Oyley of the University library contributed and helped plan and organize the most recent meeting of the Conference Group (1976), during which it was decided to publish this volume. Hazel Bartolo of the sociology department patiently and superbly typed numerous editorial revisions and drafts of the introduction. Finally, on behalf of all the contributors to this volume we would like to emphasize the research support provided in Portugal for our individual and collective endeavors: its numerous public and private institutions, libraries and their staffs, public officials, and above all the many, many citizens of that country on whom the success of these and future studies of Portugal depend.

Lawrence S. Graham and Harry M. Makler

Introduction

HARRY M. MAKLER AND LAWRENCE S. GRAHAM

Social science research on Portugal is only just beginning to emerge in both North America and Europe. As a subject of systematic study, the country has been the most neglected of Western European countries. Its relatively isolated position in one corner of Iberia, until recently its South Atlantic and African rather than northern European orientation, the lack of Portuguese-language competence among Western scholars, and a tendency for concentration on Spain rather than Portugal, even among those interested in Iberian studies, have all contributed to our lack of knowledge. Indeed, the very fact that its 1974 revolution took so many by surprise attests to this paucity. Even in Portugal itself there were few studies analyzing the country's contemporary social, economic, and political structures before the 1970s.

Portuguese social scientists and historians, unlike their counterparts in other European countries, were virtually unknown abroad. Undoubtedly, the humanistic emphasis of university education and strict censorship during the Salazar regime restricted the type of work produced, and contributed to the fact that Portugal was invisible to much of the outside world. The aging dictatorship of António Salazar weathered the *Santa Maria* hijacking in 1961, and even revolutionary activities in its overseas territories were largely overlooked by both the Western press and Western scholars.

During the early 1960s a protracted colonial war broke out in Portugal's African territories. Goa and two other Portuguese enclaves were seized by India. Unrest was echoed on the Continent in manifestations, student strikes, and massive emigration of young men seeking jobs in northern Europe and evading obligatory military service. These problems quietly simmered along for over a decade and might have gone on longer had Salazar not had an accident which soon incapacitated him and quickly eroded his rule.

The overseas problems of the 1960s continued and they were exacerbated during the 1970s as the economy became rapidly internationalized. Movement toward European economic integration was accomplished by foreign investments in Portuguese industry, which rose from 1.5 percent in 1960 to 20 percent in 1970. By 1973 the world-wide recession and increases in petroleum and basic commodity prices, plus the relaxation of price controls, dovetailed to produce a 35 percent inflation rate, one of the highest in Western Europe. Remittances from Portuguese workers overseas and tourism (which annually comprised 30% of the country's foreign currency earnings) were reduced to a trickle. The wars in Africa had become a prolonged and arduous series of sporadic military engagements which left ten thousand dead, wounded another twenty thousand, and annually absorbed half of the country's budget, stunting the growth of education, social welfare, and other domestic institutions. Salazar's successor, Marcello Caetano, tried to appease everyone—the left, right, and center. Despite his attempts at accommodation, there was increasing dissension within the governing class. General António de Spínola's book highlighted this dissension, until then internalized within the regime, by focusing public attention on the fact that the African wars could not be won and arguing that a new mode of relations with the "overseas provinces" had to be considered.[1]

Briefly put, under Caetano, the political system constructed by Salazar ceased to respond to the demands placed upon it; Portuguese politics had entered a stalemate. The regime faced so many national and international problems of seemingly equal magnitude that it could not decisively resolve any one. Nor did it appear to want to. One sensed that the Caetano government, unlike its predecessor, was transitory, almost as if it was awaiting a new "Golden Age." In the mass media, controlled such as it was, news commentators continuously debated whether it was better for Portugal to align itself with Africa, Europe, or Latin America. This indecisiveness was mirrored throughout the regime, as contributors to this volume will demonstrate.

But even now, over four years after the military coup, Portugal still is unsettled; its people are uneasy, restless, and apparently waiting for something, but they know not what. One senses that they have been disillusioned, that they have forgotten the Revolution, and indeed well they might as fifty years of authoritarian rule were followed by eighteen months of anarchy, and now, despite the restoration of the state and democracy, the country is threatened by economic collapse. As this volume goes to press, inflation is around 27 percent, unemployment exceeds 10 percent, half the food is being imported, and there is a balance of payments deficit of nearly one billion dollars, which is almost certain to increase as the country attempts to borrow two billion dollars abroad. While there are signs of recovery, these are slow and uneven. The gross domestic product rose 4 percent in 1976 after a 3.6 percent drop in 1975. Fluctuations in industrial production have been similar. The only bright spots—a factor predicted by the team of economists contributing to this volume—are increasing tourism and emigrant remittances, but these have not yet offset the other deficits. Politically, various factions are undermining governmental policies designed to curb inflation and rebuild the economy. The Communists blame the Socialist government for promoting "a capitalist recovery" at the expense of workers whose wages have been frozen at the very time that prices are rising and deregulation of private enterprises is occurring. Industrialists are critical of the government's credit policies and import restrictions as higher production costs, increasing competition, and inflation become more burdensome and European economic integration a reality. After a half century of authoritarian rule many are fearful that those in command will attempt to return to the past, resorting to unpopular measures and stifling the new experiments in representative government, free press, and political expression.

The Origins of New Scholarship on Portugal

It was within this context that a small group of scholars within and outside Portugal began to conduct in-depth research on the country's recent history, social structure, politics, and economics. Before the 1974 coup, such Portuguese scholars as António de Oliveira Marques (history), Hermínio Martins (sociology), and Manuel de Lucena (political science) conducted their labors largely outside the country, while others—for example, Francisco Pereira de Moura (economics), José Cutileiro (anthropology), and Adérito Sedas Nunes (sociology)—worked quietly at home.[2] Even though other names could be mentioned as examples of the new scholarship which was emerging within Portugal during these years, the essential point to establish is that it was largely individualistic, isolated, meagerly supported, and faced with tremendous difficulties in the context of a regime which looked askance at the social sciences and the questions they raised.

The first North American social scientists to conduct systematic studies of contemporary Portuguese society were Joyce F. Riegelhaupt (anthropology) and Harry M. Makler (sociology). Although unknown to each other, both were doctoral candidates at Columbia University and both began their research in the early 1960s. In 1960, Riegelhaupt, with a fellowship from the National Institute of Mental Health and under the sponsorship of Charles Wagley, undertook a study of peasant family life, economics, and politics in a small *salóio* village near Lisbon. In 1964, Makler, with a Calouste Gulbenkian Foundation fellowship and under the guidance of Juan J. Linz, began his study of the role of Portugal's industrialists and their enterprises in the socioeconomic development of the country.

It was not until the late 1960s, however, that informal contacts began to be developed among social scientists in the United States who were interested in Portugal. In August 1966, at an international colloquium on Luso-Brazilian studies in Cambridge, Massachusetts, Riegelhaupt commented on a paper by Makler based on his industrial elite research.[3] Another commentator was Douglas L. Wheeler, a historian at the University of New Hampshire who had conducted research on nineteenth-century Angola in the early 1960s under a Fulbright scholarship. The fourth person to become a part of the group was Philippe C. Schmitter (political science), whose research on Portugal began soon after he participated in a panel organized by Linz at the Seventh World Congress of Sociology in Varna, Bulgaria, in August 1970. At that meeting Schmitter presented a paper on interest representation in Brazil between 1930 and 1965.[4]

In May 1971, Makler and Schmitter met at the University of Chicago where they began their collaboration on a paper dealing with the integration of Portugal's industrialists into the European Economic Community.[5] Schmitter had just been awarded a grant to enable him to visit Portugal for the first time to conduct research on interest politics in the Salazar-Caetano regime and authoritarianism. Schmitter's interest in Portugal originated from his studies of corporatism and authoritarian rule in Argentina and Brazil.[6]

On the basis of his 1971 summer field research, Schmitter prepared his first paper on Portuguese corporatism, interest representation, and policy formulation.[7] He returned to the United States at the end of that summer enthusiastic about the possibilities of future social science research and cross-disciplinary collaboration. In a memorandum dated October 21, 1971, Schmitter took the initiative and formalized the sentiments that others in this group had been discussing: a collaborative volume on Portugal from a multi-disciplinary perspective, the creation of a southern European longitudinal data bank, and a near-future conference on contemporary Portugal and its problems. This memorandum was directed to Linz, Makler, Riegelhaupt, Hermínio Martins, Lawrence Graham, and Stanley Payne.

Like Schmitter, Hermínio Martins was also interested in Portuguese politics and society. While teaching political science at the University of Essex in England he produced some of the first essays in English on Portuguese fascism and political movements during the twentieth century.[8] He and Schmitter first met in England during the summer of 1971.

In the early 1970s interest in authoritarianism and corporatism led two other political scientists, Howard Wiarda and Lawrence Graham of the Universities of Massachusetts and Texas, respectively, to begin work on Portuguese politics and its evolution. Like Schmitter, both had previously conducted research in Latin America. Wiarda first traveled to Portugal to begin his studies of Portuguese politics in November 1972, with an SSRC grant to study corporatist theory and its manifestations in Salazar's Estado Novo.[9] In May 1971, Graham went to Portugal under grants from the Calouste Gulbenkian and Earhart foundations and spent eight months conducting research on the country's public bureaucracy. The following year, as a consequence of a continuation of research funding by these two sources, he extended his study to Angola and Mozambique, where he interviewed colonial officials.[10] Early in the summer of 1975 he returned to Portugal to study the role of the military in the Revolution, on which he reports in this volume (Chapter 7).

The memorandum also made its way to Stanley G. Payne, a noted historian of Iberia. In 1971, Payne, who has contributed much to our knowledge of modern Spanish history and fascism, began to turn his attention to Portugal. In June 1971, at a workshop he organized at the University of Wisconsin to encourage historical and social science research on modern Spain under the sponsorship of the Council of European Studies, Payne also encouraged the participation of Portuguese specialists. He discussed with Makler and Schmitter his interest in conducting a study of late-nineteenth- and early-twentieth-century Portuguese politics. Two years later Payne firmly established himself as a scholar of Portuguese history with the publication of his two-volume work on Spain and Portugal.[11] Moreover, he was instrumental, together with Linz, in organizing the first meeting of what soon was to become the International Conference Group on Modern Portugal (ICGMP).

THE FIRST CONFERENCE ON MODERN PORTUGAL

During the fall and winter of 1971 plans were made for a small meeting of North American social scientists who had studied or had expressed interest in studying modern Portugal. In early June 1972, with a small grant from the Council for European Studies, Payne organized and hosted an administrative meeting at the University of Wisconsin to plan a larger conference on contemporary Portugal for the following year. Among those in attendance were Linz, Makler, Riegelhaupt, Schmitter, Wheeler, Stuart Schwartz, and Thomas C. Bruneau. Bruneau, a political scientist who had also done his first work in Latin America, had met Schmitter at Berkeley, where they were both graduate students.[12] Stuart Schwartz, a historian of Brazil, had known Makler and Riegelhaupt at Columbia University and then went on to study Brazil's seventeenth-century judicial system, which involved extensive research on Portugal in its archives.

Riegelhaupt and Wheeler volunteered to organize the first conference and to act as co-chairpersons for the newly emerging group. Later that fall (1972), they submitted a proposal to fund the conference to the Council of European Studies and the Calouste Gulbenkian Foundation. Soon afterward, with grants in hand, the newly formed Conference Group scheduled its first "Workshop on Modern Portugal, 1820–1973" for October 10–14, 1973, at the University of New Hampshire's New England Conference Center.

The main objective of the conference—as well as of the two others that followed—was to encourage research on Portugal's recent history, its politics and government, its (then) colonial system, its class structure, and its economic processes. In this regard an effort was made to combine in-depth discussion with the presentation of research results by a larger group of scholars. Included were those who had already studied the country extensively, as well as newer scholars (both graduate students and professors) who were just beginning their work on Portugal.

To encourage multidisciplinary and cross-national collaboration, the organizers solicited papers from a variety of scholars on both sides of the Atlantic. With Wheeler in Portugal in 1972 conducting research, it was possible to arrange the participation of a number of eminent Portuguese social scientists and historians.

This first meeting, chaired by Juan Linz and Stanley G. Payne, was rather broad in scope, as reflected in the organization of the sessions, the disciplines, and the affiliations of the participants (see Appendix).

A number of papers from the conference were subsequently published by their authors in various scholarly journals. Others appear in this volume.[13] In nearly all cases the papers were substantially revised in the light of the coup that occurred seven months after our meeting. While our papers and discussions at the Durham meeting tended to reveal contradictions, dysfunctions, and weaknesses in Portuguese institutions, there were no hints of radical political changes. Even the most informed among us, including outspoken Portuguese intellectuals (and later political leaders), seemed resigned that the regime was firmly entrenched as its economy was relatively sound, its opposition groups were hopelessly divided in terms of both purpose and strategy, and its colonial wars in its overseas territories were stalemated.

In retrospect, a major weakness in the first program was the neglect of the military. Imagine if we had known that at the very time of our conference clandestine meetings of military officers were planning the regime's overthrow!

The most heated discussions took place in the session on Portuguese corporatism. They were largely theoretical and had more to do with the reality of academic political science than with the reality of Portugal. Two contributors to this volume, Howard Wiarda and Philippe Schmitter, had studied the same topic but had arrived at contradictory conclusions. Wiarda reported that corporatism was an "authentic" structural response, deeply rooted in Portuguese political culture, and under Caetano's guidance a meaningful element in Portuguese political life. Schmitter, in contrast, saw corporatism as having little to do with political culture (except as a *post factum* ideological justification) and as the product of deliberate public policy coercively applied. He later wrote that "its [corporatism's] structure and performance were [and long had been] an elaborate fraud and that, far from being dynamic, it was moribund; and, in fact, that its primary importance lay in what it did not do and prevented from happening rather than in what it did do."

While few of the "seasoned" scholars had any immediate plans to return to Portugal—in fact, in the corridors one often heard discussions of research prospects in Latin America—there were some "budding scholars." One was Caroline Bieler (now Brettell), a young Canadian anthropologist who was about to begin doctoral research on Portuguese migration patterns in Europe.

The coup of April 25, 1974, caught all of us completely by surprise. Bruneau, who was continuing his research on the Church and State in Portugal, was the only member of the Conference Group who happened to be "right on site" during the coup. Gradually, the members of the ICGMP returned to Portugal to assess firsthand the Revolution's impact, to "reaffirm old contacts," and to gauge the receptivity toward foreigners, especially American researchers. Overnight Portugal attracted numerous social scientists and historians who suddenly developed an interest in Portuguese politics.[14]

THE SECOND CONFERENCE ON MODERN PORTUGAL

By the fall of 1974 there were proposals for another meeting of ICGMP. It was hoped that the meeting could be held in Portugal, which would serve to clarify the causes and consequences of the Revolution and to provide opportunities to discuss collaborative research with Portuguese social scientists.

Since the political situation in Portugal remained unsettled, it proved difficult to arrange a conference there, and a small meeting was organized by Juan Linz at Yale University on March 28 and 29, 1975, with the support of Yale's Council of West European Studies. The primary purpose of this conference was to plan a cross-disciplinary study of Portugal's social structure and electorate in order to provide a sound basis for future studies and to learn about the population of a country which had been tabulated but rarely, if ever, systematically studied. There was some reluctance by the group to the idea of a large collaborative survey; the participants perceived that the Portuguese would suspect, if not outrightly resist, any social or political research conducted by a North American team. This feeling was acquired during brief visits to Portugal made by many during the summer immediately following the Revolution. Nevertheless, individual research efforts continued.[15] Riegelhaupt, for example, had begun to investigate agrarian reform, Schmitter delved into new political movements, Graham undertook new research on the military, and Wiarda returned to investigate the effects of the Revolution on corporative structure. New scholars also emerged.

Jack Hammond, a sociologist interested in voting behavior, set out to conduct a pre-electoral survey on which he reports in this volume (Chapter 8). Rhona Fields, a social psychologist, studied the political attitudes of the new military leaders; and Eusebio Mujal began his doctoral research on the Communist parties in Spain and Portugal.

THE THIRD CONFERENCE ON MODERN PORTUGAL

A year after its revolution Portugal was still very much in the news. There were countercoups, hints of CIA involvement, Socialist and Communist Party struggles, independence movements in the now-independent African colonies, and a series of economic and fiscal crises of sufficient magnitude to disturb the Western European countries and their alliances. Those who had had an opportunity to study postrevolutionary Portugal were ready to test their theories about the origins and implications of the Revolution with their colleagues. As Portuguese specialists they were also in a position to offer to the North American academic community some cogent explanations for the collapse of the Salazar-Caetano regime, perhaps in atonement for an event which none of them had foreseen. Therefore, early in the fall of 1975, efforts by David Raby (a historian of modern Mexico who wanted to study the Estado Novo epoch in Portugal) and Harry Makler to organize a meeting at the University of Toronto were enthusiastically received by the ICGMP members. With the support of the Canada Council, the Interuniversity Centre for European Studies in Montreal, and the University of Toronto, a meeting was held in Toronto, April 16–17, 1976. Unlike the previous conferences, the Toronto meeting specifically focused on the political, social, and economic aspects of the MFA revolution.[16] Specialists who had studied the breakdown of the Salazar-Caetano regime, the rise of the MFA, and the impact of the African wars were invited to participate. Nevertheless, the interdisciplinary and international character of the group was maintained and was reflected in the conference program (Appendix).

At an administrative meeting held immediately following the conference it was decided that a number of the ICGMP papers and research reports were of such quality that they merited publication. Moreover, a book on Portugal seemed timely. Not only had public interest been aroused, but it also was sustained and was still seeking explanation two years after the Revolution. Upon the request of the group, Graham and Makler agreed to collect, edit, and see to the

publication of papers which could best contribute to the understanding of Portugal's changing social, economic, and political
structure and the demise of its authoritarian regime.

The Papers Selected and the Rationale for Their Inclusion

The eleven essays selected for publication in this volume come from
a pool of thirty-five highly divergent examples of recent scholarship on Portugal. At the outset the editors requested and received
from those central to the Conference Group permission to decide
which would be the most appropriate for inclusion in a single volume. By 1976 this store of conference papers consisted of both published and unpublished materials.

The essays appearing here are those which in our judgment fit
together most effectively in providing an overview of contemporary
Portugal. As a general principle we first considered previously unpublished material of quality. Only later did we review work that
had already been published by the Conference Group. At our request, Wiarda consented to write a new paper for the book, syn-
thesizing his earlier work on Portugal and reappraising his ideas
on corporatism in light of the Revolution. In Lucena's case we found
that the paper he had prepared for the Toronto Conference, once
it was translated from the French, was not appropriate from the
standpoint of the general reader unless one were in a position to
read his larger two-volume dissertation, prepared originally for a
state doctorate in France. With the author's assistance we returned
to the original dissertation of over a thousand pages, abridged, and
translated a section from the first part of volume one which com-
plemented the other papers we had in hand. This selection makes
available for the first time material on Portuguese and Italian fascism that hitherto has been inaccessible to the English-language
reader. As a comparative study of two distinct but related regimes,
it sheds new light on both Salazar's Portugal and Mussolini's Italy.
Lastly, in order to provide proper balance to the book, we requested
and obtained permission from J. Silva Lopes (governor of the Bank
of Portugal) and Richard Eckaus to include excerpts from what has
become a much debated and highly controversial report on the Portuguese economy, an OECD–Bank of Portugal study amply commented on in the Portuguese press but hitherto of limited availability to the informed public within and outside Portugal. One wonders
whether Portugal's continuing economic and political difficulties

would have been averted had the recommendations of Eckaus been adopted. As of the summer of 1977 an MIT group was still in Portugal, continuing its studies and making policy recommendations to the government. We have also included in this volume a paper by Mario Murteira. In 1975 Murteira was minister of planning and economic coordination in the fourth and fifth provisional governments. It was during this time that nationalizations and state interventions in industry peaked. Murteira's paper represents the views of the intellectual Marxists, a group which strongly opposed the OECD–Bank of Portugal report.

SCHMITTER

The volume begins with a paper on the social, economic, and political bases of Portugal's authoritarian regime under Salazar (1932–1968) and Caetano (1968–1974). In keeping with other studies of authoritarian or fascist rule, its author, Philippe Schmitter, examines the social origins and career patterns of what he calls the "founding" political elite, that is, members of the National Assembly and the Corporative Chamber during the early years of the Estado Novo (1934–1942). He shows that Portugal's political elite was in many respects quite similar to political elites in other authoritarian regimes in that it was composed mainly of civil servants, technicians, and university professors who were self-made men of middle-class socioeconomic origin. These findings parallel and coincide with a number of those recorded by Makler (Chapter 4) in his discussion of the industrial elite.

Through examining economic and political imperatives Schmitter seeks to explain why authoritarian rule emerged in Portugal. He highlights a series of economic and fiscal crises, beginning with numerous bank failures in 1924–25, which not only led to the state's intervention, regulation, and absorption of surplus capital, but also enabled Salazar to set Portugal on course toward a "delayed-dependent" mode of economic production. In citing political causes, Schmitter notes the loss of hegemony by the dominant political class, the continuing political instability (e.g., cabinet changes, terrorist activities, strikes), and the abundance of competing ideologies. Finally, he looks at the various strategies used by Salazar to implant and consolidate his rule. In economic terms these entailed new and austere fiscal policies, centralization of authority, protective tariffs, agricultural subsidies, wage and price controls, and regulation of competition. Politically, Salazar consolidated power by abolishing political parties, replacing all class associations with corporative organizations, co-opting notables and experts into high office, and imposing strict censorship on the mass media in order to ensure ideological uniformity. The outstanding characteristics of the Salazar-Caetano regime were its success in demobilizing and imposing social control over its citizenry and its slow, non-aggressive political and economic expansion, which dulled innovation and initiative and comprised all who shared and participated in its policies.

LUCENA

Numerous facets of Portugal's authoritarian rule raised by Schmitter are historically and comparatively addressed by other authors in the volume. Chapter 2 contains an analysis of the structural underpinnings and consequences of the corporative system imposed by Salazar. Manuel de Lucena leads off his discussion by defining Salazarism as "a form of fascism without a fascist movement" and then traces its evolution in Portugal. In order to distinguish between Salazarism and corporatism Lucena chooses a comparative approach. He first outlines the emergence of fascism in Italy under Mussolini and then describes the Portuguese case. The origins, style of leadership, foreign influence, and relations with the state are vividly compared. In a section entitled "Worship of the Leader" Lucena's characterizations of Salazar and Mussolini supply new insight into the nature and persistence of authoritarian rule in each of the countries.

After re-creating an image of what authoritarian Portugal was like, Lucena describes the forces which led to its breakdown. He first acquaints us with the country's economic system: its original restructuring before the war, the impact of World War II, and the stresses imposed later by prolonged colonial warfare and integration into the postwar capitalist world. These transformations gave rise to a number of contradictions. The stimulation given to exports and domestic production by the war and the regime's association with the Allies during its final stages weakened the initial definition Salazar had given to Portuguese nationalism and to his regime. As American capital invaded Europe and many of the European states moved toward economic integration, it became necessary to abandon the original meaning given to corporatism because of its ties with fascism. But in seeking to link Portugal more closely with Europe and yet maintain a colonial empire, a new problem confronted the regime: independence movements in its overseas Asian and African territories. In order to pay for the colonial wars without weakening economic growth, the regime actively solicited foreign investment. By the mid 1960s, however, foreign capital, coupled with large remittances from Portuguese workers and tourism earnings, overloaded the system. Inflation began to mount as supply could not meet demand, salaries rose, and social and geographical mobility increased. The country was in motion and contact with the outside world accelerated, despite Salazar's endeavors to the contrary. Foreign economic relations, wars in its overseas territories, and the movement of millions to Europe and Africa, back and forth, resulted in a fluid, questioning population, one which the regime found more and more difficult to order and contain.

By 1970 authoritarian rule, now under Marcello Caetano—writes Lucena—was intermittent. Attempts were made to "liberalize" political life, censorship was less rigorous, some demonstrations and strikes were tolerated, lively debates occurred, and the state gave the industrial bourgeoisie free reign. Caetano's new course was limited in its progress, says Lucena, by factors which it unleashed. One senses that the regime gave away too much too quickly, according to its own abilities, and when it wanted to re-establish its hegemony it no longer knew to what extent it could, nor where, nor when. Portugal had been relatively isolated, but it was no longer possible to maintain this isolation. "Neither the rhythm nor the customs of Salazar could be adapted to these changes. . . . Salazarism had passed," but, states Lucena, "it remains to be known whether Salazarism was exhausted in its entirety or, on the contrary, whether it could hold to principles which could be realized in another way."

In the conclusion to his essay Lucena raises questions which observers continue to ask about postrevolutionary Portugal: What structural changes have occurred and which have not? How do we know that a regime or state is the same? Is fascism dead in Portugal? To answer these he ponders the relation between fascism and corporatism in a broader sense. He weighs the existence of corporatist movements within more modern contexts, hypothesizing, for example, that modern capitalism, with its requisites of large bureaucratic enterprises, planning, worker participation, and avoidance of social confrontations, is inclined toward corporatism, especially in Europe.

WIARDA

The questions asked by Lucena are directly related to Howard Wiarda's evaluation of corporatism (in Chapter 3) and lead him to examine in more detail some of the same topics raised by Lucena by looking at Portuguese political experience both before and after the New State.

Wiarda begins his essay by tracing the origins of corporatism in Portugal and stressing the complementarity between Portuguese civil society, governance, juridical codes, and Catholic-Thomistic emphasis on hierarchy and organicism. He argues that corporatism in the Portuguese context refers to a distinct set of attributes specific to that country's history, political culture, and development process: ". . . a value system based upon widespread acceptance of hierarchy, elitism, organicism, and authority. . . . functional representation with authority vested in the crown or central state apparatus and with the various corporate units . . . incorporated into a single, organic whole for purposes of integral national development. . . . a social order based similarly on patron-client interdependence . . . a predominantly Catholic society and political culture based upon Thomistic principles. . . . a mercantilist economic system. . . . a political system based on patrimonialism, authority, and hierarchy, with a centralized, vertical, pyramidal structure of power and decision making."

Because corporatism has become so imbedded in Portuguese social, economic, and political structures, Wiarda posits that it remains a "major persistent tradition even today." He therefore questions whether the new regime and new ideologies can "transcend or overcome" certain historic divisions, or whether they will become merely another layer of institutions and personalities imposed over the "already existing" and "perhaps dominant" corporatist model. Here Wiarda coincides with Lucena in his concern with the persistence and re-emergence of corporatist patterns in "new clothing," or what Lucena labels "neocorporatism."

It is in his discussion of the institutionalization of corporatism in Portugal that Wiarda differs with both Lucena and Schmitter. Rather than equate corporatism with authoritarianism, as a particular form of interest representation, he contrasts Salazar's initial corporative restructuring of Portuguese society with his later practices. Wiarda notes that by the mid-1930s corporatism was no longer a system of "free associability and social justice" but was rapidly becoming a means by which the state could repress, control, and contain social groups at the expense of others. For Wiarda, corporatism under Salazar was biased in that it favored employer over employee by applying and enforcing corporative decrees selectively. Various corporative organizations, such as commissions, *juntas*, institutes, and *grémios*, were used by the state to regulate the economy and its participants. Wiarda describes the attempts by the state to subordinate industry and the industrial bourgeoisie, a topic which Makler more fully explores in his paper (Chapter 4).

While Wiarda sees no necessary relationship between corporatism and authoritarianism, and hence sees the developments of the early thirties in a far more positive light than either Schmitter or Lucena, he converges with them in his evaluation of the regime by the time of World War II. He hypothesizes that a form of state capitalism linking together government and the major economic interests emerged and soon supplanted corporative structures. "With the end of the war and the general discrediting of all such 'fascistic' schemes, the corporative system was still further shunted aside, circumvented, and ignored." While there was a brief revival in the 1950s—largely owed to economic prosperity and the regime's conviction that it had accomplished economic and political stability—corporatism was already in decline.

Wiarda describes the increasing power of the working class and trade unions with the approach of the 1970s, owing to the reluctance, if not the inability, of the Caetano regime to resolve crises. Not only did the regime vacillate, but it was also inconsistent and Janus-like. In the belief that he could contain the labor movement and its increasing power, Caetano permitted the formation of Intersindical, a labor organization which soon represented twenty of the largest unions and upward of 150,000 workers. In a sense this was the "deathblow" to the corporatist system. By the time the regime attempted to outlaw the organization and purge the corporative *sindicatos*, Intersindical already had moved underground where it was infiltrated by the Portuguese Communist Party. And, when the government moved to undercut the labor movement and Intersindical by bypassing the *sindicatos* and promising wage increases directly to those concerned, it only succeeded in further de-legitimizing corporative structures and its own credibility.

In the final part of his essay Wiarda discusses the dismantling of Salazar's corporative system, but unlike Lucena he also suspects its rebirth and continuity. Indeed, he notes, while within a year "virtually the entire corporative state had been dismantled or restructured," in actuality many corporate agencies (*grémios, sindicatos, casas do povo, casas dos pescadores*) remained in existence, either being renamed or undergoing alterations in their top leadership. The new regime resurrected a new set of corporative institutions in an attempt to promote class collaboration under the hegemony of the state. That is, old systems of social, economic, and political controls were again being employed to maintain order and regulate change. Contrary to some interpretations which view corporatism as rigid and static, Wiarda sees it as malleable and evolutionary, arguing that it differed under Salazar, Caetano, and post-revolutionary governments. For Wiarda corporatism is transitional and will remain very much a part of Portuguese society regardless of its social, economic, and political changes.

MAKLER

Harry Makler's essay (Chapter 4) appropriately follows the essays by Schmitter, Lucena, and Wiarda. By thoroughly examining the impact of the authoritarian regime via the corporative system on the industrial elite, Makler not only corroborates some of the hypotheses on corporatism raised in the preceding essays but also shows its implications for Portugal's class structure and economic development.

By examining the career patterns of a large and representative sample of industrialists heading larger enterprises (50 or more employees) in 1965, during the Salazar era, Makler was able to distinguish two main groups: (a) industrialist corporative leaders who tended to be younger, propertied, upper class in origin, and affiliated with the traditional sector; and (b) industrialist national leaders who were older, university-trained engineers, nonpropertied executives of larger enterprises affiliated with dynamic sectors of the economy. It was through members of this latter group that the interlocking between government and the economy occurred and it was this group that considered the corporative system and its agencies effective. In contrast, the industrialist corporative leaders were compartmentalized by the very system they represented and were the most critical of the corporative system, even the regime itself at times. One reason for this group's compartmentalization, according to Makler, was that the regime considered them "too deeply imbedded in the rural past"; as such they did not correspond to its projection of "national interests." Whatever the motive, it was through corporative institutions that the regime was able to maintain traditional class structure and to control social mobility. On the basis of these findings Makler concludes that two forms of corporatism characterized the Salazar-Caetano regime: state corporatism for the propertied, more traditional elite sector and societal corporatism for the more dynamic and powerful ones. Here, Makler's findings modify Wiarda's hypothesis pertaining to the dynamic nature of corporatism. Wiarda notes that the corporatism of Caetano was quite different from that of Salazar and that it changed and evolved depending on societal conditions and development; Makler suggests its variability even under Salazar's rule.

RIEGELHAUPT

Whereas Makler examines in depth one of the elite groups most active in Salazar's Portugal, Joyce Riegelhaupt (Chapter 5) looks at the regime from below, through the eyes of the peasantry. Her essay on peasant political relations during the Salazar regime thereby both coincides with and complements its predecessors in this volume. While the chapters by Schmitter, Lucena, and Wiarda adopt a macrohistorical approach, with the nation serving as the main unit of analysis, Riegelhaupt takes a microapproach, asking the question: how did peasants at the village level view the regime? If Makler's analysis suggests the way in which elite groups within the regime were marginalized by the process of increasing state power, Riegelhaupt's study shows exactly how the process permeated the lower echelons of Portuguese society and why its effects were so devastating.

Riegelhaupt argues that, in general, only through a thorough understanding of a regime's structure at the grass-roots level can one explain the various forms of peasant political participation. She then provides social data showing how the country was politically organized into a series of hierarchically arranged geographical units (*freguesias*) which the central government (the state) controlled by appointing local officials (e.g., mayors, justices of the peace). Corresponding to this political structure were other public entities (e.g., *casas do povo*, or "houses of the people") whose function was to organize the economic systems of rural areas in order "to harmoniously integrate the owner and worker for the common good and avoid dangers of economic development and social change." Ideally the two systems should have encompassed and penetrated all geographical and social units, but, in actuality, there was one political authority: "*o governo*" (the government), which the peasants always tried to avoid or bypass.

By comparing two villages—one in the central part of the country and the other in the south—Riegelhaupt captures vividly how politics operated at the local level, how the peasantry responded, and the impact this "administered society" had on their traditions, their character, and their relations. Under the New State the courts, laws, police, county clerks, and even neighboring parishes were considered by peasants as belonging to *êles* ("them"), and any transactions with "them" usually resulted in conflict, economic penalties, or moral damage. The peasantry became reluctant even to press for "public goals," as they lacked both the channels and the will to communicate their needs. In this way the Estado Novo encouraged and created apathy. By promoting apathy and demobilization, the regime privatized rural life and forced patronage upon the rural population. But, as Riegelhaupt sees it, in the process of doing so, patronage, although a traditional pattern of social relations between superiors and subordinates, ceased to constitute a viable response to uncertainty in a corporatist authoritarian state where reciprocity had been destroyed and no longer had meaning. Of the two villages studied, one responded to these circumstances by closing in on itself while the inhabitants of the other begged favors. The peasantry that Riegelhaupt studied thus was subjected to the same enforced marginalization characteristic of Makler's traditional industrial elite, but unlike them it had neither the economic or the political resources to relate to the broader society.

WHEELER AND GRAHAM

Spanning the chasm separating prerevolutionary Portugal, with its politics of limited participation and induced mass apathy, from the new political order that has taken form since April 25, 1974, is the military institution. The military provides the crucial link in moving from the hierarchically structured and closed politics of the Salazar-Caetano era into a more open and competitive political system. Accordingly, two papers dealing with the military in politics have been selected from the Third Conference—those by Wheeler (Chapter 6) and Graham (Chapter 7). While the former shows adeptly the significant role played by the military in Portuguese politics both before and during the New State, the latter focuses on the internal dynamics of the officer corps and interrelations among military officers in politics and the civilian political leadership during a two-year period, extending from the initial coup in 1974 to the establishment of a presidential system based on electoral pluralities in 1976.

The merit of the Wheeler paper is the broad overview it provides of civil-military relations from the end of the First Republic in 1926 to the overthrow of the New State in 1974. It is significant to note here that military involvement in politics and factionalism within the armed forces is not a recent pattern; rather, it is one of long standing. Wheeler calls attention to the role of the military in ending the Constitutional Monarchy and setting up the First Republic in 1910, in later plotting and executing its overthrow, and in first cooperating with Salazar and later working to bring an end to the regime he established. One of the most valuable parts of Wheeler's paper is the light it sheds on the evolution of civil-military relations during the Estado Novo: from an independent role at the outset, which continued through the 1930s, to the erosion of the armed forces' autonomy after World War II and their complete subjugation to Salazar's authority during the 1950s. The upshot of this linking of the military establishment to the New State, in a fashion not dissimilar to the co-optation of the political elite and the industrial elite (described by Schmitter and Makler), was that by the time Portugal had become involved in its colonial wars many military officers felt that the armed forces had become thoroughly discredited by their close identification with the regime.

Wheeler ends his discussion of civil-military relations by comparing and contrasting military intervention in politics in the 1926 coup (which led to the establishment of the New State) and in the 1974 coup (which led to its overthrow). The similarity lies in how, in both coups, the intervention originated in unresolved internal professional military complaints and soon escalated into political stances affecting power relationships throughout the whole regime. While the ideological contents of the two movements differ greatly, the coups are quite similar in the internal military factionalism which they brought to the surface and their inability to structure a new viable national government once they had destroyed the previous regime.

Graham's paper picks up where Wheeler's leaves off, with an eye toward examining in depth exactly what transpired during the critical period of transition between the ending of the old regime and the establishment of a new one. The military grievances which served as the catalyst for destroying the Caetano regime, the factionalism and struggle for power among various groups in the armed forces, and the interaction among military and civilian leaders as they all competed for control of the decision-making centers of Portuguese government are laid out in summary fashion.

Because this is both an extremely important moment in the evolution of modern Portugal and a difficult period to assess, one of this chapter's major objectives is to set out with clarity the rapidly shifting patterns in civil-military relations, until an effective, new dominant civilian-military relations coalition could emerge—the Soares-Eanes government. Read against the background provided by Wheeler on civil-military relations before 1974, this paper offers insight into the specifics behind the decision of a major segment of the officer corps to intervene in politics to end colonial warfare overseas and authoritarian rule on the mainland. It also examines the impact on the armed forces of the attempt to democratize internal military structures and to sever ties with the old regime. In the process of change, the struggle for power among various military factions and the politicization of the armed forces as a whole had the effect of nearly wrecking the viability and the integrity of the military institution as an autonomous force in Portuguese politics. Yet these were the very goals that the original movement set out to reassert in reaction to the military's implication in the declining authority and legitimacy of the New State.

HAMMOND AND BRETTELL

In the same way that Wheeler's and Graham's chapters complement each other, John Hammond's analysis (Chapter 8) of the correlation between 1975 electoral behavior and socioeconomic cleavages and Caroline Brettell's subsequent chapter (9) on rural and small-town attitudes toward politics in northern Portugal need to be read consecutively. Much of the confusion outside Portugal in assessing the import of the events of 1974, 1975, and 1976 stems from the failure to separate and distinguish two very different processes of change: the political struggle at the top to fill the power vacuum left in a highly centralized state by the collapse of the Caetano regime, and the upheaval from below which represented for the first time the entrance of the urban and rural masses into Portuguese politics. Neither movement—the struggle to establish viable new political leadership and the spontaneous entrance of the masses into the mainstream of Portuguese national life—can be separated entirely. The instability at the top was a direct consequence of this new mass equation in national politics, and the exuberance and popular upsurge of large-group sentiments fed upon and were stimulated by the debate over who should rule and the struggle for power among new military and civilian political personalities.

Before analyzing postcoup Portuguese political behavior (voting and militancy), Hammond describes the class structure, institutions, and events during the Estado Novo period which structured politics in both rural and urban areas. The peasantry, for example,

was influenced by the Church, affected by emigration, uneconomical land holdings, and demobilization policies of the corporative
state. He hypothesizes that religion, strong in Portugal's north and
nearly absent in its south, produced different patterns of political
behavior which have persisted despite the Revolution.

His analysis of Portugal after 1974 proceeds first along regional
(north-south) and urbanization (rural-urban) lines, showing that the
parties of the right (PPD and CDS) faired better in the elections
in the north, especially in rural areas, while the parties of the left
(the Communists [the PCP] and their affiliate, the MDP) received
more support in the south, again in rural areas. The party of the
center, the Socialists (PS), was more affected by urbanization: its
vote was greater in urban than in rural areas, especially in the south.
Hammond then compares different occupational groups within
these contexts and includes some explanations to account for the
patterns. He argues that poverty (as measured by average monthly
family expenses) and emigration mainly accounted for the high conservative vote in the north. "Emigration," he states, "can similarly
be taken as a measure of prosperity, since poverty is a principal
motive for emigration."

Brettell's chapter provides further explanations for the conservative vote in the north. In her accounting for the high abstention and
nonmilitancy of rural proprietors in terms of ties to the land and
escape through emigration, we are again reminded of Riegelhaupt's
politically isolated peasantry.

However, before turning our attention to the northern vote and
Brettell's paper, it is important to seek to understand first the strong
support for the Socialist Party (PS) in Portugal's urban middle class
and among tertiary-sector employees. We signal these groups because together they are rapidly becoming the largest and politically
(at least potentially) the most powerful faction in postrevolutionary
Portugal. Threatened by growing inflation, housing shortages, un-
and underemployment, there is a real possibility they will split into
different segments supporting left and right political parties. Insight
into this dimension of Portuguese politics is also to be found in
Hammond's paper.

From his analysis of voting, Hammond weighs the militancy of
the population in 1975. He relates various political incidents following April 25, and argues that Portugal's high degree of militancy—
for example, *golpismo* by the military and relentless demands by
the citizenry—is "a consequence of the lack of stable representative
structures through which demands could be channeled." Here we

are reminded of the relative political inexperience of most Portuguese owed to the demobilization strategies of the Salazar-Caetano regime. Hammond sees a reversal after 1974: overmobilization, so much so that it is undermining agrarian reform. In urban areas, too, the long-range impact of working-class militancy, owing to the Communist Party's ambivalent role in labor struggles, remains problematical. Still, regardless of the PCP's inability to control excessive worker demands and contain strikes, it received their overwhelming support in the 1975 election in the rural south and in heavily industrialized *concelhos* south of the Tejo River. But in the north, communism was opposed because it symbolized loss of land and opposition to religion, and was "the same enemy the regime had been warning them about for so long."

By focusing on the Revolution and social change through the eyes of inhabitants of a northern rural town, Caroline Brettell is able to describe in far greater detail the forces which have tempered the Revolution. Based on conversations extending over four months with villagers in northern Portugal and emigrant workers in Paris, Brettell provides a first-hand account of the north's conservative reaction when faced with revolutionary change. Much as Hammond, she begins by painting the context and structural factors which she judges influence political behavior. "International, rather than intranational," emigration, she writes, has served to reduce "the tendency to class solidification and the development of class consciousness." So too, she continues, do different land-tenure systems. The northern minifundia system creates "minute scales of difference among rural peoples" and encourages competition rather than class conflict, while in the south because of different land-tenure systems "there has always been more revolutionary potential." We are also shown how the Church influenced the people from the pulpit, via television, and in local classrooms, encouraging a prowork, diligence, self-improvement, and acquisitive ethic.

Communism was seen as the antithesis to these values. It was the cause of *"muita liberdade"* (too much freedom), disciplinary problems, and juvenile delinquency. Brettell reports how, in the village she studied, after a brief experiment with the new liberties, the priest was given carte blanche to institute a "new regime" of order and discipline. She sensitizes us to the feelings of the peasantry and their fear of change by incorporating their attitudes into her essay.

Equally important is the insight Brettell gives us into the emigrants' attitudes. They are neither necessarily indifferent nor apathetic in their feelings toward their homeland. They have simply opted to seek their livelihood elsewhere, rather than attempt to change the system through collective action. Thus, the predilection for individualistic, rather than collective, action among the northern peasantry, through leaving the country or remaining and accepting the "system" as it is, has long served to and continues to reinforce conservative political orientations rather than promote revolutionary ones.

THE MIT GROUP AND MURTEIRA

The last two chapters in this volume—those by economists—dovetail with Brettell's discussion. Whereas she cites the conservative impact of the northern peasantry as a moderating force in the Revolution, Dornbusch, Eckaus, and Taylor (Chapter 10) and Murteira (Chapter 11) all show how emigrant remittances as a totality markedly alleviated Portugal's deficits in the late 1960s and early 1970s and how their virtual disappearance after 1974 undercut the ability of the new governments to take a more active role in the economy. Brettell presents data from the village level in the north which seek to explain how massive emigration, continued emigrant ties with one's community of origin, and regular remittances to family members remaining in the village and looking after one's interests served to retain the vitality of a traditional, conservative set of political attitudes. These chapters relate the micro to the macro setting.

The abbreviated OECD (Office for Economic Cooperation and Development) report by Rudiger Dornbusch, Richard Eckaus, and Lance Taylor, a team of American economists, adopts an optimistic and conservative view. This report, sponsored by the OECD at the request of the Bank of Portugal in late 1975, focuses on a number of "health" measures (e.g., GNP, balance of payments, consumption/investment patterns) and suggests some internal economic policies based on their projections. Although it is recognized that the economics of Portugal will remain in a state of flux for some years to come, the Dornbusch, Eckaus, and Taylor report offers a comprehensive profile of the Portuguese economy immediately prior to and after the 1974 revolution. Murteira's perspective is more focused and skeptical, perhaps because as a Portuguese economist he was closer to the situation and as planning minister (in the Fourth Provisional Government) he was overwhelmed and hampered by existing complexities. For Murteira the foreign or exogenous factor was the force which precipitated the collapse of a genuinely revolutionary alternative for building a new Portugal.

One of the most useful and permanent contributions of the Dornbusch, Eckaus, and Taylor document is the concrete data it supplies on the status of the economy in 1975. The authors compare "national income accounts" for the primary, secondary, and tertiary sectors over a three-year period (1973–1976). They note that—while postrevolutionary income redistribution resulted in an 82 percent personal consumption increase in 1974, an increase which continued into 1975—fixed capital investment was sharply declining and exports and imports were stagnating due mainly to a lag in manufacturing. The report also presents in tabular form concrete information on wages and price levels. For example, in Table 10-5 one can see marked growth in industrial employee income. Prices also increased but, according to the authors, not as much as wages. This probably accounts for the spurt in domestic consumption, particularly in durable items. Noteworthy, too, is the fact that prices and wages were already climbing prior to the Revolution. Elsewhere in the report the authors indicate that in 1975 the government "wisely supported personal consumption by *not* following 'balanced budget'" policies and that over the short run such action served to offset the loss of emigrant remittances, the impact on the domestic economy of depression in Western Europe, and the drastic reduction in exports to its former colonies.

In the second part of the report, supply constraints are evaluated. Again we are instructed that the situation was not as bleak as many made it out to be. Labor unrest, management problems, and productivity declines were exaggerated by the mass media and the political parties. Where productivity declined, it was partially attributable to the lack of demand and the inability of management to discharge employees. According to the team, labor militancy was actually "no more difficult than in most other Western European countries" throughout this period of change.

After diagnosing the postrevolutionary difficulties of the economy, Dornbusch, Eckaus, and Taylor devote the remaining part of their report to Portugal's economic future. Although acknowledging that Portugal's economic posture will be strongly influenced by the way in which the country is able to recover and reorient its international trade, the team postulates that the country's economic health "will depend crucially on *internal* events," for example, the outcome of farm production as affected by agricultural reorganization policies and climatic factors, and overall government domestic policies to stimulate economic development. By and large, based mainly on monetary indicators, the authors are optimistic about Portugal's growth rate, provided that effective domestic policies are employed by the state to stimulate national investment and reduce unemployment.

In the absence of strong export market recovery, they prescribe controls on wages and consumption, principally to be offset by increases in government deficit spending. But in making these recommendations the team recognizes that important political, social, and economic judgments must first be made. For example, regarding price controls, they argue that the application of rent controls to curb inflation could discourage private investment in real estate, especially among small entrepreneurs, and force the state into housing. Indeed, since the Revolution, there has been considerable state participation in this area in response to the influx of thousands of refugees from Portugal's former African colonies. They also advocate the decentralization of financial institutions to maximize credit allocation to coincide with recent changes in ownership and property structure at the very time that the state, for political reasons, has centralized and nationalized financial institutions. Also problematical in terms of national investment is the "cultural" response. Portugal, they remind us, "has traditionally been a country in which the government has not run a deficit," a country which had strong gold reserves and, as others in this volume have noted, a country with a sound but not speculative or flamboyant economy, at least until Caetano. Because of these factors and undoubtedly due to their exposure to other beliefs that the Portuguese have held regarding their economy, at least implicit in the authors' discussion is a concern about the willingness and the readiness of the state to adopt new economic policies. Throughout their report, however, there are tones of guarded optimism, which contrast with Murteira's generally pessimistic view that the economic crisis facing Portugal has no easy solution.

Just as Brettell sees an external-internal linkage in the political conservatism of small-town and rural northern Portugal, Mário Murteira argues—from a national rather than local level—that Portugal's political crisis and its coup d'état were and will continue to be largely dependent on exogenous factors. Says Murteira, "The economic dimension of the social process has to be understood in terms of a global interaction of different factors, some of them external or exogenous to Portuguese society." In support of his hypothesis, Murteira briefly considers the economic structure of Portugal since 1950, the changes surrounding the revolutionary period, and the contradictions presented by dependency relations; he then weighs the country's future.

In the early 1960s, undoubtedly in response to the African wars, Salazar adopted a more liberal policy toward foreign investment as he attempted to move simultaneously toward European economic integration and political and economic integration within the colonial empire.[17] As a result agricultural production stagnated; according to Murteira, this in turn caused a marked increase in food imports and massive rural emigration. Emigrant remittances together with receipts from tourism, foreign currency surpluses from the colonies, and a net increase in foreign investments enabled Portugal to equilibrate its balance of payments in the 1960s and 1970s. In fact, by the end of 1973, Murteira observes, the country had accumulated "gold and foreign currency equivalent to almost two years of imports."

What weakened the regime were the protracted colonial wars "and the total incapacity of the Caetano regime to find a political solution." By asserting this, Murteira attributes the breakdown of authoritarian rule to political failures and indecisiveness, not to overall economic weaknesses. This assertion by Murteira undercuts the popularized version of the 1974 coup, which sees the old regime as an outmoded, "moth-eaten" dictatorship collapsing under its own weight, and provides economic data supporting Graham's initial premise: that the *caetanato* was not a weak state and that to understand the rapid collapse of the old order one must move first toward an appreciation of internal military affairs and military attitudes concerning the regime.

While noting (and welcoming) the postrevolutionary movement against the major centers of private economic power, the land reform, and the destruction of the old economic order, Murteira is concerned with whether or not these "qualitative changes" are definitive in light of growing unemployment (swelled by refugees from Africa), inflation, and a huge trade deficit. In fact, in his final argument Murteira adopts the view that the changes initiated in 1974 and 1975 were not and could not be permanent without an organized mass movement seizing control of the state. Reluctantly, he sees Portugal condemned to a subordinate place in Europe and, as the weakest nation, he predicts its political and economic domination by external forces.

Conclusions

The economic overview and recommendations in Chapters 10 and 11 provide a fitting note on which to end this volume, for it is in this assessment of the short-term prospects for Portugal that the reader is equipped with an economic foundation for evaluating and understanding the alternatives open to the government of Mário Soares and any that will follow. The outcome of the 1974 coup has been such that for the present Portugal, a small dependent nation, must seek a solution to its economic, political, and social problems in an international setting where its choices have been limited by the force of events in the capitalist world. It is in recognition of this dependency and vulnerability to external factors that the pessimism of Murteira and the optimism of the MIT group meet.

This is also an appropriate point at which to conclude our collective endeavors to offer a substantive basis from which others can better understand the dynamics and dilemmas of modern Portugal and arrive at their own conclusions regarding the country's future. The first five essays—those by Schmitter, Lucena, Wiarda, Makler, and Riegelhaupt—dwell mainly on the social and economic origins of the New State and the nature of authoritarianism and corporatism during the Salazar-Caetano era. The last five—Graham's, Hammond's, Brettell's, the OECD report, and Murteira's —turn to the revolutionary and postrevolutionary period, with Wheeler's (Chapter 6) providing a link between the two eras.

The Murteira essay thus brings to an end our perusal of contemporary Portugal from the vantage point of the social sciences. Along the way the reader will encounter in these chapters analysis of the foundations of the authoritarian regime which ruled Portugal for nearly half a century, two revolutions, various social strata and classes, and the socioeconomic processes which have engendered such significant change within Portugal. In the epilogue Stanley Payne reassesses the import of these papers as a collective endeavor and signals research topics for the future which will require the attention of anyone seeking to deepen further our understanding of Portuguese society in the midst of transition.

Notes

1. António de Spínola, *Portugal e o Futuro* (Lisbon: Arcádia, 1974).
2. Much of this domestic scholarship was either restricted in circulation or remained largely unknown within Portugal until after the coup. Illustrative writings would be A. H. de Oliveira Marques, *History of Portugal*, vol. 2: *From Empire to Corporate State* (New York: Columbia University Press, 1972) (first published in English); Hermínio Martins, "Portugal," in *Contemporary Europe: Class, Status, and Power*, ed. Margaret S. Archer and Salvador Giner (New York: St. Martins Press, 1971); Francisco Pereira de Moura, *Por Onde Vai a Economia Portuguesa?* (Lisbon: Seara Nova, 1969; 4th ed., 1974); José Cutileiro, *A Portuguese Rural Society* (Oxford: Clarendon Press, 1971); Adérito Sedas Nunes, *Sociologia e Ideologia do Desenvolvimento* (Lisbon: Morais Editores, 1968).
3. This paper was published along with other conference papers two years later. See Harry M. Makler, "A Case Study of the Portuguese Business Elite, 1964–1966," in *Portugal and Brazil in Transition*, ed. Raymond S. Sayers (Minneapolis: University of Minnesota Press, 1968).
4. A revised version of the doctoral dissertation on which this paper was based has since appeared, with the title *Interest Conflict and Political Change in Brazil* (Stanford: Stanford University Press, 1971).
5. The title of this paper is "European Economic Integration and the Portuguese Industrial Elite."
6. This paper was presented at the Yale Conference on Authoritarian Brazil and was subsequently published in Alfred Stepan (ed.), *Authoritarian Brazil: Origins, Policies, and Future* (New Haven: Yale University Press, 1973).
7. This paper was later presented at the First Conference on Modern Portugal and was eventually published as *Corporatism and Public Policy in Authoritarian Portugal*, Sage Professional Papers in Contemporary Political Sociology, vol. 1, 06-011 (Beverly Hills, Cal.: Sage Publications, 1975). Schmitter followed this paper with a broader interpretation of corporatism in its cross-national setting. See "Still the Century of Corporatism?" in *The New Corporatism: Social-Political Structures in the Iberian World*, ed. Fredrick B. Pike and Thomas Stritch (Notre Dame, Ind.: University of Notre Dame Press, 1974).
8. See, in particular, Martins' article in Archer and Giner (eds.), *Contemporary Europe*; also "Opposition in Portugal," *Government and Opposition* 4, no. 2 (1969): 260–263.
9. This research, which was also reported on at the First Conference on Modern Portugal, was later published as "The Portuguese Corporative System: Basic Structures and Current Functions" in *Iberian Studies* 2, no. 2 (Autumn 1973): 73–80. After the coup he updated that article with a two-page addendum: "Portuguese Corporatism Revisited," *Iberian Studies* 3, no. 2 (Autumn 1974). These articles were preceded by "Toward a Framework for the Study of Political Change in the Iberic-Latin Tradition: The Corporative Model," *World Politics* 25 (January 1973): 206–235. The two approaches—the general and the specific—were combined in "Corporatism and Development in the Iberic-Latin World: Persistent Strains and New

Variations" in Pike and Stritch (eds.), *The New Corporatism*. His larger study of Portugal was published as *Corporatism and Development: The Portuguese Experience* (Amherst: University of Massachusetts Press, 1976).

10. The results of that research were published as *Portugal: The Decline and Collapse of an Authoritarian Order*, Sage Professional Papers in Comparative Politics, vol. 5, 01-053 (Beverly Hills, Cal.: Sage Publications, 1975). A related theoretical essay appeared in Howard J. Wiarda (ed.), *Politics and Social Change in Latin America: The Distinct Tradition* (Amherst: University of Massachusetts Press, 1974).

11. Stanley G. Payne, *A History of Spain and Portugal*, 2 vols. (Madison: University of Wisconsin Press, 1973). Among his other publications on Spain, of note are his *Politics and the Military in Modern Spain* (Stanford: Stanford University Press, 1967) and *The Spanish Revolution* (New York: W. W. Norton and Co., 1970).

12. The work on the Church and State in Portugal and Brazil by Thomas C. Bruneau, an active participant in all three conferences, warrants special mention. The paper he presented at the Third Conference was published as "Church and State in Portugal: Crises of Cross and Sword," *Journal of Church and State* 18, no. 3 (Autumn 1976): 463–490.

13. Consult the previous references to the published work of Schmitter, Wiarda, Graham, and Bruneau. The Makler paper has been reprinted here because it is linked with Riegelhaupt's work (Chapter 5), with research subsequently completed by Schmitter (Chapter 1), and with the views of Lucena (Chapter 2).

14. The most notable of these is Kenneth Maxwell, who has preferred to publish his research separately. Of note are his two articles in the *New York Review of Books*: "The Hidden Revolution in Portugal" (April 17, 1975, pp. 29–35) and "Portugal under Pressure" (May 29, 1975, pp. 20–30). See also "The Thorns of the Portuguese Revolution," *Foreign Affairs* 54, no. 2 (January 1976): 250–270.

15. Schmitter published a revised version of this paper later: "Liberation by *Golpe*: Retrospective Thoughts on the Demise of Authoritarian Rule in Portugal," *Armed Forces and Society* 2, no. 1 (November 1975): 5–33. Fields' paper and a subsequent one delivered at the Toronto Conference have been incorporated into her book, *The Portuguese Revolution and the Armed Forces Movement* (New York: Praeger Publishers, 1976).

16. The MFA stands for the Movimento das Forças Armadas, the Armed Forces Movement—the military alliance which organized the coup and dominated events throughout 1974 and 1975.

17. Francisco Pereira de Moura in a paper presented at the 1973 ICGMP meeting (6 months prior to the Revolution) also noted that soon after Caetano came to power the internationalization of the Portuguese economy occurred as a strategy designed "to overcome the reduction of the domestic market and the problems generated by the rapid technological development and resistance of the powerful importers" ("The Development of the Portuguese Economy, 1945–1973," manuscript, October 1973, p. 10).

1. The "Régime d'Exception" That Became the Rule: Forty-Eight Years of Authoritarian Domination in Portugal

PHILIPPE C. SCHMITTER

Behind this portentous title lies an embarrassing absence of reliable data and a disarming modesty of intention. The coup of April 25, 1974, which liberated Portugal from over forty years of authoritarian rule, has yet to liberate scholars from the very limited information which is available to them to explain and evaluate the bases of that protracted political experience. In fact, the sort of data which might belatedly tell us why Portugal suffered so long under such a mode of domination has become a political weapon eagerly sought and seized upon by contending forces within the Revolution. As a result we may never have access to them, or only to those parts which best indict opponents or ingratiate supporters. It seems to take defeat in war and foreign occupation really to open up the coffers of the state to impertinent scholarly post-mortems on the bases of authoritarian rule.

One reason this material is so sensitive is quite simply that such a substantial proportion of the population, especially of the relatively privileged, educated, and politicized elite, is in some way or another "incriminated" by its contents. Ironically, a regime which was manifestly exclusionist, repressive, and unpopular seems to have managed to include, if not incorporate, a great many citizen-subjects at some time in its manifold activities whether by material self-interest, ideological conviction, youthful self-delusion, or just plain personal prudence and fear. Narrowly based as the rule of Salazar and Caetano surely was, it did draw from and subsist on a wide range of class, regional, sectoral, institutional, ideational, and personal interests.

Which brings us to the theme of this article: What were the social, economic, and political bases of authoritarian rule in Portugal? As indicated above, a compelling empirical answer cannot presently be given to this question. The best we can offer is a statement of the *problématique* involved and a few tentative conclusions. Much of the literature on authoritarian rule (or more specifically on fascism and/or national socialism) places heavy emphasis on the *social origins* of individual recruits to parties and movements, individual voters for relevant parties, or plebiscites, individual appointees to state or parastate roles, and/or individual leaders in the formulation of ideologies and policies. Presumably, the root hypotheses are (a) that the social relations of production along with ethnic cleavages, religious tensions, center-periphery location, status redefinition, and spatial and occupational mobility combine to determine a given country's propensity for authoritarian rule and (b) that identification of individuals within this manifold matrix permits one to infer that they "represent" in some sense underlying collective interests and forces. Hence, if a given authoritarian movement is found to have recruited more individuals of a given social category to its ranks than were proportionately present in the society as a whole, it is said to have been, at least in part, a product of that category's needs, aspirations, or illusions.

A second theme in the literature stresses the *economic context* within which authoritarian rule emerged and/or the functional impact that policies followed by a given regime had upon that country's economic development. From this objectivist, "who needed it" and "who benefited from it," perspective, heavy emphasis is placed on such conjunctural factors as depression, inflation, and unemployment and on such structural ones as capital accumulation, concentration of ownership, sectoral competition, shifts in technology and scale of production, and international competition. These macrosystemic imperatives of the mode of production in a particular stage of its capitalist development and in relation to that of other economies are seen as inducing crises and, thereby, producing an objective need for a change in the form and role of state power—whether or not this is subjectively and accurately perceived by relevant "needy" individuals. Hence, it is argued that authoritarian *régimes d'exception* obey certain constraints and opportunities intrinsic to the capitalist mode of production even if many of their recruits, supporters, and ideologues do not come from "the capitalist-bourgeois class" and even when many of those who rule them may be genuinely convinced that they are acting to overthrow or at least overcome the contradictions and irrationalities of that system of economic exploitation.

Yet a third major interpretive theme suggests that the roots of authoritarian rule are more specifically political. In an era of generalized expectations of legal, political, and social equality and of

mass aspirations for economic "progress," fueled by invidious inter-
societal comparisons and fed by the global diffusion of revolutionary
ideologies and insurrectional techniques, liberal-parliamentary bourgeois democracies find it difficult to contain their influence and
decisional processes within the structured confines of "normal" politics. Caught in a bind between increased demands and stable or
even declining political resources, electorates get shifty, party systems fragmented, leaders indecisive, negotiations protracted, policies incoherent, implementation ineffective, and legitimacy questioned. A pervasive sense of estrangement between the *pays réel*
and the *pays légal* emerges making political life appear epiphenomenal or artificial to much of the population. Into this breech rides
the providential man-on-horseback or steps the more prosaic parliamentary dictator, and these forms of transitional, "caretaker"
rule frequently pave the way for more protracted and institutionalized authoritarian regimes. This perspective suggests that, whether
radically mobilizational or conservatively demobilizational in form
or intent, these regimes are uniquely rooted in "the primacy of the
political." Hence, they emerge in different countries backed by
quite different social alliances and motivated by substantially different economic conditions. Inversely, they do not manage to seize
power in countries at a similar level of capitalist development and
societal complexity where political structures and class hegemony
are sufficiently strong to enable ruling groups to survive comparable
economic and social crises.

Even with the best of data, no single historical case study would
permit us to choose definitively which of these three "regions" of
determination best explains the emergence of authoritarian rule.[1]
In the specific case of Portugal, the data are manifestly insufficient.
The best we can hope for is an empirically tentative and conceptu-
ally heuristic discussion of the social origins, economic functions,
and political imperatives which seem to have led up to and subsequently sustained the regimes of António de Oliveira Salazar
(1933–1968) and Marcello Caetano (1968–1974). On the purely "po-
litico-logical" level, none of these sets of factors seems exclusively compelling and all three contain highly plausible elements of
explanation.

Social Origins

The pattern of *emergence* of authoritarian rule in Portugal in the
latter half of the 1920s had certain very distinctive features which

make it virtually impossible to analyze its *social origins* in the manner routinely used for such cases as Italy, Germany, Romania, Austria, Spain, or even Norway, Switzerland, Belgium, and the Netherlands. Ironically, the *consolidation and perpetuation* of Portuguese authoritarian rule possessed other unique features which make it fairly easy to establish its subsequent *social bases*. Why, then, such a paradox?

Unlike all other regimes of this type or subtype which successfully or unsuccessfully attempted to seize power in Europe in the interwar period, the Portuguese Estado Novo was *not* the product of prior activity by a militant, self-conscious movement or party. While there were minor groups of "integral nationalists," militant "Christians," aggressive monarchists, and even a "Young Turk" youth movement active in Portuguese politics during the republican period (1910–1926), these were directly responsible neither for the 1926 coup nor for the eventual accession to supreme power of Salazar in 1932–33.

Elsewhere, authoritarian-fascist movements organized to distribute propaganda, to compete in elections, to control the streets and plants through paramilitary violence, and/or to attempt armed seizures of power. In so-doing they left a "social trace" in the form of voting patterns, arrest records, membership lists of *Altekämpfer* (early followers), even casualty reports and obituary notices in the event of violent confrontation up to and including civil war. The general pattern observed in several detailed empirical studies seems to be one of an authoritarian movement, especially of the radical-mobilizational (fascist) subtype, "vacuuming up" discontent from a great variety of sources: class conflict, urban-rural cleavages, generational discontinuities, confessional differences, ethnic competition, national animosities, status shifts, and so on in a broad historical context of instability and uncertainty. Often beginning in a fairly socially homogeneous and geographically concentrated milieu, such movements, where they were more-or-less lineally successful in the interwar period, tended to get increasingly heterogeneous in composition as they approached the seizure of power. Once they acquired control of the state, their social bases shifted even more dramatically under the impact of bandwagonners. Where these movements never broke through the established barriers to entry in the political process (e.g., Great Britain, Norway, Switzerland, the Netherlands) or where they peaked early and/or fell short of posing a continuing threat to those in power (e.g., Finland and Belgium), an inverse dialectic can be observed of a very dramatic, progressive narrowing of their recruitment basis until individual psychological, if not psychotic, disorder became the major factor.

Nothing of this sort of continuous sociopolitical dynamic can be said to have existed with respect to Portuguese authoritarian rule. Take, for example, the closest thing to a forerunner which the Estado Novo possessed:[2] Integralismo Lusitano. Although one distinguished scholar of the Republic could claim in 1969 that "integralism was the oldest of existing fascisms" (it was founded in 1914) and that it "provided the bulk of fascist ideology after 1930,"[3] there is little evidence of its participation in the coup of 1926, although *integralistas* had apparently infiltrated the military officer corps and helped to write the proclamation of the armed forces after its successful uprising.[4] In fact, their movement as a political force had crested already in 1919, was internally divided over support for different monarchist factions, and had lost its principal intellectual leader, António Sardinha, in 1925. Summarizing its position "on the eve of the 28th of May [1926]," Carlos Ferrão described them as "dispersed and disillusioned . . . dominated by a sense of patent frustration in their publications and conferences, a reading of which leaves no doubt as to the decadence of the movement already ripe to accept compromises with the winners."[5]

From all accounts, the coup which put an end to parliamentary rule in Portugal was primarily organized as a military affair but initially enjoyed widespread "popular" support. The ambiguity and breadth of its social and political base are rather well illustrated, on the one hand, by the fact that actors ranging from the extreme left to the extreme right and representatives of very varied social groups seem to have welcomed its success[6] and, on the other hand, by the subsequent persistence of sharp factional conflicts within the military establishment over personnel, ideology, and policy. The ensuing two years of military dictatorship were marked by repeated coups, continuous plotting, contradictory public policy, and even greater instability than had plagued the parliamentary republic. Despite the patent bias of his monumental study of the Portuguese Revolution, Jesús Pabón was undoubtedly correct in observing that one "would fall into an understandable and curious anachronism by attributing, in general, to the [Movement of the] 28th of May the purposes which later were to lead to the creation of the Estado Novo."[7] I would only add that it would be similarly anachronistic to assume that knowledge of the social origins of those who actually led or indirectly inspired this antidemocratic and antiliberal military uprising in some way explains the emergence and consolidation of civilian authoritarian rule in that country after 1932. In fact, some of the Estado Novo's most vigorous (if unsuccessful) opponents played a role in the 1926 *golpe*.[8]

In 1928, Salazar was "invited" a second time to become finance minister[9] and imposed such stringent conditions upon his acceptance that he in effect became de facto head of government. Not until four years later (1932) did he get around to establishing the formal constitutional outlines of his "New State" and not until 1935 were its publicly "representative" bodies, the Legislative Assembly and the Corporative Chamber, first installed. While it would certainly be an exaggeration to claim that Salazar created authoritarian rule in Portugal *tout seul et de toutes pièces*, the evidence suggests that he played a very personal and imperious role in both the direction of policy after 1928 and the selection of personnel after 1932. Of course, he must have accommodated his choices to the demands and "advice" of various privileged classes and conservative and reactionary political forces, as well as those entrenched institutional actors, most notably the military and the Church, which had not been jailed, exiled, or cowed into submission by the repressive policies of the military dictatorship, but to an extraordinary degree Salazar could create from above the "elite" to which he felt the New State could or should be held accountable. After a ritualistic plebiscite in 1933,[10] the first legislative elections were held in December 1934 and the electorate of 478,121 (only 6.7 percent of the total population)[11] was invited to vote for a single list of candidates set forth by the União Nacional, a governmental party which had been established only shortly before—and long after Salazar had firmly gathered the reins of state in his hands. All "representatives" to the Corporative Chamber were handpicked by the executive (presumably by Salazar himself). Elsewhere, I have argued that this Câmara Corporativa closely resembled "a sort of National Honor Society or functional-administrative-intellectual College of Cardinals whose members had been anointed for their service to the State," and that "given this peculiar [ontology and] composition, one could argue that an examination [of it] affords a virtually unique opportunity to peer into and analyze the dynamics of elite formation [since] the Chamber represented precisely those interests, collective and individual, which Salazar wished to reward for their fidelity to the system, or to coopt in an attempt to ensure their future fidelity."[12] While it is possible that the composition of the Legislative Assembly more closely reflected Salazar's need to accommodate and co-opt the motley assortment of monarchists, national syndicalists, Catholics, renegade republicans, "Sidonistas," and military officers left over from the fall of the First Republic, it shared many of the appointive-anointed features of the Corporative Chamber. The social backgrounds of the founding individual members of these two "representative" bodies provide the primary empirical raw material from which I will attempt to infer the social base of authoritarian rule in Portugal[13]— along with some fragmentary data on ministerial appointments.

Given its manifestly traditionalist if not reactionary ideology, its extollment of the virtues of preindustrial society, and its pretense to the promotion of a *tertium via* between capitalism and socialism, the regime in Portugal has been "identified" as a *dictature de notables* and its supposed class origins "at least at the beginning" have further caused it to be labeled as a "dictatorship of large landowners."[14] Elsewhere, it has been suggested that these large landowners were closely allied with a *"comprador* bourgeoisie,"* that is, urban financial and commercial interests acting as local agents for foreign capitalists and traders, in a dominant "historical bloc" which provided the social base for the Estado Novo.[15] Such affirmations, common and reasonable as they may seem, are based on vague impressions or aprioristic assumptions. Table 1-1 provides an admittedly very incomplete basis for testing them empirically. Its breakdown of the reported occupations of members "invited" to the first sitting of the Legislative Assembly and Corporative Chamber (1934–1938) casts some doubt on the identity of this founding historical bloc. Agrarian landowners were not particularly prominent—no more so than in the Constituent Assembly that began the republican experiment twenty-three years earlier. Granted that the veterinarians (2), a few of the engineers and physicians, and many of the lawyers may have been agents of agricultural interests, nevertheless, the proportion of *terratenentes* hardly seems excessive when over 50 percent of Portugal's population was employed in agriculture at the time. Combing the biographies for any mention of an agrarian connection, only 18.7 percent (17 members) of the Assembly could be so identified. Incidentally, most of these appear to have come from the north, where relatively small landholdings are the rule, rather than the *latifundista* south. Although no single member reported his occupation as "industrialist" or "merchant," seven of the ninety-one had some position in industry, civil construction, or transport. Banking and insurance, however, had thirteen "representatives" in the Assembly—almost as many as agriculture. Contrary to the *"comprador"* label, these propertied

TABLE 1–1

Occupations of Members of the First Session
of the Legislative Assembly and Corporative
Chamber, 1934–1938

Reported Occupation	Legislative Assembly	Corporative Chamber	Constituent Assembly (1911)
Workers*	0.0%	8.4%	1.8%
Landowners*	8.9	10.3	8.4
Military officers**	16.7	9.3	20.8
Professors and educators	8.9	15.9	10.2
Lawyers and judges	41.1	6.5	14.2
Civilian engineers	10.0	8.4	0.1
Physicians and veterinarians	6.7	3.7	21.7
Industrialists***	0.0	15.0	0.0
Merchants	0.0	6.5	3.5
Other liberal professions	7.8	14.0	19.0****
Unknown	0.0	1.9	0.0
	100.1%	99.9%	99.7%
N	(90)	(107)	(226)

Source: Portugal, Anais da Assembléia e Câmara Corporativa (Lisbon, 1935).
*Includes agronomists.
**Includes military physicians and engineers.
***Includes construction.
****Includes 25 "government employees."

interests were connected to notably "domestic" enterprises—at least at this early stage in the regime's consolidation. Particularly striking in both the Assembly and Chamber is the high proportion of engineers and lawyers, and the low proportion of physicians—especially when compared to the nineteenth Constituent Assembly. Reinforcing this impression of the prominent role of middle-class professionals (in a later period these specialists might have been called technocrats, or técnicos) is the fact that an extraordinarily large number of the new deputies were or had been employees of the state—sixty-eight, or 74.6 percent of the total! Granted that many of these had been civil governors of provinces or administrators of municipal governments (and, here, possibly closely linked to rural local notables), about one-half were working for specialized agencies of the central government.

In a sense, membership in the Corporative Chamber is less revealing. Its formal composition more or less "guaranteed" a broader sectoral spread. Hence, it contained a lot fewer lawyers and judges, a few more professors and educators (from a wider variety of disciplines and establishments—five of the eight in the Legislative Assembly were from the two law faculties), many more industrialists and merchants, and a token 10 percent of "workers" (most of whom were middle-level employees). However, when it came to public employment, the Chamber rivaled the Assembly. Fifty-two percent of its members worked for the state in some capacity or at some level.

Before taking a glance at other dimensions of the social background of this founding elite, let us make a further distinction. Given that it was the first attempt to put together a representative component to a regime which itself was barely getting started, one can infer that mistakes were made and that not all the selections "worked out." What particularly interests us are those who left after serving only a single term and those of proven reliability who went on to serve numerous terms.[16] As Table 1-2 testifies, the *procuradores* of the Corporative Chamber proved less reliable (or more occupied with other affairs). Almost one-half left in 1938 and only 9 percent served as many as five terms, whereas nearly one-quarter of the *deputados* settled in for more than twenty years of representative duty. Comparing the occupations of the short termers and those of the long termers, one discovers that among the latter were no workers or merchants and very few landowners, military officers, engineers, or industrialists. The physicians, lawyers, judges, and professors were most likely to go on to

TABLE 1–2

Tenure of Members of the First Session of the Legislative
Assembly and Corporative Chamber, 1934–1938

Length of Term in Office	*Deputados* in the Legislative Assembly	*Procuradores* in the Corporative Chamber
1. Remained only one term	28.9%	46.7%
2. Served two terms	28.9	27.1
3. Served three to four terms	18.9	16.8
4. Served five or more terms	23.3	9.3
	100.0%	99.9%
N	(90)	(107)

Source: *Anais*, 1935.

TABLE 1–3

The Survival Rate of First-Session
Representatives by Occupation:
Legislative Assembly and Corporative
Chamber, 1934–1938

Occupation	Members Who Served	
	One Term	More than Five Terms
Workers	66.7%	0.0%
Landowners	47.4	10.5
Military officers	32.0	12.0
Professors and educators	16.0	24.0
Lawyers and judges	33.3	26.2
Civilian engineers	33.3	11.1
Physicians and veterinarians	20.0	30.0
Industrialists	90.9	9.1
Merchants	42.9	0.0
Other liberal professionals	54.6	13.6

Source: Anais, 1935.

have lengthy careers as representatives. We will return later to this notion of hard-core supporters with their great longevity and multiple careers within the public and private sectors.

The tumultuous political life of the Portuguese First Republic was marked by repeated clashes between the interests and style of Lisbon and those of the rest of the country, especially the more traditional, Catholic, small-peasant-landowners of the north. The coup of 1928 was a sort of pale imitation of the March on Rome and it began in the northern cities of Braga and Porto. Although not a country having very distinctive regional, ethnic, or linguistic subcultures, it could be argued that formation of the Estado Novo in the early thirties involved the mobilization of Portugal's periphery—its provincial towns and rural masses—against its center or, more particularly, against Lisbon. The previous observations concerning the role of provincial and municipal officials in both industry and commerce (with the notable exception of finance and insurance, which were well represented), and the broad similarity in occupational background with the 1911 Constituent Assembly— all suggest that geographic location (and, with it, differences in cultural values, degree of modernization, and scale of production) may have played an independent role.

Table 1-4 demonstrates that, despite the country being treated as a single electoral district, the places of birth of the *deputados* very closely matched the general population distribution. Although the data are not available for the 1911–1926 sessions of the Chamber of Deputies for comparison, one suspects that this distribution represents quite a change. In any case, the functionally recruited Corporative Chamber was a good deal more metropocentric. Unfortunately, the hand-written cards from which these compilations were made are not sufficiently legible to identify the names of some of the less well-known cities and villages so that a full and detailed geographic breakdown is impossible. From those which can be read, the impression is one of heavier than proportionate representation from the north (but not from the city of Porto itself). This does not support the contention that Portuguese authoritarian rule was primarily a reflection of latifundist domination, most of which is concentrated in the south.[17] We are reminded, however, that place of birth is not the same as place of residence and work (although the modest rate of urbanization in Portugal from 1911 to 1930—an increase from 17 to 19 percent of the total population— implies that internal migration was not very great) and that lawyers, engineers, and physicians from other parts of the country could act as agents for *latifundistas*.

Youths, university students, junior military officers, recently demobilized soldiers, and even juvenile delinquents play a rather

TABLE 1–4

Place of Birth of Members of the
First Session of the Legislative Assembly
and Corporative Chamber, 1934–1938

Place of Birth	Legislative Assembly	Corporative Chamber	Total Population (1930)
Lisbon	13.3%	29.0%	8.8%
Porto	3.3	8.4	3.4
Rest of the country, including colonies, Atlantic islands, and foreign countries	83.3	60.7	87.8
	99.9%	98.1%*	100.0%
N	(90)	(107)	

Source: *Anais*, 1935.
*Two places of birth unknown.

prominent role in most descriptive accounts of the emergence of authoritarian or fascist movements in interwar Europe. There is more than just a suspicion that the collapse of liberal parliamentary rule was somehow related to a breakdown in the intergenerational transmission of political values and partisan allegiances. Old parties and old politicians failed to attract youthful followers, and these relatively déclassé new participants were recruited in droves by promises of a new order and the thrill of a more virile style of political activity.

Portugal is no exception to this generalization. Most of the proto-authoritarian movements which preceded Salazar's consolidation of power had their origins in university student policies. What is less well known is that Salazar and the men he gathered about him in the early thirties also represented the emergence of a new political generation. Because Portugal later developed into an extreme gerontocracy, observers tended to forget that old men were young once—and that their youth was once an important factor in their strategy of domination. At the ministerial level, Oliveira Marques has already demonstrated the significance of differences in the average age of appointments as Portugal changed from monarchy to republic to New State. During the monarchy, the mean age of ministers was over fifty and increased with time. With the advent of the Republic, it dropped to 46.5 years and then rose gradually to 49.5. The dictatorship of Sidónio Pais (1918–1919) saw a dramatic but short-lived rejuvenation (to 42.8 years), after which republican ministers tended to get older. The military dictatorship (1926–1932) only increased that trend, but when Salazar put together his "own" cabinet in 1932 its average age was only 43.7 years. More important it brought to power the "Generation of 1910" which had come of political age precisely at the moment the Republic was founded.[18]

An age and generation breakdown of the 1934–1938 "representative" elite shows an interesting difference between the Assembly and the Chamber (Table 1-5). The former was much younger—very young in fact—bringing a whole new generation into politics. Almost one-half of its members came from the same generation and its average age was only 45.4 years. The Corporative Chamber was born older and had a more normal distribution across generations. As we shall see later, this meant that more of its *procuradores* had had previous political experience during the Republic. The *deputados*, however, were more likely to have been neophytes or to have held previous government positions only during the military dictatorship.

TABLE 1–5

Age and Generational Difference among Members
of the First Session of the Legislative
Assembly and Corporative Chamber, 1934–1938

Date of Birth	Age in 1934	Legislative Assembly	Corporative Chamber
Generation of 1880 (born 1851–1860)	83–74	0.0%	2.9%
Generation of 1890 (born 1861–1870)	73–64	2.2	11.4
Generation of 1898– 1900 (born 1871–1880)	63–54	17.8	21.0
Generation of 1910 (born 1881–1890)	53–44	25.6	31.4
Generation of 1920 (born 1891–1900)	43–34	48.9	22.9
Generation of 1930 (born 1901–1910)	33–24	5.6	10.5
		100.1%	100.1%
N		(90)	(105)*

Source: Anais, 1935.
* Two unknowns.

So far, in our quest for the social origins of Portuguese authoritarian rule, we have paid attention exclusively to the 197 members selected to form the first sessions of the regime's representative bodies. Elsewhere, I have presented data on members to subsequent sessions of those two chambers which showed a rather substantial continuity in social composition over the next thirty-five years[19]— this despite the fact that both the Legislative Assembly and the Corporative Chamber increased monotonically in total size and experienced a rather high rate of turnover in personnel.[20] Average age increased, of course, as did the proportion of "workers." Landowners and lawyers increased in the Chamber and decreased in the Assembly—the inverse occurring with physicians. Military officers, industrialists, and merchants became less well represented in both, as did the proportion of "metropolitans," that is, those born in Lisbon and Porto. A substantial amount (10 percent by 1965–1969) of shuffling back and forth between the two Houses also took place.

Before summarizing our impressions, let us take a closer look at the second session of these representative bodies (1939–1942). In 1935–36, the Estado Novo took a markedly "fascist" turn. A

TABLE 1–6

Occupations of New and Previous Members of the Second Session
of the Legislative Assembly and Corporative
Chamber, 1939–1942

Reported Occupation	Legislative Assembly		Corporative Chamber	
	New	Previous	New	Previous
Workers	0.0%	0.0%	19.4%	8.4%
Landowners*	9.1	8.9	9.7	10.3
Military officers**	9.1	16.7	9.7	9.3
Professors and educators	12.1	8.9	6.4	15.9
Lawyers and judges	39.4	41.1	6.4	6.5
Engineers	6.0	10.0	8.1	8.4
Physicians and veterinarians	18.2	6.7	8.1	3.7
Industrialists***	0.0	0.0	12.9	15.0
Merchants	3.0	0.0	8.1	6.5
Other liberal professions	3.0	7.8	11.3	14.0
	99.9%	100.1%	100.0%	98.0%
N	(33)	(90)	(62)	(107)

Source: Anais, 1939–1942.
*Includes agronomists.
**Includes military engineers and physicians.
***Includes construction.

paramilitary Portuguese Legion and a compulsory youth organization were established; the infamous PVDE (later PIDE) secret police
was created; large numbers of "volunteers" (viriatos) were sent to
fight in the Spanish Civil War; the rhetoric and symbols of the
regime became more aggressively nationalistic and antidemocratic.
Perhaps in the social composition of the 95 newcomers to the Assembly (33) and the Corporative Chamber (62) in 1938 we can find
a clue to the nature of the "ultras" that accompanied, if not encouraged, this process of fascistization.

Table 1-6, however, offers very little evidence of any dramatic
shift in response to these emergency conditions, existing or impending. They did manage to find some more "workers" to fill seats
in the Corporative Chamber. Physicians (mostly from small towns)
seem to have recuperated some of the representative role they earlier played under the First Republic. Somewhat surprisingly, the
proportion of military officers declined—despite the increased emphasis on military preparedness. The second-session newcomers to
the Assembly were much more likely to have come from Lisbon

(36 vs. 13 percent), but this merely compensated for the fact that previously "elected" metropolitans were less likely to have survived the first-term cut. Their total representation, therefore, remained fairly constant. Nor was there any distinctive juvenation. In fact, the median age hardly changed. Only a trickle of the new "Generation of 1930," that is, those born 1901–1910, managed to enter the Assembly (9) or the Chamber (12) in 1938. Thus, as Portugal appeared to move toward a more mobilizational and militant form of authoritarian rule (a stance from which it prudently retreated after 1945), and thousands voluntarily joined or were compulsorily enrolled in the new fascistoid organizations, the core of social support at the individual elite level seems to have remained the same.

Of course, not all the representatives in the first two sessions of the two chambers belonged to the "hard core" of regime supporters and activists. We have already identified some important differences between the single and multiple termers. Now, let us push this search a bit further and extend it over ministerial, upper administrative, and higher party positions. In Table 1-7, I have devised a system of weighted scores for various political and adminis-

TABLE 1–7

Scoring the Founding Political Elite
in Authoritarian Portugal, 1934–1942

	Hard-Core Points
Each term in Legislative Assembly or Corporative Chamber	1
President of Municipal Council, subsecretary of state, *chefe de gabinete do ministro, presidente de junta, directório geral*	2
Civil governor of province, head of PSP, ambassador to major country, national-level leader in União Nacional, Legião Portuguesa, Mocidade Portuguesa	3
Member of Conselho Político Nacional, Conselho do Estado	4
Minister of state	5
Types of Regime Activist-Supporters	N
Total of ten points or more = hard core	(48)
Five to nine points = semihard core	(63)
Four or less points = soft core	(181)
	(292)

Source: Anais, 1939–1942.

trative positions held by this founding elite and then divided the resultant aggregated total into three categories of supporters-activists: "hard core," "semihard core," and "soft core." Complicated and arbitrary as these quantitative manipulations may seem, they do provide us with a replicable and verifiable system for distinguishing different types and degrees of "service to the authoritarian regime."

The 48 hard-core, 63 semihard-core, and 181 soft-core activists do not, however, constitute a total enumeration of all those who served to put together the Estado Novo. A very few top leaders, including Salazar himself, never held a seat in either the Assembly or the Chamber. Some who did left early for protracted tenure in a single politico-administrative position, for example, Henrique Tenreiro, the "czar" of the Portuguese fishing industry. These are therefore penalized by the scoring system of Table 1-7, which gives a sort of quantitative premium to job switchers and multiple officeholders. Finally, not all those who played a prominent founding role in the New State remained loyal to it. For example, Henrique Galvão merited classification as a "semihard-core" supporter for his recorded activity before, during, and after his tenure as a *deputado*. In 1961, he led a revolt involving the seizure of the liner *Santa Maria* in mid-ocean in one of the most colorful and well-publicized efforts to overthrow Salazar.[21]

These caveats notwithstanding, Table 1-8 provides us with an illuminating picture of the socioeconomic bases of the regime in its formative phase. The soft core consisted of temporarily co-opted workers, physicians, industrialists, merchants, and a varied assortment of liberal professionals: clerics, architects, journalists, even a sculptor and a librarian. These relative outsiders were more likely to come from Lisbon or Porto and to have had positions in the relatively modern private industrial transport, communications, or commercial sector, although there was a sizeable proportion of landowners and others linked to the agricultural sector among them. The high proportion (15.9%) whose sectoral activity remained unascertainable consisted mainly of lawyers who listed no private economic connections or public-sector positions.

The semihard-core supporters-cum-activists overlap in some ways with the soft-core—for example, a few co-opted workers and liberal professionals—but are distinguished especially by two characteristics: (a) their dependence upon the state for a livelihood; (b) their status as agents, intermediaries, or brokers for or between other interests. This was the role occupied primarily by lawyers and sec-

TABLE 1–8

Formative Political Elite in Authoritarian Portugal, 1934–1942

	Hard Core	Semihard Core	Soft Core
Occupation			
Workers	0.0%	4.8%	8.8%
Landowners	6.2	11.1	8.8
Military officers	22.9	11.1	8.3
Professors and educators	27.1	11.1	7.7
Lawyers and judges	25.0	30.2	17.1
Engineers	10.4	9.5	9.4
Physicians and veterinarians	4.2	7.9	8.8
Industrialists	2.1	3.2	11.0
Merchants	0.0	1.6	7.2
Other liberal professions	2.1	9.5	12.7
N (48)	100.0%	100.0%	99.8%
Sector of Activity			
Agriculture	13.5%	11.1%	18.1%
Industry and transport	13.5	9.5	22.9
Commerce and publishing	3.8	1.6	10.6
Finance and insurance	19.2	6.3	4.3
Public service	48.1	63.5	28.2
Other or unknown	0.0	7.9	15.9
N (52)	100.1%	99.9%	100.0%
Place of Birth			
Lisbon	16.7%	22.2%	27.6%
Porto	4.2	3.2	8.8
Rest	79.2	74.6	63.5
N (48)	100.1%	100.0%	99.9%
Age			
Born 1851–1880	14.6%	28.6%	23.2%
Born 1881–1890	33.3	23.8	28.2
Born 1891–1900	39.6	33.3	36.5
Born 1901–1910	12.5	14.3	12.1
N (48)	100.0%	100.0%	100.0%

Source: Anais, 1939–1942.

ondarily by small-town physicians or veterinarians. One suspects that the semi-hard core of the Estado Novo was not composed of the direct owners of the means of production (as was much of the soft core and the hard core in their different ways), but of relatively self-made men who saw an opportunity to mediate between the state and private-propertied groups. They were the most likely to "militate" in the União Nacional, the Mocidade Portuguesa, or the Legião Portuguesa and to have been rewarded with a few terms as a *deputado* or *procurador*, an administrative position as president of a municipal council, and/or a national agency directorship, maybe even as a subsecretary of state.

The hard core of the regime seems to have been formed by a sort of amalgam of the first two subgroups of supporters with, however, definite characteristics of its own. It too had a high percentage of career public officials (48%), but these tended to be higher-level civil servants, for example, ministers, "inherited" from the military dictatorship or even from ex-republican governments. Officers, upper echelon and older, from the armed services—both army and navy—were prominent as were tenured university professors.[22] In fact, this *catedrocracia*, especially from the University of Coimbra, constituted the major source of recruitment to the hard core. Even by 1942 many of these had already acquired important directive positions in major private firms, which brings us to this elite's most distinctive "sectoral" characteristic: the marked importance of finance and insurance, followed in a balanced way by industry and agriculture. Rounding out the distinctive attributes of the hard core in this sample were its greater provincialness and its relative youth (in 1934–1942).

Our examination of the social relations which might have promoted if not made ineluctable the advent of protracted authoritarian rule in Portugal has led to some tentative conclusions. Some are supportive of "established wisdom," others less so.

The absence of "workers" and even lower-middle-class representatives, except in the most minimal and perfunctory manner, confirms the suspicion that the emerging Estado Novo had little or no support from "popular" classes or even the *mesoi*. The high proportion of provincials, especially among the regime's hard core, suggests that its rise to power involved a mobilization of relatively privileged groups on the geographic, cultural, and developmental periphery of that society against the more sophisticated, cosmopolitan, and "progressive" elements of its metropolitan center. Rural landowners were present in substantial numbers in the founding elite but appeared to have played a rather effaced role amid the soft core and semihard core of supporters. At least in terms of personnel, the Estado Novo was certainly not a "regime of *terratenientes*."

Nor does the foreign-dependent *"comprador"* element loom very large. Unless one extends the term quite incongruously to cover those with interests in the Portuguese colonial empire, very few of the propertied elements within its ranks seem to have had extensive foreign interests or even connections. Quite the contrary. They were a narrowly provincial and rather introverted *national* elite and, as we shall see, they followed correspondingly nationalist and exclusivist economic policies, at least until quite recently.

The other most distinctive social characteristic of this founding elite (or especially its hard core) were (a) its youth and narrow generational base; (b) its dependence on public employment; and (c) its close relationship with the financial and fiscal sector of Portugal's weak and dependent capitalist economy.

The conclusion that the Estado Novo was founded and staffed in large measure by a new generation composed mainly of civil servants, technicians, and professors of fairly provincial origins who, with the important exception of the financial sector, do not appear to have *initially* been controlled by or held accountable to either a liberal, internationally linked, modern industrial-commercial bourgeoisie or a conservative, provincially bounded, feudal-landed aristocracy does not, by any means, resolve the issue of the social bases of subsequent authoritarian rule in Portugal, or its relationship to the development of capitalism in that country. To infer from the indisputable fact that by the time of its overthrow in 1974 this regime was intimately connected with Portugal's industrial, commercial, financial, and agrarian bourgeoisie that such a relationship must always have existed is to commit an elementary fallacy, that of *nunc pro tunc*, or "presentism."[23] It is to ignore the historical process and sequence by which this came about. In the Portuguese case, there is evidence that the interpenetration of public and private power came from above rather than from below— by the deliberate and systematic placement of ministers, colonial and civil governors, higher military officers, subsecretaries of state, even *chefes de gabinete*, in private or mixed enterprises *after* their period of service to the state. Often of rather modest social origins and personal fortune, these men (there were virtually no women) received specialized training in law, economics, and engineering in one of the country's few university faculties and often held teaching positions there. If loyalty, ideological orthodoxy, and professional performance were found satisfactory, they were "rewarded" with a series of ill-paying governmental positions. At the end of this *cursus honorarium* lay much more financially rewarding positions as directors of major banks, members on the board of metropolitan and colonial enterprises, and presidents of mixed corporations.

In one of the very few studies which provide some data on the economic roles of ex-political officials, Raúl Rego manages to capture some of the dynamics of this process of growing interpenetration:

> Contrary to the usual manner of the old republican, the men of the Estado Novo, with rare exceptions, interpenetrated the large economic organizations and installed themselves within them. . . . One can find whole companies transformed into veritable beehives of ex-ministers, subsecretaries of state, directors-general, and colonial governors. . . . (with dismissal from high government position) the nominations were, as a rule, not long in coming. Weeks, even days, after ministerial remodelings, commenced the dance and counterdance of placing the outgoing ministers and subsecretaries. A few go back to the places they occupied before; others go into companies for the first time, leaving their law firms, their clinics, or previous public agencies. . . . It is evident that, in most cases, these men do not enter the boards of directors because of their technical competence. It is enough to see how they pass from one company to another with completely different functions to know that the capacity that promotes them is always the same—that of being an ex-minister. . . . It appears that Portuguese public life, for many, is only a passage to the private sector; from official administrative functions they go to lucrative positions in private companies.[24]

Rego followed this description with a list of forty-six ex-ministers and twenty-three subsecretaries and the private jobs they then held.

The social basis of authoritarian rule in Portugal seems to have been founded on a very complex pattern of recruitment and elite circulation. Its hard core, far from being a mere executive committee named by a *comprador* bourgeoisie and/or rural landlords, was composed of a distinctive generation of largely self-made men, liberal professionals and technicians, who used their control over the public apparatus of coercion to penetrate (but not subordinate) the private sector. Portugal may have had the least-developed, formally public productive sector in Europe, but no other country had as extensive and systematic a system of *pantouflage* (retirement) from leading public to private-sector positions. The end result was the sort of elite symbiosis between the state and dominant economic class described in the most vulgar of Marxist treatments of the capitalist state, but it was the product of a very different historical process and masked rather different relations of influence.

Complementing this hard-core symbiotic process were other "circulatory arrangements" connecting Portuguese civil society to the state. In the semihard core, this seems to have involved local notables from the provinces, relatively minor industrialists and merchants, medical and legal professionals, as well as an assortment of priests, architects, journalists, and so forth who were offered multiple-term representative roles, positions in provincial and municipal governments, and middle-level national administrative posts in return for their support or acquiescence. This group also seems to have provided most of the active participants in the fascistoid Legião and Mocidade organizations. The soft outer core was filled with a constantly renewed set of opportunity seekers recruited from a wide variety of social groups, but it was less territorially dispersed than the other two. Positions in the syndicates and guilds of the corporative system along with minor administrative jobs seem to have been sufficient to attract and retain them. When these three core "representative" elements are combined with other regime recruits —employees in ministerial and parastate regulatory agencies, members of the National Guard and the several police forces, not to mention a very sizeable contingent of paid informants—one begins to understand how this regime could have been unrepresentative and unpopular, isolated from virtually all social formations, and undefended when the crunch came, even by its most privileged beneficiaries, and yet could have managed to implicate in its *engrenage* such a substantial portion of the population. While this analysis of social relations tells us a bit about *how* authoritarian rule may have worked in Portugal, it does not inform us very satisfactorily about *why* it occurred. For that, we must turn to other explanatory factors, such as economic functions and political imperatives.

Economic Bases

Limitations of space, time, and data make it impossible to explore thoroughly here the economic needs which may have made authoritarian rule imperative in the Portuguese case. We can only touch briefly on the issues involved.

Much of the speculation on the nature of the relationship between the mode of economic production and the form of political domination in such societies as the Portuguese has focused on two issues: their *delay* in developmental timing and their *dependence* with regard to imperial, earlier developing, capitalist countries. These themes are interrelated, in fact often treated indistinguishably. Both emphasize the three central *problématiques* of capitalist development: (a) how to accumulate capital in ever-expanding amounts from a population whose scarce command over resources inclines them to immediate consumption; (b) how to realize profitably and privately the fruits of production given the inequality in distribution of property and its benefits, hence, structural restrictions on the size of the market; and (c) how to accomplish the above within national economies in the context of growing economic competitiveness and diffusion of expectations across international boundaries. Delay, however, draws attention more specifically to changes in the scale of production and, hence, capital requirements due to ensuing technological change; discontinuities in the process of import substitution; shifts in the historical-political role of economic sectors and social classes given differences in the timing of industrialization and commercialization; and "distortions" in both production and consumption patterns inspired by emulation and mimicry of earlier developers. Dependence tends to focus more on changes in the quantity and nature of foreign capital investment; secular trends and irregularities in the volume and price of exports and imports; crises in the balance of payments and value of national currency; discontinuities and opportunities created by interimperial competition and war; penetration and subordination of "national" classes by external interests; financial vulnerability of the state due to the need for foreign loans; and manipulation of preferences through external control of media and cultural symbols.

Both of these structural perspectives suggest that at particular conjunctures of delayed-dependent capitalist development major contradictions emerge which necessitate a change in the nature of political domination, and more specifically in the nature of the regime and policy role of the state. In a nutshell, the embryonic national bourgeoisie is rendered so weak and internally fragmented that it can no longer control the processes of accumulation and profit realization through privatistic action under an established set of legal guarantees, through a stable monetary system, and within the confines of a liberal-pluralistic political process. The direct coercive power of the state must be increasingly brought to bear to replace the loss of hegemony by these propertied elites and to re-

press the threat to "order" contained in the demands of nonpropertied, exploited classes.

Is it plausible to argue that the emergence and consolidation of
authoritarian rule in Portugal correspond to the structural imperatives of such a crisis in its delayed-dependent development? The
answer seems to be a qualified "yes," but not for the reasons most
frequently advanced. No one can deny that Portuguese development
was "delayed" relative to that of the rest of Europe, but much of
the contemporary literature focuses specifically on the way changes
in the scale and type of production during a process of industrialization through import substitution produce contradictions which
can only be resolved through "imperative coordination" by the
state.[25] Portugal in 1926 or 1932, however, was a long way from
having exhausted the easy, initial stages of import substitution.
Textiles were 12 percent of its imports, not to mention 8.9 percent
in assorted manufactures (mostly finished consumer products). Capital goods constituted only 11.9 percent of the country's foreign
purchases. Not until 1936 did these figures begin to change under
the impact of the regime's protectionist policies. Textiles fell to
3.4 percent, capital goods (including armaments) remained more or
less constant at 11.1 percent, while imports of consumer goods increased to 13.0 percent.[26] Nor can one find any evidence of an impeded or impending shift in the scale of production and, hence,
need for greater capital accumulation. Industrial production was
and remained mostly artisanal (two-thirds of all establishments employed less than 11 workers); total industrial employment (only
about 130,000) had shown no marked tendency to increase prior to
1926.[27]

Nor can external dependence simply provide an alternative answer.[28] When, in 1932, the British Embassy's commercial secretary
felt it necessary to explain why Portugal had escaped relatively un-
scathed from the Great Depression, he argued:

> In many fundamental aspects commerce, industry and finance
> in Portugal are isolated from the conditions which have de-
> veloped or have been created in many other countries since
> the war. There has been until quite recently relatively little
> restriction in the operation of the normal tendencies of supply
> and demand for her principal exports such as wine, cork and
> sardines. She has not suffered the creation of abnormal condi-
> tions arising out of industrialization on such a scale that a fall
> in commodity prices, the contraction of demand and monetary
> disturbances, have imperilled the safety of the structure. . . .

> The opportunities for foreign capital are relatively limited. . . .
> Portugal has never issued a foreign loan with the minor excep-
> tion in 1896 of the unissued balance of the 1891 loan. The
> whole of the State's and the country's foreign commitments
> have been met out of her own resources. . . . The fact that the
> State has not had recourse to foreign loans and that foreign
> capital has not sought investment here can now be seen to
> have eased her burdens during the depression.[29]

To the extent there was a structural crisis in the development
of Portuguese capitalism which made a change in the mode of political domination "necessary" by the end of the 1920s, it must,
therefore, have been of a different nature than the one which seems
to lie behind the rash of authoritarian "revolutions from above"
which have afflicted Latin America in the 1960s and 1970s, perhaps closer to those which produced "populist dictatorships" in the
same area during the 1930s and 1940s. One of its elements was
a severe banking crisis. In 1924–25 twelve banks failed and almost
as many new ones were founded. This chaotic reorganization of
the private banking sector was, in turn, linked to a growing extension of public authority. A very strict governmental supervision
of banks was decreed in early 1925. Equally important had been
the rapid and steady expansion of two quasi-public banking institutions, the Banco de Portugal and the Caixa Geral dos Depósitos.
The former was beginning to compete in regular banking services
and had acquired a near monopoly of foreign currency transactions;
the latter had become by far the largest savings bank in the country and was, in effect, fixing interest rates and the volume of loans.
"The result was that the Government and the state-guaranteed
Caixa absorbed between them practically all the capital which had
not fled the country. For the normal working of Portugal's economic
system, much less for its development, little or nothing was left."[30]
To this must be added the imposition of new, higher taxes on property after 1922.

This threatening absorption of available surplus by the state was
compounded by the spectre of an eventual extension of public activity and authority over industry. The "hottest" political issue on
the agenda at the time of the 1926 coup was what to do when (in
that year) the monopoly granted to a private (Franco-Portuguese)
firm for the production of tobacco products came to an end. The
parliamentary-republican regime was ready to implement a *régie*,
state-owned, system in the teeth of fierce opposition. The issue
of public versus private ownership of railways was also in conten-

tion at the time.[31] Moreover, in 1916 a labor ministry had been established for the first time and compulsory social insurance was instituted three years later. More social and redistributive measures seemed sure to follow.

The mid-1920s also witnessed a major crisis in the regime's economic and political relationship with its empire. Administrative and fiscal decentralization and economic liberalism in the Republic's colonial policy had led to some developmental changes in Angola and Mozambique, stimulated in part by the introduction of foreign capital, but in 1924–25, there came a monetary collapse in the value of Angolan currency, a sizeable decline in exports, and the near collapse of the two private *companhias* that were exploiting Mozambique. The metropolitan state was faced with the need for large budgetary subsidies and, of course, loss of previous surplus extracted from these possessions.[32]

Finally, while Portugal did not have a large-scale foreign debt, it did have the immediate problem of paying off its accumulated war debt to Great Britain. Some £22 million were owed and the British were pressing for payment.

The salience of these issues is well demonstrated by the attention paid to them between 1926 and 1930. Banking regulations were drastically changed. The Caixa was limited greatly in its role of lender to the state and some of its functions were transferred to the Banco de Portugal or to a newly created Caixa Nacional de Crédito aimed at lending to the private agricultural and industrial sectors. The Bank of Portugal, itself, was given a new constitution making it less of a threat to private banks. The tobacco *régie* was extinguished after a few months of existence, the concession put up for auction and repurchased by the former concessionaries. Part of the state-owned railway system was turned over to an existing private line. At one point (1928), the military dictatorship even went so far in its privatizing zeal as to decree private ownership for the post office, along with all telegraph and telephone services, but this was never implemented. Once Salazar had come to power, this drive for divesting the Portuguese state of its economic role disappeared and was replaced by the more modern, "neophysiocratic" aim of using public regulatory and extractive power to subsidize the expansion of private property.[33]

The creation of a separate Banco de Angola in 1926 and a new status for the Banco Nacional Ultramarino, the bank of issue for the other colonies, coupled with tighter budgetary control over colonial government expenditures and the dissolution of one of the private Mozambique companies began to clear up the imperial mess. This was capped in 1931 by a completely redrafted Statute for Colonies which reasserted centralized, metropolitan control and raised the level of intraimperial economic preferences. In 1928 an important convention was signed in Pretoria "regulating" South African recruitment of labor in Mozambique and ensuring the *métropole* of a sizeable annual payment in gold for the transaction. Instead of being a drain on public finances and private capital accumulation, the African possessions again began to make a positive contribution to both, although Angola remained in a depressed state throughout the 1930s. Finally, the British accepted a favorable Portuguese offer resolving the war debt issue in 1926.

Fragmentary as these data are, they do support the hypothesis that the advent of authoritarian rule coincided with a structural crisis in the development of Portuguese capitalism and that policies followed by the military dictatorship and the succeeding "financial" dictatorship permitted the stabilization and eventually the growth of this "delayed-dependent" mode of economic production.[34] To two generic conflicts within the capitalist growth process—(*a*) between concentrated accumulation of savings in private hands and the fiscal and monetary imperatives of a modern state and (*b*) between "natural" private monopolies which emerge strongly in the earlier stages of development and the need for public regulation, even ownership, of this basic infrastructure of transportation, communication, and production in order that its exploitative operation will not distort or endanger further capitalist development—was added another conflict specific if not unique to the Portuguese case: a country which is simultaneously developing on the dependent periphery of Europe *and* attempting to reap the benefits of the expanding world capitalist order. Portugal's participation in World War I (and the dislocation this provoked in its economic, monetary, and fiscal situation—not to mention the direct impact this had on civil-military relations) was in no small measure a product of the desire on the part of its ruling elite to demonstrate that they were entitled to membership in the "European Concert" and, hence, entitled to maintain their colonial possessions and imperial practices.[35]

Political Imperatives

This tentative finding—that both the advent and subsequent policies of authoritarian rule in Portugal were closely related to an "overdetermined" structural crisis in that country's capitalist development—by no means precludes the possibility that the emergence of this form of political domination also had its roots in more "superstructural" imperatives. In fact, the conflicts mentioned above were peculiarly "political" in the multiple sense that they tended (a) to reflect differences of interest between and *Koalitionsfähigkeit* among fractions of the same class, for example, financial versus industrial bourgeoisie, "old" versus "new" middle class, privately employed versus public service workers; (b) to focus on alternative uses (or nonuses) of state power rather than on differences in class hegemony; and (c) to involve (at least indirectly) the asymmetric impact upon Portugal of the unequal distribution of power among nation-states. They did not involve the sort of confrontation between polarized, self-conscious *Klassen für sich* which may characterize both much earlier and later stages of capitalist development, for example, feudal aristocracy versus urban bourgeoisie, industrial bourgeoisie versus industrial proletariat.

These "fractional" conflicts and efforts at alliance formation normally find political expression within the confines of a single regime type, but Karl Marx already argued very convincingly in his *Eighteenth Brumaire* that, under certain circumstances, they could lead to regime change (without change in the mode of production) and that they did so via the breakdown of previous influence and authority relations. Sterile ideological disputes, atavistic historical attachments, resurgence of regional loyalties, provincial resentment against metropolitan predominance, "inorganic" intellectuals and interest representatives cut off from their class connections, "parliamentary cretinism," praetorianism, violence, and illegal activity by *lumpen* and déclassé elements are but some of the "epiphenomenal" manifestations Marx observed in mid-nineteenth-century France preceding Napoleon III's seizure of power. Early twentieth-century Portugal exhibited many of these signs of political collapse and several others.

Another reason for stressing the relatively autonomous role of political factors is that, in terms of specific economic *conjoncture* (as distinguished from *structure* discussed above), Portugal was not in such desperate shape. The balance of payments was no further in the red than it had been for several decades; the exchange rate for the escudo had leveled off and had even appreciated a bit; 1925 was a relatively good agricultural year and wheat imports no higher than usual; inflation had slowed down and even stopped by 1924; many industries were in crisis (e.g., textiles, cork, flour, milling, and canning) but some were expanding (e.g., cement, mining, and ceramics); unemployment does not appear to have been more serious than usual; emigration remained heavy but declined; and wages and prices had returned to their relative relationship of 1914. Most of these indicators of current economic performance got worse rather than better in the two years following the 1926 coup! These facts by no means obviate the importance of the more deep-seated impasses and conflicts, but they do suggest that authoritarian rule did not come to Portugal in the imminence of economic collapse.

The most generic political cause of the collapse of democratic-parliamentary rule in Portugal was, as the current jargon would have it, the loss of hegemony over the society by its dominant classes. Conversely, this implies that one reason for the relative longevity of subsequent authoritarian rule lay in its ability to put together a viable "political formula" (to use a less trendy but similar concept) which convinced significant social groups of the naturalness or appropriateness of its domination. Of course, given the ubiquity and ambiguity of uses of the concept "hegemony," and the unfortunate empirical fact that its loss can only be ascertained retrospectively, this is not a very enlightening argument. Its analytical weight is more-or-less comparable to saying, "The regime fell because it was insufficiently (a) powerful, (b) popular, (c) self-confident, (d) internally coherent to sustain itself, (e) some combination of the above, or (f) all of the above."

"Conquering bourgeoisies" capable of providing the material and ideational bases for their preferred, liberal-parliamentary mode of political domination have been notoriously rare in delayed-dependent developing economies.[36] Compromised by their continued and intimate association with traditional agrarian and commercial elites, unable to compete in price and quality with products exported by earlier developers, penetrated by highly visible foreign interests, badly divided internally over further import substitution, derivative in their ideas and technology, and forced by a more militant and conscious working class to cope with "premature" and inflated demands for immediate personal benefits and expanded public goods, these capitalists have trouble protecting their "right to make money," much less asserting their "right to rule." In particular, hegemony within a "bourgeois-democratic" policy depends on managing at least three general problems: (a) creating and sustaining a minimal winning supportive coalition, (b) extracting sufficient resources from civil society to cover state activities, and (c) creating and sustaining the illusion that other modes of economic production and forms of political domination are impossible or inappropriate. In all three of these "management dimensions" the Republic experienced great difficulty and the military dictatorship which replaced it in 1926 performed even more poorly. It was Salazar's ability to combine and co-opt disparate elements into this National Union, to reorder public finances, and to take advantage of the fascist ideological trend in interwar Europe and, then, the anti-communist wave of the Cold War that accounts for his relative success.

The Portuguese Republic compiled a notorious record for political instability. However, beneath the 8 presidents, 45 major cabinet shuffles, 20 "revolutions," 325 "terrorist" incidents, and 518 strikes[37] which occurred during the regime's fifteen-year existence lay a rather successful experience in political machine building. The Republican Party (PRP), or "Democráticos" as they were more commonly called, managed to combine an urban petit-bourgeois and working-class following with the support of rural *caciques* and their dependent clients. This heterogeneous coalition won every election it contested, as can be seen from Tables 1-9 and 1-10. It rarely, however, enjoyed a clear majority and suffered endemically from factionalism which made cabinet formation and legislative support difficult. The high point of this perpetual game of "musical chairs" (many politicians were reappointed to ministerial positions they had recently vacated) came in 1920–21 when there were 15 major cabinet reformations and 146 ministers! By 1925–26, however, this ultrainstability in top-level personnel had declined markedly, as had the strike rate and acts of terrorism.[38] More significant

TABLE 1–9

Electoral "Support" for Governing Party:
Percentage of Legislative Seats Won by Democrático Party (PRP),
1910–1926

	1911 (Constituent Assembly)	1912–1915 (approx.)	1915	1918	1919	1921	1922	1925
Democrático seats as % of total in Chamber of Deputies	97.9	44.4	67.9	—*	52.8	33.1	46.5	51.3
N	(234)	(153)	(156)	(155)	(163)	(163)	(159)	(156)

Source: A. H. de Oliveira Marques, *A Primeira República Portuguesa*, pp. 179–181.
* No candidates.

TABLE 1–10

Electoral Support for the President:
Percentage of Electoral College Vote for Winner on First Turn,
1911–1925

	1911	1915 (May)	1915 (August)	1918 (April)	1918 (December)	1919	1923	1925
	55.8	96.1	37.6	—*	96.8	48.1	54.8	72.5
N	(217)	(102)	(189)		(125)	(181)	(197)	(171)

Source: Oliveira Marques, A Primeira República, pp. 182–184.
* Plebiscitary election of Sidónio Pais, 513,958 votes in favor.

in terms of maintaining broad coalitional support was the defection shortly before the coup of the left wing of the Democráticos. Previously, all "hiving-off" had involved defections from the right. For the first time, the machine seems to have lost the support of the urban masses who appear to have initially welcomed the military seizure of power.

The chaotic state of Portuguese public finance rivaled the country's ministerial instability for international notoriety in the post–World War I period. Much of the public debt was inherited from the profligate monarchy and war expenses did throw the budget balance badly out of kilter, but republican politicians found it virtually impossible to contain expenditures within the extractive capacity of the state. Nevertheless, the standard, contemporary arguments about the fiscal crisis of the capitalist state hardly apply.[39] Public welfare spending was virtually nonexistent so that one cannot attribute it to concerted pressure from an aroused proletariat. Rather it was demands for government employment and pork-barrel public works from petit bourgeois and provincial notables that inflated that side of the ledger.[40] Public subsidies and credit for industry were not a major source of disequilibrium, although there were enough "political capitalists" around to have made charges of illicit enrichment through government favors and funds a credible moral weapon for right-wing "integralists."[41] Nor was the regime so tightly bound by accountability to propertied groups that it could not extract more revenue from them. The fiscal reforms of 1924 were "progressive" and successful enough so that by the time of the Republic's overthrow the budgetary balance had markedly improved. The specific conflict-cum-contradiction which contributed most to the regime's demise was the decline in purchasing power of civilian and military employees to less than one-half of previous levels. The fiscal crisis of the Portuguese state in the mid-1970s was to a large extent internal to it, rather than externally imposed by "popular masses."

Finally, hegemony was weakened by the proliferation of ideological alternatives (mostly on the right) amplified by a free and greatly expanded press[42] and encouraged by the "success" of fascist or fascistoid experiences elsewhere (especially those of Mussolini and Primo de Rivera). As long as these alternatives were divided into multiple and competing currents of monarchism, nationalism, clericalism, conservatism, integralism, corporatism, and personalism, on the one side, and socialism, anarcho-syndicalism, and communism, on the other, the core republican dogma of popular suffrage, parliamentary rule, secular education and culture, defense of private property, and social justice through gradual reform and redistribution remained that which divided the Portuguese the least. The "victors" of 1926 seem to have embraced almost all these ideological divergences and to have had no clear intention to replace parliamentary republican rule with a new hegemonic order. Only after their abject failure, did Salazar and his allies manage to synthesize and syncretize a new political formula from several of these disparate components.

The first political imperative tackled by Salazar was the fiscal crisis. So many accounts of his financial wizardry have been published, it hardly seems necessary to describe how he accomplished the "miracle" of putting Portuguese public finances in order.[43] Ruthless centralization of control, improved accounting and collection measures, a few new direct and regressive taxes, and cuts in expeditures for the navy (but not the army), the National Guard, and education plus some internal borrowing made the books balance,[44] and from at least 1933 until the 1960s the Portuguese state accumulated fiscal surpluses and paid for investments and extraordinary expenses from these "earnings." The impact of these austerity measures on capitalists was softened by a reprivatization of the banking system, new credits for agriculture and industry, higher protective tariffs and imperial preferences, subsidized prices (e.g., for wheat), and, of course, efficient repression of working-class demands.

Putting together a dominant political coalition was a more difficult imperative to satisfy. If in retrospect the transition from "exceptional dictatorship" to consolidated authoritarian rule appears to have occurred smoothly, at the time, the outcome was anything but foreordained. Resistance came from the left, the center, and the right to Salazar's gradually unfolding scheme to abolish all political parties and incorporate all "right-thinking patriots" into a single National Union; to disband all class association in favor of singular, subsidized, and state-controlled syndicates and guilds; to convert parliament into an assemblage of hand-picked notables and experts; to render executive power unaccountable, not only to the whims of competitive choice, but also to concerted elite action; and to institute permanent censorship and regime control over "the ideological apparatus." Armed insurrections, verbal *pronunciamentos*, personal resignations, and general strikes came from a wide variety of groups: some who had supported the 1926 coup; some who had opposed it; some who felt the measures were going too far in destroying the nation's political life; others who felt that Salazar was not going far enough in establishing an integral, syndicalist-fascist state.

The political composition and complexion of those first sessions of the Legislative Assembly and Corporative Chamber are uniquely indicative of the sort of hodgepodge of tendencies from which Salazar compiled "his" winning coalition which he then retained for the next thirty years or so. Of the ninety *deputados* in the founding Assembly, sixteen (17.8%) had previously been deputies, only three had been ministers in the Republic, and some eighteen (20%) had been ministers during the 1926–1932 dictatorship. Among the corporatist *procuradores*, seventeen (15.9%) had already been deputies or senators, ten (9.3%) had been republican ministers, and only seven (6.5%) had been "dictatorial" ministers. What is even more indicative than this co-optation of past politicians is the date at which the holdovers first acquired their representative position. About one-third entered politics before 1910, that is, during the monarchy. The next cohort from which Salazar recruited his representatives were first elected under the peculiar circumstances of the Sidónio Pais "popular dictatorship" (1918–1919). In fact, five of the previous monarchists re-entered politics during this period. Over one-half of the ex-republican ministers seated in the Corporative Chamber also held their positions under this prototypical dictatorship. The final cohort of any importance consisted of those elected after 1920. Of these five, two served in the short-lived parliament of 1921 when the Democrático proportion of seats fell exceptionally to 33.1 percent. In short, the representative elite of the New State, while composed predominantly of new men without previous governmental or elective experience—or of those who had held high appointive office during the frequent shifts after the 1926

TABLE 1-11

Ex-Deputies Serving in the First Session of the
Legislative Assembly and Corporative Chamber, 1934–1938

	Monarchy (Before 1910)	Initial Session Served			Republic N
		Republic (1910–1914)	Republic (1918–1919)	(After 1920)	
Legislative Assembly	5	0	6	5	(16)
Corporative Chamber	5	6	5	0	(17)*
Total	10	6	11	5	(33)

Source: Anais, 1934–1936.
* One unknown.

coup—did manage to recruit important figures from monarchist, nationalist, and various conservative parties previously active in Portuguese politics. The link with Sidonismo was especially strong. By the second session of the Assembly and the Chamber, recruitment from these pools of previous talent and experience virtually stopped (only 2 in the former, 4 in the latter), and the proportion of alumni from the monarchy and Republic dropped thereafter monotonically—despite the fact that new entrants were as a rule no younger than these anciens.

Another interesting facet of this co-optation process concerns the regional origins of the holdovers. For those for which data are available (13 of the 16 in the Assembly), all came from the peripheral regions of Portugal: seven from the north, two from the south (Beja and Evora). Not a single one had previously represented Lisbon or Porto! This is not firm evidence that the Estado Novo "inherited" the caciques who had been so important to republican politics since so many of these provincials were monarchists or Sidonistas, but it does show its lack of interest in or accountability to urban masses and their historic political leaders.

Elections, of course, continued to be held after 1934—more regularly and predictably in fact than under the parliamentary republic. They were not, however, plebiscitary devices for arousing and certifying majority support. One cynic even claimed that their principal function was to enable the police to update their records on regime opponents. Table 1-12 shows that the Estado Novo began with a constitutional plebiscite in which only 5.3 percent of the population voted. By the Second World War the registered electorate and actual voters had stagnated at 11 to 13 percent. Little or no effort

TABLE 1–12

Electoral Support for Authoritarian Rule:
Elections for the Legislative Assembly, 1934–1973

Year	1. Actual Votes	2. Inscribed Electorate	3. Total Population	4. Turnout (2/1)	5. Participation (3/1)
1934	377,792	478,121	7,148,046	79.0%	5.3%
1938	649,028	777,033	7,505,554	83.5	8.6
1942	668,785	772,578	7,830,026	86.6	8.5
1945	569,257	992,723	8,045,774	57.3	7.1
1949	948,695	?	8,333,400	?	11.4
1953	991,261	1,351,192	8,621,102	73.4	11.5
1957	1,030,891	1,427,427	8,908,766	72.2	11.6
1961	1,112,577	1,440,148	8,932,000	77.3	12.0
1965	1,211,577	1,609,485	9,234,400	75.3	13.1
1969	1,115,248	1,784,314	9,582,600	62.5	11.6
1973	1,320,952	1,965,717	8,564,200*	67.2	15.4

Source: António Rangel Bandeira, As Eleições em Portugal (Toronto:
Brazilian Studies, July 1975), p. 3; Anuario Estatístico, 1957, p. lvi;
O Século, November 11, 1973; Keesing's Weekly, various numbers.
* The 1965 and 1969 values were interpolations. The 1970 census revealed
an unanticipated net decline in population since the previous decennial
census.

was made to expand the electoral rolls until Caetano came to power
(many more were eligible than actually enrolled) and the extraordinary constancy of the turnout may have had something to do with
the fact that a high proportion of those enrolled were civil servants,
employees of parastate agencies, and other public dependents.

Nevertheless, regional or better provincial breakdowns of voting
could be interesting proximate indicators of regime support, especially when analyzed in terms of patterns of abstention and even
overt opposition on the rare occasions when candidates were run
against the official state. Unfortunately, however, such breakdowns
are only available for the last two legislative elections (1969 and 1973)
and only in the former did opposing candidates present themselves.

The data in Table 1-13, despite its temporal shallowness, demonstrate a point I advanced earlier about the social origins of the authoritarian elite. The center of gravity of regime support as measured by both relatively high turnout and low opposition vote (the
rank-order correlation between the two is almost unity) lay in the

TABLE 1–13

Regional Support for Authoritarian Rule:
Elections to the Legislative Assembly, 1969–1973

Region	Turnout		Opposition Vote	
	1969	1973	1969	1973
North and Interior				
Bragança	79.3%	81.0%	0.1%	*
Guarda	76.9	78.9	4.2	
Viana do Castelo	76.6	86.8	13.2	
Vila Real	71.8	77.3	3.4	
Castelo Branco	69.7	74.3	5.6	
Viseu	68.3	70.6	4.5	
Braga	67.9	72.2	10.9	
Portalegre	67.7	79.7	0.0	
Coastal				
Porto	63.0%	65.9%	13.1%	
Aveiro	65.1	67.2	12.9	
Coimbra	62.8	72.0	12.4	
Leiria	61.7	69.1	11.0	
Central				
Lisbon	48.1%	54.6%	24.5%	
Setúbal	47.0	56.3	36.3	
Santarém	57.6	67.7	12.6	
South				
Evora	55.2%	64.9%	9.7%	
Beja	59.8	68.5	10.2	
Faró	59.9	71.9	9.8	
Islands				
Horta	79.3%	65.3%	0.0%	
Angra do Heroismo	59.4	61.3	0.0	
Funchal	58.2	53.5	6.6	
Ponta Delgada	49.0	50.0	22.2	
Global average for continent and adjacent islands	61.6%	67.2%	12.0%	

Source: See Table 1–12.
* Opposition slate withdrew from election.

lesser developed, Catholic north and interior—the region of small landholding peasants *par excellence*. The more developed, but still Catholic, "coastal" region occupied an intermediate position. The latifundist south showed higher abstention rates (in 1969 not 1973) but slightly less opposition electoral support, while the Azores and Madeira had a more inconsistent pattern with the exception of Ponta Delgada, the most populous of the Azorean Islands.

The seedbed of opposition was clearly situated in Lisbon and, more particularly, the relatively industrialized district to its south, Setúbal. In both forms of rejection, abstention and opposition voting, they were far in the forefront. Whatever impact this might have had upon the regime was, however, systematically distorted. In addition to the usual districting arrangements rigged to overrepresent rural areas, the electoral rolls were manipulated to the benefit of those regions most likely to support the regime. Hence, in Lisbon and Setúbal, the 1969 registered electorate constituted only 74 and 36 percent of the number of families and 21.7 and 15.5 percent of the total population, respectively. For Bragança and Guarda, the two most supportive districts, the corresponding proportions were 102 and 95 percent of families and 28 and 29.2 percent of the population.

To fiscal order and electoral manipulation, the New State added a third element for its hegemonic formula: ideological control. Perhaps, no aspects of Portuguese political life were as well known and documented as its oppressive censorship, sycophantish press, docile academe, and pretentious claims to exemplifying a natural organic corporatist order, historically and culturally appropriate to that country's society and traditions.[45] The Spanish Civil War and Axis victories in the early stages of the Second World War intervened exogenously to bolster these claims and practices. After a very "uncomfortable" period marked by the Allied victory and attempted quarantine of Spain, the regime's plausibility was again given an exogenous transfusion by the Cold War. The initial emphasis on antiliberalism and extreme nationalism switched to international collaboration in the Western Christian world against Soviet and communist aggression. Not until several decades did the isolation produced by protracted colonial war and the loss of raison d'être occasioned by American-Soviet détente begin to unmask and undermine this façade, as well as promote the emergence of a strong, left-radical alternative vision of Portuguese society.

Ironically, the only previous serious challenge to its ideological and political formula came from the extreme right. As different groups jockeyed to determine what kind of regime would succeed the obviously transitory military dictatorship, an authentically fascist and radical movement emerged from the ranks of Integralismo. Calling itself "National Syndicalism," it advocated an antiliberal, antibourgeois, anticapitalist, anti-internationalist, antibolshevik mobilizational solution—a corporatist *revolução*, not just a corporatist *enquadramento*. Its social base would have been the rural-provincial middle class, the peasantry, the working classes, and *técnicos*, and their mobilized efforts would have aimed at breaking the power of "citified bourgeois," "pseudo-intellectuals," "local *caciques*," "parasitic intermediaries," and so on.[46] With its cross-like symbol expressing its "Christian" vocation, its adoption of the red flag pre-empting Communist imagery, its blue-shirted militia attracting youth, its verbal violence and xenophobia reflecting its Integralista origins, its assurance of a harmonious corporatist order within the existing property system drawing the support of some privileged groups, its promise of social welfare and a more equal distribution of income appealing to some segments of the working class, and its emphasis on technical expertise appealing to professionals,[47] the National Syndicalists seemed in 1932 to represent the wave of Portugal's future. Despite rigid censorship, their propaganda circulated freely, even in a daily newspaper, clearly indicating official sympathy and even complicity. Their leader, Rolão Preto, was a personal friend of Salazar.

Despite or because of National Syndicalism's meteoric success in attracting followers and penetrating governing and military circles, it very quickly came into conflict with Salazar's own plans for consolidating a more moderate form of authoritarian rule around a loosely structured "honorific" single party and an impotent, state-controlled set of corporatist institutions. Preto's demagogic leadership qualities may have seemed a threat to the more self-effacing, technocratically efficient, paternalist image of Salazar. In any case, National Syndicalism's "welfarism" and verbal anticapitalism would have severely compromised the plan of financial and fiscal reconstruction which was the policy core of the Estado Novo. In 1934, in a series of confused events, Preto was arrested and exiled. Shortly thereafter "the purged executive committee of national syndicalists decided to terminate its existence and called upon its members to join the União Nacional."[48] A quixotic attempt at a coup by some of its die-hards (in collaboration with anarcho-syndicalists!)[49] the following year was easily suppressed. Ironically, the

Salazar regime appropriated many of the symbols and organizational forms of the Blue Shirts when, in conjunction with the Spanish Civil War, it entered its own fascistoid period.

Conclusion

The social origins, economic bases, and political imperatives associated with the emergence and consolidation of authoritarian rule in Portugal were hardly unique for interwar Europe. Their combination, however, was rather distinctive as was the eventual outcome. In Portugal, the "exceptional" form of bourgeois domination became the rule and the regime survived longer than elsewhere. One of the primary reasons for this extraordinary longevity is that Portuguese authoritarian rule lacked or deliberately avoided many of the features which elsewhere constituted the "fascist minimum."[50] Radical, antibourgeois, and anticapitalist motivations, while present, were relatively mitigated and easily transformed by co-optation. The political authority of the bureaucratic apparatus of the state was never undermined or even challenged by a "party-army." Demobilization rather than mobilization was the intended goal of most of its "representative" institutions; obedient compliance rather than enthusiastic support was the preferred role for its citizenry. Leadership was personal and concentrated, but hardly dynamic or charismatic. The regime's nationalistic policies were aimed at cautiously conserving rather than aggressively extending its imperial domain.

In common with analogous Eastern European experiences, this form of conservative-bureaucratic authoritarian rule emerged in conjunction with a rise of financial accumulation at a very early stage of capitalist development and a double crisis in the fiscal management and ideological hegemony of the liberal state. Many, if not most, of its cadres were recruited from within the bureaucratic apparatus of that state and the ideological apparatus of its universities. To the limited extent that mass support was involved, peasants, provincial *mesoi*, and local notables on the geographic and social periphery of Portuguese society were "mobilized" against its more cosmopolitan, secular, and developed center. The absence of linguistic or ethnic minorities, the weakness of a credible Communist or proletarian threat, and the *éloignement* of Portugal from great-power competition all contributed to moderating if not obliterating some of the scapegoating, xenophobia, violence, and other extremist *bizarreries* which characterized authoritarian movements and regimes with similar social origins, economic functions, and political imperatives elsewhere in Europe.

However, the Portuguese New State did share in common with virtually all fascist and authoritarian responses to capitalist development and bourgeois modernization a number of profoundly paradoxical characteristics.[51] True, the *social origins* of its individual leaders and supporters were not dramatically different from those who founded and ran the "bourgeois parliamentary" regime they displaced—a bit younger and more provincial, yes, but basically similar in class and occupation. Nevertheless, once in power, they created new patterns of elite recruitment, circulation, and interpenetration which in the long run did radically restructure the relation between Portuguese civil society and the state. In terms of *economic functions* the Estado Novo ostensibly aimed at creating a harmonious and organic *tertium genus* avoiding the excesses of both liberal-capitalist and bureaucratic-socialist development. Instead, it presided over the establishment of an economic system with the worst features of both: extreme inequality in the distribution of wealth and income, deep-seated class enmity, and exploitation, on the one hand; stultifying administrative control and reduced capacity for innovation and initiative, on the other. *Politically*, authoritarian rule in Portugal responded to imperatives for fiscal balance, stable coalitional dominance, and ideological hegemony. It ended in financial and intellectual bankruptcy supported in the crunch by only a handful of its own secret police agents.

Notes

A grant from the Social Science Research Council in 1971 gave me an initial opportunity to conduct research on Portugal. Since then, support from the Social Science Divisional Research Fund, the Committee on Latin American Studies of the University of Chicago, and the Tinker Foundation in New York has enabled me to continue that research. A revised version of this chapter is scheduled to appear in *Who Were the Fascists: Social Roots of European Fascism*, ed. Stein Ugelvik Larsen, Bernt Hagtvet, and Jan Petter Myklebust (Oslo: Universi tetsforlaget, forthcoming). The present chapter is printed here with the consent of the author and the editors of the Norwegian volume.

1. A related difficulty concerns the "exemplary" nature of the case being analyzed. While one could hardly question the *bona fides* of Portugal as a generically authoritarian regime from 1973 to 1974 (see Juan Linz, "Spain: An Authoritarian Regime," in *Mass Politics*, ed. E. Allardt and S. Rokkan

[New York: Free Press, 1970], pp. 251–283, for the general model), one could ask whether this type of political domination is not so broadly defined that it encompasses numerous subtypes, each with its own origins and ontology. Hence, whatever generalizations are suggested by the Portuguese experience may, at best, only be valid for a subset of similar authoritarian regimes—"Demobilizing, bureaucratized, and exclusionist," as I have labeled it elsewhere ("Liberation by Golpe: Retrospective Thoughts on the Demise of Authoritarian Rule in Portugal," *Armed Forces and Society* [Fall 1975]).

2. Leaving aside the small intellectual *coterie* of "Social Catholics" which grouped around Salazar and P^e. Cerejeira (future archbishop of Lisbon) first in the Academic Center for Christian Democracy at the University of Coimbra and later (1917) in a political party, the Portuguese Catholic Center. Salazar ran for and won a seat in 1921 on this party label but made only a brief appearance in the Chamber and then resigned (H. Kay, *Salazar and Modern Portugal* [London: Egre and Spottiswoode, 1970], p. 32).

3. A. H. de Oliveira Marques, "Revolution and Counterrevolution in Portugal—Problems of Portuguese History, 1900–1930," in *Studien über die Revolution*, ed. M. Kossok (Berlin: Akademie Verlag, 1969), p. 416 n. 27.

4. Hermínio Martins, "The Breakdown of the Portuguese Democratic Republic," paper presented at the Seventh World Congress of Sociology, Varna, Bulgaria, 1970.

5. Carlos Ferrão, *Integralismo e a República*, vol. I (Lisbon: Inquérito, 1964), p. 12.

6. For a lengthy list of those who welcomed the downfall of the regime (or, more accurately, of the Democrático machine), see A. H. de Oliveira Marques, *History of Portugal*, 2 vols. (New York: Columbia University Press, 1972), 2:174; also his *História de Portugal* (Lisbon: Palas Editores, 1973), 2:286–287 for a slightly different version. Also Stanley Payne, *A History of Spain and Portugal*, 2 vols. (Madison: University of Wisconsin Press, 1973), 2:559–577.

7. Jesús Pabón, *A Revolução Portuguesa* (Lisbon: Editorial Aster, 1961), p. 574.

8. Of the thirty-three opponents active in opposing the installation of authoritarian rule from 1928 to 1931, whose brief biographies were given, nineteen were military officers (A. H. de Oliveira Marques, *A Unidade de Oposição à Ditadura* [Lisbon: Europa-América, 1973], passim). Marcello Caetano has admitted very candidly that "within the dictatorship [of 1926], in both civilian and military circles, there were plenty of nonbelievers as well as believers [in Salazar]" (*Páginas Inoportunas* [Lisbon: LibrABria Bertrand, n.d.], p. 170).

9. Previously (in 1926) Salazar had held the post for a very short time but resigned when it became clear that the government would refuse to accept his policies. According to an eyewitness account, General Gomes da Costa, head of the victorious military junta, appointed Salazar without knowing who he was (Kay, *Salazar and Modern Portugal*, pp. 38–39).

10. According to the official results as reported in ibid., 719,364 voted "yes," only 5,955 voted "no," and some 488,840 abstained (p. 49). Other

published versions have given rather different figures. In any case, abstention was high but the regime had the nerve to claim that those not sufficiently motivated to vote "no" supported its position and, therefore, counted the 40 percent abstaining as voting in favor of the proposed constitution. See Antonio de Figuereido, *Portugal and Its Empire: The Truth* (London: Victor Gollancz, 1961), p. 40, for a description of the conditions under which this "popular" consultation took place.

11. In these first legislative elections, some 377,372 reportedly voted (79% of those eligible and 5.3% of the total population). Unfortunately, district breakdowns are not available for either of these elections. For these and several succeeding contests, the country comprised a single electoral district.

12. Philippe C. Schmitter, *Corporatism and Public Policy in Authoritarian Portugal*, Contemporary Political Sociology Series, Sage Professional Series, vol. 1, no. 06-011 (1975), p. 31.

13. The primary source for this analysis is the short biographies contained in the *Anais da Assembléia Legislativa e Câmara Corporativa* (1934–1975). Dr. Manuel Cabeçada Ataíde has kindly made available to me his collection of handwritten 3" x 5" cards which record this and other information. The tabulation presented herein should be considered tentative, given problems of legibility and manual sorting.

14. André and Francine Demichel, *Les dictatures européenes* (Paris: PUF, 1973), pp. 17, 32.

15. Nicos Poulantzas, *La crise des dictatures* (Paris: Maspero, 1975), pp. 55 et seq.

16. Therefore, we are assuming that the probability of mortality was equal for all categories at the beginning of the session. Obviously, some of the one-termers did not get reannointed, for the simple reason that they had died or become ill. Since the *procuradores* of the Corporate Chamber were significantly older than the *deputados* of the Assembly, this assumption could be a source of systematic distortion.

17. Although the compilation must be considered very tentative due to legibility problems with the names of the small towns, it seems that only nine members of the Assembly and six from the Chamber were born in the southernmost provinces. With 10.5 percent of Portugal's population residing in Evora, Beja, and Faró, as of 1930, the south was slightly underrepresented in these founding sessions. Stanley Payne (*History of Spain and Portugal*, p. 574) has calculated that under the parliamentary republic "the number of leaders from the [more conservative north] was 25 to 30 percent less than its population warranted."

18. A. H. de Oliveira Marques, "Estados sobre Portugal no Século XX," *O Tempo e O Modo* (March–April 1967), pp. 270–295.

19. Schmitter, *Corporatism and Public Policy in Authoritarian Portugal*, pp. 32–33.

20. The Assembly, which initially had a lower rate of turnover, gradually became more of a revolving-door institution. By the eighth session (1961–1965) almost one-half its members were newcomers and of these 80 percent left at the end of the term. The Corporative Chamber "lost" only 56 percent of its 101 newcomers.

21. Henrique Galvão, *Santa Maria: My Crusade for Portugal* (Cleveland and New York: World, 1961). Also Warren Rodgers, Jr., *The Floating Revolution* (New York: McGraw-Hill, 1962).

22. This *catedrocracia*—prominence of tenured university professors in the elite structure of the Estado Novo—raises the issue of *agencement*, the role of these professionals in relation to other interests. Apparently, a high percentage of them were directors of financial, commercial, and industrial companies (or became so subsequently). For a listing, see Armando Castro, *A economia portuguesa do século XX: 1900–25* (Lisbon: Edições 70, 1973), pp. 197, 276–277.

23. David Hackett Fischer, *Historians' Fallacies* (New York: Harper Torchbooks, 1970), pp. 135–140.

24. Raúl Rego, *Os Políticos e o poder económico* (Lisbon: Edição do Autor, 1969), pp. 15, 16, 18, 22, 25. In his *Depoimento* (Rio de Janeiro: Record, 1974), p. 112, Marcello Caetano acknowledges (and defends) these practices. He even suggests that they constituted a sort of functional substitute for pensions!

25. Cf. Guillermo O'Donnell, *Modernización y Autoritarismo* (Buenos Aires: Paidos, 1972), and his "Desenvolvimento Político: Novas Perspectivas de Pesquisa" paper presented at the Conference on History and Social Sciences, Campinas (SP), May 26–30, 1975, for Latin American cases; Ludovic Garrucio, *L'industrializzazione traira nazionalismo e rivoluzione* (Bologna: Il Mulino, 1969), for a more Eurocentric discussion.

26. Portugal, Instituto Nacional de Estatística, *Commercio Exterior, 1947*, 1: xxi–xxv. Also Oliveira Marques, "Revolution and Counterrevolution," p. 406.

27. Oliveira Marques, *History of Portugal*, 2: 119–129, for a general résumé of the *conjuncture*. Also Stanley Payne, *History of Spain and Portugal*, 2: 573–575. Actually, industrial employment decreased in proportional terms from 1920 to 1930, as did agriculture. The residual "services" category increased from 22 to 37 percent of the economically active population. For a more complete analysis of Portugal's relatively slow structural transformation during this period, see Armando Castro, *A economia portuguesa*.

28. Portugal, like most dependent economies, did tend to have a dominant trading "partner." The United Kingdom accounted for 24 to 30 percent of imports and 21 to 29 percent of exports in the 1926–1929 period. With "invisibles," this concentration may have reached 40 to 50 percent of Portugal's foreign exchanges. British interests also controlled important public utilities, much of the wine trade, and some industries. The United Kingdom also held Portugal's war debts.

29. A. H. W. King, *Economic Conditions in Portugal*, dated July 1932, Department of Overseas Trade (London: HMSO, 1932), pp. 9–10. Other United Kingdom consular reports by S. G. Irving (1926), Leonard H. Leach (1928), and A. H. W. King (1930) were important sources for the brief description of the economic situation which follows. Also Ch. H. Cunningham and Ph. M. Cap, "Portugal: Resources, Economic Conditions, Trade, and Finance," *Trade Information Bulletin*, no. 455 (Washington, D.C.: U.S. Department of Commerce, 1927).

30. King (1932), p. 19.

31. The most detailed description of political events and issues during

this period is Damião Peres, *História de Portugal*, suppl. (Porto: Portuca-lense, 1954).

32. The best general account of colonial developments is Oliveira Mar-ques, *História de Portugal*, 2: 355 et seq. Also King (1930), pp. 57ff.

33. Although one of Salazar's "fiscal decrees" upon his taking up the Finance Ministry in 1928 ordered the devolution to private enterprise of all state activities having "a purely commercial or industrial character," there is little evidence after that date of this having occurred.

34. For a similar emphasis on the "instrumentality" of fascism for capi-talist development, see J. Solé-Tura's article in *The Nature of Fascism*, ed. S. J. Woolf (New York: Vintage, 1969), pp. 42–50.

35. Cf. A. H. de Oliveira Marques, *A Primeira República Portuguesa* (Lis-bon: Livros Horizonte, 1970), p. 78.

36. In his *Depoimento*, Marcello Caetano aims some of his most bitter remarks at the "lack of culture," absence of risk-taking, monopolistic in-stincts, and political timidity of Portugal's bourgeoisie.

37. See Oliveira Marques, *A Primeira República Portuguesa* for docu-mentation on cabinet shuffles and strikes. The other data on instability are contained in R. V. Gersdorff, *Portugals Finanzen* (Bielefeld: Verlag Giese-king, 1961), pp. 6–9.

38. Oliveira Marques, *A Primeira República Portuguesa*, p. 161. Also David Ferreira, "Greves," in *Dicionário de História de Portugal* (Lisbon: Iniciativas Editoriais, 1965), 2: 379–386.

39. Cf. James O'Connor, *The Fiscal Crisis of the State* (New York: St. Martin's Press, 1973).

40. Especially crucial was the substantial increase in state employment under the Republic and the decline in purchasing power of civil servants (Oliveira Marques, *A Primeira República Portuguesa*, pp. 58–59). The Por-tuguese case before and after the Estado Novo appears to confirm the "Di-rector's Law" which states that "Public Expenditures are made for the primary benefit of the middle classes, and financed with taxes which are borne in considerable part by the poor and the rich" (George Stigler, "Di-rector's Law of Public Income Redistribution," *Journal of Law and Eco-nomics* 13 [April 1970]: 1–10.

41. Rego (*Os Políticos*) takes indignant exception to these charges appar-ently repeated as late as the 1960s in campaign speeches by Marcello Caetano. Also, Oliveira Marques, *History*, vol. 2, refers to moralistic reac-tion to corruption, scandal, and "political capitalism" as a factor in the generalized rejection of the parliamentary republic (pp. 172–174).

42. Hermínio Martins in his "Breakdown" essay places considerable em-phasis on this communications explosion. In a country which had 80 per-cent illiterate and had a population of only 5 million there were almost 600 periodicals in 1900—more per capita than the United States or the United Kingdom. In 1926 there were 35 dailies and 283 weeklies being published.

43. For his own account, see A. de Oliveira Salazar, *A reorganização financeira* (Coimbra: Coimbra Editôra, 1930). A very comprehensive treat-ment is Araújo Correia, *Portugal Económico e Financeiro*, 2 vols. (Lisbon: Imprensa Nacional, 1938). Also useful is *Doze Anos na Pasta das Finan-ças: 1928–1940*, 2 vols. (Lisbon: Corporação do Crédito e Seguros, 1968).

44. The League of Nations, however, refused until the mid-1930s to certify that Portuguese public finances were in fact balanced since the nominal equivalence of receipts and expenditures was accomplished by domestic borrowing and juggling of categories. To make his fiscal miracle more impressive, Salazar always used the first year of military dictatorship (1926/7) as the base year, rather than the last fiscal year under the Republic (1924/5).

45. For example, Peter Fryer and P. McGowan Pinheiro, *Le Portugal de Salazar* (Paris: Ruedo Ibérico, 1963); Fernando Queiroga, *Portugal Oprimido* (Rio de Janeiro, 1958); Rudi Maslowski, *Der Skandal Portugal* (Munich: Hanser Verlag, 1971); Mário Soares, *Le Portugal Bailloné* (Paris: Calmann-Levy, 1972).

46. A. Neves da Costa, *Para além da ditadura I: Soluções Corporativas* (Lisbon: Nacional Sindicalismo, January 1933).

47. Cf. "Portugal's Blue-Shirt Fascism," *Literary Digest*, June 3, 1933, p. 14. For an excellent but brief analysis of National Syndicalism, see Hermínio Martins, "Portugal," in *European Fascism*, ed. S. J. Woolf (London: Weidenfeld and Nicolson, 1968), pp. 319–322.

48. Martins, "Portugal," p. 320.

49. Stanley Payne refers to a similar attempt in Spain at virtually the same time in which a "fascistic group" of "national syndicalists" (later JONS) made an unsuccessful appeal to the anarcho-syndicalist worker confederation (Epilogue, this volume). Presumably, both the Spaniards and the Portuguese were inspired by the success of Italian nationalists in recruiting syndicalists to their cause a decade earlier.

50. For a listing of "the fascist minimum," see Ernst Nolte, *Die Krise des Liberalen Systems und die fascistischen Bewegungen* (München: Deutscher Taschenbuch Verlag, 1966). A more limited but more reactive and negative definition of generic fascism can be found in his *Three Faces of Fascism* (New York: Holt, Rinehart, and Winston, 1965). Even more *ad hoc* are the listings in Paul Hayes, *Fascism* (London: George Allen and Unwin, 1973); F. L. Carsten, *The Rise of Fascism* (Berkeley: University of California Press, 1969); and N. Kogan, "Fascism as a Political System," in *Nature of Fascism*, ed. Woolf, pp. 11–18.

51. The paradoxical nature of fascism has been noted by others. For example, in Nathaniel Greene's Preface to his *Fascism: An Anthology* (New York: Thomas Y. Crowell, 1968).

2. The Evolution of Portuguese Corporatism under Salazar and Caetano

MANUEL DE LUCENA

António Salazar's retirement in September 1968 opened the door to a new era. In forty years, the country had changed a great deal. Although change proceeded slowly until the end of the fifties, it accelerated considerably afterward. Under the influence of two powerful forces—the colonial war and integration with the rest of Europe—Portuguese economy and society were breaking through the shell of old Salazarist protectionism. Portugal was no longer "essentially agricultural"; nor could she continue to evade the winds of history, an evasion which had only been relative anyway. Having arrived at a collective turning point in their lives, the Portuguese were being forced to understand, and understand quickly, that industrialization, decolonization, and democracy were part and parcel of the same thing.

When Salazar's successor, Caetano, inaugurated his liberal policies, this notion was confirmed. The only remaining question was whether the regime would be able to pass peacefully or would its opening to new ideas provoke, instead, breakdown and downfall? Whether one tended toward one or the other answer, the Salazarist regime itself was at death's door. The "political death" of the man meant the death of his work. Salazarism was weakened by overall decrepitude.

It was hard to believe Marcello Caetano when he spoke of "renovation in continuity." What was he promising? In almost everyone's eyes the phrase was only an alibi. For some it masked immobility, while others thought it was the necessary cover under which to liquidate an onerous heritage.

Recourse to some political lies is probably inevitable in a situation such as that in which Caetano found himself. But it would perhaps be wiser to think that Caetano wanted to do what he said he would do. His major ruse, and also his major weakness, lay in arousing irreconcilable expectations in order to divide his enemies. He was a disciple who wanted to create, and for this reason, his plan interests us here to the extent that it did not appear to be utopian.

In effect, Salazarism was already renovating itself before the departure of the master. In its underhanded, veiled, and empirical manner, the New State was altering the interior equilibrium of its forces, bending the course of the economy, trying to adapt its structures and rejuvenate its doctrine. Aided by technocrats, the industrialists took precedence over the landed proprietors: the doors were opened to foreign capital, labor and social security laws were reformed, and corporatist organization was revised. Poverty and the "small shop" were no longer eulogized. These reforms were carried out with reticence, of course, and without any apparent political overture. Salazar, vexed, said one day, "But if you want to enrich yourself . . ." He disliked our times.

The style and rhythm of Salazar had become too much of a burden. He was adapting, but without enthusiasm. Then he no longer adapted. Thus, his disappearance was important. A prudent old man who had imposed a rigid hand on everyone had departed. In 1968, it was a bit like the death of a father. Energies were liberated. But this does not mean that his order naturally followed him into the grave. Metamorphosis is also conservation.

Metamorphosis of what and what kind of metamorphosis? This is the issue that must be examined. However, it is first necessary to define Salazarism. Without knowing what its essential traits are, one cannot measure the changes which occurred. In the first section of this paper, we will define Salazarism as a form of fascism without a fascist movement, providing some explanation for this definition. Then we will pose an explicative hypothesis for the evolutionary course of the Salazar-Caetano regime. Based on a reading of Manoilesco, the hypothesis is the following: fascism is corporatist but not all corporatism is necessarily fascist. Caetano's "renovation within continuity" would precisely consist in passing from one form of corporatism to another.

In unleashing its ties with fascist structures which had been accepted to that point, the Caetano regime did not, however, renounce the principle of authority, or nationalism, or the organic collaboration of classes as foundations of the state. In this way, the troubling paradox of things which change and do not change can be explained.

In short, the "Social State" of Caetano became responsible for maintaining the essential values of the "New State" by different means and in a new context.

In this paper, we will expose very dryly our vision of the whole, though we cannot hope to provide full support for the argument in a short article.

Salazarism, Fascism, Totalitarianism

The political left has an annoying habit of calling "fascist" almost everything it considers evil. *A fortiori*, because evil is a simple matter, one no longer distinguishes, in historical reality, the diversity of which it is comprised. Within fascism there is ideology, the movement, and the state. In systematically confusing these, one impedes all possibility of analysis. Theory and propaganda are two distinct matters; without the first, the second at times becomes foolish.

Whatever it is, the concept of fascism is vague. For our discussion here, however, it is decisive and must therefore be clarified. In order to do so, we will begin with some comments on the Italian experience. Subsequently, we will be able to compare it with Portugal, so as to define Salazarism. Finally, because it is thought (wrongly) that fascism was a totalitarian regime, some ideas will be offered on that subject. The notion of totalitarian power is too important to be used with impunity.

SUBVERSIVE FASCISM AND FASCIST POWER: THE ITALIAN CASE

The original fascist program, issued from the famous meeting at the Sala di Santo Sepolcro (Milan 1919), was hardly corporatist. It was more socialist and tinged with anarcho-syndicalism, however unstructured and vague it may appear. In this program one finds the proclamation of a republic and decentralization of the executive; destruction of the bureaucracy; abolition of partisan politics as well as election and independence of judges; abolition of compulsory military service and secret diplomacy; general disarmament and prohibition of war matériel manufacture; suppression of incorporated firms; confiscation of unproductive revenues, fortunes of war, and ecclesiastical goods; administration of industry by workers and technicians; distribution of land to the organized peasantry.

This program may be subversive anywhere. It was especially so in Italy because it was incompatible with monarchy and Catholicism. Followed to the letter, it frightened the bourgeoisie, the army, the Church, the crown.

It is worth noting that this initial program was never formally shelved, but after the fascist movement seized power, it received the support of elements which were very different from those at the beginning, antagonistic even. In fact, the movement was filled to the brim with opportunists.

The landed proprietors joined first in the "squadrist" phase. They provoked an important turn to the right. The transformation of the National Fascist Movement (the MNF) into an organized party (the PNF) took place in December 1921, after the failure of the "pact of peace" with the Socialists. This pact had threatened to rupture relations between Benito Mussolini and the Agrarianists of Dino Grandi. *A posteriori*, it appeared to be a simple, expedient tactic. However, one wing of fascism saw it differently; it would have preferred the alliance of two revolutionary families, a little in the manner of the German "national Bolsheviks" of Ernes Yunger, who later on became Nazis. A pious illusion, without doubt, but a striking one. Mussolini, although he departed from the socialist revolution, remained nostalgic about it until the end.

Following this phase—in which little by little the landed proprietors, monarchists and Catholics, industrialists and bankers, and even many of the political personages of parliamentarianism identified themselves with fascism—Mussolini legally received power from the king, confirmed by a massive vote in the Chambers. He relied on the monarchy until 1943; he was economically liberal until 1929 and a friend of the bourgeoisie until Salò;[1] he made peace with the Church and managed the Roman question.

On the other hand, he never ceased to deceive his oldest partisans, either in his relaxation of the program or in his contempt for common logic. Mussolini exalted action over theory. Thus he was able to tranquilly accept doctrinaire contradictions. Antiliberalism, antibolshevism, the aggressive cult of the nation and the state—these were the concepts to which he was most faithful. In the rest, he varied. The corporative idea itself, in his hands, was everything, everything in being almost nothing. During his entire career, Il Duce made a political principle out of an absence of scruples. Salazar said once that he was, above all, a "great opportunist of action" and Giovanni Gentile cut out for him a philosophy (named "activism"), promoting efficacious instinct.

We have said that for Mussolini corporatism was everything without being anything. This is exact. But this is to say that we are dealing with an unusual instrument of ideological and political mediation. Susceptible to disparate interpretations and the most contrary of usages, corporatism united all the currents that divided the regime. To each his own version. His officials often disputed, sometimes to the point of threatening fascist stability. And then, at the last moment, Il Duce would intervene. A skilled demagogue, he was obeyed by all because he flattered the hidden designs of each, sometimes even as he renounced them brutally.

In this manner, subversive fascism began by being deprogrammed while activism (which was violent) moved delicately toward respectability. Then, the corporative idea was imposed (quietly) and became a regime, based on the dictatorship of a single party and leading the country toward an uncertain future. Under the iron thumb of one unpredictable man, the regime and the party tended ultimately toward definitive fusion. But this happened slowly: the Camera dei Fasci et delle Corporazioni was not created until 1939. Moreover, it was a political rather than a practical fusion, in which the role of fiction remained important.

It would be better not to insist too much on fascist lies. Those who limit themselves to denouncing vicious propaganda, laughing at delays and contradictions, or seeing corporatist lacuna let one essential factor escape: they do not understand that sometimes (and to a certain extent) fiction becomes reality or that an order can be efficacious because it is illogical or even "nonexistent." Corporatism can equally be conceived of as an "aide-de-camp" for private initiative as well as an impartial tutor of social classes, assuring their discipline and their peaceful collaboration, for the greatest prosperity of them all and for the sake of the country, or even as the deathblow of capitalism and the antichamber of a classless society. And so, having awakened these irreconcilable hopes, corporatist fascism would reign. Responding in some degree to the desire of all its clients, the fascist regime in Italy had a right, a center, and a left; but, while it always controlled them, it never quite fulfilled their wishes. Mixing, shaking them all again and again, was Mussolini's political art, a balance of Machiavelism and authority.

Once the monopoly of the PNF over trade unions was guaranteed, the class struggle found itself blocked at its root. This was Mussolini's main purpose. The corporations could wait and did wait. Their advent (1934) changed little; they were both the driving gear, often embottled, and the exhaust pipe for dreams. Right and left,.

capitalists and collectivists, continued to dispute this. The center, from time to time, acted in a jacobine way.

Above all this scuffling, Mussolini maneuvered according to circumstances. Until 1929, the emphasis of his economical policy was somewhat liberal. But in 1932, the country faced with a serious economic crisis, his speeches took him further: he declared that capitalism was lost, that the crisis was *of* the system and not *within* the system. At this time, at the Congress of Ferrara, Ugo Spirito produced his theory of "propertied corporations" to which the means of production ought henceforth to belong. These corporations would realize a "progressive fusion of capital and work." But, since workers and technicians, supported by the state, would be largely in the majority, the aim would be expropriation, as calm as it was inexorable. Capitalists would be enveloped and anesthetized by the organic nation. In short, there would be revolution, but without violence, thanks to fascism. But this was theory. In practice, worker representation was immediately altered: impressive, for example, was the number of prominent people charged with representing working-class interests in the corporations. Thus, Spirito's thesis remained literally on paper. But, nevertheless, aided by social demagogy, its illusion was tenacious. "National campaigns" (for wheat, literacy, swamp draining) and the din which was raised over a few partial realizations (reserve funds, family allocations, the *dopolavoro* organizations for leisure time) seduced, for a moment, many Italians.

Capitalism lost nothing, but it changed in the end. Favorable on the whole, too favorable even, to private businesses, fascism regulated them and used them for its adventures. In the context of quite heavy planning, this control was often resented as abusive coercion by the capitalists themselves. It was often thought to be a means of preparing the way for their complete absorption by the state.

Briefly, the bourgeoisie worried a great deal in the course of its long fascist march. Large capitalist interests, which played a laissez-faire game until the crisis, became afterward the major beneficiary of state intervention. They were massively sustained by public funds, protected all along. However, their visions did not always coincide with those of the state. In the context of an economy which was becoming more and more "mixed" (IRI[2] was born at this time), tensions were frequent. But these were not the cause of rupture. Such causes emerged only when the war took a turn for the worse. Then the capitalists deserted a ship in perdition. The fact that by doing this they escaped the consequences of long complicity should lead us to reflect.

Mussolini fell from power for the first time in 1943 after having been placed in the minority within the "Grand Fascist Council." Due to whom? To an opposition whose most powerful figures were those eminent men most closely allied with the crown (Federzoni), large land property (Dino Grandi), and big business (Ciano). This opposition also included the "father of corporatism" (Bottai), a man who was a typical representative of *fascismo nazionale*, the national compromise which had sustained the regime. But, in turn, at the second fall of the dictator, who died with him? Hard-core Fascists, among whom (let us note) were the most famous secretaries of the PNF: Farinacci, Starace, Scorza, Pavolini. When Mussolini, placed back in the saddle by the Germans (1943), installed himself on the shores of Lake Garda, he tried to restore himself by returning to the origins of fascism. Surrounded by the nostalgic, the desperate, and the pro-Nazis, he partially took up again the program of the Santo Sepolcro. This was the period of the Salò Republic, of "social and republican fascism" in the occupied north.

There is no need to write an epilogue to prove the erratic character of the "socialization" promised by the Salò regime. Mussolini was no more than a "factotum" for the Germans: he begged the Nazi ambassador for at least seven of the fifty trucks produced daily by Fiat; he let Hitler seize Friuli and Venezia Giulia (naming his own Gauleiters for these two provinces); and he was not even able to control his own communications or to maintain an effective body guard but had to rely on SS protection. The Italian people wanted to fight, yes, but for the Resistance, not for any vague fascist socialism. Under these conditions, the belated return to the first fascism, with its anticlerical and antiplutocratic vocation, was costly only to some priests and unfortunate businessmen—and also to the imprudent rebels of the Grand Council (Ciano and de Bono, for example) who did not escape in time. Their trial at Verona was merely a macabre parody. Nothing new was born at Salò. "Social and republican fascism," once truly unchained, made the Resistance its target. Completely isolated, it was no more than a shadow of power serving the Nazis. Naturally, things ended very badly.

Over its lengthy course, fascism presents us with a changing face. But one can, "grosso modo," discern three phases: that of its origins, that of the established regime (1925/6–1942) until the turning point in World War II, and that of approaching defeat and mortal convulsions. If one accepts this scheme, one will be tempted to say that the basic logic of the original movement emerged in its complete identification with Nazi Germany, in the Republic of Salò. *In extremis*, Il Duce attempted to respond with the plebeian and petty bourgeois attacks and passions typical of his initial élan.

Some say that authentic fascism is found at the beginning and at the end; that the rest, that is to say, almost everything, is only a long interlude; that these twenty middle years, however agitated (Ethiopia, Spain), were all in all the pale face of a necessary historical compromise riddled with treason; that corporatism as it was practiced in Italy after the Rocco Law (1926) was nothing but the regime's own N.E.P. (New Economic Policy), and so it continued to be. Twenty years, after all, are so little in the life of a people.

For twenty years, in effect, the "pure" Fascists lamented. They demanded a "second revolution," the social one to give meaning to the political revolution of 1922–1926. Through tenacious hate they were tied to those who were Fascists by mere convenience. They fought unremittingly in favor of the Axis, suspected others, and wanted to remain faithful until the end. The Axis represented, in their eyes, not only strength but also purification, because the Nazis appeared to be much closer to accomplishing certain old dreams. And it is among those belonging to the hard core of the PNF that one finds the rare harbingers of antisemitism in Italy.

All this appears to confirm the purist interpretation. It touches partial truths, but it breaks down in front of an impenetrable boundary: this pure fascism was never a regime. It was a desire, then a whim, then a defeated game. If one wants to evaluate a regime *sui generis*—that is to say, a state with a particular set of policies and programs for tying together its multiple social bases—one must dig into the "opportunist," or so-called corrupted middle phase. This phase took form between 1922 and the fascist-oriented laws of Alfredo Rocco (1926). It was then consolidated and spread throughout the country as an ambiguously designed national alliance of divergent interests.

In this alliance, pure fascism (a complicated grouping of sects) retained possession of only a part of the action. It was the presumptuous heir of the original movement, but this movement was harnessed to the state. And it was already quite enriched, that is, altered, well before it took power. Of course, the fascist movement was never completely dissolved within the state no more than was the PNF completely integrated into the state. Formally, yes: the Grand Council being the organ for integration at the upper level. But in substance a significant nuance always remained between the state and the party, expressed in terms of that famous duplication of administrative, syndicalist, and police "parallel" structures. But, on closer examination, one discovers the following: that the state prevailed and that it was only partially transformed by fascism.

In one sense, fascism conquered the state, and in this sense its original inspiration was decisive. The fascist movement influenced the state's antiliberal and antidemocratic reforms and altered its policies. Furthermore, it acted directly on society, covering it in tentacular fashion with its organizational network. But the state, on the other hand, domesticated the fascist movement—and did so in two ways. First, by forcing it to cohabit with other forces, it limited its natural, totalitarian dynamism. The militia was put under the aegis of the army, which was faithful to the king; the most rabid syndicalists and the most obstinate militants had to choose between allegiance and disgrace; those responsible for the state police itself (Bocchini, Senise, for example) were not to be identified with the convinced Fascists, and the party mistrusted them, justifiably so; they were monarchists. And Carmine Senise joined the successful conspiracy against Il Duce in 1943.

Second, the fascist state, while submitting, provided compensation. From the beginning, thousands of militants were employed everywhere: in the state bureaucracy, in the local administration, in the corporatist structure. They were honored and paid and thereby changed. Some, like Farinacci, who exiled himself to Cremona, would not abdicate from their subversive plans. But the majority resigned themselves with more or less bitterness. And some, like Rossoni, the syndicalist "leader," adapted so well to the capitalist order that Mussolini himself considered them to have sold their souls. At the height of rampant *embourgeoisement*, the left wing served propaganda purposes; it served the regime's crusades; it served finally and above all to attract youth. And it waited its hour; but when its hour arrived, fascism was finished. It finished in the hands of the Allies, but had this not occurred, it would have collapsed in the hands of Hitler. "Social and republican fascism," which was Germanic, only knew how to maintain itself as a protectorate. It renounced formally the national fascist alliance and never did have the opportunity to impose itself single-handedly over Italy.

To summarize thus far, as Italian fascism pursued its activist course, it remained, despite detours along the way, the victim of contradictions. Its great stabilizing invention was first corporatist doctrine and later corporatist organization. To some it guaranteed an end to subversion while others accepted subversion in order to maintain the flame of commitment.

Fascist fidelity has always been antiliberal, anticommunist, and nationalist. The first two, as negative passions, favor unity. As for nationalism, however expansive and violent it may have been, for a long time it remained fluid enough to avoid ruptures. At times it appeared excessive in its desire to export revolution, dreaming of a new European, even worldwide, order. But at other times it laid claim only to certain territories in a tone which was classical and unquestioning of the traditional rules of the diplomatic game. Let us clarify this point, which is of great importance.

Through all the former wars among the European powers, a new equilibrium had always been established by means of a compromising peace. But then, in these first decades of the twentieth century, fascist Italy started considering itself as the "great proletarian nation." Therefore, it wanted to hoist the flag of exploited peoples against "plutocratic" England and France in a mortal, uncompromising fight, whose final aim seemed to be the destruction of the enemy's political and social order. This was new and more dangerous, even if some thought that it was only a tactical way of reclaiming a place in the sun. However, Italian diplomacy varied so greatly that, even after Spain, the democracies awaited a new about-face, and Hitler always feared such would occur.

At a given moment it appeared also that fascist bellicosity was a "bluff" which for internal reasons was executed to assure cohesion within the regime. And it is also true that the risky and adventurous side of Mussolini's foreign policy was almost always balanced by prudence and cowardice. He preferred to fall upon the weak and the dying. It was only in this way, moreover, that he was thrown into World War II, seduced by the overwhelming military performances of nazism.

A bad guess? In this regard, some say that Italian belligerency was a mistake, an avoidable move; that there was no sufficient reason for it; and that, without preferring war, Mussolini would have lasted. Others think that Italy was doomed to war and defeat by the very nature of the fascist regime. This is a disputable issue, but the very existence of doubt (never allowed with Hitler) makes us guess the ambiguity of *fascismo nazionale*. I am inclined to support the second thesis. But one must understand why Salazar, wounded by Mussolini's decline and fall, tended to support the first. Besides convenience, the point is that he looked at all this from the point of view of his own "fascism," that is to say, on the basis of a national compromise which ignored the great tension brought by an authentic fascist movement. The time has now arrived for us to proceed to a general comparison of these two regimes.

FASCISM COMPARED

There are remarkable differences between Mussolini's Italy and Salazar's Portugal. We will review the main ones in order to arrive at an understanding of how Salazarism was a form of fascism without a fascist movement. All these differences are based upon this characteristic. Their similarities, on the other hand, can be seen almost only at the state level. It is through an examination of these differences that their similarities will become apparent.

Origins

Mussolini emerged from one of the most bitter of class struggles. He was a great socialist leader who "betrayed" the cause. Salazar, conservative and Catholic, never abandoned his original convictions. Thus, the tumultuous origins of "squadrism" are to be contrasted with Salazarist respectability. Mussolini was carried to power by an ardent movement, Salazar by a classical military coup. The Italian fascist movement preceded the conquest of power and the reform of the state. The National Union, Portugal's only party, was born of the dictatorship and grew (though little) under the aegis of the new regime. Its ideology and its structure were incomparably more lax than those of the PNF. It was not a movement of the masses, not even a party of cadres. It was more a regrouping of prominent people, an agency of the government.

This difference is not at all fortuitous. It is due to the disparities separating the two countries: their unequal development, their different levels of class struggles, their different national problems without common measure. Italy had emerged bloody from World War I, without being compensated by peace. It was an overpopulated country without colonies. Its capitalism was more advanced. Its working class, in the cities and in the countryside, more numerous and consistent, had imposed agrarian laws, occupied factories, and approached revolution. The ruin of the Italian middle classes was worse than in Portugal. Finally, Italy's national unity was recent and ambiguous: its inspiration came from the French Revolution, of course, as well as it did from the Roman Empire, and the Renaissance. In the Italian *risorgimento* all these influences operated. One has only to look at the most popular of these men, Giuseppe Garibaldi. He seduced democrats but eulogized Caesar. And the social composition of his groups (students and military men, liberal professionals, tradesmen, the petty bourgeoisie, and plebeians) reminds one of the first *fasci di combattimento*. The fascist movement injected itself into this tradition (in fact it confiscated it while distorting it) in the midst of social combat and a major national crisis. As a way of taking power and then managing it, the movement became more astute and formed a durable alliance with the "establishment." But tension remained at the interior of the regime, burning the extremes.

Italian fascism never knew how to aspire to the relative peace of Salazarism. It maintained, despite everything, a hostile attitude toward the old society, which became more and more demagogic without ever ceasing to be menacing at times. This is what makes uncertain, however, intimate, its compromises. The monarchy and the Church never felt completely sure with Mussolini. Nor did the bourgeoisie, which one must not confuse with large-scale capitalist interests, since the latter could merge with the state.

There was nothing like this (or very little) in Portugal. Salazarism was conservative to the core. His pacts with the "establishment" were natural and his love of traditions was sincere. There were, of course, the Blue Shirts of Rolão Preto. However, they recruited the majority of their leaders from the integralist-monarchists, disciples of Maurras, and had no importance except when Germany and Italy appeared to represent the future. They engineered a foredoomed revolt (September 10, 1935), they were exiled, and their national syndicalism without workers vanished without further explanation. Speaking of these men, Salazar said: "They like to live an intense, frenetic life. . . . The tumultuousness of German or Italian life, the style of Hitler or Mussolini fascinated them. They wanted me to inspire them with some sort of sacred hate toward our enemies. But that is not my purpose. I want to normalize the Nation. I want to make Portugal live habitually."[3]

These phrases illuminate an epoch. Here is what he wanted—and what he did—a man in whose eyes "men change little and the Portuguese hardly at all." Fascism in Portugal? Yes, but lymphatic. Salazar gained in equilibrium what he lost in vigor.

Before the New State came into being, a nationalism which was somewhat radical and a bit leftist took form: that of the "Octobrists." In October 1921, they seized power and held it for two months. It was a confused movement (limited to urban areas) whose history has yet to be unraveled. Its iron sword was the National Guard with its "Young Turk" officers of Lt. Col. Liberato Pinto. Its base was composed of revolutionary elements from the navy, dissidents from the democratic left, certain syndicalists, and lesser people. Nevertheless, the October coup, anticlerical and antiplutocratic as it was, appears to have been financed by the largest Portuguese industrialist Alfredo da Silva. But some of the revolutionaries wanted to kill him. Discredited by the "bloody night" (in the course of which liberal Prime Minister António Granjo and the father of the Republic, Machado Santos, were assassinated) and disunited, the Octobrists were expelled by electoral means in January 1922. They still attempted revolts without a great impact, before and after 1926, but not after 1933. They quickly resigned themselves to the New State and, afterward, some of them joined it.

Worship of the Leader

Salazar was a university professor; Mussolini, an agitator, a journalist, and a tribune. This difference was not fortuitous; nor was it by chance that the Portuguese called upon professors, jurists, and engineers while the Italian first surrounded himself with adventurers, syndicalists, and plebeians.

It is this contrast which is largely responsible for the presence in Italy and the absence in Portugal of a fascist movement. Even if there is likewise an element of unpredictable chance, one must understand that divine providence, when choosing its great men, always remembers what kind of country is to be saved. God knows, there were impetuous people in Portugal. They did not however play a major role. Leaders that would last were needed in Portugal and in Italy. But, given the circumstances, they had to have different, even opposing temperaments.

Mussolini formulated clearly his "Führerprinzip." Il Duce, according to the fascist catechism, *ha sempre ragione.* He was not *the* head of state (nor was Salazar), nor did he actually establish a legal basis for his legitimacy; it was charismatic and due to an irreproachable and mysterious "personal virtue." It was also due to fascism, of course, and therefore came from the people. But what is fascism without Il Duce? It was his own creation as the Italians themselves would be. As a matter of fact, Mussolini wanted to change the temperament of his compatriots. And then, properly speaking, his legitimacy would be evaluated in the future, not by any previous consent, even if he was plagued by a king representing the past.

Concerning the people, one must say that Mussolini recognized in them only the capacity for flashing intuition, fruits of seduction, if he said yes. But not the power to say no: this would be to err or to show weakness. In essence, Mussolini legitimized himself. Victor Emmanuel, wanting to depose him legally, had to wait for that famous meeting of the Grand Council. That is to say, he waited for the downfall of fascism when the Allies were at the door and Rome was bombarded. Otherwise he would not have dared.

In examining fascist catechism one shivers (even if one is not a believer) over the systematic usage, with respect to Il Duce, of the most intimate sacred vocabulary, vocabulary which pious Catholics reserve for the Trinity, even when it somehow occurs to them to divinize a man. In Rome, the head of Christianity, such language was sacrilege. The Church swaggered. But she also knew how to be patient with the fascists, those barbarians: she tolerated their insanities, which are usually punished in the Catholics. It was necessary for the Church to defend herself no matter what, in order to prevent Mussolini from exceeding all limits.

On the contrary, Salazar was a pious Catholic and a calm man. It is true that sometimes he let his propaganda exaggerate in praising himself. But, except for a few episodic deliriums, the official Portuguese dithyramb avoided excessiveness. Accountable to the president of the Republic, Salazar could have been dismissed at any moment. And, Marshal Oscar Carmona, a figurehead, was already the number one when Salazar came to the government. It is also true that, afterward, President Carmona became old, and (after 1951) his successors were weak. Nevertheless, the constitutional position of the head of state was very strong in Portugal (until 1959 he was elected by the people) and therefore the dictator had to be somewhat cautious.

At each new presidential election Salazar formally resigned his post, to be unmistakably reappointed by the president as the head of government. But his posture was not always commodious. As for the charismatic nature of his power, it was undeniable: Portugal in its entirety was taken in. But charisma, given as it was by God himself, always depended upon confirmation by the Church. In Salazar's case such a confirmation always arrived punctually. Nevertheless, it was by definition transitory and, according to the goals aimed at, it created some obligations for the Elected. The Holy Spirit, when it inspired this doctor, led him to consider the family and schools in a certain way, and to protect Catholic missions overseas. On these matters He would not allow Salazar to make mistakes.

For all these reasons, the prestige of Salazar took a completely different path from that of Mussolini. It relied on competence, modesty, impartiality, and legalism. Austere and melancholic, his style was hardly enthusiastic; rather, it slowly pervaded the nation. He augmented the fear of the feeble, the apathy of the poor, the precaution of the astute. Under his monotonous rule, Portugal became grey. That's a color remarkable for its tenacity.

Corruption and repression were marked by all this. The former, controlled by a technician of financial science, did not go far enough to become disruptive. The latter, which did not make much blood run, was burdensome but continuously applied. The country was so obviously repressed that true hate against the regime was rare. On the other hand, resentment was superabundant. One poet expressed this very well: "this little grief 'à la portugaise,' so soft, and almost vegetal" (A. O'Neill). Therefore, the fiercest opponents to Salazar found themselves most often very alone.

Foreign Policy

Italian fascism was expansionist and aggressive. Salazarism wanted to maintain a heritage (the colonies) and avoided as much as it could European conflicts. It did not claim sovereignty over new territories and completely missed the dynamism required by economic dominations. It stayed within ancient borders and wanted to be left in peace. Portugal was a very old nation which no longer required spilt blood to prove her unity. Then she became involved in the colonial wars. But to Salazar this conflict was an undesired one, provoked by his enemies.

Italy, on the contrary, wanted war. Its political unity was a very recent one and it considered itself amputated of certain territories. Mussolini wanted Dalmatia, Albania, Nice, the Greek islands. He also wanted to carve out an overseas empire because Italy's entrance in Africa had been both late and barely executed (1898: the disaster of Adua; 1911: the conquest of Libya, a sea of sand). In 1914–1918 Italy won the war but lost most of its battles. And national pride, apart from being very unsure of itself, was almost immediately humiliated by the cold shower of Versailles. In exchange for half a million dead (and more wounded) Italy only obtained a few small portions of the Austro-Hungarian empire. It gained nothing in Africa at a moment when its emigration (especially to American countries) was blocked off.

Years later, her peasants were attracted by the Ethiopian mirage. Their attraction is easily understandable: the liberal state had promised them everything (above all, land) because it needed soldiers. At the other end of that society, heavy industry, strongly developed by war, no longer found an outlet once the conflict was over. Economic difficulties and the social question, unresolved *intra muros*, caused Italian leaders to look for a solution farther away. This range of psychological, demographic, economic, and political problems led Italy to attack while Portugal defended itself, for its participation in the war (1914–1918) had confirmed Portuguese sovereignty over Angola and Mozambique.

It remains to be explained how Italian aggressiveness avoided undermining the friendship between the two regimes. When Mussolini talked about building an empire and hegemony, he could have spoiled Portuguese-Italian friendship. Everyone knows that the practical coexistence of nationalisms is not easy, not simple. But an explanation is easily found. Beyond similar structures and ideological convergence (propitious but insufficient in themselves), other factors were favorable to such an understanding. First, there is the fact that none of Italy's territorial claims touched Portugal. Second, there was clear evidence that Italy would not become a colossus: fascist megalomania was hardly accompanied by real force. Furthermore, Italian nationalism took sometimes a benign form, and the theory of latinity, inseparable from that of the empire, reserved for Portugal a privileged place. So, Portugal had something to win and very little to fear from Mussolini's successes. True danger arose only from Nazi Germany.

There are thus many differences between Salazarism and Italian fascism, but on the whole, and despite these differences, we must conclude that both regimes belong to the same type. But, comparing fascism and nazism, our conclusion would be just the contrary, for despite all their similarities, we are faced with substantially different things.

Before developing on this theme, it is necessary to add a further observation. Nazism was a "pan" movement, founded upon "race." Racism attacked the old idea of a European equilibrium. Nazism proposed its destruction while fascism only wanted to modify it, even when it appeared to be the forerunner of warlike delirium. With the exception (perhaps) of the British, Hitler would have submitted all of Europe to his vassalage by direct occupation or by the establishment of protectorates in the most strict sense, while Mussolini would have been content with certain territorial "acquisitions" and with a certain hegemony, both compatible with the survival of other sovereign states. Until the day when the Axis Powers were welded together definitively (one believes at times that this occurred only after El Alamein and Stalingrad), it was possible to negotiate an equilibrium with Il Duce, but not with Der Führer.

After a Nazi victory in World War II, Mussolini himself would not have survived long. Nor Franco. Nor Salazar. Consequently, the latter never wanted such a complete victory. He wanted a Nazi regime strong enough to contain the Bolsheviks in the east (to overthrow them if possible) and to hasten the crises of liberalism in the west, thus favoring regimes like his own. But that was all. During World War II, Salazarist neutralism was an authentic one.

Due not only to opportunism, this neutralism came also from Salazar's most intimate thoughts. He was strongly attached to the old concept of nation-state. And so Hitler's "new order" could not please him. Nations do not define themselves by race but by language, territory, economy, and, above all, a tradition. These historical factors are irreducible to biology. Founded upon biology, nazism could not intervene in the European crisis, except to destroy old states. Strong it could be useful; triumphant, a mortal danger.

Hitler was hardly a true nationalist. He flattered German sentiment but looked much further. In his hands the German people were only a privileged tool. Essentially he was committed to create a completely new European and world "order." And after the "final solution" of the Jewish question, he would have pursued others. By the end of the war, Hitler was already preparing, for instance, the genocide of his infirm compatriots. In one sense, one can even suspect him of being an internationalist *sui generis*. His "new order" would be one where a minority of "Aryan" lords (including some Japanese) would command a multitude of slaves (including many Germans). It was supposed to be worldwide or nothing. Under these conditions, how could one dream of durable peace with Hitler?

Such a peace was the distracted dream of Chamberlain and also the discouraged illusion of Pétain. The most wise conservative leaders, such as Churchill and De Gaulle, quickly understood that Hitler's dynamism was, by definition, insatiable. Under the boot of the old corporal, Germany was becoming a mortal enemy. National Socialism had to be exterminated, even if it would remove an eastern barrier against communism that would have pleased all the "bourgeois" states.

As for fascism, we know that Churchill cajoled it until very late. And if conquered Italy received a different treatment from the one given to Germany, this was certainly, but not entirely, due to the efforts of the Resistance. One cannot forget that fascism was intimately related to the Roman Empire and its concept of wide citizenship. This is a political, not a biological, concept. And extermination only begins when politics vanishes. Thus, the gap between fascism and nazism is a very deep one.

The States

We are approaching now the central problem. We have said that Salazarism was a form of fascism without a fascist movement. This statement has no meaning unless we are faced with two political structures of the same type. At the state level, in our opinion, no essential disparity can be discerned. If this be the case, then our definition is inadequate. It thus becomes necessary to determine these differences to evaluate their weight. There are two which can be expedited quickly, because they are unessential. Others demand more serious reflection. We shall begin with the easiest.

One state was republican, the other monarchical. Yet, in one sense, all modern states are essentially republican. What defines them as democratic or despotic is not whether the hereditary or the elective principle is used to fill the supreme magistrature. Characteristic of the modern state since the ancien régime's estates vanished is the equality of citizens before the law. Moreover, modern political leaders do not identify themselves with the state; they are no longer the law (old kings were) even when they make it almost at their pleasure. Law is general, abstract, impersonal. It can be bad (an equality may become formal), but that is another question. On the other hand, with respect to power, the presidents of some republics are at times more royal than kings. Those of the United States and France, for instance, are much more powerful than the queen of England. And so on . . .

We shall not insist on the general theory. Let us come back to our argument. The king of Italy did not govern; nor did the president of Portugal. And they were long overcome by Salazar and Mussolini. Nonetheless, both could have legally deposed their charismatical great men. It was, actually, an almost unthinkable possibility as long as these regimes retained their solidity, but it became a very serious one when crisis struck them. Briefly, the real function of both heads of state was similar: they meant moderation and a certain continuity with the past. They made sure the supporting of those regimes by traditional armies and they were the "ultima ratio," in case of great national trouble or despair.

There were two Chambers in Italy: Mussolini maintained the Senate; until 1939, he also kept a Chamber of Deputies (Assamblea Nazionale) elected from a single list. In 1939, it was replaced by the Camera dei Fasci e delle Corporazioni. In Portugal there were also two Chambers. But the Corporatist one only played a consultative role, and in the elections for the National Assembly (deputies), the opposition was allowed to concur.

Whether one compares the two regimes before or after 1939, the Portuguese regime will appear more or less corporative than the Italian and more democratic—or less authoritarian—all the time. But the first impression is illusory for, regarding workers and employers, the establishment of a new institutional framework was much more rapid and complete in Italy than in Portugal. In both countries the government dealt with the Chambers almost as if they were administrative agencies of its own; as a rule, the important laws were laws made (or inspired) by the government. Each deputy, senator, or procurator owed his place to these governments and obeyed them—in Portugal, too, even if Salazar was much more cautious and formally respectful of the deputies than was Mussolini. As far as free elections in Portugal are concerned, one must say that they occurred sometimes within the *sindicatos* (labor unions) or other social institutions. But political ones were always unfair and even tricky, held as a means of propaganda. As a matter of fact, political pluralism was banished as efficaciously in one country as in the other. One can claim that the Portuguese regime was more skillful or less logical and that its compromise with the past was deeper or that its possibilities for an internal "liberal" evolution were broader. But (without forgetting that Mussolini conserved with the king the Albertine Constitution) we must examine the record carefully, regarding what really occurred. And, in spite of some ideological and legal differences, we can hardly assume that antiliberalism was not as fundamental in Portugal as in Italy or that "democratic liberties" were less outcast there than here.

It is very remarkable how similar the two authoritarian states were in structure. Both were single-party dictatorships which put society and the state under the principle of class collaboration and were supported by an alliance of all the groups of the national bourgeoisie. In both, a single man was the undisputed leader of both the party and the state. In both, power was exceedingly centralized, relying on the police and the army and forbidding any legal opposition party. In both, corporatist organization imprisoned social classes and professional groups within its web and monopolized their representation. Finally, both were conceived in terms of stubborn nationalism. These traits are those of fascist states and fascist corporatism anywhere. And so, in this sense, we can support the thesis of a fundamental similarity between Salazar's and Mussolini's regimes. For a political regime is something stable. It is much more than a leading ideology and a strong activist movement. Against this, there are only two arguments: first, that which denies the existence of the single party in Portugal or which insists on its inner feebleness and on its dependence vis-à-vis the state; second, that which evokes the question of totalitarianism, paraded by Mussolini and rejected by Salazar. These two arguments, if they were correct, would require us to reverse our ideas. Thus, they must be examined.

In Portugal, the single party was called the National Union, not to confess its partisanship. So, it proclaimed that it was a "non-party" and declared itself open to all good patriots, while supporting a certain, very peculiar, policy. And it did of course use the means put at its disposal by the New State to defeat its enemies. But most of the time it scarcely existed. The absence, in Portugal, of a true fascist movement is evident in two ways: first, in the National Union's structure and rootedness, which were incomparably weaker than the PNF's; likewise, the "Portuguese Youth" and the "Legion" seemed lightweights when compared with the Italian youth organization or the militia. Furthermore, Salazarist syndicalism, rather amorphous, hardly depended on the party at all. Essentially, it was controlled by the Ministry of Corporations, that is, by the state.

Most often, this single party appeared to be absent in national life. Filled with prominent people, it did not include the masses, and it showed itself only transiently during electoral periods. But here we must be cautious, for absence is a form of existence. The two permanent roles of the National Union were to justify the outcasting of all other political parties and to hinder the crystallization of tendencies within the regime. The organization of distinct currents of opinion inside the party was strictly forbidden. And these two roles were very well played after all.

As for the "positive" indoctrination of the Portuguese, the National Union's capability was a limited one. Salazar himself had to recognize at once its loud fiasco. But if we look deep down we shall see that, in a certain sense, he preferred to deal with a sleeping country. And so, given the essentially negative character of this single party, it is only natural that it was never formally integrated into the state. What for?

The position of the PNF was quite different. It had a doctrine. It included millions of Italians, either directly or through an immense organizational network: organizations for the young, the women, the workers, the intellectuals, and so on. It strongly influenced the government and Mussolini had to be very attentive to its pressures. Its parallel structures often concurred with those of the public administration. It tried to influence the style of all Italian life, including the most private details, aiming to create a new culture, and even to change the character of Italian people. In short, it was a spur planted in the flanks of the state, so as to bring the fascist revolution to its logical end. Under these conditions, it was normal for the Grand Council to become an organ of the state. Let us note, nevertheless, that, politically speaking, this Council was somewhat broader than the PNF: it could eventually count among its members some cautious nonfascist men. Anyway, what a difference with Portugal where only once—between the Spanish Civil War and the turning point of World War II—something similar was perhaps becoming possible, but not so much. But let us be more precise, because our problem has just been displaced. Now, our concern is no longer with the simple existence (or nonexistence) of the single party. We are concerned now with the problem of its nature—one involving the nature of the *state*. We are facing the question of totalitarianism, which is of the utmost importance.

Within Italian fascist doctrine and within the fascist movement, the totalitarian trend is very clear. According to Mussolini, "fascism considers the state as the true reality of the individual . . . for the fascist, all is in the state, and nothing, neither human nor spiritual, exists and *a fortiori* has value outside the state." Elsewhere he says, "The fascist state is a form, an interior rule, and a discipline of the entire person. It is the soul of the souls." Certainly he defends himself from accepting that the individual will be crushed by the state. According to Il Duce, the potential of each citizen is fully developed only within the state, as that of the soldier within his regiment. Furthermore, fascism pretends to conserve essential liberties. But "in this domain only the state is judge, not the individual." Briefly, no exterior limit is admitted: "in this sense fascism is totalitarian and the fascist state—being the synthesis and the unity of all values—interprets, develops, and dominates the entire life of the people."[4]

Thus, Mussolini's thought was quite clear. Salazar's too, but he said just the contrary: "None of us would affirm in Portugal the omnipotence of the state; none of us would conceive the State as the source of all morality and justice without any respect for individual conscience, for the legitimate freedom of citizens, for the sacred aims of the human being."[5] In the same way, Salazarist thought despises proud, aggressive nationalism and proposes to replace it by a moderate one in which the notion of a beloved fatherland does not prevent a friendly relationship with other countries. Salazar goes so far as to claim that "a state, subduing all, without exception, to an ideal of nation or race represented by it could lead to an absolutism worse than that which existed before the liberal era."

In this context, it is quite clear that even the most intemperate Salazarist slogan (which says "all for the nation, nothing against the nation") cannot be considered as wholly totalitarian. According to Salazar, the Portuguese nation was by no means as divine as the Italian fascist state would like to be. Furthermore—if we agree with him—Portugal is an essentially Christian nation, that is to say a political entity intertwined with some universal values much older than the nation itself and whose definition belongs to the Church, not to any national power. In Christian terms, the human being, whose soul mirrors God, has a purpose that is identifiable neither with the state nor with the nation. The latter is a historical being, saintly indeed, but mortal, while each man's soul is immortal. Herein lies a major limit to totalitarianism.

There were some others. Family, the core of society, produces more than citizens; it provides also believers. Christ himself had mother and father. Then, the family has untouchable rights, previous to the state, sacred autonomy. On the other hand, the autonomy of all intermediate bodies from countries to corporations must be acknowledged by the state as required by natural law.

Salazarism condemned the giganticism of the modern state—whose action pervades, more and more, all spheres of human activity—as well as its absolute power. Being a decisive instrument to organize social life, the state must of course remain strong. It requires to be paid a special attention—and let us even say that it deserves a certain degree of worship. But for a Catholic leader, it will ever be no more than a "relative end," yet a means. In contrast, Italian fascist doctrines always proclaimed the absoluteness of the state.

So, it seems undeniable that Salazar and Mussolini oppose one another completely on this capital issue of totalitarianism. If they had remained faithful to what they promised, their two regimes would not have been similar. But, practical life ran otherwise, irrespective of doctrine. The New State did not attempt the creation of a new man, the control of the inner conscience, the overturning of old customs. It is true, however, that, under a Christian cloak, it liquidated political liberties, weakened immortal souls, and bullied the majority of the population. But it was conservative, whereas totalitarianism is by definition revolutionary. The Portuguese regime, however despotic, could not pretend to total power. For that, two things at least were missing: first an ideology from which to regulate all aspects of life; and second, the practical means required to destroy or subdue all social forces opposing it or not belonging to its sphere. The army, for instance, kept always a certain autonomy. And the Church was largely untouchable, its seat being in Rome. Of course, Salazarism was not conceivable without the support of the Church. In short, even supposing that he aimed at it, Salazar could never have attained total power, and the partial power he attained could not deal with everything. It was totalitarian neither in essence nor in purpose.

Such was not the case with Italian fascism, in its beginnings, at least in appearance. Certainly, it included Catholics (and, later on, Mussolini would negotiate the Lateran Agreements), but it was not linked to the Church by any umbilical cord. Likewise, it accepted the monarchy while being republican and looked to the support of the old army, though it had its own militia. But, for true fascists, all these compromises (and let us add the compromise with the bourgeoisie) were, in principle, transient. So, one can contend, always in principle, that the Italian regime was nonetheless marching toward totalitarianism: that sooner or later it would finish by upsetting the throne, subduing the army, making the pope a hostage. And, certainly, Mussolini would have liked to achieve all this.

If one looks attentively at the Italian story, one perceives, however, that all this was beyond his real forces' reach. After twenty years of the regime, the army was so little "fasciscized" that it promptly and almost unanimously overthrew Il Duce in 1943, during the first major crisis. Some months later, he took power again, but only in the north of Italy: a reprisal, essentially due to Hitler. On the other hand, the Lateran Agreements years before had made it clear that the Church, a powerful global force, external to the regime, would maintain for a long time its influence over the country. This influence was accepted and recognized in morals, family life, education. It also had to be, so to speak, tolerated in politics and even within fascist labor unions. "Catholic Action," with its organizations of all sorts, became the *bête noire* of convinced fascists. It was prudent enough, but it never ceased to go its own way.

In sum, it appears that all these compromises could scarcely be considered transient. Most probably, they were to last "sine die," as if fascist regimes could not survive without adulterating the former fascist movement. And, consequently, totalitarian ideology would not produce in fact a totalitarian state. The episode of Salò only confirmed this. In Salò, Mussolini finally—and apparently—had total power, freed from the Church, from the king, from the old army. But then, Italian fascism had already disappeared. The Italian fascist—Mussolini the first—had become the servant of Nazi Germany.

Before leaving this theme, let us only suggest three more things: first, that a true totalitarian state is always the instrument of a worldwide revolutionary dream: never, essentially, a national state; second, that (quite paradoxically) totalitarianism does not really mean a worshipping of the state: it rather promotes an idea that uses the state, reducing it to a mere, if tremendously powerful, apparatus; and third, that, even in its violent, revolutionary origin, the Italian fascist movement only partially tended toward total power. We will explain these ideas below by means of a comparison between national fascism and racist nazism.[6]

When speaking about the monarchy, the army, and the church, we left somewhat aside the Italians themselves, who nevertheless were essential. Mussolini very quickly understood that the human material he had at his disposal was not "good." He was vexed with his own people. And he tried to change them from top to bottom, aiming to eradicate a lot of Italian national traits: levity, individualism, art of compromise, softness, sympathy. Quite happily they would have "corrupted" fascism. Mussolini himself lasted twenty years because, being a true Italian, he forgot his doctrine any time it seemed useful to do so.

Out of all this, what to conclude? We will easily agree that a totalitarian tendency always remained present. But we must define fascism as a national alliance balancing a set of disparate forces, impossible to lead by *internal evolution* to total power. Totalitarianism is a completely integrated—much more than integrating—system. Often it was even rejected at the fringes and thus became ridiculous. Mussolini himself was often ridiculous; Hitler, never.

The grotesque is different from the ridiculous for it does not imply insufficiency of means.

The populace called fascism a "great bus" (*un carrazzone*). The fascists themselves lamented that the PNF, that presumptuous lance of the revolution, had become a lackey of power and had lost its bite.

As far as the question of total power is concerned, one cannot separate Salazarism from Italian fascism. As a regime, true fascism was only the so-called corrupted fascism: a national compromise whose totalitarianism remained a velleity. And to this extent, the Portuguese Estado Novo was fascist. The differences we referred to between Portugal and Italy, differences either about state doctrine or concerning the activist movement, were important indeed, but unessential. They did not constitute any deep institutional gap.

To the extent that fascism is a *sui generis* political form, to the extent that it must not be confused with traditional dictatorships and yet does not overlap with either liberalism or communism, to the extent that it creates unprecedented and stable institutions (a fact which is undeniable), Portugal had a fascist regime. It is true that a political force similar to the Italian *squadrismo* could not be seen in Portugal before 1926. But, so far as we try to define them, political forms do not depend strictly on their origins. We are perfectly aware of this with respect to many demo-liberal regimes which came into existence without local Enciclopaedias, jacobine clubs, "capturings of the Bastille," and so on. In Portugal, likewise, fascism came from above, almost "peacefully." Being much less aggressive, it became much more stable and was doomed to last much longer.

From One Corporatism to Another?

SOCIAL AND ECONOMIC EVOLUTION

Without a lost war or economic catastrophe, it is difficult to overthrow fascism. As long as it avoids these disastrous impasses, it only faces crises which are not mortal. It suffers partial defeats here and there. And it evolves, adapting itself more or less to circumstances. In Portugal it lasted for more than forty years, but, toward the end, circumstances changed; conditions were different. The regime no longer appeared to be able to assure its domination without reform, as a result of the internal evolution of the social and economic system and as a result of certain exterior forces (the colonial wars, integration with Europe). Under immobile structures, routine activities persisted and contradictions accumulated slowly. Today the old structures are cracking; they are incapable of containing developed social forces and of resolving, as they had in the past, the very problems and conflicts they had created.

These problems and conflicts were related to both past and future economic growth. Salazarism could, given fixed frontiers and a weak development of productive forces, manage a slowly expanding capitalist economy. Manpower in Portugal was abundant and underemployed, also underqualified, and easily controlled. Salaries were very low and social expenditures were kept to a minimum. Some businesses just survived; others were born or grew at the expense of the proletariat and because state protectionism took them under its benevolent wing. Both large and small interests profited from tariffs and the control of foreign investments (if not always and not in the same way). The industrial boom came late, in such a way that, among other things, it postponed the demise of outmoded industries and of an impressive number of inviable agricultural operations. A large part of the population remained in the countryside as if times had not changed (more than 40% in 1960) living as it always had, that is, badly. All this helped to some extent to control prices so that social tensions were not too aggravated, nor exports impaired, nor the stability of the currency affected. Let us add to this the colonial situation: primary products were cheap, outlets guaranteed, a vast space open to limited initiatives—all of which served to blunt internal bourgeois conflicts.

Given the above, the nature of the national fascist alliance now becomes clear. It did not treat its members in the same way. It had its poor relations, of course, Constantly, small-scale entrepreneurs were going bankrupt, enlarging considerably the ranks of the proletariat. Nevertheless, as a class, they were spared. For many it was only a respite: they were trapped; for others, the delay allowed them to settle elsewhere; for a few, it gave them time to readapt. One should not overlook these effects.

Until World War II, economic nationalism was hardly contested. Apart from certain episodes, such as the wheat policy, the regime did not strive for autarky. It acted moderately, in this as in other matters, and did nothing to impede collaboration with foreign capital, both in Portugal and in Africa. Foreign capital had long played an important role: transport and communications, the mines, insurance, colonial companies, as well as some banks, were often in its hands. It was, above all, English and little interested in areas other than extractive industries. In this respect, for twenty years, the work of Salazarism was guided by three major preoccupations: to counterbalance the influence of the English, to have the Portuguese state recognized as an indispensable interlocutor, and to integrate foreign penetration into the established order. Foreign investments increased (this was inevitable), but they were diversified, limited, and respectful of the exigencies of the economic, financial, and social equilibrium imposed by Salazar. Salazar did not want the colonies to get out of control for economic reasons, nor did he want the manner of their exploitation to depart too much from the rhythm of the metropole; he gave priority in the metropole to infrastructure: transport, communications, energy; and he tried to ally Portuguese capital closely with each new enterprise by giving it a controlling interest when possible; finally, he had to protect traditional activities (and the balance of payments) or risk creating tensions which would be difficult to contain.

All this implied slow but steady growth. Until the war, this policy succeeded for two reasons: with the economic crisis and discord among the powers, foreign pressure was not great; nor could the most ambitious Portuguese groups exert pressure, for they were dependent on the state.

The first real unrest dates from after the war. On the one hand, twenty years of accumulation and of "public works" had already set the scene for the debut of an industrial mentality. The ports were developed, the roads improved, companies of navigation founded, electrical dams built, the colonies exploited. The World War itself brought with it a boom in exports (the most famous of which was wolfram), a stimulus to certain kinds of domestic production, and money from refugees. On the other hand, the support of the regime by the antifascist Allies led to a weakening of the old nationalism. Finally, American capital invaded Europe, thereby stimulating the process of European integration. In Portugal these developments were regarded with perplexity. It was clear that the pace would change, but existing arrangements had to be carefully respected. Large capitalist interests and technocrats raised their voices against the excessive protectionism accorded to uneconomic operations. A minister of the economy became famous for having said that a country like Portugal, without industry, "is not a country but a garden plot." Some wanted to exploit more thoroughly the immense colonial wealth, for which there was not even an inventory. Salazar, frightened by the news of discoveries, is alleged to have said: "Oil in Angola? That's all I need." Those who wanted to extract iron ore had to wait, while in the metropole projects concerning steel, chemicals, and petrochemicals (as well as tourism) were held in abeyance.

More significant still (more backward too) was the situation in sugar. Groups allied to foreign capital (above all, West German) were interested in sugar production but did not want to depend on colonial cane. It would have been necessary, therefore, to plant sugar beets at home; yet the government would not allow it. This attitude also prevailed in forestry projects which could affect, sooner or later, the fundamental structure of the country.

As for the concentration of existing enterprises, there was also no clear policy. In such an important branch as textiles, the opening of new trade outlets, following Portugal's adhesion to the European Free Trade Association, gave small entrepreneurs a second chance while the large ones overexpended. No advantage was taken of the opportunity to reorganize this sector.

In spite of everything, economic growth accelerated substantially during the fifties. It did not affect agriculture, which continued to stagnate, but rather the industrial sector (where production increased at an average of 8% per year) and the service sector. Furthermore, it only affected a few poles of development (Lisbon, Setúbal, Porto); the disparity between the city and the country only increased regional imbalances. Important progress was achieved in electricity, metallurgy and machinery, certain chemical industries, cement, glass, and also within the large colonial enterprises (coffee, sugar, vegetable oils).

In the colonies, these companies changed practices and customs, creating some friction with the traditional settlers. As in Portugal the penetration of capital became more sustained, however restrained. Except for the diamonds of Angola, a long-existant exploitation, other raw materials began to attract attention, especially oil and iron. Toward the end of the decade they had started up.

Portugal was moving, in short, toward new horizons. The regime tried both to aid and to contain the movement. In 1953 the First Development Plan was initiated. In 1959, in Stockholm, Portugal obtained further respite: the European Free Trade Association accepted the country as a member, granting it privileged status. Portuguese exports would benefit from the tariff dismantling and others, but in turn the country was given fifteen years to liberalize its own restrictions. Nevertheless, it was warned that special favor would not last forever.

It became obvious also that a storm was brewing overseas: tension with India over the Portuguese possessions on that subcontinent, worry in its African provinces about the general movement toward decolonization. In all the overseas territories new questions were being asked.

The events of 1958 gave expression to a deep malaise. The electotal campaign of General Humberto Delgado disconcerted the regime. Its alarming scope can only be understood in the context of the changes discussed above. But this was only a beginning. In 1961 tensions accelerated greatly. In that year, Nehru occupied Goa, and the colonial question exploded in Angola. Guinea and Mozambique followed. In 1964, 150,000 men were fighting on three fronts at a cost far beyond the size and means of Portugal. But the regime held fast and the conflict continued for more than ten years.

At the beginning of the war it was thought that colonialism would not survive for long and that the collapse of the New State would follow the breakup of the empire. This reasoning was based on three factors: the evident lack of resources in the metropole; pressure from western Allies in favor of a compromise; and, finally, the presumed power of African nationalism, capable of making life impossible for the Portuguese there. But none of these factors worked out as expected.

In 1961–62, the regime could have fallen. The shock it received was enormous. The economy hesitated, diplomatic pressures became troublesome, and the military situation was bad. Within the regime there were those who wished to capitulate, while in the countryside opposition rumbled. The minister of defense and an ex-president of the Republic plotted against Salazar. There were worker and student strikes, serious demonstrations, and the beginnings of an insurrection in the army. On the one hand, these were incoherent actions; on the other, people believed too much in force of circumstance, in the natural collapse of the regime. But Salazar told the Portuguese that they would resist "proudly" alone as the avant-garde of a cowed West. Increasing repression, he sent them in force to Angola. He vigorously imposed his choice upon them. In short, he held on. Once the military situation was stabilized, the bourgeoisie and other powerful forces quickly understood that they had no certain and ready alternative (at least not yet).

While all this was taking place, opposition groups as well as conflicting concepts of nationalism entered into crisis. The African liberation movements, in effect, tried to create a new sense of national conscience rather than give expression to one already formed.

This is the major reason for their internal difficulties and their slow development. Those states already independent were still too weak to furnish decisive support. Portugal, in contrast, found itself powerfully supported by the Union of South Africa and Rhodesia. This "Holy Alliance" seemed to enjoy the luxury of being able to subjugate peacefully small neighboring countries like Malawi, while maintaining subversion in Zambia and the Congo. The West, with the United States at its head, played a two-faced game. Diplomatically, it ran with the hare and hunted with the hounds. Materially, it helped both sides. Portugal found herself unexpectedly advantaged by this situation.

Thus the wars continued. Much has been made of the support given to Portuguese colonialism by foreign capital. Without it, the wars would have been impossible. At the beginning, Salazar found himself faced with a new problem: how to pay for war, without weakening the rhythm of economic growth. In the midst of European integration, growth could not be postponed and was dependent on continued foreign investments and loans.

During the colonial wars, more than 50 percent of the budget went to military expenditures and to the amortization of loans. In the colonies a third of the investments foreseen by the Third Plan (1968–73) were not Portuguese. In Portugal itself, branches of large worldwide companies established automobile assembly plants; the Americans built the Tagus bridge; the Dutch and the English built the immense shipyard at Margueira; the Swedes took care of the cellulose industry; the Germans financed the irrigation of the Alentejo and became interested, along with many others, in the development of tourism in the Algarve.

The old nationalism waned when faced with such pressing needs. Foreign groups were attracted to Portugal by conditions more favorable than in the past. After 1965 a decree allowed companies with a majority, sometimes a totality, of foreign capital to export dividends and to negotiate tariff and fiscal exemptions.

Foreign capital came not only to the metropole but also to the colonies. In Angola, Belgians (Petrofina) and Americans (Gulf) began to exploit oil and the Germans (Krupp), iron ore; the South Africans established themselves at the Cunene dam and wanted to enter into the diamond trade. In Mozambique, an international consortium built the huge dam of Cabora Bassa, larger than the Aswan dam, while the English and the Japanese competed with each other over the construction of railroads. It is false to assume, however, that Portugal became merely a transmission belt for the orders of more powerful interests. It is false for this simple reason: the Portuguese state, which was strong, played off her rivals and their contradictions, as it played with its allies. No country, no group, acquired a truly dominant position. The Gaullist revolt inside the Atlantic Alliance was very well received. The enumeration above of some of the foreign interests implanted in Portugal's "economic space" is quite significant in its diversity. In short, the regime made a virtue of necessity. All in all, the war became a factor of economic growth. It even encouraged Portuguese industries connected with the army.

From an economic point of view, the decade was dominated by three major processes which set the stage for a new political development: first, the emigration to Europe of hundreds of thousands of workers—in France alone it is estimated that there are more than half a million Portuguese; second, the influx of tourists—in 1963, 300,000 foreigners visited Portugal, but by 1968 this figure had reached more than 2 million; third, the importation of foreign capital, of which we have already spoken—a million contos (about 40 million dollars) entered in 1961 alone and this reached about 6 million contos yearly by 1968. Furthermore, direct investments also increased in a similar magnitude.

What were the effects of all this? The remittances of emigrants and receipts from tourism stabilized the balance of payments. Buying power was increased, a necessary though not sufficient condition for economic development. But this increased volume of wealth also contributed to inflation as supply did not follow demand. Furthermore, the flight of workers upset the labor market. A rise in salaries was the result (more remarkable in the countryside than in the cities). This favored modernization and increased bankruptcy among small producers. An alleviation of certain social tensions also resulted since many of the dissatisfied left. But as the flood grew, the dearth of workers (especially qualified workers) constrained further industrial growth. Among those who remained, demands became more insistent, not only because they found themselves in a more favorable position but also because of the opening of the country to foreigners, the establishment of multiple contacts, and the entrance of new ideas. All these factors helped to change outlooks. The agricultural crisis itself, however propitious to capitalist development in agriculture, shook the sleeping countryside. In a few years thousands and thousands of men, who had seen only the countryside surrounding their villages, left under the Portuguese flag to fight in Angola, came back, went to France, and came back again. It was impossible to keep them leashed as they had been before.

At the same time, the process of industrialization proceeded and the pressing needs for social mobility and professional training increased. This affected not only the workers but also the system of education itself. Similarly, the question of salaries, working conditions, and living standards (urbanism, transportation, leisure) was posed. Commercial workers moved to the vanguard of active struggle. "Municipal" demonstrations increased in some cities, as did demonstrations among students. There was a growing tendency to attribute a decisive role to the proletariat. The working class was growing in number, concentrating its ranks and posing its questions. The regime wanted labor to become integrated and to participate. Speeches on income policies and on social security were proffered. Labor contracts and collective bargaining regulations were reformed, manpower services were put in order, and labor law was made more flexible.

An attempt was also made to "liberalize" political life. The elections of 1969 were slightly less rigged after having permitted the holding of a republican (opposition) convention. Censorship of the press was less cumbersome, except in the colonies. For a while the political police seemed to have become more respectful of legality and one even thought that they would spare systematically moderate opponents. With regard to this, the secretary general of the National Union (the single government party) even proclaimed that it would move toward a degree of pluralism. Finally, hopes for a constitutional revision were raised, as were those for a new press law. Reform in education went even further, at least on paper.

In fact, this "new course" was limited in its progress by the very factors which had launched it. It was not clear to what extent, given the circumstances of a full-scale war, really lively debates would be permitted or really deep divisions could be exposed. Economic growth might have been bringing these reforms, but the country was not growing fast enough. The European deadline was approaching: in this respect the adhesion of England to the European Community added further worry. Faced with economic competition from larger firms, although still in restricted numbers, too many businesses found themselves torn between defensive efforts and harsh competition.

It was necessary to contain this process and to soften the pressures. Caetano sent his emissaries to Brussels and tried to repeat, vis-à-vis the Common Market, the earlier success in Stockholm.

At the same time he hardened his position on internal problems, having very good reasons to do so. Since 1968, he had "tolerated" many strikes and these (pushed by inflation) now threatened to spread. Student protests continued. Finally, revolutionary "commandos" entered into the picture: significant acts of sabotage multiplied, aimed above all at colonial rule and NATO.

Under these conditions, it was quite likely that "liberalization" would be set aside. Even so, a return to the past seemed to be excluded. The regime would have to change in due time. If it fell, the problems posed would still be there.

It is important to understand this paradoxical set of exigencies, for it implied guaranteeing economic growth and social stability in a way which was very different from the past. Portugal could have moved slowly but was forced to move quickly. She had been relatively isolated, but then external relations were imposed. These forces were acting upon a "patriarchal" country which could no longer remain so. Men obeyed sometimes, but henceforth they would have to be convinced. Neither the rhythm nor the attitudes of Salazar were appropriate for these tasks. In this sense, Salazarism was *dépassé*. But it remained to be discovered whether Salazarism was exhausted in its entirety or, on the contrary, whether it could hold on to some of its principles which could be realized in another way.

A WORKING HYPOTHESIS

We have seen that Salazarism was a form of fascism without a fascist movement. We have also extracted the essential traits of this particular form: the dictatorship of a single party and a corporative system of social organization, both capped by a "chosen one." We have also seen that the nationalism which penetrated these regimes from top to bottom corresponds to an alliance of the entire bourgeoisie, but under the thumb of a strong state and with its different segments benefiting unequally.

Having established this definition, we traced very briefly the subsequent evolution of the Portuguese regime (of national compromise) to the late sixties when it found itself faced with new conditions and the need for reform. We know finally that this reform was pursued until April 25, 1974, under the motto of "renovation in continuity."

The question is: what changed in structural terms and what remained? To put it differently, how can a regime (or a state) be and yet not be the same? This question must be resolved in order to understand that the Caetano regime neither disguised immobility nor completely liquidated the past. Our working hypothesis will be the following: however difficult the transition may seem, fascism can be overcome or surpassed without abandoning corporatism. Let us now focus upon several essential points.

Corporatism Is Not the Same Thing as Corporative Organization

In effect, when one speaks of corporatism one refers either to a part or to a whole. The "part" is corporative organization, that ensemble of institutions *sui generis* which structures and regulates society. The "whole" is the regime which effectuates itself through this institutional ensemble, but whose principles transcend it. In the realm of the family, for example, which is not included in the corporative organization *strictu sensu*, one finds the same denial of conflict, the same principle of action: the master, the father, collaborates harmoniously with his "apprentice sons," and the wife is similar to the subordinate *compagnon* of the crafts. When this spirit dominates the entire society—and especially the relationship between classes—corporatism is thriving, whatever form it takes.

Obviously, there is no corporative regime without an embryo of corporative organization. The effective realization of integral corporatism would imply an actual coincidence of the part with the whole. The entire nation, in its most remote corners, would have produced from below or would have been encased from above in a seamless institutional network. But even so, the principles remain distinct from the organization. Historically, the latter change with time. They were only meant to be the means to achieve the former. This is particularly important to remember with regard to Portugal, especially during that period when its older corporative organization was transcended. From its institutional crisis, one might too hastily have concluded that the regime itself had been surpassed. That remained to be proven.

Corporative organization, itself, can be viewed from two perspectives. In a broader sense it encompasses the most diverse activities: economic, cultural, moral, and administrative. In its strict sense, it structures only economic activities and organizes the relationship between capital and labor. In partial corporatism this latter aspect is "everything." Integral corporatism, however, is not content with this, although it accords economic structures a privileged place. It is often thought that corporatism's sole aim is to regulate the social question to the detriment of the workers and petty proprietors, the rest being only a façade.

We do not agree entirely with this view. "Integralism" embodies an authentically global design. It is a vision of the world. Nevertheless, the economic roots of this vision are notorious. In our view, the principal attribute of all corporative systems (and the only indispensable one) consists of the imposition of a collaboration of classes and social groups in the name of national unity and the principle of hierarchy upon which it depends. In other words, it is from the domain of the economy that this imposed collaboration derives its meaning.

Corporatism Fundamentally Involves the Collaboration of Classes

In this respect let us first discard corporatism's propagandistic claim: the idea that collaboration itself is the bearer of harmony between men, of justice between classes, and of general prosperity. In disciplining conflict, corporatism pretends to be the best possible answer to the old dilemma of liberty versus authority. It even defines itself as the *tertium genus* between capitalism and socialism. Certain ideologues even affirm that it surpasses them dialectically, while incorporating what is best in both of them. This was the position of Ugo Spirito at the Corporatist Congress of Ferrara in 1932. In a world where conservatism and progress are equally costly, these promises could attract many followers. But historical reality has put them to the test and they have been found wanting.

In fact, such collaboration ensures that workers will remain dependent upon capital and assures that the latter will survive and prosper. For the bourgeoisie it provides a form of mediation between diverse strata, which in no way prohibits the dominance of the most powerful, and controls, as much as possible, the destiny of others. It gives substance to their unstable political equilibrium and expression to their conflictful alliance. Considering only the primary mechanisms of capitalism, this concern with equilibrium would seem to hinder its development. But reality is more ambiguous because this development, if it is to continue, requires social stability and strong state support which otherwise would be problematic. The bourgeois compromise represented in such a national corporatist alliance adheres to a single clause, *rebus sic stantibus*.

Corporatism's contradictions, supposedly secondary, did not disappear. It would have been quite surprising if the principal contradiction which leads employers and workers to oppose each other disappeared. "Joy at work," the slogan of the system, was short-lived, but it is no less true that the idea of class collaboration served to repress their conflict.

The adversaries were ensnarled in a thick net of public regulation. They were led to institutional coexistence and subjected to an obligatory process of conflict resolution. According to each individual case, class struggle would be regarded illegal in principle and rigorously limited in practice. In Portugal, for example, strikes were a crime. In other countries, the right to strike was maintained but so conditioned that its use was exceptional or employed only in secondary questions.

Nevertheless, Corporatism Is Not Just Any Collaboration of Classes

Any real corporative system must, in effect, be organic and permanent. It must also involve basic relations. Corporatism entails a tiered or layered domestication of the class struggle. The most brutal forms of antiworker repression do not suffice; sometimes, their presence could even be regarded a sign of the absence of corporatism. Nor is it sufficient that bosses and workers meet together (spontaneously or not), here and there, in stable entities composed of equal numbers of their representatives (for example, in a council for labor disputes or a social security institute). These are only rough approximations of the real thing. Their collaboration must not be partial or episodic but must form a coherent whole. In other words, interclass relations must become the foundation for state and society. An authentically corporative regime exists when and only when the collaboration of classes reaches this level.

But it is not necessary that the principle of interclass collaboration be formally established by governments and by constitutional law. Political calculation can intervene effectively to prevent such an open and frank disclosure. One can also be unaware of what one is doing. Likewise, it is not necessary, even if corporatism is openly proclaimed, that the anticipated institutions function in accord with its program. In Portugal, for example, it took a long time for many of these institutions to be created; they existed, for many years, only on paper. Even when they did exist, they often contradicted their own propaganda. Portuguese corporatism was hardly associative in character; it depended largely on the state. It was not pure, because neither the corporations nor the Corporative Chamber had any legislative power. It remained essentially economic in its content and provided no "integral" coverage of other interests. Finally, in no way did it reconcile employers and workers and it did not devote itself to the plight of the working man.

However, none of this gets to the essence of the system. What was important was that it muzzled deep conflicts and put immediately in their place mechanisms and institutions indispensable to its design. The rest could wait and did wait. In Portugal, at the outset, such mechanisms included unitary workers' syndicates and the "antistrike law," a few employers' associations for those branches of society which were in crisis, state organisms for economic coordination, and labor tribunals—all of which were under the control of an all-powerful executive, supported by the police and the army. In a country where pluralism was banished, corporatism applied its *vis dormitiva* to the whole society. Founded upon constraint, it could then grow slowly. But other methods are available, in some cases, to achieve the same ends.

Fascism Is Corporatist but Corporatism Is Not Necessarily Fascist

As we have defined corporatism, the obligation to collaborate may be imposed by force or by voluntary consent. Because these things are never simple (and because the culture of peoples varies) there is always a certain mixture of coercion and consent. It is more a question of knowing where to put the emphasis. The famous corporatisms of the first half of the century came in the form of single-party dictatorships. But a corporatist regime detached from them is quite conceivable.

Manoilesco, the great theorist of this system, has explained this very well. He argued that fascism is to corporatism as species is to genus. It constitutes only one possible form of the corporatist idea. Repugnant to ideological schematicism, it adapts naturally to the most diverse climates. While demo-liberal organization maintains, despite the diversity of its forms, a common schema and standard institutions, the corporative system is infinitely more complex—and more differentiated.[7]

It is possible to conclude that for Manoilesco the best corporatism would be that which emerges from a lengthy social experience: at a given moment, the qualitative political jump would merely consecrate previous evolutionary changes by bringing preformed institutions to their final stage of development. Earlier in his writings, he affirms that "it is not the state's responsibility to conquer economic life: it is for economic life, in part, to conquer the state."[8] The process of fascism is the inverse. For that writer, on the other hand, corporatism is an "inevitable historical product"[9] of the contemporary epoch. It corresponds to the real movement of history. There is nothing utopian about it, nor does it even require an excessive voluntarism. One can either help it or thwart it, but no more: it will come surely. Manoilesco refers especially to Marx, praising him for his multiple explanations of nineteenth-century development and appropriating for his own needs the concept "mode of production," which is central to Marx's work. It is at this point that his writings take on real significance.

Manoilesco's foresight lies in his analysis of the transformations underway in the world economy. First, he foresaw that capitalist development would bring to the forefront the organizational factor: "organization becomes an autonomous power and a new force, distinct from the nature of capital and work."[10] It is organization which "will gain ground and individual capitalism which will lose"[11] in proportion to technical progress and concentration.

Second—and reinforcing the same tendency—competition among nations, he argued, would become increasingly harsher. One could add to this the formation of "blocs" and the view that "all international commerce would become part of international politics."[12] The reason was simple: colonialism was entering into crisis and with it the "industrial monopoly" of the West. The time, he argued, was over for the easy subjugation of other peoples, "founded on the indefinite exploitation of agricultural countries without industry."[13] Thus, in the name of indispensable efficacity, each country will have to reduce to a strict minimum its internal conflicts and to structure as much as possible its productive activities. In this way, the "imperative of national solidarity" joins the "imperative of organization." Together they form the basis for the historical necessity for corporatism.[14] It is from these developments that the crisis of the entire world system of production and trade stems.[15]

It is an ambitious and audacious doctrine. Scientifically formulated, it tries to provide simultaneously an explanation of contemporary history and a solution which, while nationalist, would be universally valid. In the corporatism of Manoilesco, nations are not closed entities: one can easily apply these ideas to newer and larger economic and political bodies. They do not necessarily correspond to the most intimate developments in history. But they are closely enough related to force us to reflect on them.

These questions touch on the central issue with which we are concerned. According to Manoilesco's perspective, fascism "forces" history; it is to some extent premature. The Fascists first grabbed hold of the state. Then they fashioned a corporatism based on coercion with gaps, distortions. Ostensibly authoritarian, it was monolithic and incapable of tolerating conflict. What characterizes the fascist form is the elimination of pluralism and the installation (openly or disguised) of the dictatorship of a single party. It is also an attempt to clothe society with institutions it would never have produced on its own. This type of corporatism is necessarily subordinate and (at least in practice) belongs to the state. In such cases one cannot grant supreme power to the corporations, for without the state they would either disintegrate or simply cease to exist; nor could one accord to its citizens freedom of choice. Manoilesco admitted, transitionally, the idea of a guiding party and a man of providence. He charged them with responsibility for overcoming a bitter national crisis and preparing the path for integral and pure corporatism. They would lend, in short, a helping hand to history.

All this is a history of capitalism in which Mussolini died too soon. Salazar saw it ripen and thought that it was moving in his favor. He believed that corporatism would infiltrate slowly but surely all advanced countries, despite parliaments, parties, trade unions, the press, and free elections. He moved in accord, of course, with liberal-democratic traditions, but he bent them, sometimes denaturalized them, without necessarily reducing them to pure façade. Something else maintained the regime. Clearly, it was pluralism but always more and more respectful. This pluralism was the kind which extends from society to the state or which results from the interaction of the two without notable imbalance. Was this the discrete beginning of which Manoilesco dreamed?

Modern Capitalism Harbors a Tendency toward Corporatism

Certainly, one cannot predict that such will be the case. But corporatism's evolution poses this hypothesis clearly, in Europe above all. Already one can speak of a "neocorporatism" clearly linked with certain exigencies of productive systems and levels of consumption. One wonders if it doesn't correspond precisely to a system based on large enterprises (with its need for punctilious organization, periodic planning, stability); to complex national economies with their sensitivity to international competition; to the desire for security by solitary individuals who already have something to lose; to classes tired of struggling; or to bureaucratic apparatuses which strive to endure. Each nation experiences the need to unify itself. But how can it be done in an antirevolutionary way without disciplining conflict too narrowly? What could be better for this purpose than to obtain the consent of subjects?

One finds tripartite representative and advisory councils appearing everywhere. These involve salaried workers, managers, and, at times, the state. They may be initially temporary but they soon become permanent; some remain consultative but many become deliberative. One finds them at the level of individual enterprises, within branches or sectors of the economy, in regions and in different countries. Occasionally protesting, the working class delegates its power. Always protesting, it accepts the limits of the system (while engaging in "conflictive participation"). It negotiates on questions pertaining to revenue policies, demands official extension of collective agreements (which become laws), discusses changes in social security provisions, and fights for improvements in work contracts (which in turn may well end up as career contracts)—all of which become cardinal elements in labor's indefinite integration into the new order. One finds these developments again among men with experience who are represented in various economic and social councils. Yet these very same elements may well oppose, although not too strongly, the transformation of weak senates into chambers of "the productive forces," that is to say, the transformation of these state organs into corporatist organisms.

France provides many examples. But in other Western European countries the same thing has been occurring, and the patterns are often more stable elsewhere. As early as 1956 a Portuguese theorist identified with the "new wave" of corporatist thought—M. Cortez Pinto—carefully enumerated foreign corporatist developments, which he called "unavowed corporatism."[16] He began with the period before the war, not by placing emphasis on Germany and Italy but by underlining certain aspects of the "New Deal" (those laws regulating competition), the English "Joint Industrial Council" efforts, and the Dutch experience. After the war, he found a corporatist trend flourishing everywhere. At the professional level he called attention to Dutch "councils," Belgian "partisan commissions," English "tripartite commissions," the Rhineland-Palatinate's four chambers, the Swiss "professional communities," the "modernization commissions" of the French Monet Plan. At a more general economic level he analyzed social and economic councils (Dutch, Italian, French); the National Consultative Council (English); the National Labor Council and the Central Economic Council (Belgian).

At the level of individual enterprises, finally, he considered worker participation in management as a device for confirming the legitimacy of the large modern enterprise as a "corporation," a title already part of established usage in England and in the United States. Most of these developments are partial. In his eyes, in only a few small countries have these trends reached maturity—for example, in Holland, where corporatism took off as early as the fourteenth century. Elsewhere the efforts have been more timid. Above all, they have not yet reached formal political institutions. What is essential, he argued, is that these institutions already in place have not impeded the extension and progressive development of class collaboration.

One does not know where these developments will lead, nor does this question really concern us here. But we do know, in returning to the central issue, that corporatism does not ignore the fact that classes struggle. What it refuses to accept is class struggle in the Marxist sense. It refuses to regard the struggle as implacable, as providing the foundation for societies and the "motor of history," or as demanding a revolutionary, classless outcome. In addition to all this, corporatism never permits social confrontations, whatever they may be, to place national unity in danger. If social conflict can be seen as compatible with the kind of order necessary for growth, then it can be allowed. What is important is that there should be adequate institutions to subdue conflict if necessary. This is what has been attempted most recently in "free" England, be it under Conservative or Labour rule: the regulation of the right to strike tends to impose directly on those concerned a form of class collaboration which is not that of fascism.

We have almost arrived! In approaching the rest of Europe, Portugal could well pass from one corporatism to another.[17]

Notes

This article has been taken, by permission of the author, from the introduction of his dissertation "L'Evolution du Systeme Corporatif Portugais à Travers les Lois (1933–1971)," Institut des Sciences Sociales du Travail, Paris, 1971. The text has been updated to the extent that it recognizes the fall of the "Salazar-Caetano" regime in April 1974.

1. That is to say, until he was deposed on July 25, 1943. On September 11, Mussolini was rescued by the Germans and taken to northern Italy, where he set up a new government known as the Salò Republic. This was to be a puppet regime, dominated by the Germans, of short duration.—Eds.

2. IRI—the Institute for Industrial Reconstruction—was created by

Mussolini in the thirties as an investment bank, loaning money to businesses in financial difficulties in exchange for shares of stock. This particular institution survived fascism and became after World War II one of the prime instruments of the state in the Italian recovery. It has remained ever since one of the key institutions in the economy linking together state interests and private industry.—Eds.

3. Salazar, *Discursos* (volume and page citations are missing in the original.—Eds.).

4. Mussolini, *Le Fascisme* (trad. française 1933), pp. 20–25, 58.

5. Salazar, *Discursos*, 1:285.

6. This comparison belongs to a part of M. Lucena's essay which is not translated here.

7. Mihail Manoilesco, *Le siècle du corporatisme* (Paris: Lib. Felix Alcan, 1934), p. 15.

8. Ibid., p. 49.	12. Ibid., p. 34.
9. Ibid., p. 13.	13. Ibid., p. 28.
10. Ibid., p. 45.	14. Ibid., p. 32.
11. Ibid., p. 56.	15. Ibid.

16. João Manuel Cortez Pinto, *A Corporação: Subsídios para o seu estudo*, 2 vols. (Coimbra: Coimbra Editora, 1955–56), 1:40–81.

17. The end of this section of Lucena's dissertation, and hence to this chapter, presents a particular problem in translation and in updating. While the present tense is used in French and has been continued in English, this statement was made in the context of the Caetano regime before it came to its abrupt demise. The corporatism attempted by Caetano clearly ended in 1974. What is less clear, as the subsequent chapter illustrates, is whether or not corporatism as a whole has disappeared from Portuguese society: Wiarda argues that it has not. Others, such as Schmitter, have adopted the view that there is a form of corporatism that is to be closely identified with modern capitalism. Since this last section moves in that direction, beyond the limits imposed by the Caetano regime, the present tense has been preserved.—Eds.

3. The Corporatist Tradition and the Corporative System in Portugal: Structured, Evolving, Transcended, Persistent

HOWARD J. WIARDA

The term "corporatism" is exceedingly ambiguous and often loosely employed. Enjoying a certain resurgence and new-found popularity of late,[1] among both political analysts and certain political elites, it nonetheless remains a frequently confusing and misleading term and framework. Moreover, it is often a highly emotive term, conjuring up past images of Nazi atrocities and fascist dictatorships. At one time so-called corporatist regimes, with Portugal the major exception, seemed to be safely confined to the ashcans of history. Now, however, not only has the term gained a new credence and respectability but also regimes calling themselves "corporatist" have re-emerged in what are, from a policy and ideological perspective, such distinct nations as Chile and Peru. We are also discovering that regimes we are used to thinking of as liberal and social-democratic often exhibit numerous, though frequently disguised, corporative features.[2] Moreover, even those long-term and manifestly "corporatist" regimes, such as the Portuguese, remained for a long period almost wholly unstudied and shrouded in myths and misunderstandings. The time to begin clarifying both the meaning of the term "corporatism" and our understanding of how such "corporatist regimes" as the Portuguese actually function is long overdue.[3]

Corporatism as Tradition

The model for "the system" implemented during his regency (1439–1447) . . . and which was to become the standard system in the Portuguese kingdom for several centuries was that developed by Dom Pedro in his *Livro da Virtuosa Bemfeitoria*. Moreover the model developed by this Portuguese prince in the early fifteenth century is almost a prototype of what political scientists and others refer to as the corporate, patrimonial state—Sidney M. Greenfield, *The Patrimonial State and Patron-Client Relations in Iberia and Latin America*

Iberic-Latin history, in this case specifically Portuguese history, is often analyzed in terms of a presumed unilinear and universal evolution toward liberalism and democracy. This viewpoint is not surprising when it emanates from British and North American writers; occasionally, though, it finds its way into Portuguese writers as well. This perspective uses the British Parliament for its model of the Portuguese Cortes, the Bill of Rights as its model of civil liberties, the New England town meeting as its model of participatory democracy, and the liberal-Lockean tradition as its model for the ideal political system.[4]

However, the process of development in Portugal has proved to be far from unilinear in terms of such a model, and what is frequently presented as a universal framework is in fact quite particularistic. The liberal model may thus be appropriate in tracing the patterns of development of the Anglo-American democracies, but it seems to have little relevance for Hispanic and Portuguese traditions. The fact is that in Portugal the Cortes never had, nor was it ever intended to have, the independent, coequal, or even supremacist position enjoyed by the British Parliament. And while a long list of human and civil rights was usually included in a succession of Portuguese constitutions, these rights, in law and practice, have consistently been subordinated to a higher end and duty. Participatory rule has also come to be a fundamental principle of Portuguese governance, but what the Portuguese mean by participation is quite different from the unstructured and individualistic concept of Lockean liberalism. Finally, as regards democracy, the Portuguese have not historically been convinced of its efficacy or ultimate legitimacy, and, even when they have, their meaning has implied some quite different understandings than are implied in the Anglo-American conception.[5]

The narrow and ethnocentric interpretation of Portuguese history, which sees liberal democracy Anglo-American style as the inevitable outcome of a long-term societal evolution, not only clouds and obscures our understanding but also positively distorts our comprehension of key Portuguese institutions and developments. It not

...ly paints the presumed enemies of democracy, such as the Church, the Monarchy, Pombal, and Salazar, in the vilest of terms, but also generally exaggerates the accomplishments of "liberal" regimes (from 1822 to 1926) so as better to discredit and paint as wholly "reactionary" and "fascistic" the one that followed.[6]

A focus on Portugal's "corporative tradition" helps avoid some of these distortions and pitfalls. Rather than seeing Portugal's history and institutions in terms of some presumed, hoped-for, foreign, and nonindigenous tradition, or through the sometimes equally ethnocentric biases of the "developmentalist" literature,[7] this newer perspective seeks to examine Portugal on its own terms and in its own context. Because corporatism seems to be so much at the heart of the Portuguese tradition, because a kind of "natural corporatism," in Ronald Newton's phrase,[8] seems so deeply imbedded historically in the Portuguese psyche and institutions, this approach has been termed the "corporative model," or the "corporative framework."

It is at this juncture that some conceptual confusion arises, for "corporatism" is now plainly being used in two diffcrent senses. One widely cited definition is that employed by Philippe C. Schmitter: "Corporatism can be defined as a system of interest representation in which the constituent units are organized into a limited number of singular, compulsory, noncompetitive, hierarchically ordered and functionally differentiated categories recognized or licensed (if not created) by the state and granted a deliberate representational monopoly within their respective categories in exchange for observing certain controls on their selection of leaders and articulation of demands and supports."[9] Professor Schmitter goes on to contrast this kind of corporatism with pluralism, which he defines largely in terms of laissez faire, "free" associability that is the reverse of his corporatism definition, with a "monist" model à la the Soviet Union and with "syndicalism," which implies an autonomous and less structured pattern of interest aggregation.

Although the definition of corporatism offered above is useful as a description of the Salazar system at one point in time, it provides more of a static model than a dynamic one, gives a too restrictive meaning to the term "corporatism," and thus is not altogether useful for purposes of this analysis. Let us therefore recognize its utility with regard to some aspects of the Salazar regime, while also introducing the following qualifications and reservations, the first two of which have implications for our discussion later on and the third of which is of immediate concern.

1. The definition offered makes no provision for the dynamics of change within a single corporative regime, that is, from the dynamic, often social-justice-oriented corporatism of the early Salazar regime, to the repressive state corporatism of the middle years, to the moribund, "dinosauric" system of the 1960s, to the revitalized Estado Social of Caetano. It fails adequately to convey the possibility of evolution from a closed system of state corporatism to a more open and pluralist corporatism of association; indeed, by defining corporatism and pluralism in such a way that they constitute polar opposites, it negates the possibility of pluralism within a corporate society and policy as well as within a liberal one.[10]

2. The definition makes no allowance for an even more fundamental transformation from corporatism to syndicalism, nor does it entertain the possibility that the latter is a more developed, more "advanced," more socially differentiated form of the former. In the latter part of this discussion, we shall be making precisely this argument, that while the revolution of 1974 marked a significant turning point, there were some continuities as well, and that while the establishment of a form of syndicalism and socialism in the wake of the 1974 revolt implied a major reordering (or *regeneração*, in Portuguese terms), that restructuring could also be interpreted in the light of a broader corporatist tradition, now updated with syndicalist and/or socialist aspects.

3. The definition is too narrow and restrictive to serve our historical purposes. It focuses exclusively on the system of interest representation during one phase of the Salazar regime. But clearly the "corporatist tradition" as here used implies some broader phenomena. Obviously the system of interest representation is one particularly critical part of the historic "corporative model"; but it is not the only part. To describe the tradition of "natural corporatism," we prefer a broader, more encompassing definition than that.

What, then, is meant by the "corporative model," or the "corporative framework," in Portugal? Let us recognize, first, however, that to pin a single all-encompassing label on a varied national and, more broadly, cultural tradition in itself represents a series of oversimplifications. Second, let us recognize that other "key words"— *organicist, patrimonialist*—should also be employed along with the "corporatist" one to describe this system and tradition.[11] Third, let us accept the fact that, in speaking of the "corporatist model," we are employing a streamlined, paradigmatic, ideal type, only the main parameters of which are spelled out. The "corporative tradition" is used here to describe only some of the more salient features of Iberic-Latin development, particularly as that model stands in contrast to the liberal-Lockean tradition and to other social science paradigms.

The corporative tradition implies a value system based upon widespread acceptance of hierarchy, elitism, organicism, and authority. It means a pattern of corporate sectoral and functional representation with authority vested in the crown or central state apparatus and with the various corporate units (nobility, Church, military orders, universities, municipalities) incorporated into a single, organic whole for purposes of integral national development. It implies a system of bureaucratic-patrimonialist state authority and a social order based similarly on patron-client interdependence. It means a predominantly Catholic society and political culture based upon Thomistic principles. It implies an etatist and mercantilist economic system. And it implies a political system based on patrimonialism, authority, and hierarchy, with a centralized, vertical, pyramidal structure of power and decision making.

The terms "corporatist tradition" or "corporatist model," in brief, are shorthand terms used to describe some fairly distinctive features of Portuguese history, political culture, and the development process. For example, in keeping with the Catholic conception, the Portuguese state has historically been based on the reciprocity of a patron-client system—a state that was natural, moral, and just and therefore did not have to be limited by institutional checks and balances. Stratification and differentiation in the social and political sphere not only exist but also are presumed to be right, necessary, and not to be challenged. Society consisted of functionally diverse, hierarchically ordered corporate groups, each of which made its distinct contribution to the political society and was guaranteed representation in it. The nobility, the Church, and the fighting knights stood near the apex, directly below the Crown, in this vertically segmented, hierarchically ordered scheme. They constituted the higher order "corporations"; their function was to govern, to harmonize the human social order with a higher responsibility, to be responsible not just for themselves but for the good of all. The king (or, later, prime minister or president) remained unfettered by a coequal parliament or judiciary, as in the Anglo-American conception; but he too was obligated to rule in accord with a higher natural law, to govern for the common good, to respect the *foros* (rights) of the constituent corporate groups, and not to overstep the bounds which separated authoritarianism (legitimate) from tyranny (which justified rebellion). Politics usually centered on the competition among rival elites and corporate groups to capture the patrimonialist state apparatus, from which wealth and position flowed, and on the dynamic, changing relations between these constituent units and the central authority.[12]

Although this brief description does not begin to do justice to the complexities and subtleties, in law, theory, and practice, of the workings of the Portuguese corporative system historically, it does at least provide a hint as to some of the main directions. Further, it makes clear how far removed this dominant Portuguese tradition is from the dominant liberal-Lockean one of the Anglo-American nations. Although no claim is made that all of Portuguese history can be interpreted in this light, and though as with all ideal-type constructs a greater understanding of the Portuguese *Weltanschauung* is obtained at the cost of a certain definitional preciseness, still an understanding of the "corporative tradition" or of "natural corporatism" helps illuminate some areas of Portuguese development that were unexamined before or examined only in the light of Anglo-American referents. It provides a needed, valuable corrective to this other approach. Moreover, this model applies not just to the centuries of national organization and then consolidation in premodern times but also, in reconstructed and updated form, on into the "liberal" and "republican" periods of the nineteenth and early twentieth centuries. For despite the constitutional façade, Portugal remained more a corporatist than a republican regime; the power of the major corporate units (Church, army, bureaucracy, nobility) remained undiminished and even enhanced; and the parliamentary regime worked best when it was least parliamentary, that is, when it had a strong monarch or president and when the organic-corporatist conceptions prevailed. The corporative pattern of sociopolitical relations not only was thus deeply imbedded but also proved to be remarkably longlasting. It remains as a major, persistent tradition even today. "Corporatism" as a shorthand term to describe this Portuguese tradition is comparable to the use of "liberalism" to describe the dominant American tradition, and also serves further to distinguish these two national and political-cultural traditions.[13]

Some Portuguese corporatist theorists would of course go even further and dismiss all of nineteenth-century republicanism as mere façade, a temporary interruption in an otherwise dominant corporatist tradition.[14] This perspective, however, seems as inaccurate as the earlier interpretation from the liberal perspective. The "liberal" and "liberalizing" perspective of Portuguese history produced one set of distortions, but an equally unrefined corporatist perspective implies a distortion of another kind, for beginning in the eighteenth century a fissure had begun to appear in the Portuguese culture and society. On the one hand stood the dominant, inward-looking, Catholic-corporatist-traditionalist-patrimonialist conception; on the other, a European-oriented, nascently liberal-rationalist-urban-middle-class-secular one. No one viewpoint could enjoy absolute legitimacy; no one dominated entirely. Much of Portuguese history during the period 1822–1926 can be interrupted in terms of the conflict and virtually constant civil war between the two. As in Spain during this same period, two distinct Portugals had evolved and there was little basis for compromise between them.

This development has two major implications for our study: first, in terms of Portuguese history, it implies that neither the liberal nor the corporatist interpretation can any longer be used exclusively to the neglect of the other. From this point Portuguese politics and society can be understood, even on its own terms, only in the light of both models and what each tells us about two distinct, separate Portugals. It is here, where these two models and the once-parallel structures they represent sometimes meet and overlap, that perhaps some of the most fruitful areas of research lie. Second, on a more practical level, it implies that no regime coming to power in Portugal can afford to govern wholly for and in the name of one tradition and its attendant sociopolitical forces while entirely ignoring the other. When the monarchy tried in the late nineteenth century, it faced a series of republican revolts that eventually toppled the monarchy itself. When the republicans disfranchised the Church and sought to rule without the traditionalist elements, they faced a series of revolts that eventually succeeded in toppling the Republic in 1926. And, when Salazar sought subsequently to re-establish the corporatist tradition as the sole national tradition, he found he could do so only with the use of widespread repression and police-state methods; his regime and system were repudiated in 1974.

Whether the new regime that comes to power in the wake of the Revolution can transcend or overcome these historic divisions, or whether the Revolution marks the superimposition of a third layer— Marxist and socialist—over pre-existing corporatist and liberal ones, thus introducing further discord and fragmentation, are questions we shall have to weigh. But of the existence historically of a powerful, perhaps dominant, corporative tradition and model of sociopolitical organization, there can be little doubt.

Corporatism as Manifest System

> In seeking to avoid imitation of United States liberalism and of Marxian approaches in finding models for government, social relations, and economic development, much of the Iberian World has been turning increasingly to . . . corporatism.—Pike and Stritch, *The New Corporatism*

The 1926 revolution that toppled the Portuguese Republic was carried out by the armed forces with strong backing from a variety of civilian parties and movements. The chaos, disorder, and corruption of the Republic, the apparent bankruptcy of liberalism as practiced in Portugal, had led to their general discrediting. When the coup finally came, it was warmly welcomed. It had the support of a variety of monarchist, integralist, nationalist, Catholic, and center elements, together with the bulk of the middle class and many *políticos* and republicans who sought to break the patronage and sinecure monopoly of the Democratic Party. Although the military was itself vaguely integralist, corporatist, and nationalist in character, it lacked a clear-cut program. Once it had restored order, banished some of the republican political groups and politicians, rooted out corruption, and restored a degree of economic solvency—the usual practices of military regimes—it floundered for several years in search of a national formula. It was precisely such a formula that Salazar and the corporatists provided and that helps explain their ascendance to power within the context of a military regime.[15]

The corporatist system that was gradually institutionalized in Portugal over the course of the 1930s can be explained in terms of at least seven dimensions.

1. The corporatist regime represented a reaction against the chaos and disorder of liberalism and the Republic. By restoring order, stability, and national solvency, Salazar enjoyed widespread initial support. The early strength and popularity of the corporatist regime can only be understood in the light of the disorder and national humiliation that went before.

2. The corporatist regime was a strongly nationalist regime. It was nationalist in three senses. First, it was in part the heir of the Catholic, conservative Nationalist Party. Second, it represented a nationalistic repudiation of the influence of foreign institutions, chiefly British parliamentarism, which had governed the country, often with ruinous results, intermittently from 1822 to 1926. Third,

it was nationalist in its efforts to fashion a new political model upon indigenous Portuguese sources: the family, the local community, the fishermen's centers, such "natural" corporations as the Church, the army, the *grémios*, university, and so forth.

3. The corporatist regime was a middle-class regime. It marked the replacement of the older elitist and oligarchic order with a new middle-class one. That process was begun under the Republic and completed under the Estado Novo. Obscured by our attention to the political aspects of the Salazar regime is the gradual class shift that occurred; by the end of the Salazar-Caetano era, virtually every institution in the country had become thoroughly middle-class dominated: army officer corps, Church hierarchy, bureaucracy, universities, high civil service, political parties, even the trade union structure.

4. The original corporatist scheme, as envisioned by Salazar, was a fairly close reflection of the kind of society Portugal still was in the 1930s: predominantly rural and small town, Catholic, traditionalist, hierarchically structured, governed by a nationwide static. To the extent that Portugal had urbanized, modernized, and become oriented to change, and with its historic hierarchies breaking down, corporatism in the original *salazarista* sense became less and less viable with, as we shall see, wrenching social and political consequences.

5. The corporatist regime initially had a strong social justice orientation. My own investigations of the early period of the corporatist system have led me to conclude that this concern was genuine and real. It can, I think, be explained along two dimensions. First, it seems clear that the strongly Catholic orientation of Salazar and his collaborators led them to be concerned with the welfare of the poor, to feel a powerful obligation to Catholic charity, and to initiate a series of social programs, paternalistic to be sure and undoubtedly insufficient but still no less genuine, to relieve the miserable plight of the poor and to speak to the problem of alienation in the emerging mass society that Portugal was in the early process of becoming. Second, it seems clear the social justice measures were related to the efforts of the emerging middle-class system to consolidate its power, to forge an alliance with some working-class elements so as better to wrest control away from the oligarchy and the historic governing elites. Once middle-class domination had been consolidated, the old alliance with the working class could be—and was—conveniently forgotten: but for a time the middle class needed labor

support and that was accomplished by instigating a large number of programs of social justice.[16]

6. The corporatist system was designed, in Schmitter's words, to fill a certain organizational space.[17] The early 1930s were a period not only of economic depression in Portugal but also of potentially threatening revolutionary movements from below. The corporative system was designed, therefore, not, as is often alleged, as a reactionary throwback to some status quo ante, but as a way of structuring, channeling, and hence controlling the emergence of new groups, principally labor, who might otherwise threaten the entire edifice. Corporative principles of social solidarity and class harmony were emphasized as a way of discouraging class conflict, and corporative *sindicatos* and structures of participation were introduced and made obligatory, filling the organizational space once occupied by the now illegalized socialist, communist, and anarcho-syndicalist groups. Through the corporative restructuring, a middle-class-dominated change process was initiated from the top down as a way of holding in check and heading off in advance the possibility of more mass-based and revolutionary solutions.

7. The corporatist regime must also be understood in the light of the foreign inspirations and influences of the time. The Portuguese corporatists not only built on their own indigenous history and institutions but also drew heavily upon Mussolini's *Carta del Lavoro* (1927) and the encyclical *Quadragesimo Anno* (1931). More than that, however, corporatist regimes or corporatist institutions seemed to be the wave of the future, not just in fascist Italy and Nazi Germany but seemingly everywhere: Austria, Poland, Hungary, France, Belgium, Holland, even the Scandinavian countries, Britain, and, perhaps in the form of the NRA, the WPA, and the NLRB, the United States. Mihail Manoilesco was about to proclaim in a famous book of the time that, whereas the nineteenth century had been the century of liberalism, the twentieth would be the century of corporatism.[18] Corporatism's impact on Portugal must be understood in the context of a period when in the Western world corporatist solutions seemed to be becoming universal.

Once the corporatist formula had been decided upon, Salazar and the regime sought rapidly to institutionalize it. Although some of the first corporative decrees had been promulgated earlier, 1933 marked the real beginning of the corporative restructuring. In that year a new constitution was adopted proclaiming Portugal a "unitary and corporative republic" and establishing both a superior Corporative Council and a functionally representative Corporative Chamber; a new labor law was handed down that detailed the new benefits the workers were to receive as well as restructuring their participation in the political process under strong state control; and a series of decree laws was promulgated governing virtually all areas of Portuguese associational life. These encompassed the creation of a nationwide system of *casas do povo* (people's centers) for rural workers, *casas dos pescadores* (fishermen's centers) for fishing communities, *sindicatos* (syndicates) for industrial workers, and *grémios* (guilds) for business, commercial, and industrial employer interests. In the meantime a Subsecretariat of State (subministry) of Corporations and Social Welfare and the Instituto Nacional do Trabalho e Previdência were established to administer the corporative system.

This flurry of corporative legislation in Portugal in 1933 was comparable to the changes ushered in by Roosevelt in his first ninety days, and probably just as far-reaching in its implications. By 1937, with the designation of the *casas do povo* as the representative agents of rural workers and hence the creation of separate *grémios da lavoura* for landed interests, the corporative restructuring had been all but completed. The creation of the corporations themselves, nominally the capstones of the entire system, had been scheduled for late 1939, but the outbreak of war that year forced a postponement and it was not until 1956 that the regime finally got around to creating the first six corporations. For twenty-three years, hence, Portugal remained a corporative state without corporations.

Between 1933 and 1935 the regime moved quickly toward implementation. The trade unions were reorganized under the *sindicato* system; by 1935, 191 had been duly recognized by the state, and by the end of that same year, 141 *casas do povo* had been granted charters. The first *grémios* and fishermen's centers were also organized. A nationwide system of *caixas de previdência* was in the process of being established; the first elections under the corporative Constitution of 1933 were scheduled; the organizational scheme for the Corporative Chamber was promulgated; and the detailed provisions concerning workers' rights and obligations contained in the Labor Statute of 1933 began to be fleshed out.

The period 1933–35 was a heady, exciting period for the Portuguese corporativists; the corporative revolution was already *en marche*; the system was being implemented. But it was precisely at this point in the mid-1930s that the first biases began to appear in the corporative structure and the main lines of corporative development were fundamentally altered. Rather than a corporatism of free associability and social justice, the Portuguese system became a corporatism of the state, of controls and repression, and of favoritism toward one social group at the expense of the others.

Corporatism as Controls

Traditionally corporatism has been a means of providing social solidarity, avoiding class conflict, and discouraging individualism among the masses, while at the same time providing opportunities for participation by the masses in local, regional, and functional groups. In its new guise in the Iberian world, corporatism also aims at replacing an entrenched oligarchy with a more nationalistic elite whose members hope to mobilize popular support for development and greater economic independence. *Above all, it is the objective of the new corporatism to prevent a revolution from below by initiating one from above* [emphasis added].—Pike and Stritch, *The New Corporatism*

By 1935 the first biases had become clearly visible in the Portuguese corporative system. Corporatism as originally conceived, it will be recalled, had been posited on the coequal representation of capital and labor. Moreover, the corporatist solution had been proffered as a "third way," which repudiated both capitalism and socialism. In actual practice, however, corporatism in Portugal became one of the most oppressively monopolistic of state capitalist systems and it came to favor employer interests at the expense of labor to the point where industrialization was achieved by imposing its costs primarily on the industrial working class (which thus corresponds to A. F. K. Organski's definition of "fascism").[19]

The promulgation of the corporative decrees had been greeted in early 1934 by one of the most massive strikes Portugal had ever experienced. The brutal repression of the strike made it clear that, if the *sindicatos* refused to accept corporatization peacefully, it would be forced upon them. No such repression was ever practiced against employer groups (although over a long period the regime used strong leverage to subordinate capital as well as labor to state direction). Moreover, the business and fledgling industrial elements were able to make the case to Salazar that, if corporatization was to be enforced upon them as it was upon labor, it would lead to a lack of investment and the ruination of the economy. Particularly in the depression years of the 1930s, and then as the regime moved to stimulate economic development, these arguments of the business community were persuasive.

A second bias in the system may be found in the decree laws themselves. For workers, membership in a *sindicato* was made obligatory; furthermore, the *sindicatos* could gain no benefits for their members until their charters had been granted by the state and they had been reorganized in terms of corporative principles. Business groups, however, had two major "outs." First, the government had allowed the old "class associations" (chambers of commerce, merchants' associations) to continue without forcing them, as was the case with the *sindicatos*, to reorganize along corporative lines. Second, the regime provided on the employer side for voluntary *grémios* as well as compulsory ones, while on the labor side such a possibility had been specifically ruled out.

A third bias had to do with the enforcement of the corporatist decrees, and it soon became clear that the government was enforcing the corporative restructuring more on the labor than the employer side. The corporative system increasingly meant a web of controls for those on the bottom while providing for little accountability for those on top. In the urban industrial areas this implied favoritism to business and commercial interests and industrialists increasingly at the expense of labor, and in the rural countryside it implied a perpetuation of the traditional patron-client system through both benign governmental neglect and domination by wealthy landed elements of both the *grémios da lavoura* and the *casas do povo*.

Probably a fourth bias had to do with the growing security and consolidation of the Salazar regime itself by the mid-1930s, due to its institutionalization and the absence by now of major internal threats. No longer so threatened, both the regime and the broader middle class on which it rested felt no need to coddle labor. Hence, the strong social justice orientation and legislation of the early corporative regime were increasingly shunted aside.

Biases in the regime were one thing, and perhaps to be expected given the structure of wealth and power in Portugal and the corporatists' belief that they could educate the rich and the middle class to their obligations to Christian charity without wrenching social revolution; but the next step involved the development of a full-fledged system of authoritarian state corporatism, replacing the "corporatism of association" of the original conception. The move toward an authoritarian, state-directed corporatism was dictated by the fact that corporative consciousness in Portugal was still inchoate, the corporative agencies that had been created enjoyed meager support, and Salazar became convinced that something else had to be created to fill the institutional void. The continued depressed economic conditions, the perceived need for a stronger set of economic controls, the outbreak of civil war in Spain, a new series of internal conspiracies and assassination efforts launced against Salazar and the regime in 1936–37, and, I am convinced, the publication of Manoilesco's book and its dissemination in Portugal all contributed to the growth of an increasingly centralized and bureaucratic system of state corporatism.

In 1936 the regime moved to create a variety of "Organizations of Economic Coordination"—commissions, *juntas*, and institutes—which were to serve as "precorporative" intermediaries between the state and the still-nascent corporative complex. These agencies came to serve as the Portuguese equivalents for the plethora of regulatory bureaus that have grown up in other modernizing systems for the coordination and regulation of national economic life. But in Portugal the process went further. The Organizations of Economic Coordination helped set wages, fix prices, and regulate production, imports, and exports. They served as the means by which state power was extended to virtually all areas of the national economy, including control over those elusive business groups that had to this point evaded full corporatization. The Organizations of Economic Coordination were the prime instruments for the growth of etatism and state corporatism.

The relations between the Organizations of Economic Coordination and the business community were more subtle than this, however, for while, on the one hand, these agencies were used to subordinate the business elements to state control, on the other, these same business elements were moving to infiltrate and eventually capture the entire regulatory complex. Harry Makler's contribution in the next chapter documents clearly the close interrelations between the Portuguese corporative state system and the industrial elite, particularly how individual career patterns showed an almost constant coming and going between private firms and the government regulatory agencies—including the frequent holding of private and public positions simultaneously. Salazar had brought some of the major economic satrapies—the wine industry, fishing, canning, cork—under state direction, but they had also learned to manipulate him, chiefly through the argument that all his hopes for continued political stability and economic prosperity would be sabotaged if he really moved to divest this powerful, emerging bourgeoisie of its power and wealth. These arguments were even more persuasive because of the constant crises the regime faced: depression, opposition, the Spanish conflict, then World War II. The result was a sellout to private economic interests, a vast expansion of state power, and the end of the vision of a free system of corporative associability and social justice. The process in Portugal was not altogether unlike the takeover—as described by Ralph Nader, Theodore Lowi, and others—of the American regulatory agencies by the very groups they were designed to regulate.[20] And it was at this point that the Portuguese system corresponded most closely to the narrower definition of corporatism propounded by Schmitter.[21]

To the system of corporate structures and controls, Salazar now added a series of economic laws and regulations which served both to reinforce the corporative structures and, eventually, to supplant them. These laws have generally been ignored by students of the Salazar regime, but they are essential to an understanding of it and the evolution of the Estado Novo toward an increasingly state capitalist or, essentially, mercantilist form. Briefly, these laws prohibited the creation of a new economic enterprise, or the expansion of an old one, without government permission, and gave the government virtually all power to set wages, prices, production quotas, exports, and imports. They vested enormous, heretofore unprecedented economic power in the state (political and associational life had already been concentrated in the state through the new constitution and the corporative system) and gave it the power to oversee, regulate, and command virtually all national economic life.

Though these laws were "neutral," that is, adaptable to virtually any economic goal, under Salazar the purpose was concentration and consolidation of the economy under state direction. Where monopolies already existed, they were protected; in industries where they did not exist, new monopolies and oligopolies were created through the use of these laws. By the time World War II broke out, the nation's major economic sectors had all been reorganized on the basis of a great, interconnected complex of conglomerate monopolies, intimately tied to and inseparable from the government structure, linking both continental Portugal and its colonies through the same monopolistic companies, and protected against competition from local businesses or from abroad. The result was enormous economic power concentrated in the hands of the state. In this sense Portugal came ironically, given the regime's strongly anti-Communist ideology, to resemble more the centralized, state-run economies of Eastern Europe than the planned but still in large measure laissez faire systems of the West. In addition, extraordinary economic wealth was concentrated in the hands of a few rich and powerful families and of a new plutocracy—precisely those same elements who, we have just seen, had come to dominate the state regulatory agencies. A system of state capitalism thus grew up alongside, and eventually supplanted, the corporative structure as one of the main institutional pillars of the regime.[22]

Corporatism's original principles came to be abandoned more and more all across the board, and the role of the corporative complex was increasingly circumscribed, confined chiefly to some limited representational functions, the regulation of labor relations, and the administration of woefully inadequate social security. As this occurred, agencies moved to fill the vacuum. The police apparatus, whose controls previously had been sporadic and unsystematic, became increasingly brutal, total, and systematic; in so doing it developed into yet another of the prime pillars on which the Estado Novo had come to rest. The power of the state regulatory agencies, already extensive, grew even more. During the war corporative agencies were given the unpopular tasks of administering wartime austerity measures, including rationing, price fixing, and wage freezes and decreases, and their popularity declined to a new low. With the end of the war and the general discrediting of all such "fascistic" schemes, the corporative system was still further shunted aside, circumvented, and ignored. All but completely moribund, its functions and activities dwindled almost to nothing. Moreover, the "dinosauric" character of the corporative system was reflected in the regime itself, which seemed to have lost all purpose and direction. As liberal and social-democratic opposition mounted in the postwar period, the police state apparatus continued to expand and repressive, dictatorial measures were increasingly employed.

Nonetheless, a brief flurry of corporativist activity did ensue during the 1950s and 1960s and new concepts of social welfare were attempted. The old Subsecretariat of Corporations was made a full ministry. The first corporations were established and a "Plan for Social and Corporative Formulation" was initiated. Some new functions were also found for the corporative agencies to administer, chiefly in the areas of social security, but this implied a still further circumscription of the range of activities assigned to the corporative complex. These developments were probably related to the new economic prosperity in which Portugal shared from the mid-

1950s on and to the regime's conviction that, since its first-order priorities of maintaining political stability and providing for economic solvency were now accomplished, it could again move ahead with further corporative implementation.

But by this point it had become clear that corporatism and the corporative complex were no longer (if indeed they had ever been) at the base of the system, constituting, as the early ideology had proclaimed, the focus around which national life swirled. The gaps between corporative theory and corporative practice were distressingly vast, plain for all to see; and even the new social security legislation existed more on the paper of the *Diário de Governo* than in actual fact. Corporatism as a manifest system and ideology was hence increasingly ignored, both by the regime and by the Portuguese people. It had ceased to have meaning, and in fact the entire national system came to function almost as though corporatism and the corporative complex were not there.

By the late 1960s it was not just the corporative system that had increasingly gone to sleep, however, but the entire national system. Salazar was old and tired, some say senile. The fighting in Africa dragged on, by now on three fronts. The ship of state seemed rudderless, directionless. Needed decisions were not being made. Corruption had become widespread. The secret police constituted almost a separate state-within-a-state. The opposition grew and so did the terror tactics used to repress it. Both the regime and the corporative system seemed to be locked in a deep freeze. In the historic pattern the demands began to mount that something be done, not only because the regime had become "dinosauric" but also because it seemed to have overstepped the bounds between permissible authoritarianism, which was both at the heart of the historic Portuguese tradition and its most recent manifestation in the corporative regime, and outright tyranny, which therefore legitimated the right to rebellion. By the late 1960s the demand was clear: either *renovação* from within or *revolução* from without.[23]

Corporatism Revitalized

The corporative spirit lives and is practiced. . . . The Government, in remaining faithful to the Political Constitution, of necessity remains faithful to the corporative ideals.—Marcello Caetano (Secretariado Nacional da Informação pamphlet)

The regime of Marcello Caetano, it is true, was quite different from that of his predecessor, Salazar, but it did not correspond very well to the picture of it portrayed in foreign press accounts. Those accounts described Caetano as a would-be but frustrated "liberal," seeking to preside over a process of "democratization" and constantly thwarted in these efforts by powerful rightist and *salazarista* forces. The evidence, however, points to the conclusion that, while Caetano sought to update, loosen, and modernize the main pillars of authoritarian-corporate rule, he remained an authoritarian and a corporatist, and it is within that context that his rule must be judged and not in the context of some supposed desires for "liberalization" and "democratization."[24]

Caetano had inherited a government that, as one account put it, was sluggish to the point of torpor. Government, administration, decision making, public policy, the corporative structure—indeed the entire national system—had all but come to a standstill during the last years of the Salazar regime, and it would be Caetano's job to invigorate, activate, rejuvenate, and revitalize it, to evolve from "the dinosaur," to "thaw out" from the "deep freeze." Note that nowhere in this list of purposes and popular metaphors do the words "liberalize" or "democratize" appear. It is unlikely that Caetano's intentions were ever to "liberalize" or "democratize"; that idea probably represents mere wishful thinking on the part of journalists and the American Embassy, and it may hence be inappropriate to criticize him for not moving faster toward democracy when that was never his intention. Caetano aimed at broadening the directing elites somewhat but by no means at democratization; he tried to widen the base and appeal of the official party but not to provide for real choice between parties; he sought to rein in and control somewhat such "uncontrollable forces" as the secret police but not by sacrificing authoritarian control; he aimed at better implementation of the corporative system but did not intend to turn to liberalism.

Caetano changed the style of the regime more than its essence, presided over a far more open, more pluralist, more socially just system than did his predecessor, but that was done within the parameters of the corporative system and not some presumed movement toward liberalism. Caetano's goals were to adjust the system to new realities, to recognize and accommodate the new social forces that had grown up rather than turning his back on or repressing them as Salazar had done, to restore confidence in the economy and the public service that had almost disappeared under his predecessor, to wake up and invigorate a nation and system that had gone to sleep under Salazar, and to revive a slumbering, almost stagnant set of corporative institutions long neglected through disuse. It is on these criteria, not according to some imagined "liberal" ones, that his regime must be judged; and I think both the Revolution of 1974 and the judgment of history indicate that by these criteria the regime failed.

While Caetano remained a corporatist, as a leader he proved weak, uncertain, vacillating, not able to manage very well the complex divisive currents that modernization, in the face of institutional paralysis, had set loose. Although the pattern was similar in other policy areas—educational reform, governmental remodeling, African affairs, and so on—for the purposes of this study the arena of labor relations is central. Caetano's strategies may be summarized as follows: first, a tenuous opening up, then a crackdown, followed by uncertainty, vacillation, new openings, more indecision, and an ultimately disastrous temporizing. The breakthrough for labor came in June 1969 in a decree that gave the *sindicatos* the right to select their own leadership without government approval. Under Salazar the labor leadership had ordinarily been imposed by the regime. Another decree provided that, on the three-man arbitration commissions used for settling wage disputes, one member would be chosen by the *sindicato*, one by the *grémio*, and the third by the other two. Under the old system the third member had been selected by the government and had almost invariably sided with employer interests in enforcing austerity and wage controls. Another provision shortened the time limits given the *grémios* to respond to *sindicato* demands and made it impossible for the *grémios* simply to ignore these demands, which had usually been the case in the past.[25]

Within months the *sindicatos*, which for decades had been trade unions in name only, began to be transformed from amorphous government agencies into genuine instruments of the workers. For the first time opposition elements, including Communists in the case of some *sindicatos*, swept the union elections, *and the elections were allowed to stand.* Under the old regime, whenever an oppositionist had somehow managed to win a union election, the election was immediately canceled and new leaders were found who were more amenable to government direction. At the same time, the new arbitration commissions were in numerous cases deciding in labor's favor. This was due both to a general political and generational shift that had begun to take place within the state ministries (in this case the Corporations Ministry) and to explicit directions given out by Caetano's office. As the trade unions started to gather strength and some independent bargaining power, the government for the first time began enforcing the corporative laws obligating the *grémios* to respond and calling for coequal bargaining power between workers and employers. Strikes, slowdowns, and protest demonstrations, although legally banned, increased with government acquiescence. A number of new collective bargaining agreements were signed between 1969 and 1971 that provided for major wage increases. With government approval, the *sindicatos* had begun to acquire some teeth. Meanwhile, under Caetano's Estado Social, a vast range of new social programs was introduced, programs that no longer existed just on paper or *para inglês ver* but were actually being implemented. The corporative system was revitalized and for perhaps the first time started to live up to some of its original ideals.

These changes were of course related to broader Portuguese social and political developments. Accelerating industrialization had by now created a far larger and more militant work force and a real laboring *class* in such centers as Lisbon and Setúbal, as distinct from the earlier, "sleepier," deferential "servant" element of the past, on which Salazar's earlier, Rerum novarum–based conception of corporatism had been founded. Large-scale emigration and declining population had produced some severe labor shortages, thereby strengthening the *sindicatos'* bargaining position. The government's commitment to expanded production, continuous economic growth, and broadened social programs also gave it a strong interest in avoiding ruinous strikes by acceding to labor's demands. Expanded tourism and contact with the outside world, the push for entry into the Common Market, the emigration of Portuguese workers to other freer and more industrialized nations also helped break down the Salazar walls of isolation and open up the system. The freer climate, in turn, and the 1969 legislative elections gave the opposition a new impetus and stimulated it to greater organizational efforts among the workers.

Then came the clampdown. In the fall of 1970 the metallurgists, one of the most politicized of the *sindicatos*, had rejected a proffered labor contract, demanded higher wages, and called a meeting in the soccer stadium to rally support. The government banned the rally and accused the metallurgists of "fomenting class struggle." Meanwhile, other militant unions had begun following the metallurgists' lead. Employers appealed to the government to do something to halt the ferment and it responded with two new decrees, the first giving the right to appoint the third member of the arbitration commissions back to the government and the second restoring the government's right to suspend elected *sindicato* officials for activities "contrary to social discipline." The decrees opened the way to renewed state control of the *sindicatos*, and armed with this power the government moved against the metallurgists and the other militant oppositionists.

These actions failed to restore labor peace. Once the door had been opened, it proved difficult to slam it shut again. Other unions increased their demands. Since strikes had been outlawed in corporative Portugal, it was left to the government to decide whether a work "slowdown" or "stoppage" was really a "strike." Though it sounds scholastic and far removed from reality, a whole new politics grew up around the question of when a "work stoppage" was a "strike" and therefore required suppression and when it was not and could therefore be allowed to go forward. The government vacillated: it broke up with police brutality a demonstration by the clerks, but it acceded to other union demands. New restrictions were enforced but new openings were allowed also. The government gave local authorities the right to approve candidates for *sindicato* elections and, according to local labor leaders, "these petty bureaucrats used their powers unmercifully." Candidates for union elections had to meet endless qualifications, and local authorities—if they wished—could always find one that would disqualify a particular candidate. Whether the labor laws and restrictions were enforced or not depended on the play of forces at particular moments and frequently on whim. One week the government would approve an important wage increase for one sector, the next it would reject it for another. The *sindicatos* were bitter about the indecision and uncertainty, but they kept up the pressure. The regime also continued to face in two directions at once, sometimes paternal, at others brutal.

Meanwhile, as the challenges from inside the system from the corporative regime's own *sindicatos* mounted, a new and perhaps equally ominous threat loomed from without, as workers in sizable numbers began reorganizing in unsanctioned factory committees. These clandestine, nongovernment unions were organized into a broad umbrella organization called the Intersindical and had appeared in all the nation's major industrial firms. As part of its strategy to keep labor in check, the Salazar regime had consistently disallowed the creation of a strong and independent national labor

confederation, but now Caetano, believing he could contain it, tolerated precisely such an interunion group which came to represent
some fifteen to twenty of the largest *sindicatos* with a membership
variously put at between 150,000 and 200,000. Intersindical, however, was not content with the wage increases Caetano had secured and
began making stronger demands for full freedom of association and
the right to strike. By mid-1971, after Intersindical had sought recognition from the ILO (International Labor Organization), Caetano
moved to outlaw the organization and to purge its affiliated unions.[26]

But now the union movement could not be suppressed so easily
and Intersindical, having gained a strong foothold and widespread
worker support, simply moved underground, where it provided a
ready vehicle for infiltration by the similarly clandestine Portuguese
Communist Party. The government now had to deal with both a
restless official *sindicato* structure and the powerful but subsurface
Intersindical. Intersindical moved to organize "unity committees"
in numerous factories, industries, and even government offices
where it could convert worker dissatisfaction into crippling strikes.
The government responded by arranging wage increases which it
hoped would increase its popularity and undercut Intersindical's
appeal, but it was unwilling to give the unions independent bargaining power. In this way, too, it sought to preserve the essential
paternalistic and authoritarian structure of the system while at the
same time staving off discontent. When that tactic failed, however,
it continued to use riot and secret police to break up demonstrations, arrest strike leaders, and curb the clandestine unity committees. But these tactics seemed only to lead to still larger strikes.
The tendency of foreign and domestic firms to respond differently
to worker demands and pay different wage scales added to the in-
equalities and the bitterness. The foreign firms paid more and were
more responsive; domestic firms sought to resist negotiations and
relied on the state for support against the unions.

By 1973, while the government continued to provide for some
major wage increases, industrial unrest had become so rampant that
forty major strikes occurred. These strikes almost literally closed
down the economy in some cases. They undermined both the African war effort and Caetano's plans for social reform and thus led
to further paralysis. They also stimulated discontent among center
and rightist elements to such a point that they now began to plot
in earnest the regime's overthrow. As pressures from labor center
and *salazarista* forces increased, and as the question was more frequently asked whether the regime could continue to manage and

cope with these conflicting currents, the government lost all *confiança*; the plotting grew more intense; and several aborted coup attempts were launched before the final one succeeded in April 1974. Caetano had proved incapable of managing the divergent forces now loose. The regime fell; his efforts at presiding over a revitalized corporatism had ended in failure.

Corporation Dismantled, Transcended, Persistent

Corporatism is far from dead. Many continuities exist in the present regime. Corporatism may reassert itself, not just in a fascist form but in more subtle manifestations.—Manuel de Lucena

The 1961 *Programa para a democratização da república*,[27] drafted by the Portuguese opposition movement, urged that the following action be taken with regard to the corporative structure:

1. The corporations were to be abolished and replaced by institutions of a "democratic nature."
2. The various agencies and institutions of the corporative state were to be dissolved, transformed, or integrated into a new democratic order.
3. The functions of the Organizations of Economic Coordination would be integrated into the normal services of public administration.
4. The *casas, ordens,* and *sindicatos* connected with the corporate structure would be converted into genuine class associations and complete sovereignty would be granted their general assemblies.
5. The *grémios* would be converted into class associations whose leaders would be elected by the membership.
6. The *casas do povo* and *casas dos pescadores* might continue as reorganized agencies without prejudice against the rights of labor associations also to organize their members.

In the wake of the 1974 revolution, this program, in only slightly modified form, did in fact serve as the basis for dismantling the Portuguese corporative system. Not only were the control mechanisms of the Salazar regime—secret police, censorship, and the like—quickly overturned, but also the entire web of corporative agencies, the corporations, and the corporative complex were eliminated. The dismantling of the corporative system took place initially at the popular and street level and then was ratified by official decree. The initial April coup has been followed in subsequent months by hundreds of "mini-coups" in industrial plants, professional associations, and government offices. There were innumerable confrontations between workers and employers, servants and patrons, students and faculties. In scores of offices and agencies, signs appeared in the windows announcing "liberation" from the "fascists." The old official *sindicato* system broke down as the underground factory unity committees emerged, as workers seized factories, as plant managers and directors were driven out, as strikes multiplied and direct action became the means for solving disputes. The Corporations Ministry became the Labor Ministry; it was given over initially to the Communists, who used their control of the pinnacles of the labor pyramid to gain advantages for themselves while keeping the basic structure intact. The Labor Statute of 1933 was declared inoperative before a new one had been drawn up to replace it. The whole vast panoply of labor tribunals, arbitration commissions, and collective contracts was abolished; also overturned were the networks of economic regulatory commissions, institutes, and juntas. The leadership of the *ordens* and *grémios* was soon replaced, and the Communist-dominated Intersindical gained an overwhelmingly preponderant position in the trade union movement. The social services, also administered through the corporative system, were severely disrupted.[28]

Direct action in the streets was followed quickly (and occasionally anticipated) by action at the official level. Although in our attention to other, perhaps more dramatic events it has been neglected, the process by which the corporative system was dismantled in the aftermath of the April revolution merits more detailed study, particularly in the light of other, comparable experiences with post-authoritarian "decompression." Though space considerations rule out a detailed treatment here, some of the major decrees may be noted as a means of illustrating the thoroughness, flavor, and completeness of the changeovers. On May 2, 1974, it was decreed that harbor masters (generally state appointees or the servants of employer interests) would no longer serve as the presidents of the *casas dos pescadores*. On May 9 the Junta of National Salvation (the Spínola government) gave itself the power to suspend all employees of the corporative agencies and Organizations of Economic Coordination and to name all replacements. On May 27 a decree overturned the old *sindicato* structure and opened the way to the "just satisfaction of worker demands." On June 3 the Junta Central of the *casas dos pescadores* was relieved of its duties. On August 17 the corporations were dissolved. On September 9 the Junta da Acção Social of the Ministry of Corporations was "extinguished." On September 12 all corporative agencies "dependent" upon the old Corporations Ministry were dissolved and their responsibilities transferred to the Organizations of Economic Coordination. On September 25 the *grémios da lavoura* were similarly abolished; on October 23 the Fundação Nacional para a Alegria no Trabalho was "sanitized" and "restructured." On December 5 "patronal interests" were given the right to form associations in defense of their own interests. On December 23 the Federação das Casas do Povo were scuttled; in January 1975 some *grémios* were eliminated, others were to be "investigated." The "obligatory *grémios*" were replaced by a new confederation of industry, while the "voluntary *grémios*" were reorganized as private-interest associations. And so it went. Thus, by the end of the first year of the Revolution, virtually the entire formal structure of the corporative state had been dismantled or restructured.[29]

But the process was nowhere near so thorough, and the change-overs nowhere near so complete, as the analysis of the "street" action and the formal decrees implies. There was no "180° turn-about," as some of the accounts have alleged. The fact is that, while many agencies of the corporative system were abolished, a good many others (*grémios, sindicatos, casas do povo, casas dos pescadores*) remained in existence. They were reorganized, often renamed, and their leaders were changed; but a good part of the structure continued intact and, while the leadership often was turned over at the top, at lower levels the same personnel largely continued in the same old agencies. We can see this particularly in the *sindicato* structure and the Labor Ministry and at the local and municipal government levels, where a new leadership moved in but where the hierarchical, pyramidal structure was often preserved intact. The new private associations continued to act in most respects as had the old *grémios*; the *casas do povo* and *casas dos pescadores* remained almost identical to what they had been under the old regime. Obviously, this is not to discount the clearly revolutionary transformations that occurred in some agencies and some policy areas, but it is to say that there were important continuities as well. Some of the corporative agencies continued largely intact; in others the names and faces changed but the same functions continued to be performed. A close examination of the unfolding of the Revolution through both street politics and the formal decrees indicates that it may have been far less abrupt, more gradual and accommodative, more deliberate and less radical or chaotic than the United States press accounts conveyed. While no one would deny the fundamental transformations and *regeneração* that the Revolution implied, it is perhaps equally important to understand the sheer persistence of some earlier forms and practices.

Not only were some of the older corporative agencies often slow in being confined to the ashcans of history, but also the new regime moved to resurrect a new set of corporative institutions. They were, of course, called by other names but they were essentially corporative in character. In the previous chapter Manuel de Lucena has analyzed the thrust toward an ideology and structure of class collaboration rather than conflict, a feature which he correctly identifies as one of the essential features of corporatism. The movement toward an increasingly strong and authoritarian state structure, toward an increasingly state-directed economy, and toward a carefully structured and state-directed system of interest associations and representational bodies is similarly characteristic of corporate state systems. The Portuguese government and its constituent agencies are still heavily military dominated, infused with hierarchical and authoritarian structures. The regime presumes to govern for and in the name of the "common good," but it has shown little enthusiasm for democracy and genuine grass-roots participation on the liberal model, and elections carry but tentative, not definitive, legitimacy. The Portuguese state is still largely the administrative and technocratic state that it was before, heavily bureaucratic, still carefully regulated and controlled, with elaborate legal-administrative procedures left over from the old regime, still organized from the top down and governed by decree-law. Increasingly, the control mechanisms of the historic tradition have been resurrected as a way of preventing the spontaneity and joy of the early street demonstrations from getting out of hand and of channeling them, again, in preferred directions. Finally, our attention must be called to the new institutional arrangements inaugurated by the MFA and then reorganized by succeeding regimes, with their functionally representative bodies, their corporative and syndicalist tendencies, and the special place within the system given the military and other corporate groups. Thus, in this respect, too, there are some remarkable continuities with the older corporative regime, as well as some sharp departures from it.[30]

Another consideration in weighing the corporative state and the corporative tradition in Portugal has to do with the models we have used to interpret the changes underway both before and after 1974. So many of these models, implicit in the popular accounts but finding their way into more scholarly analyses as well, paint the older corporative system in rigid and entirely static terms, hence portray the post-1974 regime in generously liberal and liberating terms, and see the entire political process in Portugal in the light of a dichotomous struggle between dictatorship and democracy. Now, surely, if it is fair to call the later Salazar regime rigid and static, there were indeed some liberalizing and liberating aspects to the 1974 revolution, and there is clearly something of a struggle between dictatorship and democracy. But that is not the entire picture.

From this analysis as well as Lucena's, it becomes clear that there are various dynamic aspects to corporatism and not just static ones, that the corporatism of Caetano was of a quite different sort than that of Salazar, that corporatism is not entirely rigid and impermeable but may change and evolve depending on societal conditions and developmental transformations, and that instead of being perceived wholly through "liberal" or "liberating" frameworks the postrevolutionary regime might also be examined in the light of revolutionary, more complex, perhaps "higher" forms of corporatism. The dictatorship-versus-democracy dichotomy is too confining, too restrictive, too culture bound to provide a very useful model. It represents a false and too artificial choice, a too limited set of possibilities. It fails to recognize, for instance, that corporatism may take populist, leftist, and revolutionary directions, as in Peru, as well as conservative and rightist ones, or that even within a single country various corporative forms may be related to broader societal transformations. Where the dictatorship-versus-democracy framework is useful and bears some relation to actual Portuguese events, by all means let us use it. But let us keep open the possibility that from Salazar through Caetano to the present regime we have witnessed some remarkable changes in—as well as the persistence of—an essentially corporative system, from the conservative, rigid, unyielding Rerum novarum–Quadragesimo Anno form of Salazar to the more open, pluralist, and socially just form of Caetano to the more populist, revolutionary, socialist, and/or syndicalist forms of the present. This is a paradigm that also carries considerable explanatory power.

Finally, we return to the two senses, the two meanings, of the term "corporatism" with which we began. Corporatism has been discussed here in two ways: a political-cultural sense that implies a long tradition of what Newton called "natural corporatism," and a more manifest and explicit ideology and structure of "corporatism" that found expression in the Estado Novo of the 1930s. It has proved rather easy to dismantle the corporative institutions associated with the Salazar regime since they were often ephemeral, surface agencies that lacked deep roots, were but weakly institutionalized, and enjoyed but limited legitimacy. Whether Portugal can as easily escape the yoke of and transcend its entire corporatist tradition and political culture may be quite a different matter. From the analysis presented here, it seems clear that the continuities with and persistent features of that historic tradition remain strong even in the wake of the Revolution of 1974. Portugal may evolve toward a "higher," more "developed," more pluralist, participatory, revolutionary, socialist, or syndicalist form, but of the fact that those forms will continue to exhibit important corporatist characteristics there would seem to be little doubt. For Portugal to depart from this broader corporatist tradition would also involve shucking off some eight hundred years of history, and that seems more problematic than simply ridding itself of the corporative institutions fashioned by Salazar.

Final Considerations

The formal corporative system in Portugal from 1933 to 1974 was an incredibly mixed bag of successes and failures. Corporatism was successful in the 1930s in providing Portugal with a new national mythos badly needed after the chaos and failure of republicanism, with a new sense of national purpose and destiny, with restoration of order and stability and a set of institutions based upon national and indigenous sources, with help to restore rationality and probity to the national accounts, with provision for economic growth and development, and with help to fill the organizational void of a country whose historic, long-term problems had always included a lack of organization and a vacuum in its associational life. The re-establishment of a stable, functioning regime and the strengthening of the economy, closely related to the creation of the corporative system from 1933 on, were among the more notable and fundamental accomplishments of the Salazar regime. But after 1945, as the regime became more brutal, repressive, and fascistic, as corporatism in the earlier 1930s sense was discredited and became increasingly dysfunctional, as corporatism served more to retard national growth and modernization than to stimulate it, the failures of the system came to outweigh its earlier successes. The efforts of Caetano to revitalize the corporative system were again a mixture of successes and, ultimately, failure.

But perhaps "success" or "failure" is the wrong way to assess the situation. Perhaps we should simply take the Portuguese regime on its own terms and in its own context. In that sense the regime neither "succeeded" nor "failed"; it was rather the product of a historical period whose time had simply passed. The 1930s were probably the high point of corporatism in the global context, and the conservative Rerum novarum form of corporatism as propounded by Salazar still fitted fairly well the rural, conservative structure of Portuguese society. By the postwar period this was no longer the case. Portugal had changed and so had the international context. What was required was no longer a corporatism of control, demobilization, and selective repression but a corporatism of change and development. Corporatism in the earlier 1930s (or 1890s?) form was an idea and mode of organization whose epoch had been superseded. Time had passed the Portuguese regime by, while Salazar continued to cling to and enforce a system that had become anachronistic, even on its own corporative terms.

Here then lay the real difficulty for the Portuguese regime. It was not that it refused to move toward liberalism or socialism (neither apparently strongly favored nor enjoying the support of a majority of the Portuguese population) but that it failed to modernize even the corporative structures that it did have. The regime instead went to sleep, stagnated, became dinosauric. While other countries—Spain, Argentina, Brazil, Mexico, Peru—gradually evolved away from older Rerum novarum forms of corporatism and toward more dynamic, participatory, change-and-development-oriented, even revolutionary forms, Portugal remained locked in the older conception, in the by-now-outdated bourgeois ideal of an ordered, hierarchical, Catholic, paternalistic state and society. It failed to take account of the emerging social forces or sought simply to repress them. Caetano made some frantic and too feeble efforts to rescue and dynamize the system at the last minute, but these came too late. Portugal's chief problem was, thus, that it failed to update and restructure its ideas, programs, and ideology even within the corporative framework it had set for itself.

By the same token—and at least until the Revolution of 1974—

it was not necessarily corporatism per se that was increasingly rejected by the Portuguese population in the postwar period but the particular direction it had taken under Salazar. If Salazar had proved more adaptable, if he had modernized the nation instead of allowing it to drift, if his had not become a repressive dictatorship, and if he had been willing to recognize the changing nature of Portuguese society and the just demands of the middle and lower classes (all big *ifs*, obviously, but *ifs* that in considerable measure came to pass in the warp and woof of postwar change in other Iberian and Latin nations similarly cast in the earlier corporative mold), the corporative system might well have lasted. It became instead a symbol of dictatorship and backwardness, a thing to be despised. The outdated, discredited *salazarista* corporative conception was thus repudiated, as it deserved to be. Had that conception and its accompanying institutional arrangements proved more flexible, accommodative, and adaptable, however, it is likely that Portugal would still be a corporative system, not in the old-fashioned and now thoroughly discredited sense but in a newer, more modern sense, providing for the development of the Portuguese nation and its people. That is how development has usually gone forward elsewhere in the Iberic-Latin world; unfortunately, it did not take place in Portugal.

All this augurs ill for the future of the Portuguese system and for the possibilities of the establishment of any stable, functioning, development-oriented regime. For if it is in fact the case that corporatism in its natural, historic forms lies at the heart of Portuguese political culture and may even today be still the dominant tradition, then we should recognize the possibility that the particular Salazar practice and variant may have so thoroughly discredited corporatism that no new government will be able to build upon that heritage.[31] At the same time we must recognize that corporatism is no longer the only tradition in Portugal, that alongside it have grown up a liberal and republican tradition and, more recently, a nascent socialist one. But these latter traditions are still so new and so weakly institutionalized that they may not have sufficient support or legitimacy to serve as the basis for the establishment of a new regime either. With these three concepts and world views continuing to coexist uneasily side by side, representing wholly different ways of life and modes of organizing society and polity, with little connection between them, and with no one enjoying absolute legitimacy or even majority support, it may well be that Portugal will remain, like Argentina, ineffective and inefficient, chaotic, fragmented and disintegrated, subject to recurrent breakdowns, a kind of permanently crippled nation unable to establish any functioning system, be it liberalism, an updated form of corporate pluralism, or a newer variant of socialism or syndicalism, to replace the older form of corporatism that the new regime has dismantled.

Notes

1. Howard J. Wiarda, "Toward a Framework for the Study of Political Change in the Iberic-Latin Tradition: The Corporative Model," *World Politics* 25 (January 1973): 206–235; idem (ed.), *Politics and Social Change in Latin America* (Amherst: University of Massachusetts Press, 1974); Fredrick Pike and Thomas Stritch (eds.), *The New Corporatism: Social-Political Structures in the Iberian World* (Notre Dame, Ind.: University of Notre Dame Press, 1974); and James Malloy (ed.), *Authoritarianism and Corporatism in Latin America* (Pittsburgh: University of Pittsburgh Press, 1976).

2. Martin O. Heisler, "Patterns of European Politics: The 'European Polity' Model," in *Politics in Europe: Structures and Processes in Some Post-industrial Democracies*, ed. Martin O. Heisler (New York: McKay, 1974), chap. 2; and Leo Panitch, "The Development of Corporatism in Liberal Democracies," paper presented at the 1976 Annual Meeting of the American Political Science Association, Chicago, September 2–5.

3. The longer, more detailed case study from which much of this discussion and subsequent analysis derives is Howard J. Wiarda, *Corporatism and Development: The Portuguese Experience* (Amherst: University of Massachusetts Press, 1977).

4. An example is A. H. de Oliveira Marques, *History of Portugal*, 2 vols. (New York: Columbia University Press, 1972).

5. I am presently preparing for publication a paper defining what precisely the Iberic-Latin conception of "democracy," "representation," "participation," "pluralism," and the like implies; a preliminary statement is Howard J. Wiarda, "The Transition to Democracy in Portugal: Real or Wishful?" paper presented to the Joint Seminar on Political Development (JOSPOD), Center for International Studies, Massachusetts Institute of Technology, Cambridge, December 8, 1976, and published in the minutes of the JOSPOD Seminar.

6. Marques, *History of Portugal*, provides perhaps the clearest example.

7. One thinks particularly of the influential volume edited by Gabriel A. Almond and James S. Coleman, *The Politics of the Developing Areas* (Princeton: Princeton University Press, 1960); but much of the writings of Karl Deutsch, S. M. Lipset, W. W. Rostow, and others during this same period exhibited much the same ethnocentric and culture-bound perspectives.

8. Ronald Newton, "Natural Corporatism and the Passing of Populism in Spanish America," in *The New Corporatism*, ed. Pike and Stritch.

9. Philippe C. Schmitter, "Still the Century of Corporatism?" in *The New Corporatism*, ed. Pike and Stritch, pp. 93–94.

10. "Pluralism" is another of those terms, like "democracy" or "representation," that mean something different in the Portuguese context than in the Anglo-American one; still the possibilities for corporate pluralism should not be ruled out or defined away. Indeed, in the absence of a strong liberal-democratic tradition in Portugal, a degree of corporate pluralism may be about all that the political liberal may hope for.

11. Alfred Stepan is writing a book on Peru in which he employs the "organic state" concept; patrimonialism is of course one of Weber's categories of traditional authority and was applied to Latin America, among other places, in Magali Sarfatti, *Spanish Bureaucratic-Patrimonialism in America* (Berkeley: Institute of International Studies, University of California, 1966).

12. For further elaboration see Henrique de Gama ·Barros, *História da Administração Pública em Portugal nos Séculos XII–XI* (Lisbon: Liv. Sa da Costa, 1945); Raymundo Faoro, *Os donos do poder: Formação do patronato político brasileiro* (Porto Alegre: Ed. Globo, 1958); Manuel Paulo Merea, *O Poder Real e as Cortes* (Coimbra: Coimbra Ed., 1923); and Sidney M. Greenfield, *The Patrimonial State and Patron-Client Relations in Iberia and Latin America: Origins of "The System" in the Fifteenth Century Writings of the Infante D. Pedro of Portugal*, Occasional Paper No. 1, Program in Latin American Studies (Amherst: University of Massachusetts, 1976).

13. For the contrasting traditions see Louis Hartz, *The Liberal Tradition in America* (New York: Harcourt, Brace, and World, 1955); and Richard M. Morse, "The Heritage of Latin America," in *Politics and Social Change in Latin America*, ed. Wiarda.

14. Such Estado Novo propagandists as Augusto da Costa argued this case; so did Salazar.

15. It should be said that Salazar was also very clever in his relations with the military. Although he had incorporated many of the integralist, monarchist, nationalist, and Catholic principles into his own corporatist formula, he had not accepted one of their chief goals—the restoration of the monarchy. Instead, Salazar elevated the armed forces into the role of the "moderating power" historically reserved for the crown, thereby securing the loyalty and support of the military while at the same time retaining the backing of all but the most fervent of the monarchists, integralists, and Catholic traditionalists.

16. This analysis is clearly related to the question of the Latin American middle class and whether it is progressive or reactionary. The answer is, a bit of both, depending on the pragmatic circumstances. For the debate, see John J. Johnson, *Political Change in Latin America: The Emergence of the Middle Sectors* (Stanford: Stanford University Press, 1958); and James Petras, "The Latin American Middle Class," *New Politics* 4 (Winter 1965): 74–85.

17. Philippe C. Schmitter, *Corporatism and Public Policy in Authoritarian Portugal* (Beverly Hills, Cal.: Sage, 1975).

18. Mihail Manoilesco, *Le Siècle du corporatisme* (Paris: Lib. Felix Alcan, 1934).

19. Fascism, according to Organski, is a model of development based on a partnership between agricultural and industrial elements to carry out

industrialization but to impose its costs primarily on the industrial working class (A. F. K. Organski, "Fascism and Modernization," in *The Nature of Fascism*, ed S. J. Woolf [New York: Vintage-Random, 1969], pp. 19–41).

20. See especially Theodore Lowi, *The End of Liberalism* (New York: Norton, 1969).

21. See Schmitter, "Still the Century of Corporatism?," pp. 93–94.

22. Freppel Cotta, *Economic Planning in Corporative Portugal* (Westminster: King and Staples, 1937); Maria Blemira Martins, *Sociedades e grupos em Portugal* (Lisbon: Ed. Estampa, 1973); and George McGovern, *Revolution into Democracy: Portugal after the Coup* (Washington, D.C.: GPO, 1976), which contains important information collected by the Department of State and the Senate Foreign Relations Committee staff.

23. Implied in these paragraphs are two ideas that need to be developed at greater length. First, it seems clear that the biases that developed in the Estado Novo and the particular directions that the regime took were not necessarily inherent in corporatism per se but had to do more with the nature of power and influence in the broader Portuguese system; the priorities that Salazar and the army had established, which relegated corporative implementation to a third-order priority; and the particular choices that Salazar opted for at especially critical junctures. Corporatism in Portugal might just as well have taken a more populist, developmentalist, and pluralist direction, as it did in other nations organized initially on some similar corporatist bases. Corporatism per se seems not to be the independent villain variable on which Portugal's retarded growth could be blamed; a more likely candidate is Salazar himself. For further discussion, see Wiarda, *Corporatism and Development*, chap. 11.

Second, it seems worth considering in more detail that the regime was eventually repudiated and overthrown, not because it was corporatist and authoritarian, or because it refused to go toward liberalism or social-democracy, but because it had become oppressive, had ridden roughshod over corporate group *foros*, had violated the natural rights of its people, and had become a full-fledged tyranny—all of which constitute grounds for revolt, both in Portuguese practice and in legal theory. In short, the regime both developed and was eventually repudiated, not in terms of the liberal and democratic paradigm, but in terms of the very *Portuguese* institutions and practices on which it was based. For some orienting concepts, see Lawrence E. Rothstein, "Aquinas and Revolution," paper presented at the 1976 Annual Meeting of the American Political Science Association, Chicago, September 2–5.

24. A more detailed analysis is in Wiarda, *Corporatism and Development*, chap. 10. The assessment presented here, it should be said, is based upon considerable field research in Portugal during this period and on a series of interviews in the prime minister's office, with the Corporations Ministry, with labor elements, and with oppositionists.

25. The decrees are published in the *Boletim do INTP* for this period; see also Henrique Nascimento Rodrigues, *Regime Jurídico das Relações Colectivas de Trabalho* (Coimbra: Atlantida, 1971).

26. Based upon the field work in Portugal in 1972–73 and especially the return visits in March–April 1974 and May–June 1975. By the latter postrevolutionary date, many of the clandestine activities of the Intersindical

had been described in the numerous new journals and newspaper of the leftist parties; a useful summary may be found in the report appearing under Senator McGovern's name, *Revolution into Democracy*.

27. *Programa para a democratização da república* (Porto: Tip. J. R. Gonçalves, 1961).

28. For a more detailed treatment of these events, see Howard J. Wiarda, *Transcending Corporatism? The Portuguese Corporative System and the Revolution of 1974* (Columbia: Institute of International Studies, University of South Carolina, 1976).

29. Based on the field work and interviews in Portugal in May–June 1975. The decree laws are published in the *Boletim do Instituto Nacional do Trabalho e Previdência* for this period.

30. Most analysts feel the Spínola government sought not a complete break with the past but to turn the economy and the existing corporative system away from its close ties to the colonies and toward a new relationship with the European Common Market (that was also clear, if unspoken, Caetano policy); Portugal's latest government seems intent on following the same course.

31. Kenneth P. Erickson has suggested some of these points to me.

4. The Portuguese Industrial Elite and Its Corporative Relations: A Study of Compartmentalization in an Authoritarian Regime

HARRY M. MAKLER

Today there is a general realization that no form of interest can forget its dependence on other forms, and also that private interests must be subordinate to the general: the profession, production or the Nation. The corporative organization disciplines competition and seeks to maintain harmony and balance within each sector. Corporativism must be lived and put into practice by the whole nation. It must dominate the guidelines of companies and settle deep into the consciousness of the workers—Marcello Caetano, Ex-Prime Minister of Portugal, November 6, 1968 (Secretariado Nacional da Informação pamphlet)

Introduction

In the spring of 1974 the authoritarian regime initiated by Salazar more than forty years before was overthrown by a coup d'état. The ruling junta incorporated a variety of political persuasions into the provisional cabinet, encouraged the formation of political parties, pledged general elections within a year, and restored basic civil rights. Almost overnight censorship was eliminated, the dreaded secret police was dissolved, and Salazarists were purged from ranking civil and military posts. What will be the course of this revolution? Given the instability of the present situation, within both the state and the civil society at large, and the possibility of certain international spillovers, it would be unwise to predict the future from the present. Nor do I intend to engage in such speculation.

Reprinted, with modifications, from *Economic Development and Cultural Change*, vol. 24, no. 3 (April 1976). © 1976 by the University of Chicago.

Instead, this essay will attempt to explore some of the tendencies underlying the dissolution of the Salazar-Caetano regime. The long-term trends underlying the regime's demise are fairly well known. Since the early sixties, wars in its African territories absorbed a significant proportion of the country's human resources and nearly half its national budget. This severely curtailed domestic expenditure and infrastructural and industrial development. Industry was concerned with the prospects of the "internationalization" of the economy, beginning with the country's joining the European Common Market. Until recently industry in general and the traditional industrial sectors in particular had enjoyed the protection offered by European Free Trade Association membership. Common Market affiliation threatened economic disaster for many sectors. Many industrialists, as I have shown elsewhere, were frankly insecure about their ability to compete in the European markets.[1] Comparatively speaking, the country lacked skilled manpower; it was faced with rapid increases in wages due largely to the scarcity of labor caused by emigration; it suffered galloping inflation (21% in 1973 and 35% in the first quarter of 1974, according to OECD figures) which drastically reduced the real value of salaries and further stimulated emigration; it was threatened by the loss of raw materials vitally needed for industrial expansion (e.g., an oil embargo imposed by the Arab league); and it was hampered by dim prospects of national financial incentives and investment. The Salazar-Caetano regime clearly faced numerous problems severe enough to threaten its survival.

Could the regime have survived if different policies or strategies had been adopted? In retrospect this seems highly unlikely. Nevertheless, it could be argued that one solution would have been to intensify and broaden political mobilization among the population and to strengthen institutions and officially created voluntary associations. But the regime's fear of mobilization matched its fear of disorganization. Organization without mobilization—this was the regime's formula. And this formula required the deactivation of all organizations potentially capable of articulating and mobilizing sectors of the population for purposes of political intervention. This applied not only to the diverse political parties associated with a democracy (wherein dissent can find a limited expression) but also to the original "governmentalist" party through which support for the regime had originally been mobilized. And yet this same formula required the filling of all organizational vacuums. The various interests within civil society had to be organized in a coordinated and harmonious whole and subordinated to the state. And it was via the corporative system that the state's organizational schemes were to be realized.

The corporative system was intended to organize the interests of the various social groups and subordinate them to the interests of the state. However, we have here the germs of a contradiction. Corporatist theory maintains that the interests of these different social groups are inherently noncontradictory—that they presuppose a deeper unity within society conceived as a whole. As such the state is neither partial nor neutral. Instead it is the concrete expression of this aforementioned deeper unity, and the corporative system acts as the circuitry that transmits the differential aspects of this unity to the state. If, however, these different interests are not complementary, then the basic premises of corporatist theory are rendered invalid. The state, in fact, does not express this "basic unity" nor does the corporatist system serve to transmit this unity. Instead the interests of the state are revealed to be partial (that is, supportive of specific interests embedded within civil society and/or the specific interests of the state embedded in its own relative autonomy and positivity vis-à-vis civil society), while the corporative system serves to compartmentalize, pre-empt, and prevent "class hegemony or polarized group confrontation, and the consequent loss of state autonomy which might have otherwise been spontaneously produced as the result of capitalist development."[2] In other words, these institutions serve an essentially repressive function and can thus be quickly delegitimized in the eyes of their constituents. It was fairly obvious that the corporative institutions that "organized" the "popular classes" served this second and repressive function. But what about these corporative institutions, the grémios of the property owners (industrial, commercial, and agricultural) that served the group most favored by the regime. What functions or dysfunctions did they serve?

An examination of these questions may help to explain, if only to a small degree, why the regime fell so quickly. The relative success or failure of the Salazar-Caetano regime to develop a viable corporative system, and the reasons for this success or failure, should provide insight into the conditions which permit or prevent a corporatist solution in a traditional society like Portugal.

Portuguese Corporatism: Grémios

After Salazar's assumption of power, Portugal had a single party which played an insignificant role in politics because few elites or masses had any connection or identified with it; it had no clear ideology; no program, platforms, or propaganda; no prestige accorded to party officials; no organization at the grass-roots level. In fact, the only time one heard about political parties was during the regime's rare elections. In part, as an alternative to political parties and political mobilization, Salazar introduced corporatism in 1933 as part of the Estado Novo. Essentially, corporatism is a state-organized and regulated system of interest representation in which various constituencies, primarily grouped on the basis of their occupations or vocations, are organized into a limited number of singular, compulsory, noncompetitive, hierarchically ordered, and functionally differentiated categories. These groupings are granted a representational monopoly and autonomy in exchange for observing certain controls on their selection of leaders, articulation of their claims, and their intercorporate relations.[3]

The corporatism of Salazar has been described as *state* corporatism as opposed to *societal* corporatism. Interpreting a discussion of Philippe Schmitter: while societal corporatism has been associated with advanced capitalism and the welfare state, with a strong federal system and competitive party politics, state corporatism has been correlated with less-developed societies and authoritarian regimes, with a weak single party and repressed pluralism.[4] Portuguese corporatism, then, must be understood not in terms of its positive accomplishments but as an institution of social control which sought to permit the participation and integration of various factions while at the same time containing and regulating the emergence of new ideologies, interests, and leadership which might eventually threaten the regime's survival. Corporatist legislation established the state's right to regulate and coordinate national social and economic activity by bringing labor and capital into harmony for the common good. Through the establishment of corporative institutions (e.g., *casas do povo, sindicatos, grémios, juntas,* etc.) the regime reserved the right to intervene in economic and social activities as the arbiter and regulator of production, wages, and labor relations. By *decreto-lei* no. 23049, the regime, at its initiative, created patronal guilds (*grémios*) in each industrial, agricultural, and commercial sector and required all those operating in that sector to join, contribute, and abide by the decisions of the *grémio.* These institutions were empowered to intervene, when judged convenient, in the economic activities of the members (*agremiados*) in order to cooperate and bargain collectively with the workers' organizations (*sindicatos*) in the "progressive resolution" of work problems and social security; in the regulation of production quotas, manufacturing conditions, and pricing; and in the distribution of certain commodities essential to the country's foreign trade (wine, cork, wool) or national consumption (wheat, rice, codfish, bread).[5] However, these powers were circumscribed by the regime because the decrees also specified that *grémios* must work exclusively within the national plan "with absolute respect for the superior interests of the nation . . . and subordinate their interests to the interests of the national economy and the principles designated by the national labor statutes" (*decreto-lei* no. 23049, *artigos* 1–3). Initially, membership was obligatory for all enterprises belonging to the same sector or exercising activities in the same sector.[6] But soon after the enactment of the original legislation a new decree was enacted (*decreto-lei* no. 24715) which permitted patronal entities, at their own initiative, to petition the Ministry of Corporations for authorization to form a voluntary *grémio* after 50 percent of the enterprises in that sector had agreed to join. Once recognized, however, the regime assured the power of these corporative organizations by (*a*) officially recognizing them as the legal representatives of their respective sectors and as having a monopoly and formal access to various government councils, (*b*) stipulating that decisions taken by the *grémio* were applicable to all enterprises regardless of whether they were members or not, and (*c*) allowing them the right to impose membership on other employers in the same sector. On the other hand, the regime also assured its control over these organizations by requiring that they comply with the country's labor code, submit periodic reports for ministerial ratification, and solicit approval from the Ministry of Corporations of candidates proposed for *grémio* office (*decreto-lei* no. 24715, *artigo* 13). In this sense the *grémio*, as a corporatist artifact, paralleled similar institutions that were applied to other sectors of the population. For example, the urban working class and landowners were corporatized into *casas do povo*. However, unlike other strata, certain private industrial and commercial associations (e.g., Associação Industrial Portuguesa, Associação Commercial de Lisboa, Associação Industrial Portuense) were allowed to survive, thus offering alternative channels for interest articulation. Moreover, industrial elites, particularly some of the large, Lisbon-headquartered consortia (e.g., Companhia União Fabril [CUF], Champalimaud group, Português do Atlântico group) were able to pursue their interests via direct contact and alliances with different sectors of the state apparatus, including the military.[7]

Data on Recruitment to Leadership
˅ in the Corporatist System

A survey conducted in 1965 with a sample of heads of larger Portuguese industries (industrial elites) provides some specific evidence
for the questions raised earlier concerning the relative effectiveness
and representativity of the corporatist system under Salazar and
Caetano.[8] The data permit an analysis of the characteristics of the
heads of industries, relations between industrial sectors, and the
holding of *grémio* and other formal leadership positions. First, the
career patterns of the industrial elite will be examined in order
to characterize those elites who held formal leadership positions
and those who did not. Did the two groups differ in their social-
class origins, age, educational attainment, social mobility, or size
and type of enterprise they directed? Are they distinguishable in
terms of the relationship to the ownership and control of their enterprises? Were founders, as compared to heirs or managers, more
likely to have held formal leadership positions? Second, I will discuss the industrial elites' attitudes toward and usage of *grémios*,
the corporative institutions designed to represent the interests of
the industrialist strata. Specifically, I wish to examine which segments of the industrial elite used the *grémios* and which elites
considered these institutions effective in representing their interests. In the final section these findings will be weighed in terms
of their implications for the breakdown of the regime.

FORMAL LEADERS

In this essay formal leaders are those who held positions in government and/or in corporative interest groups. Public positions are any
public offices held at the national, provincial, or municipal levels
of government. Some examples of public positions at the national
level are cabinet positions, such as ministers, deputy ministers,
undersecretaries, directors general of ministries, *procuradores* (members) of the Corporative Chamber, or *deputados* of the Legislative
Assembly. Provincial positions are governors, provincial judges, or
assemblymen, but, since none of the industrial elite members ever
held provincial positions, this category shall be omitted from our
analysis. Municipal positions are mayors of cities, municipal councilors, and local officials in general. Public positions also include
other positions held in the government, such as a consultant to

a ministry, a delegate to an international convention, or a civil servant. Only a tenth of our sample held this type of position.

Corporative positions are ranking positions in *grémios*. To determine corporative membership, the respondents were asked, "Of the many organizations, both public and private, professional, commercial, corporative, etc., which serve or are designed to serve the interests of industry, to which does your enterprise belong and to which do you personally belong?" They were then asked whether or not they were officers in any of these organizations. Later in the interview, in order to identify public office holding we asked, "Have you ever been elected or nominated to any municipal, state, or federal position?"

From these questions four main types emerged: (a) those elites who held only corporative positions, (b) those who held only public office, (c) those who held both types of positions, and (d) those who held neither corporative nor public office. The first three types are formal leaders, while the fourth type are nonposition holders.

My tabulations show that almost half (46%) of the industrial elite members held some public or corporative office. In terms of the type of formal leaders, about a third (31%) held corporative positions and nearly as many (26%) held public positions. Considered separately (see Table 4-1), one-fifth held only corporative positions, mainly presidents of *grémios*; 15 percent held only public office; and 11 percent occupied both corporative and public office.[9]

Table 4-1 shows the relationship between characteristics of the Portuguese industrial elite and formal leadership positions.[10] The table is divided into three parts to facilitate its interpretation: (a) biographical characteristics of the industrial elite members, (b) structural characteristics of the enterprise, and (c) combinations of biographical and structural characteristics. Only the relationships which account for most of the variance shall be reported in this essay.

The most significant differences in Table 4-1 were found with respect to size of enterprise and with respect to some sectors of industry. Compared to elites heading smaller enterprises (employing 499 or fewer persons), it is apparent that heads of larger enterprises (employing 500 or more persons) were more likely to have occupied public positions at the national level of the government. Many of these public office holders were also found in the service and chemical sectors. Since a number of companies in these sectors were state owned (e.g., Sacor, the petroleum refinery), their chief executives, *administradores delegados*, were appointed by the

TABLE 4–1

Formal Leaders among the Portuguese Industrial Elite (% Distribution)

| | None | Only Corporative | Only Public | | | | Both Corporative and Public | | | | TOTAL |
			Nat.*	Mun.†	Other	Total	Nat.	Mun.	Other	Total	Total
Total	55%	20%	2%	9%	4%	15%	3%	3%	5%	11%	100%
N	(165)	(60)	(7)	(26)	(11)	(44)	(10)	(9)	(14)	(33)	(302)
A. Biographical Characteristics											
Age											
55 years or younger	55%	62%	29%	42%	55%	43%	20%	22%	50%	33%	52%
Over 55 years	45	38	72	58	45	57	80	78	50	67	48
Type of education											
Engineering	27%	22%	43%	15%	64%	32%	30%	11%	50%	33%	27%
Economics	7	5	0	0	0	0	0	11	22	12	6
Law	4	10	29	0	0	4	30	0	7	12	6
Medicine, pharmacy	4	3	0	0	0	0	0	0	0	0	3
Other university	5	3	28	4	9	9	10	0	0	3	5
High school or less	53	57	0	81	27	55	30	78	21	40	53
Socioeconomic origin											
Upper	34%	54%	43%	39%	46%	41%	30%	45%	50%	42%	40%
Middle	49	36	57	46	27	43	60	44	50	52	46
Lower	17	10	0	15	27	16	10	11	0	6	14
Social mobility											
Upward	38%	34%	57%	31%	64%	43%	30%	44%	64%	49%	39%
Static	42	46	43	50	27	43	60	56	29	45	43
Downward	20	20	0	19	9	14	10	0	7	6	18
Ownership and Control											
Founder	37%	30%	14%	54%	9%	36%	20%	45%	7%	21%	34%

	1	2	3	4	5	6	7	8	9	10	11
Heir	32	43	0	34	18	25	30	44	43	40	34
Owner-manager	15	20	0	8	18	10	30	11	36	27	16
Manager	16	7	86	4	55	29	20	0	14	12	16
Geographic mobility											
Natives	58%	62%	29%	61%	55%	54%	60%	89%	64%	30%	59%
Migrants	33	33	57	35	36	39	40	11	29	43	33
Foreign-born	9	5	14	4	9	7	0	0	7	27	8

B. Structural Characteristics

	1	2	3	4	5	6	7	8	9	10	11
Size of enterprise											
Smaller‡	66%	55%	0%	58%	9%	36%	70%	56%	29%	48%	58%
Larger	34	45	100	42	91	63	30	44	71	52	42
Location											
Northern Portugal§	55%	58%	0%	67%	27%	57%	30%	67%	36%	42%	54%
Central Portugal	45	42	100	33	73	43	70	33	64	58	45
Size and location											
Smaller											
Northern	60%	70%	0%	80%	0%	75%	43%	80%	0%	44%	62%
Central	40	30	0	20	100	25	57	20	100	56	38
N	(109)	(33)	(0)	(15)	(1)	(16)	(7)	(5)	(4)	(16)	(174)
Larger											
Northern	45%	44%	0%	91%	30%	46%	0%	50%	50%	41%	45%
Central	55	56	100	9	70	54‡	100	50	50	59	55
N	(56)	(27)	(7)	(11)	(10)	(28)	(3)	(4)	(10)	(17)	(128)
Selected sectors											
Textiles	34%	41%	0%	45%	29%	32%	17%	50%	50%	36%	35%
Construction	20	16	0	15	14	12	0	0	0	0	17
Metals||	26	30	14	20	14	18	0	0	17	7	24
Chemicals	13	11	29	5	14	12	17	0	17	14	12
Services	7	3	57	15	29	26	67	50	17	43	12
N	(118)	(37)	(7)	(20)	(7)	(34)	(6)	(2)	(6)	(14)	(203)

TABLE 4-1—Continued

		Only Corporative	Only Public				Both Corporative and Public				TOTAL
	None		Nat.*	Mun.†	Other	Total	Nat.	Mun.	Other	Total	
Technological complexity#											
T+	44%	48%	100%	19%	55%	41%	50%	22%	36%	36%	43%
T−	56	52	0	81	45	59	50	78	64	64	57
Size and technological complexity											
Smaller											
T+	51%	55%	0%	20%	0%	19%	43%	40%	75%	50%	48%
T−	49	45	0	80	100	81	57	60	25	50	52
Larger											
T+	30%	41%	100%	18%	60%	54%	67%	0%	20%	24%	37%
T−	70	59	0	82	40	46	33	100	80	76	63
C. Biographical/Structural Characteristics											
Education and size											
Smaller											
High school or less	62%	55%	0%	93%	%	87%	43%	80%	50%	56%	62%
University or more	38	45	0	7	100	13	57	20	50	44	38
Larger											
High school or less	36%	59%	0%	64%	30%	36%	0%	75%	10%	24%	39%
University or more	64	41	100	36	70	64	100	25	90	76	61
Socioeconomic origin and size of enterprise											
Smaller											
Upper	27%	53%	0%	33%	100%	38%	29%	40%	75%	44%	34%
Middle	54	38	0	54	0	50	71	60	25	56	51
Lower	19	9	0	13	0	12	0	0	0	0	15

Larger											
Upper	48%	56%	43%	46%	40%	43%	33%	50%	40%	41%	48%
Middle	38	33	57	36	30	39	33	25	60	47	38
Lower	14	11	0	18	30	18	34	25	0	12	14
Ownership and control and size											
Smaller											
Founder	43%	36%	0%	60%	0%	56%	14%	60%	25%	31%	42%
Heir	32	49	0	40	0	38	43	20	75	44	37
Owner-manager	16	12	0	0	0	0	29	20	0	18	14
Manager	9	3	0	0	100	6	14	0	0	6	7
Larger											
Founder	25%	22%	14%	46%	10%	25%	33%	25%	0%	12%	23%
Heir	32	37	0	27	20	18	0	75	30	35	31
Owner-manager	13	30	0	18	20	14	33	0	50	35	19
Manager	30	11	86	9	50	43	34	0	20	18	27
Ownership and control and location											
North											
Founder	42%	26%	0%	54%	0%	48%	33%	67%	0%	36%	39%
Heir	37	51	0	36	33	36	36	33	40	43	40
Owner-manager	12	17	0	5	0	4	0	0	40	14	12
Manager	9	6	0	5	67	12	0	0	20	7	9
N	(90)	(35)	(0)	(22)	(3)	(25)	(3)	(6)	(5)	(14)	(164)
Central											
Founder	31%	36%	14%	50%	12%	21%	14%	0%	11%	10%	27%
Heir	27	32	0	25	13	11	14	67	44	37	27
Owner-manager	17	24	0	25	25	16	43	33	33	37	21
Manager	25	9	86	0	50	52	29	0	11	16	25
N	(75)	(25)	(7)	(4)	(8)	(19)	(7)	(3)	(9)	(19)	(138)

TABLE 4-1—Continued

				POSITIONS HELD								
	None	Only Corpora- tive	Only Public				Both Corporative and Public				TOTAL
			Nat.*	Mun.†	Other	Total	Nat.	Mun.	Other	Total	TOTAL
Ownership and control and technological complexity												
T+												
Founder	33%	31%	14%	60%	17%	28%	20%	50%	20%	25%	31%
Heir	28	31	0	20	17	11	0	0	40	17	25
Owner-manager	15	28	0	0	17	5	60	50	0	25	18
Manager	23	10	86	20	50	56	20	0	40	33	25
N	(72)	(29)	(7)	(5)	(6)	(18)	(5)	(2)	(5)	(12)	(131)
T−												
Founder	40%	29%	0%	52%	0%	42%	20%	43%	0%	19%	36%
Heir	35	55	0	38	20	35	60	57	44	52	41
Owner-manager	14	13	0	10	20	11	0	0	55	24	15
Manager	11	3	0	0	60	12	20	0	0	5	9
N	(93)	(31)	(0)	(21)	(5)	(26)	(5)	(7)	(9)	(21)	(171)

Note: When the number of cases is less than 20, the observations are tentative.
* National.
† Municipal.
‡ Smaller = 50–499 employees; larger = 500 or more employees.
§ Northern Portugal = Aveiro, Braga, Oporto districts; central Portugal = Lisbon, Santarém, Setúbal.
|| Includes electrical and heavy machinery, steel, and metal products.
Technologically complex (T+) = enterprises above the mean in superior or intermediate technicians or both; technologically noncomplex (T−) = enterprises below the mean in both superior and intermediate technicians (see notes for further explanation of this measure).

government. Other calculations show that quite a few were ex-cabinet members, or ranking university professors, or both as in the case of João Pinto de Costa Leite (Conde de Lumbrales) who was *administrador delegado* of Sacor and a *catedrático* (professor) on the law faculty. In 1965, when I conducted that study, most of these services and chemical industries were concentrated in central Portugal, especially in the district of Lisbon.

In northern Portugal, those who held public positions were at one time mayors, city councilors, or other municipal officials rather than national office holders. Many were heads of textile or other light industries who, having inherited wealthy and stable enterprises, entered politics. (Most textile enterprises in Portugal are concentrated in the northern districts of Oporto and Braga.) But given the regime's tendency over the past forty years to fill top political positions with individuals from Lisbon, it would appear that northern political aspirants have had to fulfill their political ambitions at the purely local level.[11]

The group which participated least in the *polity* were those heading construction enterprises. A large proportion of these enterprises were directed by individuals who with little capital and little formal education had founded their enterprises and remained so involved in the day-to-day management of their companies that they had little time for political activities.

Corporative Leaders

In contrast to public office holders, corporative leaders among the industrial elite (e.g., presidents and directors of *grémios*) were more likely to be (a) younger, (b) upper class in their socioeconomic origins, (c) sons of businessmen or landowners, (d) nongeographically mobile (i.e., natives), (e) heirs (usually having inherited their enterprises from their fathers, who were the original founders), and (f) nonsocially mobile.[12] About half the corporative leaders had attended a university and, while most had majored in engineering, a number were also lawyers, which in Portugal has traditionally been the career chosen by the landowners' sons as a principal avenue to politics and administration.[13] Few differences in birthplace were found among the different types of formal leaders. The proportion of Lisbon-born elite members who held formal leadership positions did not significantly exceed the proportion born in Oporto, Portugal's second city and northern capital.

Structural characteristics of the enterprise, such as its size, location, technological complexity, and industrial sector, also differentiate among formal leaders.[14] For example, in Table 4-1, B indicates not only that there is a direct relationship between socioeconomic origin and corporative position but also that this is accentuated by region and sector. Those from upper-class origins, directing northern enterprises in traditional and economically more stagnant sectors, such as textiles, foodstuffs, and wood and cork products, were more likely to have occupied corporative positions. A significant number of these men were heirs.

Another noteworthy characteristic of corporative leaders was the relative stagnation of their enterprises, especially in comparison to those of most other types of formal leaders among the industrial elite. This difference is particularly apparent in traditional sectors and larger technologically noncomplex enterprises, as Table 4-1 shows. But, as I have shown elsewhere, this lack of industrial dynamism is highly correlated with inheritance among the Portuguese industrial elite.[15] Despite the fact that heirs were from upper-class origins and have inherited larger enterprises, some let their businesses remain idle or even dwindle in terms of technological capability and recruitment of personnel. Other calculations reveal that these industrialists were "backward" in their managerial structure, as relative to enterprises of comparable size they had small managerial teams and were reluctant to delegate authority. This pattern, incidentally, is not peculiar to Portugal but has been noted by other students of entrepreneurship and economic growth. For instance, Charles P. Kindleberger, in discussing the British family firm, notes that "the founder who emerged from poverty is replaced by the son or grandson 'without exceptional energy' and 'brought up to think life easy.' The first obstacle [to economic growth] is the desire for the quiet life, or for public esteem. . . . In Britain the descendants of the founder were typically statesmen first and businessmen second."[16]

The predominance of this type of participant in ranking corporative positions has consequences for the grémio's effectiveness. It suggests that the grémio's function was more honorary than effective. In fact, often the entrepreneurs (founders) in our studies criticized their grémio leadership for being unaware of, or oblivious to, the problems which confronted their sector. Most founders thought that participating in or presenting problems to their grémios was a waste of time. Very few, as I will show, saw the grémio as effectively representing their interests.

Public Leaders

Thus, corporative industrial leadership in 1965 was principally the haven for those from upper-socioeconomic-class business and land-owning origins, inheritors of family businesses, those with a secondary education or law training, and those who had always lived in the same geographical area. The composition of those who held *public positions* was different. Compared to corporative leaders, they were more likely to be (a) older (55 years of age or more), (b) middle class in socioeconomic origin and individuals whose fathers were from a variety of occupational backgrounds (i.e., more white-collar, professional, and working-class population), (c) upwardly socially mobile, (d) individuals with engineering, technical, or liberal arts training, and (e) managers, especially those heading larger enterprises.

In addition to size of enterprise, other structural characteristics of the enterprise combined with biographical characteristics in locating those who held only public office among the industrial elite members. There are two distinct groups who have held public positions. One group held leadership positions at the national level. It was composed of managers of larger, centrally located, technologically complex enterprises, such as those found in state petroleum and utilities (e.g., electricity, transportation, water) sectors. Over half were migrants of middle- and lower-middle-class origins who had come to Lisbon from the north to pursue a career in engineering. Although many of these national public leaders were employed in these state-owned industries, a number were also associated with the large consortia in private sectors. The second group was composed largely of nonuniversity-educated, middle-class founders or upper-class heirs who were directing mostly northern, technologically noncomplex enterprises belonging to traditional sectors of the economy. This group held ranking municipal government positions. Their political activities were more local in scope and more community oriented. In contrast, the managerial types holding positions at the national level were more technocratic in training and outlook. In their day-to-day activities they devoted more time to planning, establishing norms and policies for their enterprises, and obtaining information about external trade and market conditions. The founder and heir types were more "inward" oriented and more "immediate" in their activities. They tended to handle problems as they arose in their enterprises; they spent a great deal of their time inspecting their factories' operations and giving orders; and they exhibited a more paternalistic concern with the workers, their workers' families, and the local community.[17]

A third group also emerged in the analysis. This was comprised of those elites who held "other" public and corporative public positions. Mainly they were industrialists who held nonpolitical positions at the national level, such as a functionary in a ministry (e.g., economic technician), a member of a national or international commission (e.g., permanent committee member on National Industrial Progress commission, delegate to the International Labor Organization Congress, OECD representative, adviser on Angolan vegetation), a university professor, or an administrator of a state-owned enterprise. Those who held this variety of positions were more likely to be (a) evenly distributed in terms of their age, (b) university graduates in engineering, (c) from upper socioeconomic origins, (d) upwardly socially mobile,[18] and (e) managers of larger, centrally located enterprises in both traditional and modern industrial sectors.

Since this large group resembles those who held national positions, I will group them when analyzing the relationship between the industrial elite and the *grémios*.

Corporative and Public Leaders

A tenth of the industrial elite held both corporative and public positions. Comparatively speaking, those who were both corporative and public leaders were older than those who held only corporative or public positions, suggesting that age and position holding in corporative and public institutions vary directly. As a whole there was a greater proportion of university-educated elites among this group and more hailed from middle-class origins, but, as Table 4-1 shows, very few (12%) were managers. Corporative and public leaders were more likely to be associated with technologically noncomplex enterprises, particularly in the textile sector.

But similar to the patterns which emerged in describing public leaders, the greatest differences are found between national and municipal leaders rather than between those who held dual positions and those who did not. Corporative-national leaders look very much like those industrial elites who held only national positions. Even more alike are corporative/municipal and only municipal position holders, as the figures in Table 4-1 show. The primary attributes of these types of industrial elites are their ownership and control (as founders or heirs) of technologically noncomplex, northern enterprises associated with traditional industrial sectors. The overlap of roles at this local level could be interpreted as evidence of attempts by this propertied elite to consolidate its power in order to be able to influence policies affecting industry which, as I shall show, were not influenced through the corporative system or its organizations. But further research on the relationship between *grémios* and municipal politics is necessary to clarify the extent and nature of interlock between these two institutions.

Nonposition Holders

Finally in my profile are those who held *no* formal positions. This group comprised half of the elite. This indicates that the largest proportion of industrial elite members have not been involved in public or corporative office holding, nor as I shall show in the following section did they seek the support of, or articulate their interests through, their *grémios*.

The nonposition holders were (a) concentrated more in smaller, northern, construction, textile, and other traditional and technologically noncomplex enterprises; in terms of their biographical characteristics they were (b) evenly divided in secondary and university educational attainment, (c) more likely to be middle class in their socioeconomic origin, (d) more upwardly mobile, (e) mainly founders or heirs, and (f) nongeographically mobile (i.e., natives).

The ownership and control factor perhaps best characterizes the nonposition holders. I found that they were mainly upwardly mobile founders of smaller construction companies; heirs of northern technologically noncomplex textile, foodstuffs, or metallurgical companies; or from a small group of managerial directors of smaller, centrally located, technologically complex, and recently founded enterprises. As newer enterprises, either these had not been incorporated into a *grémio* or, more likely, they belonged to an industrial sector which had not been corporatized. Other calculations indicate that, of those who were managers, many were foreign born, which would preclude their holding corporative and public office.

Thus, the formal leaders among the Portuguese industrial elite were a mixed lot. The corporative leaders (*grémio* leaders) could be characterized as younger, propertied (founders, heirs, owner-managers), from upper-socioeconomic-class origins, divided between nonuniversity and university trained, geographically nonmobile, and directors of technologically noncomplex enterprises mainly associated with traditional industrial sectors. Among public leaders, two groups can be distinguished: municipal and national. Those who occupied municipal positions displayed the same characteristics as the corporative leaders, except that as a group they tended to be older, more middle class in origin, nonuniversity educated, and more concentrated in technologically noncomplex northern enterprises. In contrast were the national leaders. They were older, university-trained engineers or nonpropertied executives of major, centrally located, and technologically complex enterprises often connected with important Lisbon-headquartered consortia.

My findings indicate that there was some interlocking between the polity and the economy. At the very least there was an interchange between what C. Wright Mills labeled top-command posts in government and those positions at the top of the industrial world.[19] The chief executives of a number of Portugal's largest, most modern enterprises at one point in their careers held ranking positions in the regime. Other calculations indicate that the movement was from top political and civil service positions immediately into the presidencies of large corporations, similar to the pattern in France.[20] The typical career path to a modern corporation in Portugal started with an assistant professorship at a university, particularly under the tutelage of a well-known *catedrático*, movement into an undersecretarial (deputy minister) position, and then either from there to a top industrial post or continuation in the government, moving into a ministerial position, and then into industry. The predominance of academics was undoubtedly due to Salazar's and Caetano's influence. During their political careers both retained their full professorships at the University of Coimbra, Portugal's oldest and most famous university.[21] My impression is that the professoriate in Portugal enjoys high prestige. For example, as I have shown elsewhere, university professors were accorded higher social prestige by the industrial elite than ranking civil servants (deputy ministers), military officers (active colonels), and even prominent leaders in their own class (directors of enterprises employing more than 400 individuals).[22]

I found no evidence that there was a movement in the other direction, that is, from the executive suite into ranking national government posts, as is sometimes the pattern in advanced industrial countries like the United States. In fact, a recent study of Portuguese corporatism has shown that, while industrialists comprise about 20 percent of the Corporative Chamber, very few were members of the much more important national Legislative Assembly.[23]

Nor were industrialists to be found at the cabinet level.[24] Thus, at least formally, the regime seems to have limited the mobility of this class and confined them to corporative organizations. However, that the regime precluded the industrial elites from directly participating in the polity did not mean that this class had no influence on government policy. The very fact that the largest private, modern enterprises recruited ranking civil servants can be construed as a means by which this group attempted to contact and influence the government at the national level. At the local level there seem to have been more linkages between the polity and the economy. Members of the traditional propertied class among the industrial bourgeoisie occupied top municipal or *grémio* positions either simultaneously or at one time during their terms as enterprise heads. Thus, there was more of a two-directional "flow" between industry and the polity at the municipal level than occurred at the national level. However, neither was there upward mobility from the municipal or the *grémio* arena into cabinet legislative positions nor, as I shall also demonstrate in the next part of this essay, was the regime particularly receptive to the claims from this group.

FORMAL LEADERS AND THEIR *GRÉMIOS*

In the previous part of this essay the characteristics of industrial elite members who held corporative and/or public office were identified. Here I will examine the attitudes of the industrial elite toward their *grémios* in order to evaluate the nature and function of these organizations. For example, what proportion of the industrial elite use their *grémios*? What proportion consider them to be effective in defending their interests and why?

Spokesmen for the Salazar-Caetano regime would have maintained that the industrial *grémio* served to transmit the interests of its constituents to the state. At the same time they would have stressed the complementarity of interests between the two. The potential contradiction between these two statements was hidden by the very organization of the *grémio* system. The latter was constructed as if the interests of the two parties were indeed complementary, which in practice meant that the *grémios'* functions were narrowly circumscribed by the state. Indeed one part of the corporatist legislation states that the *grémios* "must subordinate their respective interests to the interests of the national economy, in collaboration with the State" (*decreto-lei* no. 23049, *artigos* 1–3).

And Pedro Theotónio Pereira, one of the principal architects of Portuguese corporatism, in discussing corporative leadership stated that corporative organizations should be "directed by neutral elements who have the confidence of the Government."[25]

If this contradiction was implicitly recognized in the legislation of the regime and in the statements of its ideologists, what was its status in the actual functioning of the grémio system? One would expect that the continued viability of the grémio system would depend ultimately on the "flow" of demands moving from the entrepreneurs to the state; on whether or not there existed regular opportunities for different groups within the industrial elite to openly compete for leadership positions; or, at the very least, on whether or not the majority of the industrial elite made use of their grémios and considered them effective in articulating their interests. This problem can be analyzed only by an examination of the nature of the relation between the grémio system and its constituents. And this opens the door to a larger problem: the relation between the government and the various components of the patronal class.

In my study of the Portuguese industrial elite I asked each respondent with what frequency he presented problems to his interest group or grémio (for those who indicated that this was the interest group most directly related with the defense of their enterprise's interests) and to evaluate the designated organization's effectiveness in representing his interests.[26]

Table 4-2 shows that use and effectiveness of grémios are correlated with formal political leadership in interesting and revealing ways. First, except for those who held corporative and public positions, the industrial elite's evaluation of their grémios outweighs their actual use of these organizations. For example, while 64 percent of those who held public office reported that their grémios were effective in defending their interests, only 44 percent actually used them. The same pattern appears among those who held no formal leadership positions and among those who held only corporative positions, although the percentage difference is not as pronounced. Second, industrial elite members who held public office were more likely to have considered grémios to be effective than those who held only a corporative or no leadership position. This was especially the case among those who held national positions. In fact, this even suggests that corporative office holding might be inversely related to positive evaluations of the grémios.[27] Some attitudes of formal leaders and nonposition holders substantiate these quantitative findings.

There were a variety of responses to the question, "In which ways does this *grémio* effectively defend your interests?" Criticism centered on reservations about leadership, "*personalismo*," lack of cooperation and trust among members, government receptivity, *grémio* mandate, and corporatism itself. Consequently, many were led to circumvent the system and either to articulate their interests directly to ranking government officials or to do nothing at all. Here are some examples of these criticisms.

Some industrialists expressed little or no confidence in leadership. Typical in this regard was the opinion of the manager of a large Setúbal cork products plant who, in discussing the Junta Nacional da Cortiça,[28] said: "How can it protect us? It doesn't do that at all. These organizations suffer from organic deficiencies. Our branch of activity has never had any protection from the state or any of its organs. Its leaders are neither acquainted with our branch nor surrounded by technicians who could elucidate them. As a result, we sometimes receive statistics on exports in which cork is not even mentioned. This is absurd considering that cork is one of our largest sources of income in this country. Therefore, as this is a difficult branch and government lacks technical background, they simply avoid us. The president of the Junta da Cortiça asked me for suggestions in December of 1961. Nothing ever came of it! Since they have no technicians, they can neither help us nor try to reorganize the branch. I told them we could have avoided the competition of other countries but it was no use. What is wrong with this country is that we have 'doctors' without specialization in the branch and we lack technicians to help us with the problem. It is not like France or the USA. In those countries one can count on technicians for advice" (manager, Setúbal, cork products, giant-size enterprise). And an heir of a small northern textile mill told us this about his *grémio*: "The *grémio* still does not protect our interests because it is a very young organization, but I don't think it ever shall. The guilt lies with the officers. If there was leadership of the *grémio*, perhaps one could already have seen the results of its action. I do not trust the *grémio* as a solution to our problems, because I do not agree with its leaders. They are not qualified enough to deal with problems in our sector" (heir, Oporto, textiles, medium-size enterprise).

Some industrialists doubted *grémio* effectiveness because of the

TABLE 4–2

Formal Leaders Who Used *Grémios* and Considered Them Effective

		Only Corporative	POSITIONS HELD Only Public			Corporative and Public			TOTAL
	None		Mun.*	Nat.†	Total	Mun.	Nat.	Total	
Leaders who used *grémios*	28%	51%	39%	57%	44%	75%	79%	78%	55%
N	(97)	(51)	(18)‡	(7)	(25)	(8)	(19)	(27)	(200)§
Leaders who considered *grémios* effective	44%	55%	61%	71%	64%	62%	65%	64%	52%
N	(101)	(51)	(18)	(7)	(25)	(8)	(20)	(28)	(205)‖

* Municipal.
† National; also included in "national" are those who held "other" positions.
‡ Limited number of cases (20 or fewer) permits only tentative observations.
§ Twenty-two reported using other organizations which best represented their interests (12 used private interest groups [e.g., Associação Industrial Portuguesa], and 10 used other corporative organizations [e.g., *juntas*]). Half of the remaining 41 cases were not affiliated with any interest groups and the responses of the others were not codable.
‖ Thirty-four reported that other organizations were effective (22 indicated private interest groups and 12 used other corporative organizations). The remaining cases were not affiliated with any interest group.

TABLE 4–3

Formal Leaders Who Frequently Contacted Government

		Only Corporative	POSITIONS HELD Only Public			Corporative and Public			TOTAL
	None		Mun.*	Nat.†	Total	Mun.	Nat.	Total	
Leaders who frequently contacted government	30%	40%	23%	80%	44%	11%	64%	48%	35%
N	(142)	(58)	(26)	(15)	(41)	(9)	(22)	(31)	(272)

Note: Unlike Table 4–2, this table is not restricted to those who indicated that *grémios* best represent their interests but includes other interest groups as well.
* Municipal.
† National.

strong individualism, distrust, and competitive relationship among the members of the same sector. Typical is a foodstuffs manufacturer who remarked that "the directors of the *grémio* are too worried about solving their own problems. We discuss problems dealing with prices, financing, work, discipline; but most of the time, I am against their opinion. The leaders of the *grémio* are all bad competitors. After all, we are all in the same business, and there are sufficient consumers to sell all our production" (founder, Oporto, food products, medium-size enterprise). And a Lisbon executive explained that "the *grémio* is too slow. There was a time when the Associação offered better guarantees. But the government tried to limit its power so that the *grémio* could take over most of its functions. The problem is that the members of the *grémio* are too suspicious of one another. Therefore, they restrict themselves to discussing general problems which do not involve confidential information. The Portuguese never trust their competitors. Generally, there was more cooperation in the Associação Commercial" (manager, Lisbon, mining, large-size enterprise).

More serious, perhaps, were industrialists who felt that the *grémio* was ineffective because the government ignored, or was insensitive to, its claims. Typical in this respect were the complaints of two owners of large northern textile mills. One said that "I go to the *grémio* to discuss problems of general interest that are fundamental to our industry, such as the labor contract which was written without our being consulted. We only were officially informed there would be a 40 percent raise in salaries one week, after the government's decision" (owner-manager, Braga, textiles, large-size enterprise). And another commented that "I don't see much point in going to the *grémio* since it can't help me much. Besides its being too young as an organization, the minister does not pay attention to what the *grémio* requests and sometimes he does exactly the opposite" (heir, Oporto, textiles, giant-size enterprise).

An owner of a Lisbon metallurgical products factory spoke much in the same vein and also hinted at those whom the propertied class considered the regime to favor. "The *grémio* presents its reports to the Corporação da Indústria which takes them to the government. However, the government does as it pleases, paying no attention to these reports. Instead of asking the opinion of people with experience in the field, they would rather confer with technocrats" (heir, Lisbon, metallurgical products, medium-size enterprise).

Still another source of criticism among members of the industrial elite centered on limited mandate of *grémios*. For example, a founder of a relatively small (185 employees) metallurgical products plant remarked that "the institution of *grémios* has brought few benefits to our industry. It is true that the *grémios* are not well organized. They should be in permanent contact with industrialists. However, the *grémios* have not been given a definite function in our industrial structure. The *grémios* lack autonomy and are not powerful as representative organs should be. For example, right now a labor agreement is being discussed at our *grémio* but the Minister of Corporations has already promised longer vacations to our workers before we could say anything about it. There is no coordination. I also knew that in other branches of industry *grémios* have been trying to introduce export bonuses, such as the ones in Spain. Our *grémio* hasn't succeeded because it is not given enough consideration. As a consequence certain Portuguese industrialists prefer to invest capital in Spain where these bonuses exist" (founder, Lisbon, metal products, regular-size enterprise).

Finally, some industrialists expressed strong skepticism about the corporative system in general and participation in *grémios* in particular. Notice that in the following criticism a Lisbon executive indicates the necessity to increase his *grémio*'s political and financial power through conglomeration (the formation of a national *grémio*) and the establishment of its own financial institution (an industrial bank). "There seems to be a tremendous lack of coordination between several of our industrial organizations. The problems we discuss at the *grémio* are taken to the Corporação, which takes them to the ministry. Later on the problems are referred to the Direção Geral da Indústria, and finally they come back to the ministry. The whole process may take years. Nothing is solved, first, because our public servants are ill paid and, second, because there is no coordination of functions. A corporative system without coordination is anarchy. There are six or seven *grémios* for the metallurgic industry. This is why they have been discussing the labor contract for three years without success. There should be a national *grémio* since we all share the same interests. Later on this *grémio* should organize an industrial bank" (owner-manager, Lisbon, metallurgy, large-size enterprise). And one founder and owner of a giant foodstuffs company outrightly remarked that "I don't believe in *grémios*. I don't agree with the way they are now organized. They are good for nothing. During the [second] world war corporatism didn't remain faithful to its principles of self-directedness. Theoretically, the *grémio* should act as a link between the industry and the government, but that hasn't really happened. The Grémio dos

Oleos Vegetais, for instance, only deals with technical problems. It does not protect our interests. Whenever I need something, I'd rather go to the ministers directly" (founder, Lisbon, food products, giant-size enterprise).

One pattern that clearly emerges is that the propertied elite members—the founder, the heir, and to some extent the owner-manager—were far more critical of the *grémios* than were the hired managerial types among the industrial elite. Particularly critical were the propertied elite who also held *grémio* office. Many were northern Portuguese textile elites.

Enterprise founders, in particular, tended to criticize *grémio* leadership. This is understandable since, true to the mold of the Schumpeterian entrepreneur, they were usually assertive, self-made, risk-taking individuals who would be unlikely to tolerate ambiguity, lack of leadership, and indecisiveness, especially among their industrial colleagues, in their negotiations with ministries and other government institutions. Inevitably, during our interviews with founders they would say, "I wish our *grémio* was more powerful in its dealings with official organizations," or, "Our *grémio* leadership is afraid to take a position or does not persist with our claims." Other calculations show that even industrialists who had been *grémio* officers and/or had attempted to articulate their interests through these organizations gradually became discouraged and began to adopt other strategies. The principal one seems to have been contacting ranking government officials or ministries directly. Some indicated that they contacted the appropriate minister or ministry whenever they had to resolve a problem. One owner said, "It is much easier to deal with the government directly than with organizations like *grémios* which are supposedly protected by the government" (heir, Lisbon, transportation, giant-size enterprise). But being able to contact government officials in Portugal depended upon "whom one knows." In this regard Table 4-3 clearly indicates that the majority of those elites who held national positions were in frequent contact with the government.[29] To recall, most of these were once senior civil servants who were recruited by the country's important consortia to head their major technologically complex enterprises. In marked contrast are the remainder: those who held only corporative and/or municipal positions. Only a small proportion of this group reported that they contacted officials in higher government circles. These were the propertied elite—the heads of smaller companies mainly associated with traditional economies in northern Portugal—who neither used corporative organizations or private industrial associations nor contacted officials in higher government circles.[30] Most were really "outsiders" in terms of being able to articulate their interests. Consequently, when questioned on how they resolved problems paramount to their enterprise's survival the reply "I do nothing" was not uncommon.

Summary and Conclusion

These different types of formal leaders among the Portuguese industrial elite give the impression of a certain degree of heterogeneity. But upon closer inspection one discovers that the different sectors of the industrial elite were confined to relatively homogeneous compartments. The main participants in the national arena were technocrats: deputy ministers, middle class in origin, once professors who were co-opted into senior civil service positions and then into the executive suites of Portugal's largest, newest, mainly state- or consortia-owned enterprises. Participating in the municipal and *grémio* arenas were the propertied elite—the less educated, wealthier founders, owner-managers and heirs of mostly traditional, technologically noncomplex enterprises. Mobility was also truncated. Technocrats moved into larger, newer enterprises from government posts but rarely from there into municipal and *grémio* positions. There is little evidence that once in industry they were co-opted back into ranking national posts. The more traditional propertied elite, in contrast, moved in and out of municipal or *grémio* office but were rarely recruited into the higher command posts of the regime.

What, then, is the relation between this apparent stratification of the industrial elite and the *grémio* system? On the basis of the above paragraph it can be seen that the *grémio* system did not serve as a staging or socializing institution from which the regime recruited its future leaders. None of the industrialists who held *grémio* positions were co-opted into national posts; in fact, only a few industrialists could be found even in the Corporative Chamber, where academics and bureaucrats have been consistently and heavily overrepresented.[31] Indeed, it would suggest that the function of the *grémio* system was its ability to enforce such compartmentalization. This becomes evident when we examine the *grémio* system in terms of its ability to represent its constituents' interests.

In our brief excursion into opinions about the effectiveness of the *grémios*, it was often the smaller, more traditional, propertied elite that was the most critical. And of these it was often those most integrated into the corporative system, the *grémio* leaders, who offered the most poignant complaints. Some viewed the government and its ministers as a haven for technocrats who understood little about the actualities of industrial life, others expressed reservations about the possibility of cooperation among competitive units, while others complained about the *grémio's* lack of mandate. In this connection it should be noted that the *grémio* system provided the only means by which this group could articulate its interests to the government. They did not, on the whole, have access to the older, private patronal entities or the semipublic *juntas*— the latter being used by only a small proportion of the industrial elite. Nor could they bypass the institutional structure and present their claims directly to the government. They simply did not have the power or the "connections." In short, they were forced to channel their interests through an institution that could not, in their eyes, effectively represent these interests.

In this case, it could be argued that the *grémios* served as a placating and buffer institution. As noted earlier, they could be considered at the organizational level as an alternative to political parties and political aspirations for a system which, on the one hand, after nearly three decades of political turmoil, wished to maintain a maximum of political demobilization but, on the other hand, had to satisfy the ambitions of certain sectors of the industrial class. *Grémios* and even municipalities permitted the regime to offer controlled political expression to the propertied elite. This was a group to which the regime was beholden but wished to keep at arm's length, a group on which the regime's power was based but which was accorded little power of its own. It could be argued that the regime blocked the participation of this group in the national arena in order that it not come into conflict with the professoriate and lawyers who had been recruited for their technocratic or bureaucratic expertise. Perhaps it could be better argued that the regime felt that the interests of this group were too deeply embedded in the rural past and as such did not correspond to the projected "national interests."[32] Whatever the case, it appears that the regime attempted through compartmentalization to both maintain and contain the traditional class structure.

However, not all components of the industrial elite were critical of the *grémio's* effectiveness. Our study has revealed that the closer a leader was to the "top" (a national position) the greater the likelihood he would both evaluate the *grémio* as effective and use it.

That a larger proportion of this group tended to laud their *grémio*'s effectiveness than actually to use it suggests that the interests of these more powerful sectors largely coincided with those of the state. If we presume that these interests were totally congruent, then we would have to conclude that the *grémio* system was for this group totally redundant. However, such an assumption would be unwarranted. It would be better to suppose that there existed a whole range of issues where the interests of these industrialists neither coincided nor conflicted with those of the government. And it would be in terms of representing these interests that the *grémio* could acquire its function. Yet this group tended to bypass the *grémio* structure and penetrate the government by more private and direct means. This suggests that the *grémios* were too cumbersome to be effective organs of interest representation. Nor did the *grémios* serve to contain the political interests of this group—and thereby secure the state's autonomy. The more powerful elements in the industrial elite seem to have been able to pursue their own interests by supporting various cliques in different intragovernmental struggles.

In sum we could say that the compartmentalization noted earlier with respect to intraelite mobility finds its echo in the compartmentalization of interest representation. According to Schmitter, the Portuguese regime was characterized by state corporatism for the smaller, more traditional propertied elites and societal corporatism for the more dynamic and powerful members of the industrial elite.[33]

One wonders if the corporatist system could have effectively represented the interests of the industrial elite—even in the best of all corporatist societies. The growing complexity of the economy, the spawning of new economic sectors and subsectors would, according to corporative theory and practice, necessitate the creation of new *grémios*, and new *sindicatos* to enter into negotiation with the *grémios*, and new government agencies to oversee both the *grémios* and the *sindicatos*. Such a quantitative extension threatened not only to overtax government resources; it also threatened a bureaucratic proliferation whose internal rigidity could only hamper enterpreneurial activity. While such considerations may not apply to those operating in the more backward and stagnant sectors, their importance is quite considerable for those firms facing heavy competition in the more advanced sectors. In essence, corporatism violated that flexibility required by the more dynamic forms of capital accumulation. It comes as no surprise, then, that after the first and original spurt of corporatization the *grémio* structure became an object of unofficial, benign neglect on the part of both the government and the industrialists.[34] It has already been noted that this process was most advanced among the most powerful and dynamic groups. And this process could be accelerated only by the proposed "internationalization" of the Portuguese economy. In fact the *grémio* structure was, on the whole, not enlarged to include the more recently established sectors of the economy. In short, the *grémio* system was in decline. It was gradually being reduced to a purely formal façade that neither reflected nor organized its underlying reality. Of course this process had not been completed. The *grémio* system still remained repressive for some, irrelevant for others, and cumbersome for all. One could almost hear the sighs of relief that followed this institution's demise after the coup: "We suffered from the economic archaism of the old regime: corporatist and patronal unions, *grémios*, and protectionist measures that prevented free competition."[35]

The above discussion provides some evidence for the regime's lack of legitimacy, for the reasons behind its failure to find support among those who had the most to lose after its demise. After all, those who were forced to bear the brunt of the corporatist system were marginalized by that very system. However, it would be a mistake to suppose that the regime's stability could have been enhanced by incorporating a wider span of elites. To equate stability with elite "pluralism" is to make a number of assumptions that do not hold in the Portuguese case.

In the first place, it presupposes that the exclusion of certain elites from the centers of power would result in their active opposition to the latter. While they may have resented the *grémio* system, there is no evidence to suggest that they played a role in the coup of either an active or passive nature. To recall, a large proportion of those groups which were marginalized were from the north, the traditional stronghold of Portuguese conservatism. And it was to this group, among others, that General António de Spínola appealed during his attempted countercoup in September 1974. Nor is there any evidence that this group, if incorporated, could have proposed alternative solutions regarding Portugal's chronic difficulties. In fact this possibility was unlikely since many among these groups were associated with family enterprises embedded in the traditional economies, often characterized as resisting any changes in the economy which would threaten their already precarious position. Indeed, other calculations show that compared to elites associated with dynamic sectors the traditional elites were isolationist. Over half opposed Portugal's economic integration into Europe and nearly 60 percent even opposed the country's economic integration with its African territories.[36]

In the second place, it presupposes that these groups would not be marginalized by the "spontaneous" evolution of the Portuguese economy. Yet, given the concentration of this group in the more backward and stagnant sectors, we must assume that the opposite is the case. In fact, if we are to attribute a progressive role to the *grémio* system, it could only be in terms of the enforced (political) marginalization of certain groups that still play an important and even dominant role in the economy. In this sense the *grémio* system may be an eminently transitional phenomenon.[37]

A more relevant hypothesis than the pluralist one could be advanced in the other direction: that the regime's instability was due not to its failure to incorporate a broad range of elites but to its failure to control those interests which were able to infiltrate the state apparatus itself. In this sense, because there were no reliable and institutionalized channels of interest articulation, those groups interested in influencing government policy did so by allying themselves with various cliques in their intragovernmental struggles. It is in these machinations, internal to the state, that the immediate causes of the coup are to be found. However, these immediate causes cannot be divorced from the larger context.

The various alliances and conflicts which were focused within the government were manifestations at the political level of problems that had much deeper roots.[38] Portugal by the 1970s had accumulated a variety of problems—colonial wars, relations with the European Economic Community, severe inflation, massive emigration—which remained unresolved. While certain of the more powerful consortia (or, more specifically, conflicts among these consortia) had a role in precipitating the events that led to the coup, it would appear that these consortia have been bypassed by subsequent events, particularly after the demise of General António de Spínola.[39] The continuing intervention of the government can only erode the economic and political position of the industrial elite (or at least its leading sectors). At present the government has nationalized the banks and much of basic industry—including petrochemicals, heavy metal-mechanic industries, the largest trucking

firms, cellulose, cement, tobacco, steel, and electric industries—
and has also recently intervened in other ways, for example, in the
appointment of state administrators over private firms, *saneamentos* (purges), control over credit, price and income policies, and so
on. However, it would be premature to write this class's obituary.
Its future role will depend on political developments within and
perhaps outside Portugal, particularly the outcome of the conflict
between the Communist and Socialist parties during the next few
months, to say nothing of the emerging conflicts within the military.

Postscript[40]

In July 1976 and again in June 1977, I returned to Portugal to study
the status of the 306 enterprises (whether intervened or not) and
their leaders (their whereabouts) whom I had studied more than a
decade earlier. This was accomplished through the Associação Industrial Portuguesa and the Associação Industrial Portuense (the
manufacturers' associations of Lisbon and Oporto, respectively);
data from the Instituto das Participações do Estado (the Institute
for State Participations); consulting government legislation and
daily reports of its official activities as reported in its *Diário do
Governo* (later, *Diário da República*); or telephoning companies
directly. A year later, in June 1977, data on the profits and losses
of each enterprise in the three years immediately preceding the
Revolution was sought (and eventually obtained in December 1977)
from the Ministry of Finance's taxation department, and in-depth
studies of a few enterprises were begun.

In this postscript some structural characteristics of the enterprises and the career patterns, attitudes, and beliefs of the industrial
elite will be correlated with data on interventions and the status
(or whereabouts) of the industrial elite in order to determine which
enterprises were intervened or nationalized and which industrial
elites left their positions.

Earlier I established that the Salazar-Caetano regime had recruited
technocrats from managerial positions of the larger, modern-sector
companies in Lisbon and through its corporative system marginalized the propertied industrial elites, the wealthier founders, heirs
and owners of the mostly traditional sector, technologically backward enterprises, many of which were situated in Portugal's north.
Although ten years later, from the rhetoric and legislation, it seemed

that the same propertied class was the target of state control and marginalization, my recent study of the industrial elite and their enterprises indicates that the tables have turned. Others bore the brunt of the political order that emerged soon after the revolution of April 25. This postscript will merely show the impact on industrial elite and its enterprises.

From the broadest perspective, 27 percent of the enterprises and 19 percent of the industrialists were directly affected by the state's intervention policy. Eight percent of the enterprises were nationalized or became public companies, 15 percent were intervened financially and/or administratively, and 5 percent were no longer in business (Table 4-4). Among the industrialists, 19 percent had quit their positions, 2 percent had been purged, 8 percent had retired, and 16 percent had died (Table 4-5).[41] Many of those who had quit their positions migrated to Latin America, especially Brazil, where they apparently had little difficulty in locating lucrative positions.

Focusing first on enterprises, Table 4-4 indicates that the larger enterprises and those in central Portugal were more likely to have been nationalized and intervened than were smaller enterprises or those in northern Portugal. Indeed, the larger the enterprise the more likely it had been nationalized, and this was particularly true if the firm was situated in central Portugal. Larger enterprises in central Portugal also tended to belong to the economy's modern, newer economic sectors. Indeed state intervention was greater in the modern sectors of services, chemicals, steel, and metal products than in the country's traditional sectors of textiles, construction, and nonmetallic minerals. Correspondingly, nationalization was higher in technologically complex enterprises, particularly among those which employed a greater proportion of superior and intermediate technicians. This implies that perhaps the state had unwittingly moved against the bulk of the technocratic class, most of which were employed in the new sectors.

The calculations on what happened to the industrialists largely mirror the firm.[42] Excluding those who retired or died, one finds that size of enterprise is inversely correlated with still being director. For example, in small enterprises (50–99 employees) only 15 percent of the industrialists had quit as compared to nearly three times the proportion (43%) in the larger. In the giant firm (1,000 or more employees) more than half had quit.[43] Regionally, too, the difference is remarkable. Among the larger (500 or more employees) enterprises in central Portugal, 54 percent had left the enterprise.

In the north the majority of the industrialists still held their positions. This was particularly the case in the outlying districts of Aveiro and Braga. However, four of the five industrialists in this region had actually been purged from their factories.

Among the principal industrial sectors, services (e.g., public utilities, transportation) saw over half (54%) of their industrialists leave. In fact, the proportion was approximately double that of any other sector. As previously discussed, most of these firms were nationalized in the spring of 1975 and, therefore, their entire board and top executives were replaced by state appointees. When an enterprise was affiliated with one of the large consortia the industrialist left long before nationalization occurred. For example, José Manuel de Melo, the head of Sociedade Geral de Comércio, Indústria e Transportes, the country's largest trucking company, fled Portugal in the fall of 1974 with other owners and top executives of Companhia União de Fabril (CUF), Portugal's largest consortium.

Part B of Table 4-5 also identifies the affected industrialists according to their biographical characteristics. Here the impact on the upper classes is vivid. The calculations show that the higher the socioeconomic class origin the greater the likelihood that the industrialist had left his firm. But, the more upwardly mobile also were more likely to have quit than those who were downwardly socially mobile. A number of these were *comprador* industrialists, that is, loyal hirelings of the large consortiums from middle-class origins, university-educated sons of the petit bourgoisie. Others were state *compradores* who moved from an assistant professorship (usually in law) from the university into a deputy and later a full cabinet (or national-level) position and then were recruited to direct one of the consortia-owned firms or were appointed *administrador delegado* (delegate administrator). The statistics pertaining to ownership and control and public office (Table 4-5, Part B) corroborate this pattern. A much larger percentage of managers (52%) compared to owners of production (i.e., founders [18%], heirs [21%], and owner-managers [32%]) and a larger percentage of national-level politicians (63%) compared to municipal (8%) or nonoffice holders (26%) had left their enterprises. Other calculations show that these managers received the highest salaries among the industrial elite. When originally interviewed in 1965 most were making between U.S.$17,500 and $35,000, compared to most founders, who reported earning $9,000 or less a year. Not long after the Revolution a maximum income of U.S.$12,000 a year, from all sources, was estab-

TABLE 4-4

State Interventions in Portuguese Industrial Enterprises by 1976
(Percentage Distribution)

	Nationalizations	Interventions in: General	Financial	BD Directors	Management	Other	Not in Business / No Interventions	No Intervention / Not in Business	Total
Total	8%	6%	4%	2%	2%	1%	5%	73%	100%
N	(23)	(18)	(12)	(6)	(7)	(2)	(14)	(224)	(306)

	Nationalizations	Interventions	No Interventions	Not in Business	Total (N)
Size of Enterprise					
Smaller[a]	2%	8%	84%	6%	(176)
Larger	15	25	58	2	(130)
Giant (1,000 or more employees)	19	27	54	—	(69)
Location					
Northern Portugal[b]	2%	11%	79%	8%	(165)
Central Portugal	14	18	67	1	(141)
Size and Location					
Larger/Central Portugal	23%	23%	54%	0%	(73)
Selected Sectors					
Services	44%	8%	48%	—	(25)
Chemicals	20	8	72	—	(25)
Metals[c]	2	19	77	2%	(51)
Textiles	—	12	75	13	(72)
Construction	—	—	91	9	(34)

Traditional/Modern Sectors
and Date of Foundation[d]

Traditional: before 1928	5%	18%	69%	8% (88)
Traditional: after 1928	5	8	82	5 (112)
Modern: before 1928	15	18	67	— (48)
Modern: after 1928	21	10	67	2 (58)
Technological Complexity[e]				
Technologically complex (T+)	14%	15%	69%	2% (134)
Technologically noncomplex (T−)	2	16	76	6 (172)

[a] Smaller = 50–499 employees; larger = 500 or more employees.
[b] Northern Portugal = Aveiro, Braga, Oporto districts; central Portugal = Lisbon, Santarém, Setúbal.
[c] Includes electrical and heavy machinery, steel, and metal products.
[d] Traditional = mining, nonmetallic minerals, ceramics, glass, cement, wood, cork, foodstuffs, beverages, textiles; Modern = steel, heavy metal products, electrical machinery, chemicals, services, paper products.
[e] Technologically complex (T+) = enterprises above the mean in superior or intermediate technicians or both; technologically noncomplex (T−) = enterprises below the mean in both superior and intermediate technicians.

TABLE 4–5

Percentage of the Portuguese Industrial Elite
Who Quit Their Enterprises by 1976

	Quit	Still There	Died	Retired	Total
Total	19%	57%	16%	8%	100%
N	(60)	(173)	(49)	(24)	(306)

A. Selected Structural Characteristics[a]

	Quit	
Size of Enterprise		
Smaller	15%	(144)
Larger	43	(89)
Giant (1,000 or more employees)	55	(44)
Location		
Northern Portugal	18%	(139)
Central Portugal	37	(94)
Size and Location		
Larger central Portugal	54%	(46)
Selected Sectors		
Services[b]	54%	(11)[c]
Metals	28	(43)
Textiles	25	(64)
Construction	21	(24)
Chemicals[b]	7	(14)[c]

B. Selected Biographical Characteristics[a]

	Quit	
Socioeconomic Origin		
Upper	46%	(92)
Middle	22	(100)
Lower	21	(33)
Geographic Mobility		
Natives	25%	(142)
Migrants	24	(72)
Foreign-born	42	(19)
Social Mobility		
Upward	32%	(85)
Static	25	(100)
Downward	15	(46)
Education		
High school or less	16%	(129)
University or more	33	(104)

Ownership and Control

Founder	18%	(84)
Heir	21	(80)
Owner-manager	32	(38)
Manager	52	(31)

Public Office

National level	63%	(8)[c]
Municipal level	8	(25)
Other government	29	(14)
None	26	(186)

Corporative and Public Office

Corporative and public	20%	(33)
Public[d]	23	(26)
Corporative	22	(50)
None	28	(133)

[a]This table excludes 73 cases who died (49) or retired (24).
[b]Half retired or died in these sectors.
[c]Limited number of cases permits only tentative observations. Ten of the original 18 in this group had died or retired.
[d]Eighteen individuals or nearly half of this group had died or retired.

lished. Considering what the income level of the same managers must have been by 1974 would alone explain why they were no longer in their positions.

Few differences were found when corporative office holding was considered. Designed early in Salazar's Estado Novo to regulate economic life, the corporatist system became an object of unofficial and benign neglect for both the industrial bourgoisie and the state. While it certainly was bypassed by the larger industries and consortia who had direct access to the state, it served as a placating and buffer institution for the propertied industrial elite—the less educated, the founders, heirs, and owner-managers of mostly traditional, technologically noncomplex enterprises. These were not the industries or bourgoisie that the left was interested in containing. Although the corporatist system was dismantled soon after the Revolution, those industrialists who held corporative office did not fall with it. This attests to the innocuousness of the system under Salazar and Caetano.

However, the firms of ex-corporative leaders did not entirely escape intervention. Indeed, the extent of administrative and financial intervention among this group was higher, suggesting that corporative officers might have been so involved in corporative affairs that they neglected their enterprises, or that they might have become politicians in an attempt to revive their failing businesses.

In summary, it was *not* these local propertied, traditional-sector elites that the government moved against. It was their polar opposites: the managers of larger consortia-owner enterprises in the modern sectors whose firms were nationalized and who, in turn, left their positions. Under the new regime the technocrats and their modern-sector firms were marginalized and controlled. However, as a result of a series of economic and political crises which were not directly related to the conflict between the state and the industrial bourgoisie, the pendulum has swung back. By the summer of 1976 deinterventions began and, as I have recently discussed, the state was attempting to resurrect the technocrats and their patrons.

Notes

The first version of this paper was presented at the workshop on modern Portugal, University of New Hampshire, October 10–14, 1973, and a revised version was presented at the mini-conference on contemporary Portugal, Yale University, March 28–29, 1975. The generous support of the Canada Council (grant no. S73-0668), the Council for European Studies, Yale University, and the Humanities and Social Science Committee and the International Studies Program of the University of Toronto enabled my participation at these conferences. I wish to acknowledge the Calouste Gulbenkian Foundation (Lisbon), which originally supported this study. I am also grateful for the comments of Juan J. Linz, Joyce Riegelhaupt, Michael Rodell, Philippe C. Schmitter, and Douglas L. Wheeler, and especially the revisions suggested by Brian C. J. Singer and Kenneth N. Walker.

1. This is clearly shown in an essay Philippe C. Schmitter and I prepared entitled, "The Portuguese Industrial Elite Faces the European Economic Community."

2. Philippe C. Schmitter, *Corporatism and Public Policy in Authoritarian Portugal*, Contemporary Political Sociology Series, Sage Professional Series, vol. I, no. 06-011 (1975).

3. This is a composite of definitions offered by Philippe C. Schmitter and James M. Malloy (see Philippe C. Schmitter, "Still the Century of Corporatism?" pp. 93–94, and James M. Malloy, "Authoritarianism, Corporatism and Mobilization in Peru," pp. 55–59, in *The New Corporatism: Social-Political Structures in the Iberian World*, ed. Fredrick B. Pike and Thomas Stritch [Notre Dame, Ind.: University of Notre Dame Press, 1974]). Also see the historical essay by Howard Wiarda in the same collection.

4. Schmitter, "Still the Century of Corporatism?" pp. 103–105.

5. The latter functions were the property of the *juntas*. For a detailed discussion of Portuguese corporatism and its history, see Corporação de

Comércio, *As Corporações na Economia Nacional* (Lisbon: Companhia Nacional Editora, 1971).

6. Corporative legislation specified four types of *grémios*: (*a*) national, which are obligatory, e.g., Grémio Nacional dos Bancos e Casas Bancárias (National Guild of Banks and Banking Houses); (*b*) regional, whose domain coincided with a political administrative area of a metropolitan territory; (*c*) district, usually representing commerce or industry; and (*d*) municipal, farmers or commercial *grémios* (see Corporação de Comércio, *As Corporações na Economia Nacional*, pp. 28–29, 92–94).

7. "O Fim da Noite Salazarista," *Opinião*, May 6, 1974, p. 5. Also see Robin Blackburn's recent essay for a discussion of the linkages between the large consortia and the regime ("The Test in Portugal," *New Left Review* 87–88 [September–December 1974]: esp. pp. 7 and 14).

8. In 1965 a survey of 306 heads (chief executives, presidents, etc.) of manufacturing and service enterprises in Portugal's six most industrialized districts (Aveiro, Braga, Lisbon, Oporto, Santarém, and Setúbal) was conducted. A stratified random sample of enterprises employing 50–999 individuals was drawn, using statistical information from an industrial census (Instituto Nacional de Estatística, *O Inquérito Industrial de 1957–1959*, General Volume [Portugal, n.d.]), and manpower data from files provided by the Ministry of Corporations (*Fundo de Desenvolvimento de Mão-de-Obra de Ministério das Corporações*). The sample was augmented to include all enterprises employing 1,000 or more persons, considering the importance of this stratum to the economy. Although enterprises having 50 or more employees constituted only a small fraction of all manufacturing and service enterprises (this is true even in the most industrialized countries), because they employed a large share of the labor force (66%) their heads were defined as members of the Portuguese *industrial elite*. In all, 6 percent of the elites heading enterprises employing 50–99 persons (small enterprises), 16 percent of those employing 100–499 (regular and medium enterprises), 54 percent of those employing 500–999 persons (large enterprises), and 100 percent of those employing 1,000 or more persons were interviewed. The sources of these data were detailed, systematic tandem 2–3 hour interviews, half of which were in central Portugal (the districts of Lisbon, Santarém, and Setúbal) and half in the northern part of the country (the districts of Aveiro, Braga, and Oporto). The study included questions on the internal organization and decision-making processes within each enterprise; labor relations and manpower; interest group affiliations; and attitudes toward and experiences with banks, government agencies, foreign investment, and international economic blocks (e.g., European Free Trade Association, European Economic Community). Also included were questions pertaining to the socioeconomic origins, career patterns, self-image, and opinions of the industrial elite. For a more extensive discussion of the sampling, survey design, and analysis techniques, see my study, *A "Elite" Industrial Portuguesa* (Lisbon: Calouste Gulbenkian Foundation, 1969), appendix A.

9. Very few, perhaps three or four, elite members held ranking offices in other interest-group organizations, such as *juntas*, *federações*, or the private commercial or industrial associations.

10. My preference in this essay is to treat formal leadership positions

as the independent (or causal) variable, although most biographical and structural characteristics antecede leadership, e.g., socioeconomic origin.

11. Schmitter established that from 1934 to 1969 a greater proportion of Corporative Chamber members were born in Lisbon than in Oporto (Schmitter, *Corporatism and Public Policy*, table 5).

12. Social mobility was determined by comparing the socioeconomic origins of the respondent (as measured by father's occupation and his evaluation of the economic status of his family during his youth) with the size of the enterprise he directed at the time of the study. An example of a downwardly mobile industrialist would be an individual who characterized the economic situation of his family during his youth as "prosperous" and whose father was a large landowner, but at the time of the interview the industrialist directed a small enterprise in a traditional and economically more stagnant sector (e.g., foodstuffs, ceramics, wood and paper products). In contrast, an upwardly mobile industrial elite member would be someone who described the economic situation of his family during his youth as "poor" and whose father was a minor public functionary but who himself rose to head a larger enterprise.

13. Hermínio Martins, "Portugal," in *Contemporary Europe: Class, Status and Power*, ed. Margaret S. Archer and Salvador Giner (London: Weidenfeld & Nicolson, 1971), pp. 67–68, for a more detailed discussion of avenues to power during the Salazar-Caetano regime.

14. Technological complexity was measured by determining the number of intermediate and superior technicians relative to other enterprises of similar size (number of employees). Those which were above the mean derived for any of the five categories (small, regular, medium, large, or giant) either in superior, intermediate, or both types of technicians were considered technologically complex; those below the mean in their size category were considered technologically noncomplex enterprises. A further discussion of this measure and its derivation appears in chapter 10 of my book *A "Elite" Industrial Portuguesa*.

15. Ibid., pp. 115–118.

16. Charles P. Kindleberger, *Economic Growth in France and Britain* (Cambridge, Mass.: Harvard University Press, 1964), pp. 124–127.

17. Makler, *A "Elite" Industrial Portuguesa*, pp. 274–276.

18. This is explained by the regime's tendency to have recruited technicians from middle-class origins to direct its public utility corporations.

19. Further studies of other elite groups (e.g., Portugal's political elite) are necessary in order to establish the *extent* of interlocking among the polity and the economy. Preferably, this should be done over a span of years.

20. See Henry Ehrmann's study, *Organized Business in France* (Princeton: Princeton University press, 1957), for a discussion of the movements between civil service and industrial leadership.

21. In fact, Caetano's career itself has been characterized as typical of the interlocking among academics, the polity, and the economy. Martins has noted that Caetano was co-opted: ". . . a conservative monarchist of non-upper class origin, he had a distinguished academic career in Law via the professoriate, whence he joined the Cabinet, and played other political

roles . . . ; and by marriage into a leading Republican business family whose wealth and Republicanism date back several generations" (*Contemporary Europe*, pp. 71–72).

22. Makler, *A "Elite" Industrial Portuguesa*, pp. 238–240.

23. It has also been argued that the Corporative Chamber is an innocuous institution. Schmitter notes that "the Chamber could be abolished completely and it would neither radically disturb the pattern of policy-making, nor seriously threaten the persistence of the 'corporative complex'" (*Corporatism and Public Policy*, p. 21).

24. Martins, *Contemporary Europe*, pp. 70–71.

25. Pedro Theotónio Pereira, *A Batalha do Futuro* (Lisbon: Livraria Clássica, 1937), p. 128.

26. Specifically, the questions measured relevance, effectiveness, and use. In sequence they were "Of all the organizations that you have just mentioned which one is most directly related with the defense of the interests of your enterprise?" "In which ways do you think this organization effectively defends the interest of your enterprise?" and "Aside from routine matters how often do you present problems to this organization?"

27. This hypothesis only holds for *grémios*. Other calculations show that elite member assessment of private industrial interest groups (e.g., Associação Industrial Portuguesa) is more positive and more consistent among formal leaders and those who held no formal position in government or corporative organizations.

28. A *junta* was a national corporative organization established mainly to coordinate the commercialization of a product or service very important to the national economy.

29. The questions used to determine frequency of contact with the government were "With what frequency do you contact official entities, directly or indirectly, regarding problems confronting your enterprise?" and "Which entities do you approach?"

30. Those who used the private patronal associations (e.g., Associação Industrial Portuguesa) and the *juntas* tended to perceive them as more effective and actually used them more often than those incorporated into the *grémios*. However, only a small proportion of the industrial elite were associated with such institutions (10%). The group belonging to the private associations were the heads of the larger, modern, technologically complex enterprises situated in Lisbon; those incorporated into the *juntas* belonged to the traditional export sectors, such as cork, wine, and fish products, which the government protected in order to guarantee a correct balance of payments.

31. Schmitter shows that civil servants and professors have been well represented in Portugal's Corporative Chamber since its first session in 1934 (*Corporatism and Public Policy*).

32. In his essay on Portugal, Schmitter paraphrases Marx and suggests that authoritarian rule was the only possible form of rule when neither the bourgeoisie nor the working class had yet acquired the ability to rule, but the transition from precapitalist to the capitalist mode of production was imposed upon the nation from without. In this sense the compartmentalization of the traditional elites could be seen as an attempt by the

government to bypass this group without destroying it in order to further economic growth and capitalist development in the absence of a vigorous and autonomous national capitalist class (ibid.).

33. The Portuguese case thus appears to be a hybrid. However, at the formal level the Portuguese polity was characterized by state corporatism. It was only at the informal level that societal corporatism reared its head, and as such the inordinate influence of powerful economic groups was not exercised via formal associational intermediaries (Schmitter, "Still the Century of Corporatism?" pp. 103–105).

34. Schmitter, *Corporatism and Public Policy*.

35. Quoted from Morais Cabral, member of the executive commission of the Confederation of Portuguese Industry, cited in Yves Hardy, "Portugal: Anatomie du Nouveau Pouvoir Militaire," *Les Temps Modernes* 30 (December 1974): 544.

36. Most isolationism was found among those who held only municipal positions. Seventy-three percent opposed European economic integration and 63 percent opposed integration with the country's African territories. In contrast, among those who held national positions, 60 percent favored European economic integration and over half favored economic integration with the territories.

37. In this case one could argue that the *grémios*, by containing the traditional sector, permitted that space to develop within which more modern economic sectors could emerge. However, further study of the system would be necessary to substantiate this hypothesis.

38. This does not mean that these intragovernmental conflicts were mere reflections of long-term trends. The short-term and immediate causes cannot be reduced to the long-term causes. In this sense there was no "necessity" in the coup that can be traced to, say, the "political economy." However, these longer-term trends would result, and were resulting, in changes whose importance should not be underestimated. After all, the transition from feudalism to capitalism did not necessitate the occurrence of the French Revolution.

39. Kenneth Maxwell argues that Spínola supported the consortia and their vision of a Portuguese economy "rationalized" along Western European lines, while the Portuguese Communist Party (PCP) and Armed Forces Movement (MFA) support "the small, archaic, and uncompetitive enterprises that managed to survive under the old regime." This argument, while formally correct, can be misleading if it suggests that (a) small enterprises will flourish under the new regime and that (b) the government will not "rationalize" the Portuguese economy. The present economic difficulties and the measures necessary to combat these difficulties point in the opposite direction (see Kenneth Maxwell, "The Hidden Revolution," and "Portugal under Pressure," *New York Review of Books*, April 17, 1975, and May 29, 1975, respectively).

40. Harry M. Makler, "The State Versus the Industrial Bourgeoisie since the Portuguese Revolution," paper presented at the Ad-Hoc Committee on Economy and Society, Ninth World Congress of Sociology, Uppsala, Sweden, August 16, 1978.

41. So far as I know none of the industrialists were killed as a direct

result of the Revolution or its aftermath, although it is believed that some suffered cardiac arrest, had nervous breakdowns, and/or became alcoholics.

42. There were deviations from this pattern that will only be alluded to in this essay. Fifteen percent, or 34 of the 233 active industrialists, quit their enterprises, although their firms were not intervened, and 9 percent, or 20 industrialists, saw their enterprises intervened but remained at their posts.

43. Among the giant enterprises 23 percent of the industrialists that I interviewed in 1965 had died. This is understandable, as the average age of this group was older than the average age (53 years) for the entire sample. Age and size of enterprise varied directly.

5. Peasants and Politics in Salazar's Portugal: The Corporate State and Village "Nonpolitics"

JOYCE FIRSTENBERG RIEGELHAUPT

In order to be wholeheartedly on the side of the people and to foster its steady material and moral improvement, we need not believe that the origin of power resides in the mass of the people, or that the justice of the laws is derived from mere numbers, or that the government can be undertaken by the multitude and not by an elite whose duty is to direct it . . . and sacrifice itself for the common good.—António Oliveira Salazar, *Prime Minister of Portugal, Says* (Lisbon: SPN Books, n.d.), p. 26

The Portuguese Revolution of April 1974 ended almost fifty years of dictatorial rule and brought political and social freedom to a nation that had been organized as an authoritarian and corporatist state. In the first elections held on the Revolution's first anniversary, over 93 percent of the population voted in a massive display of political participation. The first few years "post April 25" (as the Revolution is called) have seen a proliferation of political parties, a high level of electoral participation, and innumerable other political activities: strikes, land occupations, worker and tenant councils, neighborhood committees, and so on.[1] This widespread participation stands in sharp contrast to the half century of apparent political apathy and acquiescence that characterized Portuguese political life under Salazar's Estado Novo.

In this article, I shall examine the manner in which the Estado Novo controlled peasant participation by effectively eliminating all possibilities for local-level participation in the political arena. I shall argue that only through an understanding of a regime's structure can one explain the forms of peasant political participation. The ethnographic material analyzed is based on field work done in

São Miguel[2] and on the data from Vila Velha in José Cutileiro's excellent monograph *A Portuguese Rural Society*.[3] By comparing these two parishes, which have very different ecological bases, land tenure systems, and social structures, the pervasive manner in which the corporatist authoritarian government of prerevolutionary Portugal determined peasant participation in politics will be demonstrated.

State Structures and Village Life

Portugal's authoritarian political system has been described by H. R. Trevor-Roper as clerical conservatism: "... the direct heir of the aristocratic conservativism over which the liberal bourgeoisie triumphed in the second half of the nineteenth century . . . The *Rerum Novarum* remains its charter. [And it exemplifies] the conservative ideal of the 1890's: an ordered, hierarchical, undemocratic, 'corporative' state."[4] As has already been made clear in previous chapters, Portugal became an efficient mercantile dictatorship under Salazar and Caetano. Leo VIII's philosophy, modified by Pius XI, provided the ideological basis for the establishment of a state dominated by mercantile elites and bankers. This regime was explicitly "anti-democratic, anti-parliamentary, and anti-liberal."[5] The primary aim of its leaders was to establish order and stability, and the pursuit of order and stability (both politically and economically) remained its hallmark.

Under the Estado Novo, Portugal was organized into a series of hierarchically arranged geographical units. The smallest political unit was the parish (*freguesia*). Parishes varied in size and could comprise a number of hamlets, villages, and towns. A large town or city contained several parishes. Each parish had a local government body, the *junta de freguesia*. A number of contiguous parishes formed a county (*concelho*) governed by a mayor (*presidente da câmara*), appointed by the central government, and a municipal council (*câmara municipal*). The three hundred odd counties were combined into sixteen districts, each led by a governor, selected by the minister of the interior. Ideally, the system was autarchical and decentralized; in fact, it was a highly centralized political system.

Portugal's corporatist structure envisioned a close tie between economic and political institutions. With varying degrees of success, the state attempted to organize the total economic system into groups (*grémios, sindicatos*, etc.) based upon industrial, commer-

cial, or agricultural interests which, with a minimum of state interference, would operate to harmoniously integrate owner and worker
for the common good and avoid the dangers of economic development and social change. In the countryside, there was to be a *casa
do povo* (house of the people), a corporative institution bringing
together landowner and farm laborer. According to the law (D.L.
23,051) each rural parish should have a *casa do povo*; in fact, in the
early 1960s, less than 20 percent of the parishes had *casas do povo*.
In the two parishes we are examining, Vila Velha had had a *casa do
povo* since 1945, São Miguel did not have one. Membership in the
casa do povo was compulsory for owners and workers. Only laborers, however, were eligible for the free medical service, pharmaceu-
tical discounts, and unemployment and sickness benefits which the
casa do povo was supposed to provide.[6] The attitude expressed by
the Vila Velhanos about the *casa do povo* typifies the peasants'
assessment of much of the corporative state: "The Casa do Povo is
like every other organized body, alien to [our] interests, and is
in fact a cross between a tax-collecting office and a charity organization."[7]

Although the Estado Novo can be defined as a corporatist state
with interlocking economic and political institutions, it is possible
to separate out an institutional sector which can be referred to as
"political." That area of decision making and control which was
regulated in the Portuguese Constitution and the Administrative
Code was recognized as "political" by the people. Ideally, the socioeconomic corporations should have, at all points, intersected with
the geographical and social units (individuals, families, households)
to provide other means of representation in the syndical and corporative organization of society. This remained an ideal; for the
people there was a very real sector of political organization that they
called "*o governo*" (the government), and it is on that sector at the
local level that the remainder of this essay will focus.

Local-Level Politics

Political relations between the central government in Lisbon and
the parishes were based on the direct appointment by the state of
lower-level officials and direct elections of National Assembly
members.

Only two legislative bodies were directly elected: the National
Assembly and the parish *junta*. Individual citizens were enfran-

local-level political activities, for, under the Estado Novo, no lower level of the political system had any leverage on a higher level. Local "politicians" existed only at the sufferance of the higher level, and the only resource they could bring to the central system was information about local discontent. They were unable to mobilize voter or popular support as in other electoral systems.

For Portuguese constitutionalists, the governmental system was autarchical and reinforced the two central units of the society: the family and the community. Individual welfare was subsumed under the social welfare of the group, for the individual under the Estado Novo was not considered a basic unit of society. As Hugh Kay, a proregime analyst, wrote, "There are no abstract rights of man, only concrete ones. Thus representation is organized not through artificial groups or parties, but by real and permanent elements in the national life."[8]

The ideological basis and the form of government institutionalized by the Estado Novo led to a system in which the separation between "administration" and "politics" was very evident at the local level. If we consider "politics" to refer to decisions on public matters and "administration" as referring to the execution of previously decided upon policy, then we find that at the parish level most of what appears "political" is, in fact, "administrative." This distinction used by M. G. Smith,[9] among others, was at the heart of the Portuguese governmental system. Unlike most anthropological descriptions of "local-level politics,"[10] the local level in the nonparty, authoritarian, corporate state was characterized by minimal and trivial politics, a far cry from the reported dynamic nature of political behavior in other small communities.[11] Constraints on local-level political activity in the Portuguese state emanated from the governmental administrative process and the manner in which decrees were enforced at the local level. Although the *junta* was, ideally, a "political" body and the *regedor* an "administrative" position, they were both, in effect, administrative agencies. Power and decision making within the parish were inconsequential, while the administrative bureaucracy was of utmost importance in the lives of the villagers. Marcello Caetano, Salazar's successor as prime minister and a leading constitutionalist, echoed this when he said, "I am fully aware of the value of politics, but I am equally clear that this worth can only be attained through good, effective administration."[12]

In the ethnographic section that follows, the major concern will be to see how this governmental system which precluded local-level politics operated. The Estado Novo eliminated the parish as an "arena" for discussion, debate, and decision making on matters of public policy and the differential allocation of power. Instead, the corporate state substituted a highly centralized, bureaucratic administration. Peasants were subject to centrally decreed policy; politics, for them, consisted of searching for leverage in an attempt to influence policy implementation.

Two Village Case Studies

The rural parishes to be analyzed are São Miguel, located northwest of Lisbon in the province of Estremadura, and Vila Velha, in the Alentejo, the mid-south of Portugal. While both are agricultural parishes, they are characterized by very different socioeconomic arrangements but, I shall argue, by very similar political processes under the old regime.

The parish of São Miguel consists of thirty-four nucleated settlements, villages, and hamlets, inhabited primarily (and traditionally) by small agriculturalists who utilize their household labor force in the growing of wheat, grapes, and garden vegetables, as well as in wage labor in nearby stone quarries. There are no large or dominant landowners in the parish, and most agriculturalists work scattered fields, some owned and others rented from neighbors. During the 1960s, they, as did many Portuguese, increasingly moved out of agriculture and in many instances out of Portugal into the Western European labor force.

Interpersonal relations in São Miguel are adaptive to an agrarian system of small-scale farms, worked by family labor with paleotechnology, in which the marketed proportion of the crop is either consigned to government purchasing agencies or sold at local markets by household members. The area is not densely populated. Throughout the last century new land, previously scrub, has been put into cultivation with the slow introduction of farm machinery. Parish endogamy predominates and partible inheritance has been the rule for the last hundred years. While Portuguese society is a class society, differences in wealth within the parish of São Miguel have not led to local class differentiation.

Within the socioeconomic structure of São Miguel, the important units are households, which maintain balanced reciprocal relations with their neighbors. No one in the community is in a position of dependence on anyone else; no agriculturalist is in the permanent employ of another. In fact, the optimum model of relations in São

Miguel is that good relations depend upon their symmetry; no one should give more than is received, and the objective is to return a like amount as soon as possible. Unlike George M. Foster's model of the "dyadic contract,"[13] São Miguel households prefer that all relations come to relatively rapid closure rather than being open-ended and continuing. The worst position for a São Miguelito is to be in debt, either economically or socially.

The dominant mode of interpersonal relations between households within villages, and between villages within the parish, is what Marshall Sahlins has called "balanced reciprocity."[14] In this system of reciprocity, careful accounts are kept and each item received is returned as soon as possible. This general mode of equivalences and closure also operates in interpersonal relationships between São Miguelitos and other parish villagers.

As one moves through geographical space to the county seat, one also moves through social space. It is in the county seat that the wealthy, the professionals, the bureaucrats, and the businessmen live. The dominant mode of interpersonal relations between the peasantry and the urban "elite" is not balanced reciprocity but, on the contrary, negative reciprocity in which each party seeks to take advantage of the other.

The anthropologist's model of "reciprocity," viewing the relations between segments (and strata) within a society, is reflected in the villager's linguistic usage, suggesting a similar view of interpersonal relations. Fellow villagers are referred to as "we," and other communities in the parish as "ours." Neighboring parishes are often given uncomplimentary nicknames. But the people in the county seat, the clerks and the others in the town hall, in fact almost all other members of Portuguese society are referred to as *êles* (they or them, depending on context). One avoids *êles* and one should never be in debt to them. It is a term, in effect, of fear and is characterized by avoidance and negative behavior. However, it is among *êles* that individuals representing, or in contact with, the governmental system are found. Throughout the last century, internal balanced reciprocity and external negative reciprocity was an adaptive mode for the maintenance of economic and social security within the parish. However, under the Estado Novo, this pattern of interpersonal relations operated to cut São Miguelitos off from any access to the governmental system.

The Alentejo parish of Vila Velha consists of six nucleated villages surrounded by large wheat farms, latifundia, which dominate the agrarian system. The social structure of the parish is characterized by a rigid economic and social stratification system, which dates from the nineteenth-century period of rapid agricultural development and consequent local social mobility. None of Vila Velha's latifundists are descendants of old ennobled Portuguese families. Most of Vila Velha's population is landless, earning a precarious living as either day laborers (*trabalhadores*) or sharecroppers (*seareiros*). About two dozen men qualify as *proprietários* (landowners), having sufficient land to periodically employ day laborers, but also working the land themselves. Latifundists own very large farms and employ sharecroppers, day laborers, and farm managers. None of the latifundists live in Vila Velha. They all maintain homes in Vila Nova, the county seat, and in the past provided important links between the parish and the county.

Although derived from entirely different economic arrangements, the agricultural basis of life in both São Miguel and Vila Velha puts households into competition with one another. In Vila Velha, the establishment of sharecropping arrangements resulted in competition among *seareiros* vying for choice lands. This competition led, historically, to the establishment of ties between sharecropper and latifundist—the vertical ties so characteristic of Mediterranean society. In São Miguel, the villagers' traditional roles as producers and sellers in the marketplace create competition. São Miguel is characterized by autonomous households with social relationships coming to rapid closure, leading to a lack of ties between households. This lack of horizontal ties is combined with a social structure that limits the possibilities for establishing vertical ties. In both socioeconomic systems, it is difficult for members to express communal goals. Neither community is corporate or characterized by factional conflicts and consequent mobilization.

Conflict between households and between individuals in São Miguel is avoided by careful accounting between parties, by the avoidance of debt relations, and by interlocking kin ties. In contrast with many southern European peasant societies, Portuguese rural life is not characterized by a great amount of litigation between parties over land, family matters, insults, or any of the other myriad events that keep courts crowded. People avoid getting involved with *a justiça* (the law) and try to avoid having any conflict come to *o tribunal* (the court). Fights that occur within households are usually patched up through the intervention of kinsmen, although there may be many threats to take a case to court. Acts of physical violence are rare in Estremaduran Portugal. In fact, the few fights that did occur during our stay in the village were always initiated by women. Only toward their conclusion were men involved. When men get drunk they may become verbally abusive, but they usually refrain from physical fights. When a fight or argument gets out of hand, a frequent resolution is for the parties to stop speaking with one another.

Individuals break off social contact with other villagers over conflicts ranging from presumed personal snubs to disagreements over land and water rights. Kinsmen may concur with terminating relations if they feel that their relative was "right," although they are not required, or even expected, to break relations with the other parties. At any given time, someone in the village is not on speaking terms with someone else. Much time and gossip is expended at the washhouse (o rio) and the wells discussing the who, what, and whys of interhousehold relations. The rio and well are centers of social control, where everybody's private life (carefully viewed through the shuttered windows) is washed publicly along with the laundry. Current incidents and conflicts are recounted by village women, and public resolutions are agreed upon.

The case that goes to court brings the villager into contact with lawyers and legal requirements. Going to court costs money and time lost from work. Villagers feel that the whole legal system is designed to cheat them. They do not file inheritance claims, except minimally, and only when they feel that they have been truly wronged do they venture a trip to the county courthouse. These few excursions into the court system are constantly being recounted, with the villager usually describing the manner in which he or a neighbor was taken advantage of by the system. A miller told me of the time that he went to court to collect a large debt owed to him by an outsider. His lawyer told him that he needed two witnesses to sign certain papers. On his next trip to the county seat, the man persuaded two of his friends to accompany him and act as witnesses. When they met the lawyer in the courthouse, the miller was told that his witnesses were not acceptable and that the miller would have to use the two witnesses that the lawyer had conveniently brought with him. The miller objected, pointing out that his friends had come all the way to town with him, but the lawyer insisted upon using his witnesses. After the witnesses had signed, the lawyer then told the miller that their fee was five escudos for the "service." The courts and the law are part of "THEM," and at all costs the São Miguelito attempts to avoid contact.

Compared to many social systems, Portuguese rural society experienced minimal conflict before April 1974. The dominant pattern

of interpersonal relations was balanced reciprocity and, because relations outside the parish are minimal, social control was maintained within the parish with little outside interference. External
enforcement of the law was provided by the highway police and
the Republican Guard (Guarda Nacional Republicana). The highway
police patrolled the main road that cuts through the parish, giving
summonses for two people riding on a motorcycle or to truck drivers
carrying passengers illegally. Both types of summonses served to
limit the mobility of the villagers since few families owned more
than one motorbike and there was limited public transportation.

The Republican Guard periodically patrolled the parish, once a
week walking through each village and hamlet. Two guards always
patrolled together—one good guy, the villagers say, and one bad
guy. Armed with rifles, wearing stiff grey uniforms and high black
boots, they marched, on the lookout for infractions—unleashed and
unlicensed dogs, animals wandering about, or any construction
underway without a proper license or authorization. Villagers were
also on the lookout for the police, and as soon as they were seen
walking on the road from one of the hamlets, information was
passed through the fields and into the village. Pet dogs were hustled
into the house, other infractions were hidden as well as possible,
and the villagers went indoors to avoid the Guard.

Although the PIDE, the Portuguese secret police, did not operate
within the village, the use of informers was a widespread system
of getting information. Being seen talking to the Guard was tanta-
mount to being considered a police informer. Civil servants were
prime targets for such accusations, and villagers generally believed
that police knowledge came from information received from state
employees, such as ditch diggers and road repairers. Local people
believed that a civil servant reporting an infraction to the Guard
received a percentage of the fine. It is not clear if this was the case
for every reported infraction, but the villagers were on the right
track. According to Article 725 of the Administrative Code, 50 percent of a fine collected in the parish went to the person who drew
up the official report. While reporting an infraction was not the
same as writing the official report, the villagers assumed that all
civil servants shared in the collection of fines. Since fines and other
minor harassments operated to keep the population constantly on
guard, the idea that there was a bonus for reporting irregularities
heightened the sense that everyone was watching everyone. Everyone was watching everyone, but it is doubtful that they were reporting what they saw to the Guard. Instead, the law served several

purposes; one was to supplement the salaries of lower-level officials and to discourage the acceptance of bribes; another was to maintain an atmosphere of "informing" as a mechanism for social (and political) control.

Cutileiro does not discuss the quality of interpersonal relations within Vila Velha. Several factors suggest, however, that, despite the stratified latifundist-*proprietário*-sharecropper-laborer structure that exists in Vila Velha, there is a value system operative in which the Vila Velhano would prefer to see himself and others on an equal footing. Vila Velhanos do not accept the "naturalness" of the social order. Just as the São Miguelito maintains egalitarian and avoidance relations with his neighbors, so too does the Vila Velhano attempt to maintain this balance. Thus, petty thievery is supported by the villagers as preferential to begging, for begging is a dependency relationship. Institutionalized charity, often pointed to proudly by the latifundists, is not welcomed by the peasants, who see themselves "morally damaged by it." [15]

Cutileiro's description of the villagers' relationships with the Guard and the description of the court system quoted below are highly reminiscent of the attitudes and behavior found in São Miguel. On the police, Cutileiro writes: "In many instances they [the Republican Guard] are looked upon almost as employees of the latifundists, although they are paid by the State . . . However, when poorer people enter into patronage bonds with Republican Guards they are singling themselves out from their group and establishing alliances which will always be regarded as having the sole purpose of securing leniency in legal matters. These cases are therefore regarded as instances of collaboration with the outside force of the State with implicitly harmful effects for the rest of the community" (p. 181).

As to involvement with the judicial system: "Going to court is considered a great nuisance and complication, and *andar metido em justiça* (to get involved with the law) is an expression frequently used to describe the whole process. To the people of the freguesia 'justice' . . . conveys the notion that a person has become involved in an unknown, hostile, and money-consuming world with its own set of rules. It also implies that in the hands of lawyers, court clerks, and judges, whether the case is lost or won, a man undergoes an ordeal from which he emerges certainly the poorer and usually the wiser" (p. 184).

In Vila Velha, as in São Miguel, local conflicts were not brought to the attention of outside authorities, nor were they resolved through local tribunals; rather, the social system's patterns of inter-personal relations served to keep these activities out of the public sphere.

In a processual approach, the diagnostic markers of the "political field" are the publicly articulated goals and the distribution of power. According to the political structure of the Estado Novo, the parish was the smallest political unit, and examination of field data from São Miguel demonstrates that it was, in fact, a unit for the articulation of public goals. The three examples that follow illus-trate, however, the limitations that the state placed on the realiza-tion of communal goals. While public goals could be articulated, the parish did not have the power to accomplish any public goals. To the reader, the objectives may seem trivial and inconsequential; to the villagers, they were important and critical. However, there was under the Estado Novo no way to directly and effectively com-municate village needs into the governmental system, let alone act upon such needs locally.

During the summer of 1961, São Miguel's central fountain, the main source of village drinking water, was damaged. It had to be fixed; but who would (or, better, could) fix it? The villagers went to the *junta*, but the *junta* said that, since the fountain was county property, they would have to ask the town hall to send a repair-man. Fixing the fountain would have been very easy. It was not the difficulty of the job that precluded *junta* action; rather, it was the question of property and principle. Since the fountain was not the property of the parish, the *junta* had no right to do repairs. All the *junta* could do was ask the mayor and the municipal coun-cil. Whenever a villager—or his wife—encountered a *junta* mem-ber, he or she would ask, "Well, why isn't it fixed yet?" "We asked," would be the reply. "We will just have to wait." Finally, several weeks later, some workmen sent from the county seat fixed the fountain.

The water supply, electricity, road conditions, postal matters, education, health and welfare benefits, and all other community needs (with the exception of common lands) were outside the con-trol of the *junta*. Instead, all facilities and benefits came from the municipal council, on which the parish was not directly represent-ed, or from higher levels of the state bureaucracy.

The second example points up the weakness of the *junta* as a representative body. It had long been felt that São Miguel's large central plaza would be an appropriate place for a monthly Sunday fair. On the second and fourth Sundays of each month there was a fair in the county seat, and on the third Sunday in another parish in the county. Thus, the first Sunday of each month could have been the date for a São Miguel fair. It would bring activity to the parish, save the villagers from having to make trips to other fairs, and bring a cheaper and greater variety of goods closer to home. In this case, the only objections came from the local shopkeepers, who saw the fair as competition for their small general stores. It is not surprising that, since the three members of the São Miguel *junta* were the baker and two shopkeepers, the *junta* never acted on this idea. This lack of action denied a good source of revenue to the parish.

The *junta* members found themselves in the quandary in which all officials found themselves within the Estado Novo. They were not "representatives" of the villagers and they gained little, formally, from their positions. Consequently, in any situation in which their private interests and the public good conflicted, their private interests usually prevailed. *Junta* members remained private individuals whose public roles could not be called into question by their constituents; only their superiors who appointed them could supervise their actions.

The third case has an even more futile cast, for the *junta* could not even be appealed to as a first resort. In this instance, the parish of São Miguel was stocked with rabbits and designated as a hunting area during the month of September. Throughout the rest of the year, rabbit hunting was prohibited, but during September the entire region, without respect to property boundaries, was opened to licensed hunters. Aside from the fact that rabbits are agricultural pests, and that it is a bit unnerving to work or walk in fields when hunters are about, the dates for the opening of the hunting season coincided with the grape harvest (*vindima*). Grapes are an important local crop, and the peasants looked on as their fields and vines were damaged by outside hunters. In this instance, one could not even appeal to the mayor or the municipal council, for decisions like setting hunting seasons and licensing hunters were not county-level decisions.

The data from Vila Velha are quite similar. There, the view was openly expressed that *junta* members worked only for themselves or *êles*. In São Miguel, the villagers were more charitable. *Junta* members, they said, were honorable men, but nobody listens to us, or them. Membership on the São Miguel *junta* rotated among the more affluent and out-going community members and the idea of a competitive election for the *junta* was viewed as inconceivable. From the villagers' viewpoint, those who were the selected *junta* members would also have been selected by local choice.

These three examples demonstrate that, while there were local public goals, the Estado Novo governmental system closed off any communication (let alone decision) pertaining to these objectives into the higher levels of the system. From the parish to the municipality, hardly any information flowed. From the county to the parish, communication usually took the form of arbitrary directives. The government removed all initiative from the parish and instituted, instead, administrative decrees which local bodies merely enforced. What characterized local political life was the degree to which administrative regulations curtailed every action that the individual villager may have wanted to take.

There is a question whether a public political arena in the Portuguese parish really existed. The *junta* hardly ever met even though it was required to do so by law. When it did meet, its deliberations were usually perfunctory. Local goals could be communicated and barely acknowledged only through occasional special pleadings, for in the parish of São Miguel no one (with the exception of the priest) could mobilize any resources which would make the political system respond or even pay attention to local demands.

In terms of decision making or problem solving, the parishes were monuments to autarchy. Despite the presence of the *junta*, the parish was effectively cut off from the political arena. The center of local governmental authority in Portugal was the town hall in the county seat. The mayor appointed the members of the municipal council and the town hall was staffed by professional civil servants. The mayor was usually a man of wealth and status. The position paid a minimal salary, and the position, although it was not sought after, conferred prestige (and problems) on its incumbent. Unlike administrative personnel, the mayor could not be bribed by villagers; he had to be appealed to. On the basis of appeals, public goals could be realized. Villagers recognized this by identifying public improvements in the parish with the name of a particular donor, despite the fact that decisions were governmental.

Peasants had to visit the town hall for marriage certificates, payment of local taxes, license applications, and payment of fines; to fulfill many of the other bureaucratic requirements; and to fill out the myriad of "papers" which a Portuguese had to have. The town hall was thereby a political center, housing the mayor and the municipal council, but more importantly it was the administrative center of the local governmental system.

Operating in the political arena was virtually impossible for the villagers; operating in the administrative arena was a constant fact of life. The Estado Novo actively encouraged political apathy on the parts of individuals and prohibited the formation of political groups. Little information was available to the public about political leaders or their doings. While the official literacy rate was about 70 percent, the effective literacy rate in rural areas was much lower. All mass media were under government control and censored. Instead of participating in local or upwardly directed politics, the Portuguese villagers were constantly being presented with and harassed by a series of administrative decisions. One could almost use as a rule of thumb in Salazar's Portugal that "anything that is not expressly permitted is probably prohibited." Or, if a given act was not forbidden, then one probably needed a license to undertake it. "Portugal," one São Miguelito said, "is the most advanced country in two things: licenses and fines." Cutileiro echoes this: "If all regulations were observed the life of the country would be paralyzed in twenty-four hours" (p. 199). Not all regulations were, obviously, enforced, but the villager could never be sure, and the very selective enforcement of the law itself created an atmosphere of uneasiness and unsureness.

The need for licenses in Portuguese daily life was omnipresent: owning a cigaret lighter, a television set, a radio, a motorbike, or a mule cart, building a house, repairing a house, widening a room, fixing a wall—all required a license; the list was endless. If the peasant was caught without the proper license, he had to pay a fine. The cost of the license plus the trip to the county seat to get it, the queues in which one would have had to stand, and the insults and disdain with which the clerks treated the peasants were extremely discouraging to the villagers. Cutileiro reports that the peasants in Vila Velha and the clerks in Vila Nova had an agreed-upon scale of bribes. My experience in São Miguel suggests that within that Town Hall no such knowledge was widespread, and many a villager reported a fruitless day spent standing in lines, during which his papers were never called or processed.

Endless papers flowed through this bureaucracy and each request or application for a license had to be presented to the appropriate clerk on official, stamped paper, known as *papel celado de vingt cinco linhas* (stamped, twenty-five–line paper), which was sold in only one store in the entire parish. Rather than file the proper papers and get involved in the intricacies of the bureaucracy, many a villager preferred to pay the fine which, if one adds all the costs involved in securing a license, may in fact have been a saving.

The View from Below: Authoritarianism and Village Life

Until its abrupt ending in 1974, political life in Portugal was relatively tranquil. The sporadic coup attempts throughout the Salazar years were confined to segments of the military and urban populace.[16] As Cutileiro notes, "political calm [was] achieved . . . through the control of information, of education, of access to the Civil Service, and a nation-wide police network."[17] In addition, I would add the noncompetitive electoral nature of the political system. Those elections that were held served more to ferret out elite discontent than to mobilize the population.[18] There was no need ever to mobilize a voter either for or against, or to make, however insincere, a promise to a community that a road would be built or a school opened. The only way to get anything accomplished was by having a contact or paying a bribe. It became extremely difficult to realize any public goals; instead, the achievement of private ends was pursued. A contact had to be someone with the leverage to get an administrative officer to alter the execution of a decision. The Portuguese term *cunha*, meaning wedge, is used to describe the leverage that one's contact used in manipulating the system.

The Estado Novo virtually perfected a system which actively encouraged the political apathy of its population. Minimal mobilization was practiced. Political leaders rarely appeared publicly. In many ways Salazar's reclusive nature was imposed on the people as a model of political activity. Apathy was further strengthened and was a direct outgrowth in turn of the structural powerlessness of the villager. Apathy, however, was not a sign of depoliticization, if depoliticization refers to the degree of perception of relevance of governmental functions for daily life. Quite the contrary, the corporate state attempted to "politicize" all aspects of social and economic life. While the political arena could not be entered, the administrative arena had to be constantly manipulated in order to accomplish goals. It was to "patrons" that one had to turn. Manipulating the administrative sector had to be sub rosa and therefore was only suitable for accomplishing private objectives, allowing an individual to resolve his own difficulties with some government decree or regulation. In fact, patron-client relationships, particularly in the Mediterranean, which take peasants into the public arena are usually activated for the accomplishment of private ends and not as a means of securing local public and communal goals. Thus, avoiding conscription, getting immigration papers, getting a driver's license, repairing a house, selling crops—all of these required interaction with the government, not through political means, but through a series of individual dealings with the administration. When peasants were successful they succeeded not in participating in the making of policy but in manipulating the imposition of already decided upon regulations or programs.

That patronage should be operative in a Mediterranean society is scarcely a new finding. However, the Portuguese corporate government succeeded in establishing a system in which patronage was an appropriate mode of manipulation and, at the same time, an undesirable relationship, from the perspective of either the patron or the client. For the villagers in both São Miguel and Vila Velha, "patrons" were not easily available. The role of "patron," which involves some kind of enduring relationship, is not appropriate for São Miguel and is rare in contemporary Vila Velha, although Cutileiro uses the term; nor are "mediators" or "culture brokers" available as institutional linkages. The Estado Novo made it extremely difficult for rural villagers to make the appropriate types of contact—to use the patrons, mediators, and brokers, whom they needed—and thus the state, effectively, reinforced the powerlessness of the peasantry.

In neither São Miguel nor Vila Velha can one identify a patron with a number of clients. Given the corporatist authoritarian state, there was no reason in Vila Velha for anyone to want to serve as a patron. In São Miguel, there was no one, even if the structure of interpersonal relations were different, who could have served in that role. In addition, both communities were characterized, as was virtually all of Portuguese society during the Estado Novo, by an absence of political, religious, labor, or even social associations which in any way could have provided for the articulation of individual interests or provided group leverage. In short, Portuguese at almost all levels of society could not organize or mobilize to influence. Hence, the villagers were thrown on their own individual resources.

In Vila Velha villagers were constantly looking for *amigos*, while in São Miguel they were always looking for *conhecimentos*. The difference in these terms relates directly to the variation in community social structure. *Amigo* means friend, while *conhecimento* means someone you know (who knows someone). The Vila Velhano was willing to put himself in a subordinate position to a "friend"; the São Miguelito would use and pay for a *conhecimento*, but would never indebt himself to a friend. By definition *amigos* or *conhecimentos* would do something for you that you could not do for yourself, and, when you are barely literate and without financial resources, there was much you could not do.

Given the social stratification of Vila Velha, we would expect to have found patrons, and in the past they were present. For a period of time in the late nineteenth and early twentieth centuries, the economic and political conditions provided an impetus for the latifundists to act as local *caciques*. During that period the patron-client model operated rather smoothly, with sharecroppers and day laborers providing manpower, economically and politically, for the latifundists. Today, however, sharecroppers are not needed as a labor source on the more highly mechanized latifundia and the latifundists do not need votes. Despite the fact that Portugal had scant experience with "democracy," it was, nevertheless, necessary periodically to mobilize voters. Even in corrupt political systems, the ballot can be a valuable commodity. Aside from labor service and moral dependency, it is one of the few resources that the client brings to the patron-client relationship.

Under the Estado Novo, the villager could bring no resource to the persons whom he used as *amigo*. The Vila Velhano was always in the position of making a *pedido* (requesting a favor, begging). As Cutileiro puts it, "deprived of any capacity to reciprocate, a man is reduced to begging for favors . . . the only thing that he can offer in return is his moral dependence."[19] One could argue that the Vila Velhano was fortunate in having access to a few who would help even in return for "only" his moral dependence. But moral dependence, this role of clientage with minimal resources, had its costs for the Vila Velhano. As one old woman told Cutileiro, "What I ask for is not a favor; it costs me my shame" ["Isso que eu peco não é favor; minha vergonha me custa"] (p. 245).

The moral dependence implicit in the subordination of the client was an inconceivable relationship within the structure of São Miguel society. Within the parish through the mechanism of "balanced reciprocity" the São Miguelito avoided indebting himself to a neighbor. Households closed in on themselves and the only times when it became necessary to go outside the immediate household—as in the establishment of *compadrasco* (godparent) relations—the preference was to reinforce pre-existing kinship ties. In the search, thus, for *conhecimentos* to manipulate the governmental system, the

São Miguelito had to look outside the local parish. He had to make contact with *êles*, individuals from the very groups with which relationships of negative reciprocity had been established. What São Miguelitos attempted to coalesce at particular moments of need were less like patron-client ties and more like action sets, or networks. That is, they attempted to weave their way out of the parish and into the realm of *êles* by taking small steps, each one of which was potentially repayable, rather than placing themselves under the moral dependence of or in a subordinate position to a patron. As can be imagined, this was a slow and often unsuccessful enterprise. Even if a *conhecimento* of a *conhecimento* could be found, it was usually necessary to pay for any assistance. In establishing these contacts, the villager was forced to weigh the balance between the degree to which he was exploiting the relationship for his advantage and the degree to which he might subsequently be exploited by the contact. Even with repayment, the São Miguelito envisioned the social risks a potential dependency relationship.[20]

Inevitably, when a villager was able to overcome an administrative decree, receive a low tax rate, obtain papers to emigrate, or avoid a fine for repairing a wall without a license, rumors would abound on how a *conhecimento* was used to accomplish these goals. However, for the most part, villagers paid fines, paid taxes, and served in the army, for they had no linkages that they could mobilize in their search for *conhecimentos* and had no political or material resources to offer such *conhecimentos*. São Miguel had a social system which closed in on itself and which was adaptive in maintaining the economic self-sufficiency of each household. It was not an adaptive social system for the political reality of the Estado Novo. To be effective, one had to have a *cunha*, but unlike the peasants of Vila Velha, São Miguelitos were not willing to beg, and, one can ask, even if they were, to whom would they have gone?

Conclusions

Vila Velha and São Miguel, two parishes with different types of local social structure—the former part of a highly stratified latifundist tradition, and the latter a community of small peasant proprietors—each encountered, under the Estado Novo, great difficulties in communicating both individual and communal needs to the larger political system. To accomplish political objectives, individuals in both communities needed contacts. However, because of the centralized, authoritarian, nonparty, and nonelectoral features of the Portuguese state, and because there were no local resources of any worth, there were few "patrons" available to serve as contacts. Moreover, in the case of São Miguel, the patterning of interpersonal relations discouraged the establishment of the dependency ties which are characteristic of patron-client relations.

There is today an extensive anthropological and political science literature discussing the prevalence of the patron-client model of political organization in Mediterranean, Latin American, and Southeast Asian societies. In many of these works, the authors assume that the position of economic dependency, or subordination, of the peasantry is structurally transformed into a political role of client dependency; this role, that of client, is then viewed as the preferred goal for the peasant.[21] The data from two Portuguese parishes suggest that the mere presence of economic inequality, and even the presence, as in Vila Velha, of rigid social stratification, does not in itself create an attitude of, or a preference for, dependency on the part of the peasantry. The appearance of clientilism is not automatic; the analyst must first carefully examine the political structure of the state as well as the local social structure, the resources available locally (both human and material), and the dominant patterns of interpersonal relations before assuming that peasants will "naturally" seek out patrons. At the same time, a similar analysis must be performed on the nonpeasant sectors of the society in order to determine whether there are, or could be, willing candidates for the role of patron.

The Portuguese governmental system institutionalized by the Estado Novo presents a paradox. Its overbearing administrative bureaucracy was ideally suited for the development of widespread patronage, yet in São Miguel it did not exist and in Vila Velha it existed at great social costs to the individuals involved. São Miguelitos would not indebt themselves to a potential patron. In Vila Velha, despite the presence of latifundists, there was no advantage for anyone to be a patron. Effectively, therefore, these rural villagers were as impotent in the informal operations of the Estado Novo as they were when operating through the formal structure of the *junta* and the municipal council.

Villagers were marginal actors in the Portuguese political system; they were integrated into a political process which granted them a minimal role of apathetic acquiescence. The Estado Novo prevailed for almost fifty years by enforcing apathy; it permitted only the articulation of private goals and provided no means for the presentation of communal goals. Peasants individually and severally were made powerless in a system that gave little to them, but also asked little in return. Moreover, by not allowing interest associations to develop, the corporate state acted to encourage the establishment of vertical personal ties as opposed to horizontal linkages in the society. However, patronage was curtailed by the lack of resources (both economic and electoral) that the rural communities (or individuals) could mobilize. Patronage was seen as a burden, for there was little anyone could gain from playing the patron's role. To paraphrase Fred Bailey,[22] Portugal's authoritarian corporate state was a system in which rural villagers could mobilize no spoils and hence had no stratagems. The Estado Novo decreed parish and village "nonpolitics." Perhaps, even more than Marcello Caetano realized, from the peasant's perspective, Portugal was an "administered society."

Notes

Earlier versions of this paper were read at the American Political Science Association meetings, Washington, D.C., August 1972; Columbia University Seminar on the State, December 1972; and the Workshop on Modern Portugal, Durham, N.H., October 1973. I am grateful for the comments made by participants at those meetings. Many of their ideas have been incorporated into the current version. I am particularly grateful to Shepard Forman, Gloria Levitas, and Jane Schneider for their comments and criticisms.

1. John Hammond, "From the 'Urnas' to the 'Ruas,'" paper delivered to Crisis in Portugal Conference, University of Toronto, April 1976 (Chapter 8 in this volume is a revised version of this paper—eds.).

2. Joyce Firstenberg Riegelhaupt, "In the Shadow of the City," Ph.D. dissertation, Columbia University, 1964; idem, "Saloio Women: An Analysis of Informal and Formal Political and Economic Roles of Portuguese Peasant Women," Anthropological Quarterly 40, no. 3 (July 1967): 109–126; idem, "Festas and Padres: The Organization of Religious Action in a Portuguese Parish," American Anthropologist 75 (1973): 835–852. Field work in São Miguel (a pseudonym) was conducted under a Public Health Fellowship (MF 12,036) from 1960 to 1962. Return visits were made to Portugal during the summers of 1964, 1968, 1971, and 1976. Additional short field work trips have been made by Edward Riegelhaupt in 1966 and October 1974.

3. José Cutileiro, A Portuguese Rural Society (Oxford: Clarendon Press, 1971).

4. H. R. Trevor-Roper, "The Phenomenon of Fascism," in European Fascism, ed. S. J. Woolf (New York: Vintage Books, 1969), pp. 24–25.

5. Jean Meyriat, La Peninsule Iberique (Paris: Université de Paris, Institut d'Etudes Politiques, 1957), p. 594.

6. Cutileiro, *Portuguese Rural Society*, p. 154.

7. Ibid., p. 155.

8. Hugh Kay, *Salazar and Modern Portugal* (London: Eyre and Spottiswoode, 1970), p. 56.

9. M. G. Smith, *Government in Zazzau* (London: Oxford University Press for the International African Institute, 1960).

10. See especially Marc J. Swartz (ed.), *Local Level Politics* (Chicago: Aldine, 1968).

11. Ibid.

12. Marcello Caetano, *No One Can Shirk Fulfilling His Duty to the Homeland*, speech delivered in Oporto, Portugal, May 1969 (Lisbon: Secretaria do Estado da Informações e Turismo, 1969). This distinction is useful in analyzing the legal constraints on peasant political activity within the Estado Novo. Historically, the circumstances under which peasants take political action through banditry, rebellion, and revolution have often been in reaction to the imposition of administrative decrees (taxation, military drafts, food seizures, etc.). Consequently, I am not arguing that administrative decrees cannot provoke political behavior, but that within the constitutional framework of the Portuguese state there was no way for peasants to act politically in a legal manner.

13. George M. Foster, "The Dyadic Contract: A Model for the Social Structure of a Mexican Peasant Village," *American Anthropologist* 63 (1961): 1173–1192; idem, "The Dyadic Contract in Tzintzuntzan, II: Patron-Client Relationship," *American Anthropologist* 65 (1963): 1280–1294.

14. Marshall Sahlins, "On the Sociology of Primitive Exchange," in *The Relevance of Models for Social Anthropology*, ed. Michael Banton, A.S.A. Monograph, no. 1 (London: Tavistock Publications, 1965), pp. 139–236.

15. Cutileiro, *Portuguese Rural Society*, pp. 75–76.

16. Douglas Wheeler, "The Honor of the Army," paper delivered to the Annual Meetings of the Society of Spanish and Portuguese Historical Studies, Johns Hopkins University, April 1976 (Chapter 6 contains an updated, expanded version of this paper and the one presented at the 1976 Toronto Conference on Portugal—eds.).

17. Cutileiro, *Portuguese Rural Society*, p. 220.

18. Philippe C. Schmitter, personal communication, 1976 (see Chapter 1 for data and interpretations confirming this view—eds.).

19. Cutileiro, *Portuguese Rural Society*, p. 244.

20. Even in highly stratified Vila Velha, such social costs must be considered. "The cost of buying material advantages through moral submissiveness may be extremely high . . . People who are known to ask for the patronage of wealthier individuals too often or to ask for too much acquire a reputation for shamelessness. Yet anyone seeking patronage has to be shameless to some degree" (ibid., p. 245).

21. Another approach frequently seen in the literature refers to the replacement of the patron-client tie with party patronage. It is not my intention to cast doubts upon the wealth of Mediterranean, Latin American, and Southeast Asian studies, but instead to suggest that the Portuguese case, while it may be unique, forces us to re-examine the presumptive "patron-client" pattern of particularistic bureaucratic systems as well as the unilineal developmental model which leads from patron-client to po-

litical-party patronage. Alex Weingrod, following Silverman, refers to this transition in the following: "Patron-client ties can be seen to arise within State structures in which authority is dispersed and State activity limited in scope, and in which considerable separation exists between levels of village, city, and state. Party-directed patronage, on the other hand, is associated with the expanding scope and general proliferation of State activities and also with the growing integration of village, city, and state" ("Patrons, Patronage, and Political Parties," *Comparative Studies in Society and History* 10 [1968]: 377–400).

In this context, the Portuguese corporate state was a particularly interesting form. It was a centralized system with "an expanding scope and general proliferation of state activities" but one which made no structural or processual allowances for the presumed transition from a client system to a constituent system. In the Estado Novo, the peasants were not "constituents" and there were great limitations, as we show, to patronage. It will be interesting to see if under the postrevolutionary republican and multiparty form of government a party patronage system develops. If it does, the process will not be a transformation of patron-client relations, but rather the result of a new structuring of party-government relations and resource allocation.

22. Fred Bailey, *Stratagems and Spoils: A Social Anthropology of Politics* (New York: Schocken Books, 1969).

6. The Military and the Portuguese Dictatorship, 1926–1974: "The Honor of the Army"

DOUGLAS L. WHEELER

The situation of the Portuguese army, from the point of view of moral considerations, or of the material, is absolutely wretched. The state of neglect, misery, and degradation to which the public force has arrived would by itself justify a thousand revolutions. . . . The army is . . . the most powerful guarantee of national sovereignty, internal peace, and external respect.— Lt. Jorge Botelho Moniz, rebel officer in eighteenth of April 1925 abortive coup, in his book, *O 18 de Abril*

If, before 1961, the armed forces were not openly affected adversely in their prestige, or were not so affected in a very violent form, it is because the internal crises of the regime had not yet reached an especially acute stage. However, beginning with the fall of India, and above all in the manner in which the wars in Africa were prolonged, the armed forces discovered, not without fear on the part of many soldiers who saw things clearly for the first time, the true separation from the nation. The armed forces are, therefore, humiliated, discredited, and presented to the country as if they were those mainly responsible for the disaster.—(February 1974) First Manifesto of the "Captains" of the Armed Forces Movement, as cited in text published in *Textos Históricos da Revolução* (Lisbon: DiAbril, 1975), p. 16

Among Western states, Portugal's experience with military intervention in politics and government appears to be unique, with the possible exception of Spain's experience, 1923–1939. Twice in the twentieth century, the Portuguese military has overthrown a civilian-dominated regime: in 1926 and in 1974. Twice, following each military coup, the armed forces' officer corps not only dominated government activities but also took part in the administration of the country: in the years of the "pure" military dictatorship, 1926–1928, and again in the aftermath of the coup of the twenty-fifth of April 1974, during the period May 1974 to April 1976. In both cases, the Portuguese military chose, for a variety of reasons, to return to the barracks and to give over the lion's share of power to civilians.

Any analysis which deals with the Portuguese military in politics and government must, of necessity, deal with the phenomenon of the extensive period of the Portuguese dictatorship, often known as the "New State 1926–1974." Since a definitive study of the New State is not feasible at this time, this article must be limited in scope. There will be a preliminary inquiry into the major trends in the history of the Portuguese military during the period between the two coups of 1926 and 1974.

Two key questions will then be asked and material will be provided to answer them: What were civil-military relations during this era? More to the point, what was the political relationship between the Portuguese military, chiefly the officer corps, for the purposes of this study, and the New State government? What were the most important factors which can be clearly identified in the process which led to the active intervention of the armed forces in governing the country?

The Role of the Military in Creating and Destroying the Republic

No analysis of the history of the Portuguese military in recent times is complete without a discussion of the experience of the military during the first Portuguese Republic, 1910–1926. The Portuguese army officer corps, in effect, initiated a *pronunciamento* tradition after 1820. In a series of coups, officers overthrew regimes and played an important role in high politics until the relatively quiescent period of 1851–1891. As the Constitutional Monarchy lost popularity and its cohesion disappeared, the armed forces reflected the growing political crisis. Rather apolitical as of 1890–91, the officer corps underwent gradual politicization through the revival of the *pronunciamento* tradition through the activities of middle-class republican militants, both civilian and military; discontent among laboring and commercial classes in the towns and cities exacerbated the role perceptions held by the military leadership. Should the military continue to support the Monarchy? Should the

Monarchy alter its strategy and use a clique of rightist, militarist army officers, including Maj. J. Mousinho de Albuquerque (1855–1902), in order to defeat the rising tide of republicanism and to regain authority for the weakened Monarchy?

There was an increasingly shrill debate in Portugal over the role of the armed forces in society. In effect, variants of two conflicting models (the "aristocratic" and the "democratic")[1] were being debated among monarchists and their republican antagonists. Many republicans desired a military which would conform to a "democratic" model closely resembling civil-military relations in France's Third Republic and in the older Swiss Republic. Republican leaders argued for a "nation in arms" concept where civilians held top authority. In this model, all male civilians regardless of class were obliged to participate in military service. By this scheme a "national conscript" force would include all males between the ages of 17 and 45; this force would be trained by a smaller professional force.[2]

In Portugal, the Monarchy, by tradition, was closely associated with a military which possessed authoritarian tendencies and an aristocratic base for its officer corps. Civil-military relations were troubled by a rising wave of public violence, coup plotting, and conspiracies which threatened to overthrow the Monarchy. Militant republican citizens, not military personnel, were most active in inciting the military to revolt. Many republican militants were members of the Carbonária, an auxiliary force of the Republican Party, secret, anarchistic, yet a republican society.[3] After many abortive plots and coup attempts, on October 5, 1910, a largely civilian-manned insurrection, beginning in the capital, succeeded in gaining the support of the armed forces. After some fighting, and despite the fact that only a handful of regular officers and a minority of the key Lisbon garrison actively supported the coup, the armed forces in the end refused to defend the Monarchy; republican forces triumphed and much of the public in the main towns hailed the victory of the civilian-dominated republican group.[4] It should be noted that in the final years of the Monarchy the civilian and royal leadership mistrusted the reliability of the bulk of the army and navy and came to depend upon paramilitary forces for security and last-ditch defense in the towns.[5]

Under the first Republic (1910–1926), excessive instability and conflict characterized government, politics, the economy, and society. The armed forces underwent unprecedented pressures: a relatively high level of public violence, civilian attempts to incite armed forces units to insurrection, civilian orders to repress both military and civilian insurgency in towns and rural areas, a wave of violent strikes, and combat in Europe on the Allied side in 1917–1918 and in Portuguese Africa in 1914–1918. There was a brief civil war in northern Portugal in early 1919, and the country suffered greatly from the hardships inherent in a collapsing economy.

The Portuguese military experience in World War I, both in Europe and in Africa, had profound consequences. Civilian leadership became more dependent upon the military, and, at the same time, the military leadership became increasingly dissatisfied and frustrated. The country was forced to sustain what was then the most massive mobilization effort in its history (see Table 6-1). Some military personnel believed that the war provided new opportunities for improved training, experience, pay, promotion, and professional expertise. Many others, however, resented the politicization of the officer corps and ranks, civilian intervention in military affairs on many occasions, political partisan strife in the government and politics, maladministration in general, and the military program of the republican civilian elite.[6]

A considerable portion of the Portuguese professional officer corps was highly critical of one aspect of the Republic's well-meaning but abortive attempt to create in Portugal a "nation in arms," by means of a new universal draft system and a militia program. Both plans broke down for want of means and military support.[7] During World War I and its aftermath the militia program assumed new features. A substantial portion of officers were commissioned under the new militia program. There was friction between the regular officers and the supposedly temporary militia officers; for political and professional military reasons regular officers resented what they believed to be favoritism shown by the civilian and military republican leaders in the parliamentary system toward partisan militia officers who were retained in service at the rank they had held at the end of the war. This alleged favoritism encouraged the majority of antirepublican officers to protest and eventually to plot military overthrow of the First Republic. Although there were a number of important professional and economic grievances, besides an increasing dissatisfaction with the political situation, the professional officers' collective resentment felt concerning the 1921 militia commission law provided a clear, powerful initial rallying point among officers with divergent political beliefs and membership commitments to different political parties.[8]

Army officer resentment toward the civilian leadership, and toward officers who were considered to have "sold out the army" to

TABLE 6–1

The Portuguese Army: Numerical Strength

Year	Numerical Strength	(includes both regular and active militia forces)
1910	12,000	
1911	11,690	
1914	12,000	
1918 (November)	110,000	(in foreign combat theaters at end of WWI, plus garrison troops at home; total estimated, 120,000–125,000 troops)
1920	23,000	
1921	16,432	
1925	30,000	(approximately)
1926	27,255	
1927	34,947	
1928	34,236	
1929	32,663	
1933	12,000	(not including 25,000 annual conscript draft)
1961	80,000	(including conscripts, at onset of insurgent war in Angola)
1967/68	120,000	(including forces in Portugal, Atlantic islands, Angola, Mozambique, and Guinea; excluding colonial civilian militia)
1971/72	130,000	(in Angola, Mozambique, and Guinea, not counting perhaps 15,000 in Portugal as part of under-strength two infantry divisions "assigned" to NATO)
1974 (April 25)	140,000	(not counting mobilized African regulars, militia forces in colonies)
1976 (March)	40,000	
1977	32,000	(redesigned army, as planned; Staff Draft Plan, 1976)

Sources: For figures in the years 1910–1933, see Wheeler, *Republican Portugal*, chap. 11; for figures in years 1961–1968, see Wheeler, "The Portuguese Army in Angola," *Journal of Modern African Studies* 7, no. 13 (October 1969): 429–436; for figures in years 1971–1974, see Wheeler, "African Elements in Portugal's Armies in Africa (1961–1974)," *Armed Forces and Society* 2, no. 2 (Winter 1976): 237–246. Figures for March 1976 force and projected new army (consisting of an "Intervention Force" [regular] and "Territorial Corps" [conscript 15–18 month term]) for 1977 on, from discussion of Army General Staff Plan discussed in public in an article in a weekly newspaper, "Corpo Voluntário de Intervenção . . . ," *Expresso* (Lisbon), March 6, 1976, p. 13.

the politicians, built upon a series of factors which went beyond specific professional grievances. In attempting to answer the question, Why did the military overthrow the First Republic's parliamentary regime and take over the state in 1926, it is important to discuss briefly four key factors which can help to explain the importance assumed by the military in 1926: (a) a revival of Portuguese militarism in officer circles, (b) a revival of active colonialism in Africa, (c) a new professionalism among officers, and (d) the growing influence upon public opinion and among officers of conservative political ideologies, including Portuguese nationalism, integralism, and several varieties of fascist and Catholic thought.

Inherent in the new militarism, a phenomenon with strong roots in the nineteenth century, were two key ideas: First, the armed forces, most especially the army, represented the most vital institution in Portugal. An increasing number of officers had come to admire the opinion of a rebel officer, young Lt. Jorge Botelho Moniz (1898–1961), whose sensational attack on the parliamentary regime included the statement that "the army is . . . the most powerful guarantee of national sovereignty, internal peace, and external respect."[9] Second, there was the increasingly accepted belief and idea that only the army was "unified" and capable of coping with the problems which the parliamentary Republic had failed to solve.

The increasingly important influence of a revived colonialism, a new professionalism among officers, and antiliberal, antidemocratic, and antiparliamentary ideas became naturally combined with a growing trend internationally: the rise of fascist or semifascist regimes in Italy (1922), Spain (1923), Greece (1925), and Poland (May 1926).

The parliamentary regime was overthrown by a military coup which began on the twenty-eighth of May 1926 in Braga. Support for this movement then spread to all military units in the country. The details of the coup plotting and operation are discussed elsewhere,[10] but it is worthwhile indicating several important features of the "28th of May." First, it was a bloodless coup which was received with some enthusiasm initially in both urban and rural areas. Second, it was a coup which featured almost exclusively junior regular officer corps participation (the first year or two of the subsequent dictatorship are often described therefore as the "regime of the lieutenants").[11] Third, the coup plotters were severely divided politically, and their partisan divisions roughly approximated the political fragmentation of the nonmilitary elite. Plotting and organizing the 1926 coup, in fact, involved not one main *junta*, or coup committee, but *two*. One, a largely "monarchist" committee, led by the "18th of April" (1925) group of rebel officers, was dominated by younger integralist and nationalist officers and was oriented toward maintaining power by means of force and authoritarian methods. The second committee, broadly "republican," was dominated by Radical Party member-officers and some old-line republican conservatives in the Cunha Leal splinter party (Liberal Union) and proposed a "presidentialist" but liberal, democratically oriented republican regime.[12]

The history of the Portuguese military during 1910–1926 generally raises some key points which, if viewed in the longer perspective of twentieth-century politics and government, suggest that the conventional models of scholars and the cultivated "myths" of the new state regime and their opponents must be severely qualified and perhaps abandoned.

While Janowitz' models of civil-military relations in the industrial nations (aristocratic, democratic, totalitarian)[13] may fit some national cases, they do not fit the Portuguese case. While Portugal failed to achieve the conditions and goals of a "democratic" model armed force, in 1926 the army actually replaced civilian control over the state with military administration based upon officer corps consensus or votes of officers in regiments or smaller units. "Barracks parliamentarism,"[14] in fact, was in stark contrast to all precedent in Portuguese civil-military relations. Later, when the New State government civilianized control of the government, and the military returned to the barracks, civil-military relations came to resemble Janowitz' model for new nations: "authoritarian-personal control." Since the New State did not establish a true mass party, and since the political secret police terrorized the officer corps increasingly after 1945, in Portugal the authoritarian–personal control model must take into account a secret police as the key replacement of the armed forces in maintaining the regime in power and keeping "order."[15]

A major problem with the "ideal type" analysis, of course, is that in the case of the Portuguese military there was no "one army" or service. There were, in fact, several. The officer corps, for example, contained personnel with differing political beliefs and creeds; within the army itself, as in a parliament or congress, then, power, decision making, image building, and control issues were debated and a struggle for dominance by one group was an almost constant process.

With these tendencies in mind, a student of the Portuguese military in politics can be safely skeptical of the well-known New State myths concerning the military: "only the army is unified"; "only the army is capable of unifying the country"; "the army is 'allowing' the premier to manage the country, while it supports his program"; and, after 1968, when Caetano replaced Salazar as premier, "the army is neutral or apolitical but supports the authority of the state." In a related point, sociologist Hermínio Martins suggested that the only two institutions in the new state with any measure of autonomy were the Church and the armed forces.[16] After close reading of the forty-eight–year history of the Portuguese dictatorship, however, historians must qualify this generalization. In fact, after 1936, with the creation of a series of paramilitary organizations, the increasing power of the secret police to intervene in armed forces' business, and the rise of fascist and authoritarian controls in general, the armed forces became merely one more co-opted and subordinated institution. Whatever relative autonomy it may have had, or groups of its leaders may have had, during the 1926–1928 "pure" Ditadura Militar and up to 1936, it was severely restricted by the end of World War II.[17]

It is true that *golpismo* continued, especially during the years 1926–1962. The military became part of plots to overthrow the dictatorship (see appendix, "Permanent Conspiracy"); nearly every year during the entire era there were one and often two plots concerning the idea of inciting one or more military units to rebel against the state and change the *situação* in the interests of *opposicionistas*. In most of the cases, however, fewer than a dozen regular officers were involved in the plots, and in many cases largely republican civilians were the plot leaders. Especially after 1945, however, as occurred during the 1926–1931 wave of *pronunciamento* plots, *chefes* selected to head the *juntas* or *comités* were professional officers of high rank. As in the traditional form of plotting by both civilians and the military, the choice of leader, *chefe*, was a crucial problem. Whoever became the designated leader, the officer destined to take power if the coup succeeded, largely determined which officers and which units and which political factions or parties would be willing to support the movement and work for its success. *Personalismo*, or the allegiance to persons over ideas and institutions, as in parliamentary and presidentialist republican politics, also played a key role in barracks or military politics.[18]

The continuation of coup plotting and *golpismo*, nevertheless, did not mean that the armed forces enjoyed significant autonomy vis-à-vis the New State rulers. After 1936, as was suggested above, the status and privileges of the military were diminished. An excellent example is the question of the immunity of officers to police arrest. During the early years of the regime, during the military dictatorship, the military were a privileged caste. On April 16, 1929, the headquarters of the Portuguese Masons in Lisbon was assaulted and raided by state police, civilians, and units of the paramilitary GNR (Guarda Nacional Republicana). All masons (or "freemasons") apprehended in this raid were arrested and jailed, "with the exception of army officers." [19] In a 1932 published interview, Premier António Salazar stated openly that the military were "a little privileged" group compared to others in the country at the time. This was because, he suggested, the military earned privileges during World War I and they were "keeping peace" in Portugal. Salazar concluded by stating, "I think that the country has an open debt with the army which will not be easily paid off." [20]

After his successful moves to woo and to appease the leaders of the officer corps, Salazar and his circle of Coimbra peer professors gained greater control of the reins of power and decision making in the state. The army returned to the barracks. Indeed, the New State elite was largely civilian, and, after 1933 when the Constitution was "ratified" and put into law, the state machinery at top levels underwent extensive civilianization. [21]

Civil-Military Relations under Salazar

If the models and official myths are suspect, what was the essence of civil-military relations under the more "vigorous" period of the dictatorship, 1933–1962? The New State civilian elite, dominated by the person of Salazar, demonstrated that in governing and in surviving threats pragmatism, opportunism, and the "art of ruling" [22] took precedence over doctrine and ideology. As Martins has carefully documented, even the "favored" integralists had a very limited autonomy. [23] The armed forces leadership after 1933, and especially after World War II, was increasingly controlled by the state. Like all the other New State institutions, the armed forces were co-opted and were influenced by a process of "divide and rule."

It is useful at this point to turn briefly again to the question of officer immunity to arrest. This became a more common officer grievance after 1940. Before, during any crackdown on oppositionists, officers might be immune to arrest by civilian police. After 1945, the state unilaterally imposed self-generated laws which eliminated this same immunity. Secret police powers were increased. In a law of October 13, 1945, PIDE was given the power "to arrest and detain anyone suspected of political activity" for forty-five days without charge and was given discretionary power in legal proceedings and the release of suspects.[24] On June 1, 1947, the government had published in all Portuguese newspapers an "official" reminder note that by "Decree no. 25317, dated May 13, 1945, the Government had taken to itself the powers to dismiss officers of the armed forces who failed in their duties to the established institutions . . ."[25] While the state did sometimes compromise on the severity of its use of the police and on legal sentences and penalties against officers involved in plots and conspiracies (i.e., after the 1962 abortive Beja coup), the general autonomy of the officer corps diminished in succeeding decades.

Another major feature of civil-military relations was the manner in which the state co-opted groups of officers by employing them in positions which identified them or, indeed, the "army" with the regime. At a high level, a close crony of Dr. Salazar was the monarchist-nationalist officer Fernando Santos Costa (1899–?). A "cadet of Sidónio" in 1918, Santos Costa was a member of the group of young, prointegralist, profascist officers who organized the twenty-eighth of May 1926 coup.[26] Involved in training and leadership in a paramilitary force, the Legião Portuguesa (1936–1974), Santos Costa soon became a leading member of the inner circle around Salazar. In 1944 he was appointed to the key post of minister of war, having been Salazar's personal "interim" minister of the army. In 1958 he was replaced after the brief oppositionist flurry surrounding the presidential elections in which the regime's candidate, Adm. Américo Tómas, was openly opposed by air force Gen. Humberto Delgado. Becoming the new minister of national defense in 1958 was another "Cadet of Sidónio" and a "Lieutenant" in the 1926 coup, Gen. Júlio Carlos Botelho Moniz, brother of Jorge Botelho Moniz, cited above.[27]

Santos Costa remained a key man in the Salazar regime's subordination of the armed forces to the will of the state. His personal talents were primarily political and conspiratorial. Increasingly, professional, less political officers viewed Santos Costa with hostility.[28] Santos Costa epitomized for the opposition the mediocrity and cronyism which infected the New State appointments. He indeed symbolized a case of how the New State co-opted army leadership and promoted officers not for military prowess but for political reasons and loyalty to the regime.

The state recruited officers from the army and navy, and later also from the new air force, to fill middle- and low-level posts in the home administration and in the colonies. This practice provided rewards for the government and compensation to those officers who were loyal to the regime.

Armed forces officers' support and collaboration roles with the New State fell into at least six sectors. These were areas in which thousands of officers were employed in full or part-time, paying positions which were not "conventional" military jobs.

1. Officering and manning the key paramilitary organizations of the New State, training duties, auxiliary consultations, etc.
   a. State correctional, prison services (guards, jailkeepers)
   b. Legião Portuguesa (1936–1974)
   c. Mocidade Portuguesa (1936–1974)
   d. GNR (Guarda Nacional Republicana; "second army," in effect)
   e. PSP (civil police)
   f. Secret police (PIDE/DGS)
   g. Guarda Fiscal (customs, frontiers, immigration, etc.)
2. Volunteering for the Legião Portuguesa campaign ("viriatos") in the Spanish Civil War, 1936–1939, and fighting; estimated 20,000 "volunteers" sent; 6,000–8,000 dead
3. Officers in state censorship service (usually as second positions, "moonlighting," in effect)
4. Holding office as cabinet ministers, under-secretaries of state, in ministries; in central, district, and local administration in Portugal and the Atlantic islands
5. Holding office as minister of war, defense, navy, or air force; at high levels in government
6. Fulfilling assignments in colonial service in African or Asian colonies, at all levels from "governor-general" or "high commissioner" down to local chefes do posto; seconding of officers to fill a variety of colonial posts, an old tradition; naval officers dominating upper levels of colonial administration by tradition until the twentieth century, when army officers came to dominate the major colonial posts in Angola, Mozambique, and Guinea; after the 1961 insurgency war began in Angola, post of governor-general normally filled by lieutenant colonels and colonels from the army

Benefits enjoyed by the regime included compromising and co-opting military leaders by identifying their employment and even livelihoods with the status quo of the political situação; obtaining needed technical and nontechnical skills from officers for jobs; and keeping officers occupied and perhaps somewhat removed from the barracks while, at the same time, their employment made them more vulnerable to regime demands, requests, and police surveillance. For individual officers, the initial and probably major attraction of such employment beyond their normal military duties was, simply, money. During the Salazar regime military pay was very low, except in some instances in later years when service in the African wars offered special bonus payments. To survive or to advance, officers sought second or superior jobs or attempted to be posted from their regular slots to special positions with better pay. Aspects of the military role in the state bureaucracy were already traditional as early as the First Republic and military pay, by tradition, was low in Portugal. It was largely the lower- and middle-ranking officers (from company grade up to lieutenant colonel) who came to find employment in sensitive positions more and more common. Some officers came to consider such work "degrading."[29]

Two other areas of civil-military relations remain to be discussed: the extent to which the army was rewarded in terms of armament and equipment purchases by the state, and the role the officer corps played in "nominating" or selecting candidates from their profession for top state posts which were traditionally reserved for the military—the presidency of the Republic and the military ministries (defense, army, navy, and air force).[30]

There is not space here to discuss post-1961 developments in armament and, indeed, these events are better known. It is worthwhile, however, to analyze a specific case of rearmament from the 1930s. In 1926 both the army and navy commands were anxious to employ state funds for the long-overdue purchase of new equipment. The army's equipment was obsolete and most of it was originally second-hand equipment granted to Portugal by the Allies in 1919. The navy's situation was even worse. By 1928 Portugal was bankrupt; a contemporary technocrat, Dr. Salazar, was given financial control. Salazar had a choice of options. He could delay indefinitely the rearmament programs for both services but then incur more unpopularity. Or he could rearm one service, or both. No decision had been made when the regime was shaken by the 1931 oppositionist insurgency in the Madeira Islands. A timely naval expedition from Lisbon, commanded by the minister for the navy himself, turned the tide and, in effect, saved the regime from a strong threat. A grateful regime thereupon decided to use funds from a foreign loan, beginning in 1932, to re-equip the navy with British-made warships.[31] The army would have to wait for its new equipment.

Army command reaction to this decision was hostile, and certain groups of junior officers in Lisbon plotted the overthrow of Salazar and his replacement by a prime minister to be approved by President (Gen.) Oscar Carmona, who would be more sympathetic to the army's perceived need for new armament.[32] Salazar effectively squashed the budding plot by delivering a threat of resignation in person to General Carmona. The president then reiterated his personal support for Salazar and in 1934 gave him authorization to replace an independent minister of war, one in fact hostile to Salazar.[33]

The army thus took second place to the navy in getting new equipment. But there were some positive decisions made in order to mollify officers. In May 1934 the government authorized the dispatch of a Portuguese military mission of four senior officers to England in order to study methods of military education.[34] Three years later authorization came for the rearmament of the army by means of purchases of largely British equipment.[35] In this way, the New State leadership balanced pressures from contending rivals for rewards in the system (see Table 6-2). Nevertheless, after 1929 the New State severely reduced the military budget and increased it only when necessary—in 1940–1943, when there appeared to be a German threat to the Azores, and after 1961 with the African wars. Even after the African wars drained over 40 percent of the annual budget, Caetano's New State reduced the metropolitan contributions to the military budget. The "Overseas Provinces" budgets were manipulated so as to have the African territories pay ever larger portions of the costs of the war.[36]

The officer corps' role in selecting high officials (president of the Republic) and the military ministers is an important topic which remains poorly researched. Certainly, it was Gen. Oscar Carmona who helped to select Salazar as prime minister and to maintain him in office. Throughout the 1930s, when more than one challenge from military circles assailed Salazar, Carmona stood by him. However, there is evidence that, as Carmona aged and became less aware of and not in command of his prerogatives, he grew to dislike Salazar and may have considered dismissing him, a power he had under the 1933 Constitution.[37]

There is some evidence that in 1945–1947 Carmona discussed with some oppositionists the idea of a "poll" of leading officers

TABLE 6–2

Armed Forces Defense Budgets, 1913–1974

Year	% of Revenue Spent on Armed Forces	
1913	13.1%	*(army only; naval expenses not included)*
1917	30.0	*(approximately)*
1926	40.0	*(approximately)*
1928/29	23.42	
1938	22.4	
1961	36.5	
1962	38.5	
1963	37.3	
1964	38.3	
1965	40.9	
1966	41.3	
1967	41.9	
1968	42.4	
1969	40.7	
1970	38.9	
1971	36.5	
1972	33.4	
1973	30.0	
1974	27.6	
1975	?	

Sources: For figures for budget in years 1913–1926, see Wheeler, *Republican Portugal*, chaps. 10, 13; for 1928/29, see Figueiredo, *Portugal*, p. 63; for 1938, 1961–1974, see sources cited in article by Schmitter, "Liberation by Golpe," *Armed Forces and Society* 2, no. 1 (Fall 1975): 17. It is difficult to obtain reliable evidence on this subject, but for speculation on possible moves to reduce budgeted military expenses after the 1974 coup, see the Portuguese press, e.g., the Lisbon press during the week of January 7–15 when it was suggested that the MFA and the provisional government promised a 40 percent reduction in the spending on the armed forces in 1975.

on the issue of retaining or dismissing Salazar. Dr. José Magalhães Godinho, head of the committee which drafted the 1974 Electoral Law under the postcoup regime, recalls an interview with Carmona in 1945 where the question of dismissing Salazar was discussed. As a young, democratic oppositionist, this lawyer-to-be urged the president to fire Salazar; to which the ageing Carmona replied, so this version goes, that this could happen but only if leading armed forces officers organized a *junta* and demanded this action.[38] There is also evidence from the affair known as "National Liberation Board," 1946–1947. A group of officers plotted the proclamation of a Junta da Libertação Nacional after the abortive 1946 Mealhada coup attempt (see Appendix). The officers planned the dismissal of Salazar, repeal of the 1933 Constitution, and abolition of the PIDE and other paramilitary, New State organizations. Some generals were in on the plot, but the secret police were made aware of the plot through an informer. The coup never reached the streets, since arrests were made, while Salazar remained safely ensconced in a loyal army unit barracks in Lisbon. There followed the 1947 government note reiterating the applicability of the May 13, 1945, law ending officers' immunity to arrest by the PIDE.[39]

After Carmona died in office (1951), Salazar could manipulate a personal choice of successor. The officer corps did play a role in indicating individuals who might be appropriate for the military ministries. But after 1951, these officers had less influence. Gen. Craveiro Lopes, president of the Republic, 1951–1958, evidently was too independent for the tastes of Salazar and his circle and in 1958 he was replaced by the regime's man, the passive, accommodating, and compliant professional navy officer, Adm. Américo Tomás.[40]

In summary, the New State got the best of civil-military relations during the dictatorship. Primarily after 1933–1936 and the intensification of civilianization, the imposition of interlocking and multiple controls and co-option, and the increasing power of the secret police, the armed forces leadership became less independent. Even the generals, of whom there were relatively few for the size of the forces, could be manipulated, frightened, and corrupted. Some were even murdered. There is evidence of murder in the case of Gen. Marques Godinho in the 1940s[41] and, definitely, in the case of Gen. Humberto Delgado, the officer murdered by PIDE in 1965 on the Luso-Spanish frontier.[42]

Not a few officers bitterly resented many similar acts and incidents. One of the more expressive written protests is the book published by "ex-Lt." Fernando Queiroga, *Portugal Oprimido*. Discussing a similar reaction by officers a few years after the 1946 Mealhada abortive coup, a fellow officer, Lt. Col. Luis Calafate, wrote trenchantly of the feeling of ruined "honor":

Officers in the MMI (Movimento Militar Independente [precursor of the MFA]) . . . were . . . angry with the events which late-

ly had stained the uniform of the Portuguese soldier—the po-
lice-like functions of the regiments, in support of a regime of
One Party; the odious exhibitionism of combat cars in Lisbon
squares (to frighten the citizen who trusted the army to defend
him and who finally saw it [the Army] betray him] . . . there
was the affront to the President-elect Humberto Delgado, from
whom the general's decorations were stripped without any
trial and his uniform torn from him as if it were a mere piece
of cloth—not being able any longer to put up with the vicious
insults, they had decided to protest to the president of the
Republic and to submit their resignations.[43]

Factors Influencing Military Intervention in 1926 and 1974

In foregoing sections of this article, I suggested that in the political
sense there was not one Portuguese army or armed forces but, in
fact, many. Not only was the army officer corps not unified; it was
also factionalized. If sections of the body were "apolitical" there
were also a number of politicized factions, both monarchist and
republican. More to the point, these political groups can be divided
into three types for the sake of discussion: authoritarian (*situacio-
nistas*), nonauthoritarian (*opposicionistas*), and passive, apolitical,
or conformist (*barriguistas*). Whether under the First Republic, the
military dictatorship, or the New State, the majority of officers have
been largely indifferent to politics while small factions of officers
have struggled for position in order to get their views accepted or
their candidates for office "elected" by top leadership.

With this factionalization of the officer corps, the armed forces
reflected the broad political trends of society. Before 1945, a larger
group of activist officers was authoritarian. After 1945, and the tri-
umph of antifascist forces in Europe, more officers found themselves
in the ranks of the opposition. Thus, new grievances based on new
conditions arose.

In this final section of the article, there will be a tentative attempt to answer the question posed at the beginning: what are the
most vital factors which can be clearly identified in attempting
to understand the process which led to the active intervention of
the armed forces in the government and politics of Portugal? One
way of approaching the problem is to outline the similarities between the grievances of the officer corps in 1926 and in 1974.

Initially, we may identify what I would describe as a major factor, or "master grievance," of the officer corps: professional discontent based upon the belief that the "honor of the army," or of the armed forces, as an institution had been severely compromised by its role as a defender of the now-discredited regime and as a collaborator in a major effort which failed or was about to fail. The master grievance in both the 1926 and 1974 cases is apolitical, professional in nature. The 1926 "Lieutenants" desired to end the militia program and deeply resented the effects of the 1921 militia commission law. By the same token and in oddly similar circumstances, the 1974 "Captains" movement began to organize around a consensus concerning a specific professional grievance: Decree-Law 353/73 of July 13, 1973, designed to ease the shortage of trained officers, became a cause célèbre among junior officers and elicited a series of written and verbal protests.[44] The law provided new measures for encouraging militia officers with little time in rank to assume commissions in the regular cadre. In fact, the first "Manifesto" of the "Captains" addressed this issue as a grievance, and it aroused immediate support from a variety of officers with varying political views.

The master grievance, therefore, naturally provided plotting officers with a clear rallying point of agreement, one which could gain the sympathy of both conservatives and liberals. What began, then, as a professional grievance could develop into something more. Traditionally, the next discussion points in coup plots which came out of initial discussions were "minimum" program,[45] a *chefe* to head the movement,[46] and a plan of operations to oust the regime in power.[47]

In outline form, then, here is a fundamental exposition of a comparison of factors impelling the officer corps to intervene directly in the governance of the state.

1926	1974
1. *Professional Grievances*	
1921 militia law	1973 militia law
Low pay	Low pay
Bad duty	Bad duty
"Honor" of individual and armed forces at stake	"Honor" of armed forces at stake
Discontent with militia system in general	Shame in wearing uniform in streets of Lisbon

Unprofessional officers, "dead wood"	Corruption of officer corps through collaboration with New State, overseas and at home
Pay increases too "democratic"	
Promotions too "political"	Inadequate facilities in Africa
	Promotions too "political"

2. *Economic Grievances*

Purchase power of pay cut by half 1915–1926	Severe inflation (30%, 1973–1974)
Severe inflation	Severe price rises
State seen as corrupt and incompetent	Business and industrial elites better off than armed forces officers
Price rise extreme	

3. *General* Situação *in Politics*

Repressiveness, oppressiveness of state	Secret police power over individual and groups (PIDE/DGS)
Power of PIDE's predecessors, core state police of 1926	New State under Caetano not going to liberalize significantly
Politicians viewed as corrupt, venal, incompetent, and antimilitary	New State losing its grip at home and in Africa
Army blamed in World War I defeats and disgraces in Flanders and Africa	African wars cannot be won, only prolonged
Politicians "responsible" for failure to lead or to equip forces adequately to meet German threats	Army in danger of being blamed for failure of state
	Heavy emigration to avoid low pay, draft, and service in Africa draining country
Fear of loss of African colonies to imperial rivals: Britain, Germany, Italy, and Spain	Skills needed in Portugal drained to wars in Africa

Some of the similarities between the 1926 and 1974 intervention causes can be observed in an analysis of the Appendix. There are striking resemblances on just two points: the World War I mass mobilization and increase in the size of the armed forces and the even larger effort to meet the challenges of the post-1961 African wars, and the outlay of budget for military purposes.

In conclusion, the Portuguese military's relationship with the dictatorship, which was Europe's longest surviving authoritarian system, was both complex and troubled. Only briefly, during the years 1926–1928, did the army make the major decisions in government; by 1928 it was apparent that the so-called National Revolution was in grave danger. Leading officers were neither allowed to nor capable of solving the key financial problems, and public distrust of military rule had burgeoned. If the military's record in governance was poor in the 1920s, it was at best "mixed" in the period 1974–1976. In late February 1976 the army leadership, symbolized by President of the Republic (Gen.) Francisco Costa Gomes, signed a pact with the civilians to hand over all but advisory and consultative powers after 1976 parliamentary and presidential elections.[48]

The Portuguese military experience exhibited *continuidade* in yet one more respect. The "Draft Plan for Restructuring the Armed Forces" in 1976 was strangely similar to army reform laws in the late nineteenth century and to the Army Reform Law of 1911. This plan called for a return to the barracks and a nonpartisan, nonpolitical role for the armed forces. For the army, however, there would be an additional function besides those of defense and internal security: "development of the territory," in effect, "nation building." A small, volunteer "Intervention Force" of professional regulars would train a revolving "Territorial Force" of draft conscripts who would serve from fifteen to eighteen months.[49]

At best the record of the military as rulers has been mixed. As many African armed forces learned to their dismay, it is one thing to overthrow a regime and take power but quite another to govern and rule effectively.[50] In Portugal, in two distinct cycles at different times in history, the armed forces have ruled briefly and then withdrawn from power, finding the burdens of ruling too great.

The New State managed to manipulate the armed forces while at the same time producing endless streams of promilitary rhetorical propaganda. In 1962 Salazar was quoted as stating that the army was "the last bulwark which in the most serious crises defends the destiny and conscience of the nation."[51] The New State institutionalized its controls over the armed forces, yet it never succeeded in working out a mutually satisfactory set of civil-military relations. The danger of the army turning on the regime was always present, a *siege* mentality always latent. Once even the New State's paramilitary defenders went "neutral," the regime's end was near. There is a possibility that the regime's final defenders believed their own propaganda. As the ill-fated Fifth Regiment of Caldas da Rainha began its "unauthorized military parade" (the government's official explanatory term),[52] a new era in Portugal began.

Appendix

PERMANENT CONSPIRACY

Military Coup d'État Attempts against the Portuguese Dictatorship, 1926–1974

Date	Principal Locations	Military Units Involved	Civil-Military Organization Supporting Attempt	Casualties	Results
February 3–9, 1927	Oporto, Lisbon, Amarante, and Penafiel (Minho)	Several units in Oporto and Lisbon	PRP; PCP; Republican opposition	300 dead; 1,000 wounded	Brief civil war; rebels lose; widespread arrests
August 15, 1927	Lisbon	?	?	?	Arrests; groups exiled
July 20–21, 1928	Lisbon, Setúbal, and Castelo Branco	Caçadores 7	Integralists wing under Filomeno da Câmara	?	Arrests; collapse of rebels
March 1930	Luanda, Angola	One regiment of infantry	Radical wing of integralists	1 dead; several wounded	Collapse of revolt; arrests and dismissal of High Commander, Filomena da Câmara
April 4–May 2, 1931	Madeira Islands, Azores, Portuguese Guinea, Lisbon	Local garrison units; junior officers in Madeira and Azores	Republican opposition led by General Adalberto de Sousa Dias	Madeira Islands: 27 dead; 100 wounded	Collapse of revolt; arrests; exile of rebels to African colonies

Date (duration)	Location	Participants	Opposition	Casualties	Outcome
August 26, 1931 (duration 9 hours)	Lisbon and Alverca airfield; Almada (bombardment)	Attacks on barracks of 1st Mach. Gun 3rd Art. Regts.	Republican opposition in Paris; Spain unit under Lt. Col. Fernando Machado	5 dead; 300 wounded	Surrender of rebel unit; arrests of rebels; over 500 arrests of suspects
1934, plotting	Lisbon garrison	Junior officers of major units	Attempt to have Salazar dismissed by Pres. Oscar Carmona	Several deflated egos	Plot squashed as Pres. Oscar Carmona fires minister of war for intriguing with junior officers; Salazar triumphs
September 10, 1935	Penha da França; warship in Tagus River, Bartol. Dias	Mixed army detachment at Penha da França; crew of warships	National Syndicalists under Dr. Rolão Preto; dissident officers	?	Arrests of scores of Syndicalists; collapse of plot
January 13, 1934	Lisbon and Marinha Grande; other towns; bombings of military installations in Coimbra and Setúbal	Guarda Nacional Republicana at Marinha Grande	Portuguese workers and Communist Party (PCP); anarchosyndicalists; workers' groups	Several wounded	Collapse of general strike plan; dismissal of workers compromised in plot; arrest of PCP leaders; ranks depleted heavily
September 9, 1936	Ships in Tagus harbor	Sailors in crews of two warships: Dão and Afonso de Albuquerque	?	Several wounded; 208 sailors arrested	Collapse of revolt and attempt to "hijack" vessels

Appendix—Continued

Date	Principal Locations	Military Units Involved	Civil-Military Organization Supporting Attempt	Casualties	Results
1945, plotting in association with October 1945 election	Lisbon and Oporto	Lisbon garrison units	Republican opposition in exile and in country MUNAF (and Gen. José Norton de Matos)	?	Coup attempt fails to reach streets
October 11, 1946	Oporto area and south to Mealhada	Caçadores 6 Regt., Oporto junior officers and militia officers led by Lt. Fernando Queiroga	Republican opposition	?	Rebels surrender at Mealhada; failure and arrests
April 10, 1947, plot collapses	Lisbon area	Junior officers and two former commanders of Azores, Gens. Marques Godinho and Ramires; Adm. José Mendes Cabeçadas, leader of 1926 coup	?	?	Failure and arrests

Date	Location	Units	Organizations/Leaders	Casualties	Outcome
May–June 1958 and July 17, 1958, plots in association with Presidential elections of 1958	Lisbon and Oporto	Lisbon units and four officers; letter by Gen. Humberto Delgado urging they overthrow Salazar	Movimento da Unidade Democrática (MUD), Movimento Nacional Independente (MNI); Gen. Humberto Delgado and officers (juniors mainly); Pres. Francisco Craveiro Lopes	None	Failure to reach streets
March 11–12, 1959	Lisbon area	1st Mach. Gun Regt.; 2nd Lancers; 1st Inf.; and 2nd Cav. Reg.	Civilian oppositions (including Catholics) and Movimento Militar Independente (MMI); Capt. José Almeida Santos; Capt. Vasco Gonçalves	Arrests; jailings	Plot fails, but Minister of War Fernando Santos Costa replaced by republican Gen. Júlio Botelho Moniz
January 22–February 3, 1961, hijacking	High seas between Venezuela and Brazil, Portuguese ocean liner, *Santa Maria*	None; attempt to win over crew of *Santa Maria* during hijacking	Capt. Henrique Galvão, and Gen. Humberto Delgado; Spanish revolutionaries (DRIL group)	One crewman dead; several wounded	Ship interned in Brazil; rebels' asylum failure

Appendix—Continued

Date	Principal Locations	Military Units Involved	Civil-Military Organization Supporting Attempt	Casualties	Results
March 1961	Lisbon area	Lisbon garrison main (junior officers) units	Leading officers and some junior officers attempt to pressure Pres. Américo Tómas to dismiss Salazar	None	Failure; dismissal of plot leaders, including Gen. João Botelho Moniz, Chief of Staff
January 1, 1962	Beja	3rd Inf. Regt. junior officers attempt to take Beja garrison; military leader, Capt. João Varela Gomes	Gen. Humberto Delgado's exiled opposition group of junior officers in central-south; Catholic liberals under Manuel Serra	3 dead; 4 wounded (including Lt. Col. Jaime Filipe de Fonseca, Under-Secretary for Army)	Surrender of rebels; collapse of plot; 78 persons arrested; prison sentences for 65; 10-year-sentence for Manuel Serra, 6 years for Capt. João Varela Gomes
February 1965 plot for coup, PIDE murder of General Delgado at Spanish border	Alentejo and Lisbon areas	None directly	Gen. Humberto Delgado's exiled opposition group from Algiers	3 dead (1 PIDE agent, Gen. Delgado, and Brazilian personal secretary)	Collapse of plot and weakening of exile organization

1970–1973	Colony of Portuguese Guinea (Bissau)	Portuguese garrison; junior officers	None; discontented junior officers led by Capt. Otelo Saraiva de Carvalho	None	Plots, no definite plans
March 16, 1974	Caldas da Rainha	Inf. Reg. no. 5 attempts to begin coup; marches on Lisbon; turned back	Movimento das Forças Armadas (MFA), following plots and conspiracies beginning September 1, 1973	None	Arrests of over 150 soldiers; surrender of unit
April 24–25, 1974	Lisbon and all areas	All major units under Maj. Otelo Saraiva de Carvalho; Maj. Vasco Gonçalves, committee	Junior officers in MFA, principally (ca. 200 officers)	5 dead; 15 wounded	Success; overthrow of New State

Notes

1. For the purposes of discussion, I am referring to the "models" introduced by Morris Janowitz, in *The Military in the Political Development of New Nations: An Essay in Comparative Analysis* (Chicago: University of Chicago Press, 1964), pp. 2–5.

2. See articles critical of this system in the professional military journal *Revista Militar* (1922–1927) and in Jorge Botelho Moniz, *O 18 de Abril* (Lisbon, 1925), pp. 53–55, 103ff; also David Magno, another junior officer of that generation, *A Situação Portuguesa* (Lisbon, 1926). For an outline of the 1911 army reform, see articles in *Revista Militar* (1911–1913).

3. On the rise of republicanism and Carbonária activity, see Jacinto Baptista, *O Cinco de Octubre* (Lisbon, 1965), and my article, "The Portuguese Revolution of 1910," *Journal of Modern History* 44, no. 2 (June 1972): 172–194.

4. While the "Founder of the Republic," Naval Commissary (Warrant Officer) Machado Santos, was an officer in the regular cadre, only a handful of others followed him initially and the republican forces consisted mainly of some enlisted men, some N.C.O.'s, sailors, civilian riflemen, and bomb-carrying teenagers. Most of the casualties during the fighting of October 3–5, 1910, were in fact civilian, and few officers risked their lives on one side or the other.

5. See Jesús Pabón, *A Revolução Portuguesa* (Lisbon, 1961), p. 48; see also the account of the last premier under the Monarchy, Teixeira de Sousa, *Para a História da Revolução*, 2 vols. 2: 355–358, 449–450.

6. See criticism found in Melo e Athayde, "O Pais e o exército no actual momento," *Revista Militar* (May 1919), pp. 288–295; F. Cunha Leal, *As Minhas Memórias*, 3 vols. (Lisbon, 1966–1968), 2: 363–365, 380. Article by Major A. Branquinho in *Revista Militar*, no. 4 (April 1922), p. 217; *O Século*, May 4, 1911; *A Noite*, April 17, 1926.

7. See also some professional military criticism reflected in the book by J. C. Vasconcelos, *O Movimento Nacional de 18 de Abril* (Oporto, 1925); also Anselmo Vieira, *A Crise Nacional* (Lisbon, 1926).

8. See my *Republican Portugal: A Political History, 1910–1926* (Madison: University of Wisconsin Press, 1978), chap. 10.

9. Botelho Moniz, *O 18 de Abril*, p. 33.

10. See my manuscript, "Politics in the First Portuguese Republic," chap. 12, "The Twenty-eighth of May."

11. See the interesting French account of 1926–1927, George Guyomard, *La Dictature Militaire au Portugal* (Paris: Les Presses Universitaires de France, 1927), pp. 23, 106–107.

12. Jorge Campinos, *A Ditadura Militar, 1926/1933* (Lisbon: Don Quixote, 1975), pp. 53–54. See Portuguese daily press, May 28–June 17, 1926, e.g., *O Século* and *Diário de Notícias*.

13. Janowitz, *The Military in the Political Development of New Nations*, pp. 2–5.

14. Guyomard, *La Dictature*, p. 23.

15. For material on the function of the secret police in the dictatorship after 1933, see Hermínio Martins, "Portugal," in *European Fascism*, ed.

S. Woolf (London: Vintage, 1969), pp. 312–328; António de Figueiredo, *Portugal: Fifty Years of Dictatorship* (New York: Holmes and Meier, 1976), pp. 105–158 ff; Mário Soares, *Le Portugal Bailloné* (Paris: Calmann-Levy, 1972). A recent sensationalist "dossier" by an anonymous writer contains some useful photostats of documents and photographs of prisons: "Reporter Sombra," *Dossier P.I.D.E.* (Lisbon, 1974); many similar accounts emerged after censorship was lifted in late April 1974.

16. Martins, "Portugal," pp. 307, 328.

17. See only a few accounts of some officers who experienced "administrative terror" in the 1940s and 1950s: Fernando Queiroga, *Portugal Oprimido* (Rio de Janeiro, 1958: repr. Lisbon: O Século, 1974); Humberto Delgado, *Memoirs of General Delgado* (London: Cassell, 1964); Henrique Galvão, *Santa Maria: My Crusade for Portugal* (New York: World, 1962); Captain Sarmento Pimentel, *Memórias* (Lisbon, 1973).

18. See the anthology of documents edited by A. H. de Oliveira Marques, *A Unidade da Oposição a Ditadura, 1928–1931*, História do Portugal Contemporâneo, Documentos, vol. 1 (Lisbon, 1973); and an expanded anthology with a larger focus, Oliveira Marques, *O General Sousa Dias e as Revoltas Contra a Ditadura, 1926–1931* (Lisbon, 1975).

19. A. H. de Oliveira Marques (ed. and comp.), *A Maçonária Portuguesa e o Estado Novo* (Lisbon, 1975), p. 52.

20. Campinos, *A Ditadura Militar*, p. 172.

21. Martins, "Portugal"; and Campinos, *A Ditadura Militar*, pp. 148–160.

22. A major thesis of Jorge Campinos' recent scholarly study, a translation from the French of his political science dissertation at Poitiers, is how little the New State depended on ideology as opposed to the "art of ruling" (*A Ditadura Militar*, pp. 163–170).

23. Martins, "Portugal," pp. 309–320.

24. Figueiredo, *Portugal*, pp. 118–119.

25. Ibid., p. 124.

26. "Cadets of Sidónio" were those young military cadets and officer-candidates who were followers of President (Major) Sidónio Pais (1917–1918). Though their hero was assassinated in 1918, many of his "Cadets" remained loyal to his memory and to his ideas, some of which were adopted in the New State regime.

27. General Júlio Botelho Moniz was dismissed by the New State government in April 1961, after becoming involved in a coup plot to have Salazar dismissed. See Figueiredo, *Portugal*, pp. 210–211; Mário Soares, *Portugal's Struggle for Liberty* (London, 1975 English translation by Mary Gawsworth of French 1972 ed.), pp. 128–130.

28. Queiroga, *Portugal Oprimido*, pp. 42–160; Delgado, *Memoirs*, and Galvão, *Santa Maria*, pp. 34–35. Galvão notes that Salazar's men could "mobilize" the armed forces at election time, as in the "threatening" episode of 1968, in order to "demonstrate" loyalty at a key moment. I well remember the public declaration made by the army commanders in Lisbon, widely publicized in the daily press, on the occasion of the National Assembly elections in early November 1961. By this statement just before the vote, and by the menacing attitude of troops lining the streets on polling day, the regime's point was clearly made. The troops seen at

the time appeared to be independently menacing, not "servile" as Galvão later described them.

29. Josué Da Silva, *Legião Portuguesa: Fôrça Repressiva do Fascismo* (Lisbon, 1975); Martins, "Portugal," pp. 327–328.

30. Queiroga, *Portugal Oprimido*, pp. 92–105. This account documents the penury cum corruption of certain high-ranking officers, such as one "General Ramires." When approached for a commitment to back a military coup in his sector, "Ramires" pleaded poverty and promised to work with Queiroga in the plot only if he received 1,500 contos (p. 105).

31. Public Record Office (PRO), London, F.O. 37119729 (Confidential), #14687, March 1, 1935, Amb. Russell to Sir John Simon, p. 2; see my *Republican Portugal*, chaps. 10, 13. See also PRO, F.I. 371/F, F. Lindley to A. Henderson, April 18, 1931, pp. 1–2; also, letter, previous day, April 17, 1931, and F. Lindley to A. Henderson, May 1, 1931. União Nacional, *28 de Maio: Comemoração em 1935* (Lisbon, 1935), pp. 117–160. Gen. Ferreira Martins, *História do Exército Portuguez* (Lisbon, 1945). Arquivo Histórico Militar, Lisbon, 1 Div., Sec. 35, Box 1264, Pasta 2, "Reorganization do Exército (1919)," telegrams, letters doc. no. 2 (December 13, 1918), Chief of Staff of Army to Chief of Dept. of Office of Minister of War, etc.

32. PRO, F.O. 371/18589 (Confidential), #14467; *Portugal: Annual Report, 1933*, Sir Claud Russell to Sir John Simon, February 1, 1934, pp. 40–43.

33. Assis Gonçalves, *Intimidades de Salazar: O Homen e a sua Epoca*, rev. ed. (Lisbon, 1972), pp. 189–197.

34. PRO, F.O. 371/19729, *Portugal: Annual Report, 1934*, Sir Claud Russell to Sir John Simon, March 1, 1935, p. 23.

35. Martins, *História do Exército*.

36. Note the decrease in the percentage of the annual budget devoted to war costs after 1968/69, in chart cited in Philippe C. Schmitter, "Liberation by Golpe," *Armed Forces and Society* 2, no. 1 (Fall 1975): 17. See United Nations, General Assembly, "Report of the Special Committee on the Situation with Regard to the Implementation of the Declaration on the Granting of Independence to Colonial Countries and Peoples" (A9023/ Add. 3*, September 19, 1973, Angola section), pp. 60–96, etc.

37. Oliveira Marques, *History of Portugal*, 2 vols. (New York: Columbia University Press, 1972), 2: 211–219.

38. Figueiredo, *Portugal*, pp. 120–122; Soares, *Portugal's Struggle*, pp. 72–72. My information on a Carmona suggestion for an officers' informal "vote," in effect, derives from personal conversation-interviews with Dr. José Magalhães Godinho, lawyer-oppositionist and Socialist Party member, whose political activity went back to the mid-1940s, when he interviewed Carmona himself (conversations, Lisbon, October 1972; March 1973).

39. Figueiredo, *Portugal*; Peter Fryer and Patricia McGowen Pinheiro, *Le Portugal de Salazar* (Paris: Ruedo Ibérico,1963), p. 100 (French ed. of *Oldest Ally*).

40. Soares, *Portugal's Struggle*, p. 106.

41. Figueiredo, *Portugal*, p. 123; Soares, *Portugal's Struggle*, pp. 53, 72.

42. Queiroga, *Portugal Oprimido*; Lt. Col. Luis Calafate, *Liberdade tem um Preço* (Lisbon, 1975), pp. 28–29.

43. Calafate, *Liberdade*.

44. See memoirs of ex-Premier Marcello Caetano, *Depoimento* (Rio de Janeiro, 1974), pp. 184–186.

45. See Queiroga's memoir, *Portugal Oprimido*, and the volumes by Delgado, Galvão, Soares, and Calafate cited above. The problem of selecting a *chefe* for the 25th of April 1974 movement is discussed in the useful, comprehensive journalistic account by Avelino Rodrigues, Césario Borga, and Mário Cardoso, *O Movimento dos Capitães e o 25 de Abril: 229 Dias para Derrubar o Fascismo*, 3d ed. (Lisbon, 1975), pp. 255–338.

46. See also the brief account, in the form of an interview, Otelo Saraiva de Carvalho, *Cinco Meses Mudaram Portugal* (Lisbon, 1975).

47. See also Lt. Col. Luis Ataide Banazol, *A Origem do Movimento das Fôrças Armadas* (Lisbon, 1974).

48. "New Lisbon Pact to Bring an End to Military Rule," *New York Times*, February 27, 1976, p. 1.

49. *Expresso* (Lisbon), March 6, 1976.

50. William Gutteridge, *Military Regimes in Africa* (London: Methuen, 1975).

51. Quote from Salazar speech, May 28, 1962, cited in vol. 6 (1959–1966), *Discursos e Notas Políticas* (Coimbra, 1967), p. 220.

52. Reported in international press as official statement issued by Lisbon to "explain" Caldas da Rainha incident, March 16, 1974; see *New York Times*, March 17, 18, 1974.

7. The Military in Politics:
The Politicization of the Portuguese
Armed Forces

LAWRENCE S. GRAHAM

During the period extending from January 1974 through January 1976, the armed forces played a crucial role in the political transformations sweeping through Portugal and her former African colonies. Abandoning their posture as supporters of the old regime, a majority of the officer corps had by the end of 1973 opted for the overthrow of the incumbent government of Marcello Caetano. But, as individual officers became involved in the events which resulted in the dissolution of the old order, opinions came to diverge sharply when these men had to face questions regarding the country's political future. For a brief period after the coup d'état on April 25, 1974, military conservatives dominated the scene. Then, with increasing rapidity the balance of power within the officer corps shifted away from those identified with conservative postures to those with revolutionary ones. From late 1974 until the end of 1975 almost everyone commenting on events in Portugal spoke of the country in revolutionary terms and it seemed to many observers as though the new commanders of the Portuguese military establishment would be successful in transforming the armed forces into an agent of revolution. Then, as suddenly as the left-oriented Armed Forces Movement (the MFA) had emerged as a major political force identified with the goals of fundamental social, political, and economic change, the Movement dissolved and moderate officers gained control. Consequently, by early 1976 talk in Portugal of revolution was replaced by concern with the revival of right political forces, and the military, reversing its earlier stance as revolutionary agent, emerged as an advocate of rule by a constitutionally elected government in accord with majority sentiment and the formation of a middle-of-the-road civilian regime.

This particular sequence of events and the shifting political postures adopted by those in command of the country's armed forces make the Portuguese case an extremely interesting one to examine, not only from the vantage point of those elements of the unique which belong peculiarly to Portugal—a relatively little known and little studied European country before April 1974—but also from a wider comparative perspective. What is it specifically that took place within the military institution during this period of rapid change? Can we learn anything from recent Portuguese experience that is relevant to the general study of civil-military relations?

Before delving into the particulars of the Portuguese case, it would be helpful to review briefly what has taken place more generally in the study of the military. Over the last three decades, within comparative politics and more especially in writing on the Third World, numerous scholars have devoted attention to the involvement of the military in politics. In this literature, which spans political experience in Asia, Africa, the Middle East, and Latin America, a perennial theme has been concern with militarism. Although the term itself has been used somewhat unsystematically to refer to a variety of military actions, what is of note here are those instances in which the military has moved actively into politics, overthrown an incumbent civilian government, and exercised a dominant voice in the formation of the successor regime.

In one world region, Latin America, interest in military governance and its identification with new forms of authoritarianism reached a new high in the late 1960s. In the wake of the collapse of sundry civilian regimes, ranging from moderate, somewhat conservative governments (such as the Fernando Belaúnde Terry regime in Peru) to Salvador Allende's Chile (where the governing coalition sought to bring about radical changes within the polity), there were by the mid-1970s only two civilian governments left in South America: those of Colombia and Venezuela. Prior to this, the literature on the causes of Latin American militarism had linked military coups and dictatorships with the phenomenon of the caudillo and personalism in the armed forces and had advocated the development of professional standards patterned after U.S. experience to mitigate these factors.[1] Reacting to these events and re-examining the premises underlying earlier writing on the military in politics, more recent scholars have demonstrated conclusively how the new professionalism, instead of promoting apolitical action, has actually engendered new forms of military participation in politics and has become synonymous with the revival of authoritarian rule.[2] Prototypical of these developments and the new authoritarianism are the Brazilian case since 1964 and the Peruvian since 1968.

In the comparative analysis of the military in politics, recent Portuguese experience has the potential of contributing valuable new insights into the nature of civil-military relations under conditions of rapid change. There the circumstances which led the military to overthrow an incumbent regime and the outcome of military attempts to reshape civil society in the aftermath have led not to a new authoritarianism but to the country's first real attempt to make party government meaningful. While the South American cases provide insight into the conditions leading from the breakdown of government by political parties to authoritarian governance, the Portuguese case can be cited as an example where the military has served as a primary agent in the destruction of dictatorship and as a catalyst for revolutionary change.

Despite this potential, the emphasis in writing on Portugal, whether popular or academic, has focused on the idiosyncratic. Numerous writers have called attention to the old regime's outdated commitment to the maintenance of a colonial empire (despite the costs of a three-front war in such divergent regions as Guinea-Bissau in equatorial Africa, Mozambique in East Africa, and Angola on the Atlantic side of the continent). Still others have stressed the radicalization of the younger officers as a consequence of fighting a losing battle with guerrilla forces, the impact of this experience on their political outlook, and their determination to liberate mainland Portugal by eradicating all vestiges of colonialism and removing from power previously dominant economic and political elites.[3] Although any empirical case that one chooses to examine will always contain elements of the unique, the time has come to look at Portuguese experience in broader comparative perspective and to inquire as to its relevance to the development of greater understanding of the military in politics in contemporary society.

In comparative terms, three arguments can be advanced from the Portuguese case. First, there is the need to analyze national military forces from an organizational vantage point, so that more attention will be given to the development of concepts and methods focusing on military bureaucracy and to how internal military affairs interact with and influence external political events. Equally important is the utility of adapting group analysis as it has evolved in the study of U.S. politics and in general comparative work to the identification of military factions. Finally, it is essential that analysts seek to develop more fully diachronic perspectives (i.e., a temporal, or sequential, view of politics) in the evaluation of civil-military relations.

Of these three projections from Portuguese experience, the most difficult to develop on the basis of existing data concerns the structure of the Portuguese military and how its organizational evolution since World War II and tensions within a complex set of military organizations (here termed "the military institution") influenced political outcomes. Yet, because in contemporary society group behavior is shaped increasingly by the impact of such large-scale formal organizations as mass-based political parties, governmental bureaucracies, the institutional church, modern military establishments, and business corporations, our analysis of Portugal must begin here before we can proceed with an examination of military factions and the sequence of events which were responsible for rapid shifts in the posture of the military over a relatively short period of time.

The first point to establish regarding military bureaucracy in Portugal is its ties with old-regime institutions and personalities. The long-lived authoritarian government, created by António Salazar in the 1930s and continued under the leadership of Marcello Caetano, shaped the outlook of several generations of Portuguese leaders, civilian and military, and limited decisively their recourse to political action. What is sometimes forgotten today is that, although the Portuguese military served as the catalyst for ending repressive rule in 1974, decades earlier it played an equally important role in bringing an end to parliamentarian government and in laying the foundations for that very same authoritarian state it was later to overthrow. The intervention of the military in politics in 1926 was no less decisive than it was to be later in 1974 in the eradication of the previous political order. In both instances the decision to intervene cannot be isolated from the failure of the military, once having seized power, to form a viable government. In the late twenties catastrophic economic conditions and the failure of the military to deal with them successfully were resolved by calling upon Salazar to assume the portfolio of finance and later by the military's withdrawal from power, confirming Salazar as prime minister and retaining control only of the presidency. In the mid-seventies, having destroyed the old regime and liquidated the overseas empire, the military proved just as incapable of constituting an alternative regime and coping with abysmal economic conditions left in the aftermath. Once again, demonstrating its incapacity to govern with or without the support of civilians, the military has turned effective power over to a new generation of political leaders, retaining control once again only of the presidency. Yet, in all this, there is one obvious and notable difference: military intervention in the twenties resulted in the formation of an authoritarian regime based on limited participation; in the mid-seventies, after national trauma and the threat of revolution, it led to the formation of a popularly elected regime and made possible the first real mass mobilization in Portuguese history.

On the eve of the coup, the organization and internal hierarchy of the Portuguese military institution reflected more the norms and values of late nineteenth- and early twentieth-century Europe than it did those of a modern, post-World War II fighting force. The old army was essentially a class-based organization in which the senior officers were primarily men of upper-class background, while the average enlisted man came from the peasantry or the country's small urban working class. Its symbols of authority, the formal military dress used, the military education provided, the elaborate system of rewards supplied through membership in military societies and decorations, the easy entrée into top business and governmental circles—all served to reinforce social distance within the armed forces between officers and enlisted men. Even though Portugal's participation in the North Atlantic Treaty Organization and the establishment of Comiberlant (the South Atlantic Naval Command) in Alges outside Lisbon exposed the Portuguese military to new professional standards, provided advanced staff training outside Portugal, and made modern military equipment more accessible, it was prolonged guerrilla warfare in Portuguese Africa which wrought the real internal changes within the country's armed forces.

The old class structure of the armed forces, the decline of the attractiveness of military careers for youth with elite status, and the obligation to serve in Africa had the effect of creating a serious leadership vacuum within the middle ranks of the officer corps. Not only did young men find far more attractive jobs and opportunities within mainland Portugal in business and banking as a consequence of economic expansion after 1968, but also the prospects of longer and longer African sojourns, coupled with exposure to guerrilla warfare in remote areas and less pay, reduced the appeal of military careers. For the most part, the senior military—generals, commanders, and admirals now in their sixties and seventies—preferred their comfortable lives on the mainland where, in addition to the respect they commanded because of age and seniority, they enjoyed privileged access to government and business circles. Those in the senior military who did respond to the challenge presented by guerrilla warfare—such men as Kaúlza de Arriaga, António de Spínola, and the Silvério Marques brothers—recognized the need to modernize the nation's armed forces as rapidly as possible. They were dismayed by the conditions with which they had to contend: the shortage of competent junior officers, complacency within the New State bureaucratic establishment, the dearth of military equipment, inadequate training and preparation, and the extensiveness of the campaigns they were obliged to conduct in three very different areas of Africa.

Given the incapacity of those in command of the New State regime to alter its bases of power and the drain on public resources presented by commitment to retaining all Portuguese territory in Africa, the pressure on the military became unbearable. To defend adequately core population and economic centers in Portuguese Africa over the long haul required reorganization and conversion of Portugal's armed forces into highly mobile tactical units and willingness on the part of governmental authorities to permit the military to abandon defense of peripheral zones.

As Philippe C. Schmitter has demonstrated in his analysis of the 1974 coup, there is nothing in data presently available which demonstrates that economic conditions in metropolitan Portugal made revolution inevitable. The causes were essentially political and involved primarily the military. Although the regime had to face large military expenditures, declining productivity in metropolitan agriculture, and widening trade imbalances within the empire, the GNP continued to grow and general economic prospects were quite favorable.[4]

Also notable is the fact that, while the military budget continued to increase in absolute terms, it began to decline percentally after 1969 as the costs of fighting a major portion of the African wars were shifted increasingly to the provincial budgets of Angola and Mozambique (see Fig. 7-1). The strains on the regime which ultimately led to its destruction, thus, were twofold: the refusal of the far right (the *ultras*) to permit Caetano to abandon Guinea (where costs had far exceeded any benefit to be derived by the metropole in holding on to the territory) and the pressure placed on the military establishment as it became apparent that it would have to continue fighting guerrilla movements on three fronts indefinitely.[5]

Within the armed forces the pressure to meet those demands fell most heavily on the junior officers, among which there was a shortage of qualified personnel. One dimension of this problem is to

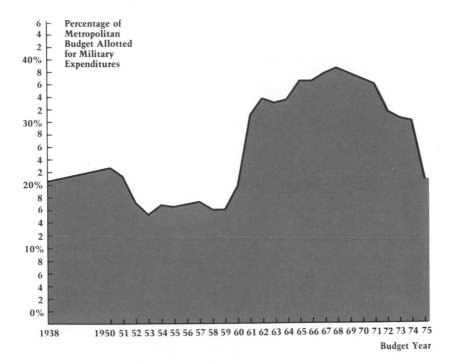

Figure 7-1. The military budget as a percentage of Portugal's total metropolitan budget (*Anuário Estatístico*, various years).

be captured by examining the number of students enrolled in the military academies: the Academia Militar and the Escola Naval. Taking 1945 as a base line, both schools registered overall a growth in enrollments until the mid-1960s, as did higher education generally in Portugal (see Table 7-1 and Fig. 7-2). The initial response to the outbreak of guerrilla war in Portuguese Africa in 1961 took the form of patriotic gestures throughout the civil and military establishment. Military school enrollments had been on the increase since the late 1950s and continued to rise after 1961, with peak enrollment being reached in the Naval School in 1964 and in the Military Academy between 1963 and 1965. Thereafter, while overall higher education enrollments continued to climb, both academies underwent a steady decline. Most notable was the experience of the Military Academy, where enrollments had dropped back to post–World War II levels by 1970. Combined with this were com-

TABLE 7–1
Military and Civilian Academic Enrollments, 1945–1973
(*Numerical Representation*)

	ACADEMIA MILITAR*		ESCOLA NAVAL		Total Higher Education
Year	Enrolled	Graduated	Enrolled	Graduated	Enrollments
1945	232	109	41	0	10,787
1946	237	86	58	25	11,893
1947	304	100	52	16	11,976
1948	257	151	55	15	11,959
1949	263	83	50	18	12,019
1950	302	70	53	21	12,771
1951	360	83	62	19	13,489
1952	454	116	68	16	14,070
1953	461	132	98	23	14,131
1954	456	307	108	46	14,563
1955	475	126	135	25	17,866
1956	416	115	104	50	18,626
1957	423	105	80	63	19,161
1958	433	221	49	22	19,880
1959	491	129	103	14	20,904
1960	— — — — — (No yearbook published) — — — — — —				
1961	548	121	177	14	23,877
1962	744	103	231	83	25,077
1963	842	93	206	0	26,924
1964	843	143	258	50	29,788
1965	851	146	247	126	31,575
1966	781	216	153	43	33,972
1967	575	267	194	40	35,933
1968	498	134	201	26	38,647
1969	475	77	173	42	41,969
1970	330	91	185	0	46,019
1971	285	95	174	35	49,461
1972	290	84	204	46	51,510
1973	264	64	210	22	53,999
1974	The year of the Revolution: education disrupted				

Source: *Anuário estatístico*, various years (Lisbon).
* The Academia Militar was earlier known as the Escola Militar.

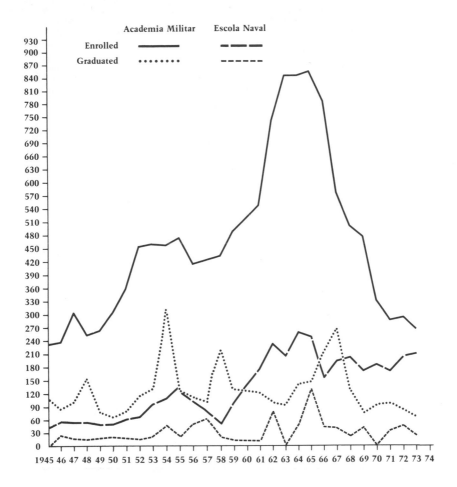

Figure 7-2. Military enrollments—graphical representation (*Anuário Estatístico*, various years).

plaints regarding deterioration in the quality of instruction at the Military Academy.

Thus, at the very time when the military alone was being called on to make the sacrifices necessary to continue the African campaigns indefinitely, the number of new officers entering the armed forces was decreasing. Because military service was required of all male Portuguese citizens, the draft ensured an adequate influx of new enlisted men; hence, the difficulty did not reside in total numbers. While the African wars were hardly popular among the citizenry, there was no choice for young men regardless of social-class origin: either one served overseas and returned to service when called back for additional tours of duty, or one emigrated. With more than adequate mass recruitment continuing, the absence of a sufficiently large number of younger officers at middle-range levels— those of captain and major—came to create a real bottleneck, since it was these men the senior officers depended on to provide leadership in the field and expected to lead small contingents of troops on forays against the guerrillas into the back country.

When the Caetano government took action to resolve this problem by opening the lower officer ranks to recruits with fighting experience but without formal officer training, it alienated the very military elements it most needed to continue in power. What became a revolution, sweeping away the old order in Portugal, thus began quite simply as an internal military affair in which two distinct currents of military opinion merged: the one made up of junior officers; the other, restricted to conservative senior officers disaffected with the policies of the Caetano government.

Of the two, the larger movement was the one organized by a relatively small number of dissident captains, the majority of whom had fought in the Guinea campaign at the time Spínola was military commander and had had contact with him. Referred to originally as the Captains' Movement, after the coup these men called themselves the Armed Forces Movement (the MFA) and began to seek ways of giving institutional expression to their ideas and goals.

As career officers who had fought for extended periods in Portugal's African campaigns, not only had these men become convinced of the futility of further efforts to stop the independence movement in Guinea-Bissau, but also they resented greatly the attempts of the Caetano government to blanket into the officer corps men from outside the career service in order to meet the demand for more lower-ranking officers in the field. Having received accelerated training and gained combat experience in Africa, many of these draftees (called *milicianos*), often of a different social-class background, aspired to the same privileges and compensation as the regular officers and, if permitted, would have entered the career service at a rank immediately below the captains (as first and second lieutenants).

The second group involved older men of more senior rank who really did not make up a cohesive faction. More appropriately a cluster of individuals, they wished to see an end to the Guinea campaign, as did the junior officers. But, whereas the captains came to identify their aspirations for change with abandonment of all overseas possessions and liberation of the mainland, the former wanted only to see Portugal cut its losses overseas. Above all, they favored consolidation of resources in such a way that Angola would remain under Portuguese sovereignty. While ambiguous over the disposal of Mozambique, they assumed that the status quo could be continued in the country's island dependencies for the foreseeable future. What was more important at the time the coup was being planned was the fact that, insofar as internal military affairs were concerned, these senior officers sympathized with and supported openly the captains' professional grievances.

By late 1973 both groups advocated replacement of the Caetano government. As planning advanced and they became aware of shared goals, both abandoned the more limited and moderate postures they had adopted in the beginning. Frustrated by the rigidity of the old regime in its military and civilian manifestations and antagonized by the class bias of the senior military, the junior officers were the most receptive to radical postures and ideas once the military took power and they realized how easy it had been to remove Caetano. Over the next year and a half their movement leftward was accelerated by the revolutionary forces they helped unleash but could scarcely contain.

Documents since published by the military and accounts prepared by observers of the MFA detail the evolution of these sentiments and views within the military institution during the ten months preceding the actual coup.[6] In this literature there are two distinct themes. One emphasizes a particular view of Portugal's African wars. In the absence of a sufficiently large enough pool of middle-range officers to staff overseas positions, career captains and majors were called on repeatedly to take African assignments. As they studied counterinsurgency materials, assessed field situations in the areas to which they were assigned, and led raids into the interior, they came to question the utility of these efforts. Aware of the defeats already suffered by the French in Indochina and Algeria and the Americans in Vietnam, they frequently contrasted the limited resources held by Portugal with the affluence and military superiority enjoyed by the United States and France. Through their NATO ties, they were struck by the fact that this power had been of little avail to those countries in dealing with similar movements of national liberation. Increasingly they saw their assignment less as one at the service of higher concepts of national interest, defined in terms of a multiracial society and a greater Portugal incorporating vast expanses of non-European territory, and more as personal sacrifices they were called to make on behalf of an authoritarian establishment which benefited in no way either them or the black majority under Portuguese rule overseas or impoverished rural and urban masses on the mainland. Once they began articulating these views among their comrades in arms, they soon discovered that sizable contingents in the air force and navy shared the same feelings. The majority of these men simply had had enough of the day-to-day fighting and sacrifices they were called to make in isolated military encampments.

The second set of grievances, while more specific in character and limited to the army, was equally important in the formation of a new and more radical military outlook on Portuguese affairs. On July 13, 1973, Caetano issued Decree-Law 353/73. Confronted with a decree granting full officer status to officials who had completed their required military service overseas and wished to remain in the army, the captains reacted strongly. As graduates of the Military Academy in Lisbon, they protested against what they perceived to be an attempt by civilian bureaucrats to admit into the officer corps men without proper training.

From the viewpoint of the Caetano government such action was necessary to fill vacancies overseas. By the early seventies the Military Academy was no longer able to provide a sufficient number of career officers to meet all of Portugal's commitments in Africa. Combining these grievances with earlier ones resulting from repeated, unsuccessful efforts to obtain more competitive and equitable salary scales, the captains appealed to Generals António de Spínola and Francisco Costa Gomes to intervene on their behalf. By the time the Caetano government withdrew this particular decree a little more than a month later, all parties to the dispute had become alienated.[7] The arbitrary fashion in which the Caetano government handled the affair, as well as the confusion ensuing when career officer status was granted to the *milicianos* and then rescinded, convinced all that there was absolutely no way to improve conditions within the military or to end fruitless military campaigns overseas without replacing the incumbent regime in its entirety.

Reform without Revolution: The Ascendancy of Spínola

Once the coup was over, a conglomeration of civilian political figures belonging to the center and the left entered the political arena and joined the ruling military coalition in what became a prolonged struggle for control of the centers of power within the Portuguese state. What had begun as a military movement expanded quickly into a complex political game in which the integrity of the military institution was to be called into question and right, center, and left forces vied for power.[8] The new government reflected these developments. From the outset it was little more than a loosely knit coalition of military and civilian groups opposed to the old regime, focused around two decision-making centers: the military *junta*, called the Junta of National Salvation, and the first provisional government, formed on May 15 under the premiership of Adelino de Palma Carlos. What was less obvious at the time but of great import for the future was the fact that this initial arrangement guaranteed a dominant role for the military and a secondary one for civilians in the struggle to create and consolidate a new political order. The military was not to withdraw effectively from power until eighteen months later, when the politics its officers sought to control had so politicized the armed forces as to threaten its institutional integrity.

Within the military *junta*, advocates of a negotiated solution to the African wars and of a continued Portuguese presence in Africa continued in uneasy alliance with opponents of the colonial system throughout the summer of 1974. While left-wing MFA officers never considered this arrangement to be anything other than an expedient one, a substantial number of commissioned and noncommissioned officers within the military institution, if not the majority, were not so certain as to what they desired. Because they were prepared for professional careers in the military and trained for apolitical roles in Salazar's New State, politics was alien to most of them and was, more often than not, a term identified in their minds with the factional infighting and governmental instability characteristic of the Old Republic. For them General Spínola was no mere figurehead. As newly appointed president of the Republic and symbolic leader of the coup, he represented for many the prospects of evolutionary rather than revolutionary change in dismantling the old regime and in moving Portugal from authoritarian to democratic governance.

To understand fully this dimension of the Portuguese revolution and the impact that politicization was to have on hitherto apolitical military officers, one must focus attention on internal military affairs, seek to understand the nature of the revolutionary myth that became identified with the MFA, and take into account rapidly shifting perspectives among military men in positions of command as they experimented with political rule.

The first military *junta* reflected the ambivalence of the officer corps regarding Portugal's future. Included in the new government were conservative generals, such as Spínola, who while opposed to the arbitrariness of the dictatorship favored the creation of a political democracy in which the interests of the propertied would be defended; centrists, such as Mário Firmino Miguel, who while linked to Spínola desired to see a fully representative democratic regime similar to others in Western Europe come into being; and radicals, such as Vasco dos Santos Gonçalves, who argued that meaningful change was impossible without the creation of conditions of social equality.

With the reactionary generals, the *ultras*, displaced from their command positions at the apex of the military institution, opinions began to diverge within the officer corps. By July, views had coalesced around two opposing perspectives: a centrist one which, while conservative in ideology, was no longer authoritarian and a radical one that stressed eradicating all structures and removing from power all individuals identified with the old regime. Because of the dominant role played by Spínola at the time in aligning center forces, those who favored limiting change to the granting of formal political rights and liberties became known as *spinolistas*. They advocated the elevation of Spínola to the status of national leader, the dismantling of the MFA, the return of the military to the barracks, and the inauguration of a civilian-dominated regime committed to political democracy. Avoiding identification with a single personality, radicals favored institutionalization of the MFA, adopted the slogan "MFA-Povo" to symbolize their alliance with the masses in promoting revolution throughout Portugal, and applied the label "fascist" to any and all tainted by ties with the previous regime.

Within the Junta of National Salvation centrists predominated. These included Generals António Sebastião de Spínola, Jaime Silvério Marques, Carlos Galvão de Melo, and Manuel Diogo Neto. Outside this group stood General Francisco Costa Gomes and Vice-Admirals José Batista Pinheiro de Azevedo and António Alva Rosa Coutinho, men identified with the MFA.

During these initial months Spínola enjoyed wide-scale popularity within and outside the military institution. Such a personality cult constituted an anathema to the left officers; they were determined that in postcoup Portugal old-style personalism and paternalistic, conservative leadership would not continue to dominate national politics. For "conservative democrats," whether military or civilian, Spínola soon became a liability from which they could not escape. So close were his ties to the centrist position that, when he was finally displaced from power and discredited as a public figure, this grouping collapsed as an alternative power center. It was not to re-emerge as an effective power contender until late 1975 and only then after it had freed itself from much of the Spínola legacy.[9]

The civilian branch of the new regime reflected the same reformist, rather than revolutionary, perspectives. Of the sixteen members named to the May Government, seven adopted centrist positions (this included Premier Palma Carlos); one represented those favoring constitutional monarchy (the group called Convergência Monárquica); and four could be classified as socialists—António de Almeida Santos, an independent, and three members of the Socialist Party: its leader Mário Soares, República editor Raúl Rego, and Francisco Salgado Zenha. Representing the revolutionary left were two members of the Portuguese Communist Party (its secretary general, Alvaro Cunhal, and Avelino Gonçalves) and Francisco Pereira de Moura (for the alliance known as the MDP/CDE). The single military appointee in this first provisional government, Defense Minister Lt. Col. Firmino Miguel, was also a centrist.

While the junta alignment between spinolistas and MFA officers remained unaltered until September, tensions between centrists and revolutionaries in the external political system led to the naming of a new provisional government on July 7. In this second government, military participation was increased by seven, with allotments being made specifically to the MFA. The most significant of these appointments was the naming of Vasco Gonçalves as prime minister.

Despite these changes, the second provisional government continued to represent a broad range of interests. Although weakened by the exit of Palma Carlos as prime minister and four of his cabinet ministers, centrists remained in the majority. Two of Palma Carlos' ministers were reappointed (Joaquim Magalhães Mota and Firmino Miguel); José Silva Lopes (an independent without party affiliation, identified with the Europeanist faction in the precoup Caetano government) became finance minister; and Maria de Lourdes Pintassilgo (the first female minister in Portuguese experience and a Catholic without party designation) accepted the portfolio for social affairs. Joining them were Emílio Rui Vilar as economy minister (the founder of SEDES, the Association for Economic and Social Development, and a technician identified with the previous Europeanist faction) and António Almeida Santos (reappointed as minister of interterritorial coordination), men who were identified with a left-center outlook. Even though Spínola as president found it necessary to move more quickly on the Guinea question than he preferred and by the end of July had announced that independence would be granted without delay, there were few signs at the top that revolutionary changes within the metropole would soon be forthcoming.

The Displacement of Spínola and the Expansion of MFA Influence

The events of September 28, 29, and 30 changed the postcoup balance of power decisively. Yet this particular affair began in a fashion not much different from other popular manifestations convoked so frequently after April 25.

Groups on the center and right had scheduled a large public meeting in Lisbon for the twenty-eighth to demonstrate their support for Spínola and to express opposition to left influence within the government. With rumors in circulation that a countercoup by the right was in the making, left groups organized opposing demonstrations in favor of the MFA and against Spínola's continuance in power. At this point left-wing officers identified with the MFA intervened and pressured Spínola to cancel the meeting and to prohibit all demonstrations. On the grounds that a countercoup was forthcoming, pro-MFA military forces proceeded to block entrances to Lisbon and a small group of revolutionary-minded officers, under the leadership of Brig. Otelo Saraiva de Carvalho (military governor of Lisbon and commander of COPCON, Continental Operations) took command.

The consequences of these actions were immediate. For the first time, MFA officers were able to seize control of the military institution. Left without a power base within the military, General Spínola resigned as president of the Republic. With this resignation the viability of a centrist coalition among military officers and civilians collapsed. Generals Galvão de Melo, Diogo Neto, and Silvério Marques exited from the military *junta* and Colonel Miguel and Major Sanches Osório resigned their positions in the second provisional government. Within the *junta*, officers from the next echelon identified with the MFA—Brig. Carlos Fabião and Lieutenant Colonel Lopes Pires in the army and Colonel Pinho Freire and Lieutenant Colonel Mendes Dias in the air force—filled the vacancies left. Of the senior military only Costa Gomes survived. Although it was agreed within the *junta* that he would become president, Costa Gomes did not constitute a focus for the creation of an independent power center. He had neither the wide popular appeal enjoyed by Spínola among center groups nor the desire to pull together military moderates into an effective alignment to offset MFA influence among lower-ranking officers and enlisted men. His primary objective was to survive and to do so he would collaborate with the MFA.

In this context, with two sets of commanding officials removed from positions of authority (first the old regime *ultras* and now the centrists), discipline within the armed forces began to break down as politicization spread throughout the ranks. The concern expressed over the following months with institutionalization of MFA authority reflected recognition of the need for a new set of symbols to re-establish military unity and for a program to transform newly developed political awareness in the armed forces into an effective set of relations within the officer corps and between officers and enlisted men, if the military was to serve as the primary agent of revolution. Just as hierarchical authority in civilian politics was identified in the eyes of many with old-regime authoritarianism, so too within the military, once MFA officers began to speak of internal democracy, orders issued by ranking officers no longer had the same binding effect on subordinates. The issues of the day centered around the destruction of fascism, popular mobilization, and the construction of a new society.

In the place of military hierarchy and unquestioning obedience to commands issued by superiors, MFA leaders advocated decision making within the military institution by consensus through assemblies and representative committees. Those in command were no longer to exercise their commissions by virtue of authority ascribed to them from above, but by the consent of those serving under them. While such an outlook became an essential part of the strategy for building a new political order, it played havoc with internal military affairs. It became all too apparent that politicization of lower officers and enlisted men would not lead to the formulation of a uniform revolutionary outlook.

With Costa Gomes as president and Vasco Gonçalves as prime minister, a left regime came into being, centered around revolutionary-minded military officers and those parties which could be identified as progressive forces: the Popular Democrats (PPD), the Socialists (PS), and the Communists (PCP). This was to be a period of close collaboration between the newly formed political parties and the MFA.

While the dominant civilian groups within the fourth provisional government were clearly the PPD, the PS, and PCP, there were three other minor civilian alignments whose participation became important because of the support they offered the military: the Movement of the Socialist Left (MES), the MDP/CDE alliance, and the independents. Made up of left-oriented intellectuals in large part, the MES characterized itself as a revolutionary movement, independent of and hostile to the PCP. Its significance lay not only in its appeal within the MFA to left officers suspicious of the intent of the major parties but also in its being a source of ideas and a pool of talent from which the military could draw civilians to staff policy positions in subsequent governments. Most prominent among these individuals, many of whom broke officially with the party and became known as the ex-MES group, was João Cravinho, minister of industry in the fourth provisional government. In contrast to MES, the MDP/CDE favored and promoted collaboration with the PCP. Originally an antigovernment electoral alliance during the New State era, it attempted to form an electoral front immediately after the coup. Failing in this strategy, by fall 1974 it had become a distinct political party on the left whose small size was offset by the fact that in the power vacuum left after Caetano's demise it had seized control of the majority of local government offices throughout the country. Its most prominent figure was the economist Francisco Pereira de Moura, who held ministerial posts in the first and fourth provisional governments. Apart from these groups stood the independents, such men as Finance Minister José da Silva Lopes, who prided themselves in their technical skills, maintained minimal political party involvement, and sought to convince Portugal's new rulers that their old-regime ties had not inhibited them from developing new loyalties. While hardly a formal group, this cluster continued to provide managerial talent on which the military could draw without having to deal with the parties.

The most significant development during this phase of the Revolution (which extended from October 1974 to March 1975) was the attention given by the MFA leadership to institutionalization of their movement within the armed forces. In order to understand what occurred during this period and why these men perceived MFA institutionalization to be so important, however, one must call attention first to ad hoc organizational arrangements made during the preceding summer to contain Spínola's influence.

Realizing that the senior military as well as a number of civilians in the Palma Carlos government had been more interested in seeing the MFA disbanded than consolidated, MFA officers in the *junta* and the third provisional government early attempted to consolidate their newly acquired positions of power by creating an autonomous set of organizations. Cognizant of the fact that the Council of State mechanism fashioned in May to guide the Revolution would never function as intended, they opted for the formation of two new military institutions: the Council of 20 (the Conselho dos Vinte, which soon became known in more formal terms as the Conselho Superior do MFA) and the Council of 200 (the Conselho dos Duzentos). Once Spínola and other centrist generals were removed from power, the Junta of National Salvation ceased to operate as a decision-making center and the weight of executive authority shifted in the direction of the Council of 20.

In order to retain a distinct identity for their movement in the months immediately following the coup, MFA officers established a clear-cut distinction between their twenty-five–member Coordinating Commission and the Council of State, a Spínola-created entity to which the MFA was assigned seven representatives. As Spínola's attack on the integrity of the MFA became more open, officers at the helm of the movement sought to create a more cohesive organizational structure by establishing an additional organ for coordination at the top: a seven-member directorate within the Coordinating Commission which coincided with its seven representatives on the Council of State.

Once Spínola was isolated and ousted from power, these organizational distinctions ceased to have much meaning. Without formal action being taken, after September 30 the Council of 20 became the effective center of power, not only within the military institution but for the country as a whole. Represented within it were the president (Costa Gomes), the premier (Vasco Gonçalves), the military ministers within the provisional government, and the seven officers from the MFA's Coordinating Commission.

While these shifts within Portugal's armed forces had a direct effect on policy and were an integral part of the effort to structure the MFA into an organized force and to consolidate its political control, it was not all that clear at the time that a basic realignment was underway. On the surface there was little difference between the second provisional government (in power July 17 through September 28) and the third (in office November 3 through March 11, 1975). Except for the naming of a military premier, there continued to be no more than seven military ministers in the cabinet and substantial civilian representation (eight altogether). Furthermore, the same general division of power established at the outset continued, with the military exercising the dominant voice and the provisional government, with its ministers, secretaries, and undersecretaries of state, occupying secondary status.

Although MFA leaders had made considerable progress in institutionalizing their movement by January 1975, conflict over policy and the course of the Revolution was becoming more and more apparent. Commitment to democratic principles within the armed forces led to extensive debate over their actual content just as the need to provide substance to what had been announced as a revolution required concrete programs and specific actions. This debate over internal and external military policy resulted in the formation and articulation of three distinct viewpoints within what were recognized in early 1975 as the MFA's official organs: the Council of 20, the Coordinating Commission, the Council of 200 (which was by then also being called the Armed Forces Assembly), and individual assemblies elected within each of the three branches of the armed forces.[10]

Leading the left wing of the movement, from October 1974 until his fall from power in September 1975, was Vasco Gonçalves (then a brigadier who was promoted to general in early 1975). Supporting him were a number of individuals within the Junta of National Salvation, a majority of the Coordinating Commission, and several of the military ministers in the third provisional government. Within the armed forces he could count on a majority of the engineering corps as well as a substantial part of the infantry and artillery corps and a majority of officials in the marines.

Despite the ascendancy of officers identified with revolutionary expectations, a second group could still be defined as centrist. While much more extensive before September, those who continued to identify themselves with this perspective in early 1975 were centered in the cavalry, although a number of officials in the infantry and artillery corps also retained a similar identification. Even though Spínola had been displaced from the presidency, he retained support within the armed forces from those officers and enlisted men who were conservative or neutral in their politics.

The third group, led by Maj. Ernesto de Melo Antunes (a minister without portfolio in the third provisional government), was the dominant faction from October through February. These men favored collaboration with the progressive parties—those who most actively supported the concept of building social democracy. Aligned with them were numerous officials in the air force and the army, many of whom were recognized as original members of the April 25 movement. These officers wished to see a socialist state constructed, but without sharp ruptures in Portuguese society. They aspired to meaningful national independence in economic as well as political terms and would have Portugal stress its commitment to a policy of decolonization in building closer ties with the Third World.

The elusiveness of this effort to institutionalize the Armed Forces Movement and to arrive at consensus within the armed forces is nowhere better demonstrated than in the general MFA assembly held on February 17. There a major attempt was made not only to establish clearly which would be the MFA's official institutions, what their linkages with each other should be, and how they were to relate to external political mechanisms, but also to pull together divergent military views into a single official policy expressed in terms of support for the MFA's program.[11]

By February commitment to representation within the various MFA organs meant the election of delegates from within the armed forces at large and no longer limitation of participation to those identified with the April movement. Such a development had the effect of increasing the plurality of views expressed within the armed forces and, to the dismay of the more radical officers, continued to provide representation for those favoring Spínola's outlook. Yet, even then, at this high point of support within the MFA movement for democratic pluralism, the principle was maintained that military and civilian power should be distinct and separate and that civilian government should be accorded only limited responsibilities and confined essentially to administrative and financial affairs. There may well have been important civilian participation in the new government, but in the eyes of those military officers dominant at the time the Revolution remained essentially a military affair.

Revolutionary Breakthrough and the Reign of the Radicals

The events of March 11 marked a culmination of the realignment of political forces within the military which had begun on September 28 as well as the point of departure for a new phase of the Revolution. While the exact circumstances behind the attempt to overthrow the revolutionary government on this date remain unclear, the results were conclusive. Responsibility for leading the movement to overthrow the incumbent government was assigned to Spínola. Having been maneuvered into a position where he did join procoup forces, Spínola and his closest associates had no choice but to flee the country when the movement failed. Shortly thereafter those officers most closely identified with his position in the military were purged. At this juncture commitment to building socialism within the military and without became dominant and it seemed as though revolution had begun in earnest. Debate now centered around what kind of socialism was most appropriate for Portugal: democratic or one of a number of its authoritarian variants.

Within the military institution radical officers took command. In their attempt to ensure that commitment to revolutionary change would be irreversible, the MFA leadership followed with three policy pronouncements.

First, they reorganized military governance. Supremacy of military over civilian authority was once again reasserted, this time in terms no one could ignore. The Junta of National Salvation, the Coordinating Commission, and the Council of 20 were merged into a single revolutionary executive authority: the Council of the Revolution (the Conselho da Revolução). Its power was further increased by granting it responsibilities previously assigned to the Joint Chiefs of Staff (the Conselho dos Chefes de Estado Maior Geral das Fôrças Armadas—the CEMGFA). While implementing legislation provided for a maximum of thirty members, the Council began operations with the twenty-five officers who had been instrumental in firming up these new arrangements.

Rationalization of executive authority was followed by reorganization of the MFA's representative assemblies. The Council of 200 became known officially as the Armed Forces Assembly and its membership was expanded to 240. Representation was extended beyond the commissioned officers to include sergeants and enlisted men. The same pattern was repeated in each of the individual services. For example, the Army's Assembly was assigned 120 representatives: 60 commissioned officers, 30 noncommissioned officers, and 30 enlisted men.

Insofar as executive authority was concerned, the secondary status assigned to the Council of Ministers, now in the form of a fourth provisional government, became even more apparent. As a consequence, full meetings of the Council were held less frequently. More often, policy discussions involving civilians occurred within what was called the Conselho Restrito (the "restricted council"). These sessions varied according to the particular items of business on the agenda. For example, when matters related to the political parties were paramount, the prime minister met with his ministers without portfolio. In terms of the new hierarchy of authority, the ministers without portfolio generally were accorded a status superior to that of ministers assigned to individual ministries. In the fourth provisional government these men were Alvaro Cunhal for the Communist Party, Mário Soares for the Socialist Party, Francisco Pereira de Moura for the MDP/CDE, and Joaquim Magalhães Mota for the Popular Democrats. On economic matters the prime minister met with those ministers responsible for various sectors of the country's economy.

The second policy pronouncement concerned the economy. In order to bring about the transition to socialism, the MFA leadership moved to destroy what they perceived to be the core of the Portuguese capitalist establishment: banks and insurance companies throughout the mainland were nationalized. This was to be but a first step. In the ensuing months they nationalized large-scale industrial and commercial firms owned by Portuguese interests on a sector-by-sector basis. In pursuing such a policy, however, they were careful to exclude international concerns. Where joint endeavors, such as the Lisnave shipyards, were involved, the government took control only of that percentage of stock held by nationals. By July most of the economy was under state control. All that remained of the private sector was a series of small and medium-sized firms whose operations had always been independent of the large conglomerates (such as the Companhia União Fabril and the Champalimaud and Espírito Santo interests).

While nationalization was accomplished relatively easily and the old economic elite found much of its wealth confiscated in a matter of weeks, the running of nationalized enterprises became no easy matter. Not only was there a scarcity of trained technicians in the public bureaucracy to administer the state's newly acquired entities, but there also were few if any managers in the private sector to whom the government could turn. Those who had not already exited discreetly were now fleeing the country as rapidly as possible. Into this vacuum created by the military moved a variety of worker committees, men who for the most part had little understanding for day-to-day business operations. As far as they were concerned, what was essential was the fact that the military government had guaranteed the payment of their salaries. In terms of the Marxist rhetoric which the official news organs of the state now espoused, workers were taking control of the means of production in order to ensure that the Revolution would not be undercut by subversive economic forces.

The third major policy pronouncement was directed at the political parties. Bringing to a head negotiations initiated before March 11, the MFA leadership issued a party pact on April 2 to which the parties were expected to adhere. Forty-eight hours later, in exchange for an MFA commitment guaranteeing that Constituent Assembly elections would be held, the twelve parties who had announced previously their intent to enter candidates (should elections be held) accepted the conditions established by the military. In writing a new constitution, they agreed, appropriate provisions would be made so as to grant the MFA a supervisory role over Portuguese politics for a transitory period extending from three to five years. The pact was signed and elections for the Constituent Assembly were held on April 25.

Ample publicity has since been given to the outcome of Portugal's April 1975 elections and to the fact that afterward the two parties with the most votes (the PS and the PPD) found themselves isolated within the fourth and fifth provisional governments. Even though the Socialists did amass 38 percent of the vote and the Popular Democrats 26 percent, what was forgotten by many persons during the summer of 1975 was that from the perspective of the military these elections had been held only for the purpose of electing an assembly to write a new constitution. In no way were they linked to the formation of a national government.

For the radical officers, now in command, the decisive date was March 11. It symbolized the defeat of Spínola and his supporters, the institutionalization of the MFA, the consolidation of their command over the military establishment, and the saliency of the country's armed forces in determining the course of the Revolution. As far as they were concerned, elections were a civilian affair, guaranteed by the military, and of secondary importance.

While the Socialists and the Popular Democrats continued to participate in the provisional government until mid-July (the Socialists left the government on the eleventh, followed by the Popular Democrats on the sixteenth), it became a question of time as to how long a coalition government of military leaders, operating through an autonomous set of institutions, and the civilian parties, restricted primarily to the Council of Ministers and the Constituent Assembly, could function. The confrontation between military authorities and the Socialist Party over the newspaper *República* was symptomatic of the crisis at hand.

The role the radical officers assigned to the MFA as guardian and arbiter of the Revolution proved to be incompatible with the idea of government by majority consent. MFA leaders conceived of themselves as a revolutionary vanguard whose task was to carry revolution to the countryside. Accordingly, they sought to establish their authority as supreme and to abrogate any challenges to the way in which they wished to define the rules of the new political game. The difficulty with this stance was that among the parties represented in the fourth provisional government—the Socialists, the Popular Democrats, the Communists, and the MDP/CDE—neither the Socialists nor the Popular Democrats would accept such conditions. Their image of a socialist Portugal envisioned the establishment of a parliamentary republic with regularly and duly held elections, whose government leaders would be determined by popular majority and in which democratic freedoms as traditionally defined in the West would be respected.

The attack on the editorial staff of *República*, a newspaper associated with the Socialist Party, by typesetters working for the paper raised the issue of press freedom. Although this action represented a direct assault upon the right of an opposition press to exist, what was at stake here was not the suppression of the last independent newspaper in Portugal, as much of the foreign press stated the issue at the time. At the height of the crisis there continued to be accurate and complete reporting by other independent papers in Portugal: the Lisbon daily *Jornal Novo;* the weeklies *Expresso* and *O Jornal*, also in Lisbon; and Oporto's daily *O Primeiro de Janeiro*. Furthermore, party-sponsored papers opposed to the government, such as the official organ of the Socialist Party, *Portugal Socialista*, continued to appear.

What this affair did reflect was the seriousness of the confrontation among those forces seeking to give more precise definition to the course of the Revolution. In seeking to consolidate their control, post-March MFA leaders found it impossible to arrive at consensus within the decision-making organs they themselves had established for the military. In the process they changed sides numerous times and their attempt to give final resolution to the matter, by turning the paper over to worker control at the end, remained at best a random and arbitrary action.

The Socialists and Popular Democrats were fighting for the right to articulate opposing views on the course the Revolution should pursue and the right, even if they went against the wishes of the MFA leadership, to have voice in determining policy outcomes commensurate with popular wishes, as expressed in the April elections. In contrast, neither the Communist Party nor the MDP/CDE would adopt public stances challenging the authority of the military. On the occasion of each confrontation they merely reaffirmed their support for the military, thereby convincing the radical wing of the MFA that they alone were amenable to working within the Revolution according to the MFA's definition of its parameters.

However, even though the Socialists and Popular Democrats finally did withdraw from the government, an effective alliance between the MFA and the Communist and MDP parties never did materialize. Within the MFA there was no longer present even the semblance of unity, for the summer crisis split the Movement into four distinct alignments.

On the left, two distinct groupings appeared. At the forefront of the dominant faction stood Vasco Gonçalves, who favored open collaboration with the Portuguese Communist Party and the MDP/CDE. In counterpoint stood another group of officers led by Otelo Saraiva de Carvalho. While continuing to support the Vasco Gonçalves government, they favored the creation of a left-oriented military regime. For them alliance with the PCP and MDP/CDE was a convenient and temporary necessity, essential if the military was to retain its dominance, but they were adamant on the point that the civilian parties cooperating with the military remain in secondary place. Supporting Vasco Gonçalves were a number of distinguished MFA names: Capt. Ferreira de Macedo, Lt.-Capt. Carlos Contreiras,[12] Capt. Martins Guerrero, First Lt. Miguel Judas, Col. João Varela Gomes, Com. Ramiro Correia, and Vice-Adm. António Alva Rosa Coutinho. Com. Jorge Correia Jesuíno, Maj. Aventino Teixeira, Capt. Duarte Into Soares, Gen. Morais da Silva, and Adm. José Batista Pinheiro de Azevedo could readily be identified with Otelo's stance.

The cluster of interests dominant before March 11, which had been called social democratic, continued to constitute a distinct undercurrent of opinion, and Maj. Ernesto de Melo Antunes and Brig. Vasco Lourenço retained their visibility. Considering them a threat to their plans, radical officers within the MFA sought to discredit them by giving the label "social democrat" antirevolutionary connotations. During May and June the Portuguese press consequently rarely referred to them as social democrats, preferring instead to call them *terceiro-mundistas* (those with a Third-World orientation who would have Portugal opt for a neutral stance in world politics).

To the right of this group stood moderate or independent officers, many of whom could have been identified earlier with a centrist outlook. Some of them may well have favored Spínola originally, but by summer 1975 they had ceased to think in these terms. For the most part these were men who placed high value on the concept of a professional military and were appalled at the havoc politicization had wrought with internal military discipline and order. Lacking leadership and crippled by the label *spinolista*, they did not at the time constitute a force to be contended with. From May through August, continuing in their posts within the armed forces, they found themselves in an ill-defined and difficult position, between the left democrats and those conservatives who had openly supported Spínola.[13]

Aside from these four major alignments, there was a fifth grouping: various officers identified with civilian movements left of the PCP. Of them Lt. Col. Manuel Franco Charais and Gen. Carlos Fabião were the most visible. Neither, however, could be identified with a distinct faction. In the context of the struggle which culminated in the naming of a new provisional government in mid-September, their participation took on meaning only in how they aligned themselves with the major groups. The former eventually opted for Melo Antunes, while the latter to his detriment ended up in Otelo's camp.

The most significant aspect behind these developments, however, lies not in specifying further how the MFA split into several distinct groupings and the way in which moderate officers continued to hold on to positions of importance within the armed forces, but rather in the fact that the radical officers had lost control of the Revolution they had sought to create. In the context of anarchy and the power vacuum developing at the top during August and September, the extremist parties formed the Frente Unida Revolucionária (FUV)—the United Revolutionary Front. Prior to the Front's formation, MRPP activists (one of the groups joining the movement) already had attempted to mobilize enlisted men by going directly into the barracks. As these groups accelerated their activities and the Front took shape, rumors began to surface inside and outside the armed forces of the possibility of uprisings within the barracks. The Front's objective was to trigger revolutionary upheaval by having recruits rebel against the officers and join hands with the radicalized working classes. When these activities finally jelled, they took the form of a movement among ordinary soldiers who were for the most part themselves of peasant or urban working-class background: Soldados Unidos Vencerão (SUV)—Soldiers United Will Conquer.[14] With the disintegration of authority and discipline in bases and camps in or near Lisbon, the SUV challenged the very integrity of the military institution.

Had the FUV and SUV achieved their objectives by inciting enlisted men to revolt against their superiors, had the PCP abandoned its alliance with Gonçalves and the left-wing MFA officers supporting him and opted for a genuinely revolutionary stance by joining the revolt initiated on November 25, the civil war so many feared during the fall might actually have broken out. Such conflict at this point would undoubtedly have destroyed the capacity of the military to continue as a distinct power contender. But mass uprisings did not occur. Once again maneuvering at the top was sufficient to halt further deterioration. Into the vacuum left by the radical officers stepped the Melo Antunes group. Very quickly, with the support of troops outside Lisbon removed from the radicalization which had been occurring in the capital and its immediate environs, these officers took command. How this happened necessitates concentration on maneuvering among officers within the military institution and cabinet-level politics, not on mass movements in the north or in Lisbon itself.

The Revival of the Forces of Social Democracy and the Shift to the Right

On July 25, in response to the withdrawal of the Socialists and the Popular Democrats from the fourth provisional government and after extensive meetings of the Council of the Revolution and the Armed Forces Assembly, the commanding group of radical officers announced the naming of a triumvirate, composed of President Costa Gomes, Prime Minister Vasco Gonçalves, and COPCON Commander General Otelo Saraiva de Carvalho. The idea was that by joining forces these men could amass sufficient political and military power to deal effectively with the crisis. A prolonged stalemate followed, as the Socialists, Popular Democrats, and other popular forces protested against these men's attempt to form an outright military government with close ties with the PCP and the MDP/CDE. Although Vasco Gonçalves was able to put together a short-lived fifth provisional government on the eighth of August, it had neither effective power nor the capacity to function.

At the height of this controversy, the Melo Antunes group acted. On August 7, Vasco Lourenço delivered to Costa Gomes and Otelo a manifesto stating the views of nine influential officers and defending the ideals of social democracy. Calling for a halt to revolutionary excesses, these men asserted that the time had arrived for ending ambiguities within the Revolution, for placing constraints on the course of action embarked on by Vasco Gonçalves, and for reaffirming the alliance of the military with progressive civilian forces.

From August 7 up through September 6, when Admiral Pinheiro de Azevedo attempted unsuccessfully to form another government, the Group of Nine, as they became known, followed the strategy of gaining the widest possible support for their document from among military officials. Bowing to what became inevitable pressure, Vasco Gonçalves, Otelo, Fabião, and Pinheiro de Azevedo finally accepted the fact that they did not command sufficient support within the armed forces to continue in office. Signifying their recognition of defeat was the announcement on the morning of September 19 that the Council of the Revolution would abandon in large part its executive functions and permit the formation of a sixth provisional government with real powers, giving full expression to social democratic perspectives among military officers and civilians.

A new set of military leaders, made up of social democrats and moderates, now came to the fore, men who agreed for the first time to the formation of a government in accord with popular wishes (as expressed in the April 25 elections) and to the sharing of power with the leaders of the majority political parties. Accordingly, in the sixth provisional government four positions were assigned to left democrats within the military institution (most notably Melo Antunes and Vitor Alves, two of the Nine); four, to the Socialists; three, to independents; two, to the PPD; and but one, to the Communists.

When the deliberations of the Council of the Revolution were made public, the significance of those changes became even more apparent. Not only did the Council announce its abandonment of general executive responsibilities, in the political arena, but it also stated that in the future its oversight over military affairs would be reduced. Furthermore, the Fifth Division (the vehicle of the radicals for carrying the Revolution to the countryside) was to be placed under the direct command of the Joint Chiefs of Staff (the CEMGFA).[15]

Throughout October and November the transfer of power from the radicals to left democrats and moderates accelerated. The climax came on November 25, when revolutionaries left of the *gonçalvistas* and the Communist Party attempted unsuccessfully to execute a countercoup centered on an airbase north of Lisbon known as Tancos. Within an hour's time rebel troops seized command of Tancos, bases in Monte Real and Montijo, the air force's communications center at Monsanto, and staff headquarters in Lisbon. There the revolt stopped. The marines remained loyal to Admiral Azevedo, and army troops for the most part refused to enter the affair. Without their support the movement collapsed.

Despite the fact that Fabião, commander of the army, and Otelo, head of COPCON (the unit most actively identified with defense of MFA ideals), did not join the movement, their ties with the far left and their image as men willing to play with forces committed to revolutionary upheaval made them particularly vulnerable. Equally liable to attack was Rosa Coutinho, a naval officer who because of his identification with the MFA radicals and his pro-MPLA attitudes in Angola had become known to many as the "Red Admiral." Moving quickly and deftly that same night, the left democrats and moderates took command of the situation. Suppressing procoup forces and establishing their control over the military institution, they ousted Fabião, Otelo, and Rosa Coutinho from the government and from their positions of authority within the armed forces.[16]

A swing to the right ensued. The Gonçalves and Otelo factions were finished as effective power contenders. The viability of a coherent radical stance within the military thus became as remote after November 25 as that of the *spinolistas* had proven to be after March 11. So quickly did reaction set in that in the aftermath even the Melo Antunes faction remained far too radical for those officers who controlled the more important military contingents outside Lisbon. The Revolution had come full circle. Into the vacuum left by the exit of the radicals came the moderates, now joined by many of those who earlier in the year could be identified as centrists.

What is most intriguing about this set of events and interplay of personalities is how irrelevant the Communist Party had become in influencing the course of the Revolution at the time of its greatest crisis. The *bête noir* of the right and influential circles in the United

States, the PCP of Alvaro Cunhal found itself confined to self-imposed isolation. Having eschewed the course of violent revolution independent of the officer corps and tied itself to what were perceived to be impressive left centers of influence within the military institution, it discovered all too late how limited and ephemeral the real power of the MFA was. Unwilling to promote insurrection among enlisted men in the army for fear of direct foreign intervention at a time when it knew full well it could not count on support from the Soviet Union, the PCP moved to disassociate itself from the regime it had sought so earnestly to help create and influence. Henceforth the only course of action that seemed rational for the Party to pursue would be the electoral route: building civilian support and seeking to influence politics within the framework of a competitive constitutional order.

For the first time since the Revolution had begun military leaders favoring disengagement of the military from active intervention in politics took command of the military institution. Without delay the remnants of the MFA apparatus were dismantled and the Portuguese Joint Chiefs of Staff (the CEMGFA) was re-established as the supreme military authority—first under the command of President Costa Gomes and shortly thereafter under that of Gen. António Ramalho Eanes. Gone were many of the officers identified with the Revolution they had begun a year and a half earlier. Quietly but effectively Eanes extended his authority over the military institution, and before long civilians found the military speaking, in more traditional terms, of its role as guarantor of civilian government. So great was this shift that men like Melo Antunes who had been so influential in making these changes possible also found themselves isolated because of their earlier advocacy of revolutionary change within the military and external civilian society.

Conclusions

Despite these developments, one should not presume that we have seen the last of the military in politics in Portugal. Previous experience both in the country and elsewhere with the military as a power contender in national politics makes virtually certain its reinvolvement, if civilian leaders step outside the boundaries defined by military leaders as legitimate and should civilians fail in the task of reconstruction lying ahead. For the time being, emphasis will certainly remain on the building of civilian government. Underscoring this commitment to civilian governance was the issuing in early 1976 of a new military-civilian pact, ending the principle of military supremacy and guidance of the Revolution. Congressional elections were successfully held in April, and these were followed by presidential elections in June. Thus, for the first time since April 1974, when civilian political forces articulated the goal of a popularly elected government, the political parties received a free hand in the electoral campaign and meaningful party government became a distinct possibility.

These then are the particulars of the Portuguese case and how by combining analysis of military bureaucracy, the group approach, and a diachronic perspective we might gain fuller insight into the military in politics in a crucial period of Portuguese politics. From this analysis, four observations of relevance to the general study of civil-military relations might well be made.

First, even in small countries like Portugal it is important to consider the military not as a single power contender but as containing a variety of groups and outlooks. Under conditions of rapid change and politicization what would normally be simply differences in perspectives becomes the basis for distinct political factions and leads to a variety of possible combinations between military and civilian forces. The old-regime military was no more the exclusive vehicle of the *ultras* than was the postcoup military the property of the MFA.

Second, despite the significance of identifying military groups and factions, analysis of varying alignments of officers and enlisted men must recognize the organizational context within which such actions take place. The parameters of the military institution are fixed and clearly defined. Accordingly, one cannot ignore identifying the particular patterns of socialization which develop within national military organizations. What made shifts in political orientation within the Portuguese military possible was the recognition among those in the officer corps that there was a shared outlook which mitigated against purges and expulsion of those identified with opposing viewpoints unless they violated the integrity of the military institution. During the ascendancy of the radicals, moderate officers remained loyal to their military superiors and moved against them only reluctantly. Even then those removed from power were the men most active in distinct political roles; it was only after severe crises that action against such persons as Costa Gomes, the supreme military commander, was taken and that he was replaced. Likewise, MFA officers during the highpoint of their domination of the military institution continued to deal with and interact with officers with quite different political orientations.

Third, military involvement in politics does not necessarily result in the building of new authoritarian governments. This is hardly an original point, but in light of the current literature, especially the writing on the military in South America, it warrants repeating: there is no necessary correlation between military intervention in political affairs and authoritarianism. Portugal has had its instances of authoritarian military personalities, but it also has produced military figures who have stood solidly behind the principles of party government. Had a faction within the military not become involved actively in politics in 1974, the authoritarian state with which Portuguese citizens were saddled for so long would most probably still be in existence. It was not a weak state and it was not inevitable that it should collapse.

Fourth, in times of political crisis the military constitutes a major force to be reckoned with. Despite attempts to link the military establishment with the New State and efforts to make the armed forces apolitical, political awareness within the officer corps and dissatisfaction with the status quo continued to grow throughout the late sixties and early seventies. As a consequence of the African wars, the drafting of large numbers of men of diverse social backgrounds, and the attempt to field a more professional fighting force produced an army which was far more representative of all social strata than had ever been true of the previous organization. The shift in social-class background within the officer corps over time from older upper-class to new middle-class elements, joined with the articulation of diverse social, political, and economic perspectives, set the scene for change from within. External pressure, in the form of military campaigns which could not be won, served as the catalyst for an internal revolt by bringing these changes to a head.

Revolutionary change thereby came first to the military institution and from there spread to the larger society. In turn, the military was influenced by the mass movements it unleashed; in fact, it came very close to being overwhelmed by them. However important these mass movements may be in assessing politics after April 1974, what is essential is to understand how the demise of the New State arose not from the inevitable but from the action of a small group of military officers and how, consciously or unconsciously, their actions contributed ultimately to the prospects of representative government and made possible for the first time in Portugal widescale citizen mobilization and the organization of mass-based party organizations.[17]

Notes

1. Representative of this perspective would be the works by Lieuwen and Johnson. See, especially, Edwin Lieuwen, *Arms and Politics in Latin America* (New York: Praeger, 1961), and John J. Johnson, *The Military and Society in Latin America* (Stanford: Stanford University Press, 1964).

2. Consult, for example, Alfred Stepan, "The New Professionalism of Internal Warfare and Military Role Expansion," in *Authoritarian Brazil*, ed. Alfred Stepan (New Haven: Yale University Press, 1973), and Luigi R. Einaudi, "Revolutions from Within? Military Rule in Peru since 1968," *Studies in Comparative International Development* 8 (Spring 1973): 71–87. While it is not my purpose here to review the literature on militarism in its entirety, a systematic review of the literature is to be found in Douglas J. Murray, "The Current Status of Research on the Latin American Military" (one of two unpublished essays submitted for the master's degree, University of Texas at Austin, 1970), and "In Quest of Professional Militarism: An Issue in U.S. Civil-Military Relations" (unpublished essay prepared for the doctoral program, Department of Government, University of Texas at Austin, 1976).

3. Of these articles, the most complete accounts dealing with the particulars of the Portuguese case are to be found in Gerald J. Bender, "Portugal and Her Colonies Join the Twentieth Century: Causes and Initial Implications of the Military Coup," *UFAHAMU* 4, no. 3 (Winter 1974): 121–162, and in Kenneth Maxwell's two articles, "The Hidden Revolution in Portugal" and "Portugal under Pressure," *New York Review of Books*, April 17, 1975, pp. 29–35, and May 29, 1975, pp. 20–30. See also Jane Kramer, "Letter from Lisbon," *The New Yorker*, September 23, 1974, pp. 101ff.

4. Philippe C. Schmitter, "Liberation by Golpe," *Armed Forces and Society* 2, no. 1 (November 1975): 16.

5. For an analysis of trade imbalances within the empire and the burden presented by Guinea-Bissau, see Lawrence S. Graham, *Portugal: The Decline and Collapse of an Authoritarian Order*, Sage Professional Papers in Comparative Politics, 5, 01-053 (Beverly Hills, Calif.: Sage Publications, 1975), pp. 20–28. By 1973, in addition to the military fiasco in Guinea, military leaders had to contend with a rapidly deteriorating situation in Mozambique. Tied down with substantial commitments in Guinea, there was no way to shift further matériel and men into East Africa.

6. These are contained in "O Movimento das Fôrças Armadas e a luta pela libertação do povo português," *Movimento: Boletim Informativo das Fôrças Armadas*, October 25, 1974, pp. 1–5, and Avelino Rodrigues,

Cesário Borga, and Mário Cardoso, O movimento dos capitães e o 25 de Abril: 229 dias para derrubar o fascismo (Lisbon: Moraes Editores, 1974).

7. On August 20, 1973, Caetano issued Decree-Law 409/73, which altered substantially his earlier decree, No. 353/73.

8. To understand shifting patterns of power and alliances within the Portuguese military and to separate these patterns from mass politics, it is important to keep in mind the distinction between a particular group of military officers as a government and the military as an institution. A military government refers to a limited number of officers who become involved in specific political roles at a particular time, whereas the latter refers to the larger set of military organizations which retain a separate identity from civil society. For further details concerning this distinction insofar as a Brazilian politics is concerned, consult Alfred Stepan, The Military in Politics: Changing Patterns in Brazil (Princeton, N.J.: Princeton University Press, 1971).

9. The "power contender" phraseology adopted there and used throughout this article has been adapted from the work of Charles W. Anderson (Politics and Economic Change in Latin America [Princeton, N.J.: D. Van Nostrand Co., 1967], pp. 104–114). For a discussion of the relevance of his approach to Latin America politics in the analysis of politics in southern Europe, see Lawrence S. Graham, "Latin America: Illusion or Reality? A Case for A New Analytical Framework for the Region," in Politics and Social Change in Latin America, ed. Howard J. Wiarda (Amherst: University of Massachusetts Press, 1974), pp. 242–243.

10. The following analysis of MFA factions, while based originally on Expresso, March 8, 1975, p. 1, has been adjusted in accord with information collected in thirty-one elite indepth interviews conducted by me in Lisbon with civilian and military personnel in May and June 1975.

11. In assessing these developments the most important bellwether of the drive to mobilize support behind the radical officers' definition of the MFA program was the Fifth Division's Commissão Coordinadora do Programa do MFA bimonthly publication, Movimento 25 de Abril: Boletim Informativo das Fôrças Armadas. Equally significant is the fact that after November 25, 1975, the date when the back of the MFA was broken, publication ceased.

12. For those interested in military terminology, it should be noted that Contreiras is a navy officer, not an army officer. A lieutenant-captain (capitão-tenente) in the Portuguese Navy is the counterpart of a lieutenant in the U.S. Navy.

13. At the time interviews were being conducted (May–June 1975), I found this particular grouping the most difficult to assess. Only in hindsight, after the events of November 1975 and moderation of the Revolution did the content of these interviews take on meaning for me. The respect that several of these officers had shown for Costa Gomes as head of the Joint Chiefs of Staff (the CEMGFA) originally led me erroneously to identify Costa Gomes as the most visible member of this cluster and to overlook the real message contained within this set of interviews: the high value placed on discipline, professionalism, and reform of the military institution (through further modernization of the armed forces, basic revision of instructional methods in officer training programs, and depoliticization).

14. This discussion of the SUV is based on Jane Kramer, "A Reporter at Large: The Portuguese Revolution," *The New Yorker*, December 15, 1975, pp. 92 ff. She provides a much more coherent account regarding the significance of this movement than is to be found elsewhere in the existing periodical literature, both within Portugal and outside.

15. Since January 1976 and especially since General Eanes' election as president, the Council of the Revolution has come to function in accord with the moderating power granted to it in the new constitution. With the influence of radical elements within the military checked since November 1975, the Council under Eanes' direction has assumed a dual role as guarantor of democratic institutions and as the supreme political and legislative organ for military affairs. See Maurice Duverger's discussion of the link between the presidency and the Council in "Portuguese Presidency: Power to Make or Break the Regime," *Manchester Guardian*, July 11, 1976, p. 11. Specific accounts of the Council's actions during late 1975 and early 1976 are to be found in *Expresso;* see especially November 22, 1975, pp. 1 ff., and January 31, 1976, p. 1.

16. See Kramer, " A Reporter at Large," for details surrounding the November 25 affair.

17. For research support permitting me to return to Portugal in May and June 1975 and to purchase research materials unavailable in Austin, I would like to express my gratitude to the Earhart Foundation. I would also like to acknowledge my appreciation to John Vincent-Smith (at the British Institute in Lisbon) and Thomas Bruneau (at McGill University in Montreal) for their critiques of an earlier version of this article, and to Sam Wolfson (my research assistant) for assistance in preparing the table and figures.

8. Electoral Behavior and Political Militancy

JOHN L. HAMMOND

When on April 25, 1974, the junior officers of the Armed Forces Movement dealt the coup that ended forty-eight years of fascism in Portugal, neither they nor the Portuguese people anticipated the strength of the forces for change that would be unleashed. Even those who had planned to institute democratic liberties were surprised by how immediately and enthusiastically those liberties were exercised. The celebrations of May Day; the *saneamentos* of local governments, enterprises, and trade unions; and the rapid foundation of more than fifty political parties were among the immediate expressions of popular political activity. Portugal resembled and even exceeded many countries which have experienced "a rapid escalation in political participation," a "burst [of] explosive energy" when civic freedoms are restored after a long period of repression.[1]

The explosion of participation continued. It has been presented with two faces in the Western news media: on the one hand, Portugal held its "first free elections in fifty years" (more accurately, as Wheeler points out, the first free elections ever)[2] with a 90 percent turnout and a centrist majority. On the other hand, the country experienced an unprecedented wave of "violence," with cars blown up, political rallies attacked, factories and farmlands occupied, and a siege of rural violence against the political parties of the left.

At first glance, these two phenomena appear contradictory to western eyes. Properly understood, however, they are part of the same process. In Portugal between 1974 and 1976, the same political demands were expressed through institutional (in this case, electoral) and noninstitutional means. Different population groups expressed politically the diverse interests which derived from their different locations in the class structure. These expressions took varied forms as a consequence of half a century of authoritarian rule and the fluid authority structure which succeeded it.

To explain the forms and content of political behavior in Portugal over this crucial two-year period, accordingly, one must begin with an outline of Portuguese class structure and the political experiences of the relevant classes under fascism. Because this article is concerned with popular political behavior, the discussion will be restricted to the most numerous classes, omitting the owners of major productive resources in agriculture and industry.[3] In the agricultural sector, at the risk of oversimplification, one can make a broad distinction between two regions. The dominant form of agricultural unit in the north is the small holding, owned or rented (in many cases, a single farmer controls both owned and rented parcels); in the south before 1975, it was the large holding, in which most of the labor force works for wages. These different social structures led to widely different opportunities for political organization and, hence, to different levels of ideological formation under fascism.

In the south, where the regime disciplined the labor force for the benefit of industrial and agricultural employers, the wage relationship made possible the clandestine organization of political opposition. The rural proletariat was receptive to the organization of opposition based on economic grievances but upon which the regime, through repression, forced a political definition.[4] The Communist Party, taking an almost exclusively economist line, represented their interests through the organization of illegal strikes and through the expression of counterregime demands for improvements in conditions.

In the north, in contrast, small landholding led to a peasant political mentality, reinforced by years of demobilization through the Church and the regime. As has often been pointed out, the social situation of the isolated peasant does not lend itself to political organization.[5] The traditional political passivity of peasants is in part tactical: their situation is such that no change suits them best, and thus there is little for them to advocate. When they do undertake political activity, they tend to respond primarily to outside leadership and are therefore often available for instrumentalization in the interests of other classes.[6]

The traditional demobilization of the peasantry has been accentuated in recent years by four circumstances: the role of the Church, emigration, the uneconomical size of holdings, and regime policy. To Caroline B. Brettell's discussion of the depoliticizing influences of the Church and emigration in the following chapter can be added the remark that emigration has provided an important economic support to Portuguese society as a whole through remittances and decreased pressure on its cities. Many landholdings are so small that they produce less than necessary even for the subsistence of the family, which is accordingly not vulnerable to market fluctuations that elsewhere have generated rural protest.

More importantly, the Portuguese peasantry was subjected to a deliberate policy of demobilization under the corporate state. The regime, in defense of the interest of large landholders, prevented a transformation of agrarian patterns[7] and prevented northern peasants from emerging from their poverty and backwardness—the large numbers of emigrants and their concentration in the north are the best testimony to the corporate state's failure to serve their interests. That same regime reinforced peasants' characteristic individualism through a political system which permitted (and often in effect required) their use of personal connections for private gain, but which made the definition and achievement of collective goals nearly impossible. Government slates were usually uncontested in the periodic nominal elections, and the state maintained a dense network of police and informers who not only impeded political opposition but also interfered in the most minute details of local life. Under the twin leadership of corporatism and the Church, the peasantry had been effectively deprived of any sense of opportunity for or potential benefit through political activity.[8]

Rural social structure thus predisposed southern agricultural workers to opposition to the fascist regime and contributed to the development of a radical political consciousness, largely channeled by the Communist Party, while northern small holders were predisposed to apolitical but implicitly conservative views. These patterns carried over to some extent to urban industrial workers in north and south, since migrants to cities tended to come from the rural areas nearest those cities. Structural conditions in industry further contributed to making southern industrial workers more radical than northern industrial workers: though the north is proportionately slightly more industrialized than the south, its industry is more dispersed, industrial enterprises are somewhat smaller,[9] and many industrial workers are able to maintain small plots of land. The southern industrial workers are concentrated into larger plants and are geographically concentrated in the Lisbon-Setúbal belt.

Moreover, the north remains the stronghold of the Catholic church, while active religious affiliation has largely given way to secularization in the south—a pattern that has characterized the country at least since the early twentieth century.[10]

These two social contexts, as already implied, produced very different patterns of political activity during the forty-eight years of fascism: the passivity of northerners contrasted dramatically with the focal points of opposition in the south. These different traditions, as I will show, have been continued in the respective political patterns of the two regions since April 25, 1974.

The 1975 election of a Constituent Assembly occurred on the first anniversary of the Armed Forces Movement's coup. During the intervening year the explosion of political activity had been accompanied by the destruction of what had at first appeared to be a remarkable consensus on national goals. The assertion of MFA hegemony over colonial policy in July, the ousting of António Spínola following September 28, the trade union dispute in January, and the institutionalization of the MFA and the signing of the political pact following March 11 had led to a deepening uncertainty over the course of the Revolution. Each of these events had brought a further radicalization of the Revolution and an increasingly open alliance between the MFA (or its then-dominant segment) and the Communist Party. Nationalizations, factory occupations, and latifundio takeovers made some Portuguese increasingly enthusiastic and others increasingly disturbed. The political pact threatened to deprive the election of any significance—and even at that, the election was twice postponed, causing some to fear that it would not be held at all.

Nevertheless, that year was the most open year in the living memory of most Portuguese, and probably the most open year in Portuguese history. Even some who were increasingly alienated by the rapidity of the apparent advance toward socialism exulted in the freedom to speak, to express their opposition, and to organize. Portugal was undergoing what Philippe C. Schmitter has described as a "civic orgy," and the election marked its peak—if also perhaps its end. A newsweekly article about election day was entitled "The Elections Were a Festival." The article recounted that the election was disparaged by conservatives and by some radical intellectuals, but for those who knew the difference between the repression of fifty years and the freedom of the year just ended, the election was the symbolic capstone of liberation: "O Povo sabe empìricamente o que ela [a liberdade] pode representar [the people know empirically what liberty can represent]."[11]

What else did the *povo* know? Some things about their political consciousness, their sense of national direction, and the goals they wished to pursue through politics can be inferred from the way they voted. I will argue that the same political consciousness and the same goals expressed in the voting booth have also been expressed in what some choose to regard as "wildcat" political activity, and that both demonstrate a surprisingly well-developed sense of class consciousness and a use of politics in the pursuit of appropriate interests. This relatively high articulation of class interest and its expression through the vote and other political activity is surprising from the standpoint of a tradition of comparative politics which argues that without a history of electoral experience an electorate's development of partisanship and the relation between partisanship and interests must be somewhat random. Philip E. Converse has argued that only several generations of competitive elections and party development will permit fixed party allegiances—whatever the social bases of the cleavages that ultimately develop.[12]

Converse's argument arises from his observations that party identification in Germany and Italy, where electoral democracy was interrupted, is much lower than in the United States and Britain, where it has been continuous, and that women old enough to have come to adulthood without the opportunity to vote have very low party identifications. He finds a high correlation between the exposure to electoral politics and the degree of party identification in nation-age cohorts.

Converse is arguing about stability of individual party identification over time. Portugal of course does not yet provide an opportunity to test that stability.[13] It is not unreasonable, however, to infer from his argument a prediction about the outcome of the first democratic elections in a polity: if individual party identifications are highly labile, the static correlations between social statuses and party choice should be somewhat random.

Others have argued that there are systems where party choice is instrumentally determined by voters' involvement in social and economic conflicts.[14] In such instances, stable party allegiance develops only to the extent that voters judge parties to represent their interests in such conflicts. If they do find parties representing those interests, there should be a clear correspondence between social position and party allegiance even at the time of creation of a competitive system.

Data from the 1975 election show a clear correspondence. The vote for the five parties receiving the highest proportions is neatly distributed into areas of very distinct social composition. The analysis of the social composition of the 1975 vote is based on aggregate data from the 274 *concelhos* of continental Portugal (a data base which excludes the Azores and the Madeira islands). This analysis is based on the relation between the vote and the distribution of the active population into sectors—primary, secondary, and tertiary, and within the primary sector, self-employed versus employed by others. The results of this analysis must be considered rather tentative: the relation between sectoral distribution and the vote ignores the inactive population;[15] the division of the primary sector into employed and self-employed is derived from the merging of two data sets not entirely consistent with each other; and the sectoral breakdown is of course different from the class breakdown which I will use as an indicator. In discussing the analysis of voting statistics directly, I will speak of "sectors"; later, I will discuss "classes," assuming that the correspondence between sector and class, though not perfect, is close enough to draw such inferences.

For purposes of analysis I have stratified continental Portugal into four groups of *concelhos* by geography (north/south) and urbanization.[16] I have analyzed the vote for the five parties receiving the highest number of votes: the Socialist Party (PS), the Popular Democratic Party (PPD), the Communist Party (PCP), the Social Democratic Center (CDS), and the Portuguese Democratic Movement (MDP). I have also analyzed the "party" of abstainers (in which I include those who cast blank or void ballots, as a percentage of the total number registered). Table 8-1 shows the distribution of votes for these six groups within the four region/urbanization strata. The regional distribution is clear: the two parties of the right (PPD and CDS) did considerably better in the north, and the two parties of the left (PCP and MDP), in the south. Within regions, the vote for these four parties was more accentuated in rural than in urban areas: within the region in which each party did best, it received a higher vote in rural areas, and within the region where it did poorly, it received a higher vote in urban areas. Abstentions were higher in the north than in the south; but within each region they were higher in rural than in urban areas. The PS is the only party on which urbanism has a consistent effect: its vote was greater in urban than in rural areas; the regional effect, however, was as great, with the PS doing better in the south than in the north.

The analysis of the party vote by sectors and by other socioeconomic characteristics which follows must be understood in the light of this regional variation. Though differentiation by class is considerable, it must be remembered that (within the limitations of my data, in which class is measured inadequately) it is overshadowed by differentiation between regions. Regional differences within sectors are probably due in part to inadequacies in the data and

TABLE 8–1

Vote for the Constituent Assembly, 1975

(*Distribution by Region and Size of Place*)

Region*	CDS	PPD	PS	PCP	MDP	Abst.†	Number of Concelhos
Rural north	11.0%	38.2%	30.1%	4.2%	3.3%	17.3%	156
Urban north	9.7	27.5	41.6	7.2	3.8	12.7	25
Rural south	2.4	8.6	41.5	28.1	6.8	14.6	72
Urban south	4.3	12.6	45.1	22.3	4.7	12.9	21
Continent	7.7	24.7	38.6	13.1	4.2	14.6	274

*Urban *concelhos* are all those that contain a district capital or a city greater than 10,000. The south includes the Algarve, the Alentejo, urban *concelhos* of Lisbon district, and agrarian reform *concelhos* of Lisbon, Castelo Branco, and Santarém districts. Figures (except for abstentions) are percentage of total vote.

†Including blank and void ballots, as a percentage of the number registered.

in part to two factors to which I will return below: the effect of predominant sectors on other sectors within regions, and the differences in levels of organization and political consciousness arising out of the regions' different histories under corporatism. But it remains the case that regional differences are great and that my explanations are to some extent speculative.

Table 8-2 shows the sectoral breakdown of the party vote. The aggregate data indicate the following rough breakdown: tertiary-sector workers voted PS and (though to a much lower degree) PCP. Agricultural workers divided into two groups, according to whether they were self-employed (owners or renters) or workers; the former voted for the parties of the right, the latter for the parties of the left. Secondary-sector workers were divided: in the north they voted more like rural proprietors and in the south more like rural workers, though in both regions there was a tendency for them to move to the center.

Two other sets of observations should be made about the party vote: one relating to economic level, the other relating to religion and general backwardness. The parties of the right were supported in rural areas of lower prosperity and higher Catholicism—cultural and economic conservatism were closely related.

When the vote is analyzed more closely, there is a sharp contrast between the parties of the right and the left on nearly every dimension. The CDS and the PPD can be analyzed together, for, although the vote for the latter was nearly four times that for the former,

TABLE 8–2

Labor Force Distribution and the Vote

Sector	CDS	PPD	PS	PCP	MDP	Abst.
Rural North						
Primary, self-employed	20%	63%	2%	−3%	3%	24%
Primary, employed	13	45	22	2	0	21
Secondary	18	45	25	3	2	9
Tertiary	−16	−20	92	21	10	17
Multiple R	.315	.522	.666	.411	.243	.552
Urban North						
Primary, self-employed	25%	51%	9%	−3%	12%	13%
Primary, employed	−5	9	40	16	−1	37
Secondary	12	24	48	5	3	7
Tertiary	5	30	44	11	4	15
Multiple R	.335	.330	.545	.401	.385	.814
Rural South						
Primary, self-employed	4%	20%	45%	−18%	14%	38%
Primary, employed	2	2	32	55	4	7
Secondary	3	16	46	15	10	13
Tertiary	2	8	60	9	7	15
Multiple R	.179	.503	.329	.558	.210	.692
Urban South						
Primary*	6%	14%	59%	1%	4%	16%
Secondary	−4	−3	30	59	6	11
Tertiary	9	20	51	7	5	13
Multiple R	.756	.524	.448	.554	.187	.300

Note: The figures in this table represent estimates of the percentage of voters in each labor-force category who voted for each party. The estimates are derived from a regression analysis of each dependent variable by three variables representing the percentage of each *concelho*'s labor force in three of the labor-force categories (the fourth is omitted because it is linearly dependent on the other three).

The cell entries are derived from the regression coefficients in the following manner: for the three variables included in the regression, the cell entry is $a + b_j$, where a is the intercept and b_j is the variable's raw regression coefficient. For the omitted category, the cell entry is a.

Under ideal conditions, this transformation provides an estimate of the proportion of each sector voting for the party. That conditions are not ideal is demonstrated by occasional anomalous values less than zero; these anomalies indicate the margin of error of the other estimates as well. Errors are due to several factors: the differences between the labor force and the voting population, inadequate estimates of the independent variables, and they were distributed in much the same way. They will be contrasted here with the PCP, and the discussion of the PS will be postponed briefly.

The conservative parties were overwhelmingly supported by self-employed farmers, both north and south. Though rural owners and renters gave most of their vote to the PPD, they nevertheless constituted a large majority of CDS voters as well. Agricultural workers voted strongly for the PCP, especially of course in the south; in the north they gave a fairly large vote to the PS and PPD. Though the PPD won many votes among secondary-sector workers in the north, these workers rejected both conservative parties in the south and in the urban south voted overwhelmingly in favor of the PCP.

Apart from occupational composition, the conservative vote was concentrated in the poorer, more remote, and more backward areas of the country, although differentiation along these dimensions was much greater in the north and in some instances was reversed in the south. With prosperity measured by average monthly family expenses, the conservative parties were supported in the poorer areas. Emigration can similarly be taken as a measure of prosperity, since poverty is a principal motive for emigration. The areas that produced the most emigrants also produced the most conservative voters.

In the urban south, poverty and conservatism were negatively related: the conservative vote was concentrated in the wealthier *concelhos*. (As Table 8-2 shows, the vote for these parties among tertiary-sector workers in the urban south was also relatively high.) Even though the conservative parties principally attracted poor voters elsewhere, professionals and the high bourgeoisie concentrated in certain *concelhos* of the Lisbon area also gave them a high vote.

As already noted, urbanization was differently related to the vote in the two halves of the country. In the south, the conservative vote was slightly more urban; in the north, it was overwhelmingly rural (so that in the nation as a whole it was more rural than urban). The converse is true of the PCP. A measure of the penetration of

---

contextual effects within regions. (For a discussion of such anomalies in inferences from aggregate data, see John L. Hammond, "Two Sources of Error in Ecological Correlations," *American Sociological Review* 38 [December 1973]: 764–777; idem, "New Approaches to Aggregate Electoral Data," *Journal of Interdisciplinary History* [forthcoming, Winter 1979].)
*Because of their small numbers in the urban south, it is not possible to derive reliable estimates for farmworkers and self-employed farmers separately.

modernization and social services is the number of births without medical assistance. Voters were more conservative in the areas with poorer medical attention. Again, this relationship was particularly strong in the north; in the south it was much weaker and more inconsistent.

Finally, the religious influence on the vote was very strong. Catholics voted strongly for the two conservative parties and overwhelmingly rejected the PCP. In the north the relation between religion and vote was greater in the rural than in the urban *concelhos*. In the south (where the relation was in general much weaker) it was stronger in the urban than in the rural *concelhos*.

One peculiarity of the CDS vote is, as Jorge Gaspar and Nuno Vitorino note,[17] that it varies enormously among *freguesias*, even among those that are socioeconomically and geographically similar. They suggest that this variation may be due to the influence of local *caciquismo* in some *freguesias*.

The vote for the MDP can be summarized briefly: its relation to the PCP vote was rather surprisingly low; in the south, in fact, it was negative, and the MDP (though its vote in all sectors was slight) had a surprising attraction for rural proprietors. Electorally, at least, the MDP was not a mere substitute for the PCP, as some argued (as I will mention directly, the PS came closer to playing that role in the north). Gaspar and Vitorino point out that the MDP vote, like that for the CDS, varied widely among *freguesias*. They suggest that in the case of the MDP this is less likely to be due to *caciquismo* than to localized traditions of opposition dating back many years.[18]

The internal homogeneity of the vote for the other leading parties is not matched by the distribution of the vote for the biggest vote winner, the PS. As has been noted, the PS was in the south a conservative choice, and in the north a left choice.[19] The only nationwide constant in the PS vote was the overwhelming favor it received from people employed in the tertiary sector. Among other sectors PS preference reversed itself in north and south: it was supported by rural workers in the north and by rural proprietors in the south; it received a large relative share of secondary-sector workers in the north and, in the south, though its vote among those workers was substantial, it was overshadowed by the PCP. Secondary-sector workers in both regions voted similarly to primary-sector workers in the respective regions, but in both there was a tendency for them to move to the center—that is, to the PS. In terms of

family expenses and emigration, the PS won votes in more prosperous *concelhos* in the north and (though the differentiation was
slight) in the less prosperous *concelhos* in the south. It was rejected
in Catholic areas, though to a much lesser extent than the PCP; and
in the urban south the preference for the PS was strikingly high
in Catholic *concelhos*—higher than for the PPD, almost as high
as for the CDS. The PS, which ran an American-style campaign,
evidently won its victory by presenting a contradictory image and
attracting very different types of voters in different areas.

The abstentions and blank ballots (combined, they amounted to
nearly 15% of registered voters) tended to be distributed like the
conservative vote: the correlations with the PPD and (negatively)
PCP votes were quite high; the correlation with the PS vote was
also negative, but not so high. Abstention tended to be least among
secondary-sector workers, although it was especially low among
southern agricultural workers. It was, moreover, notably high among
rural proprietors. It was also greatest in the poorest and culturally
remotest *concelhos*: it was greatest in the zones of emigration, poor
medical care, and Catholicism. Once again, the PS vote was more
like a left vote in the north and more like a right vote in the south:
in the north it was negatively correlated with abstentions, and in
the south positively. A last-minute campaign encouraged blank ballots as a vote for the MFA. There is little reason to suppose, however, that the campaign had much impact. The count did not distinguish between blank and void ballots, which were in any case
closely correlated to abstentions. And, given the ideological tenor
of the MFA at that time, the concentration of blank ballots in conservative areas makes it unlikely that many of them represented
endorsement of it.

The distribution of the vote, then, suggests that the parties (except probably the PS) did present consistent images to voters, and
that voters reacted to those images in terms of their social statuses.
The Communist Party won strongly in those areas where it had long
been strong and among voters who could assume, on the basis of
both its program and its past history, that it was their representative: rural wage earners and industrial workers in the southern industrial concentrations. The PPD and CDS were most attractive to
rural proprietors, to Catholics, and to the culturally remote, although they also did well among the urban bourgeoisie in the south.
The class base of these parties and the regional base overlap:[20] the
support of each party was concentrated in the region where the

dominant mode of agricultural production corresponds to its class base. Moreover, in their respective regions of maximum support, they won disproportionate support from other classes as well.

The PS won consistently among tertiary-sector workers. Though this is the most heterogeneous occupational category, its attraction to the PS probably represents above all the approval of the petite bourgeoisie and public functionaries for the social democracy which the PS has increasingly espoused, and which in northwestern Europe has indeed principally benefited those who command education and skills but little capital. The PS also attracted the votes of workers outside the dominant mode of agricultural production—industrial workers in the north and rural proprietors in the south. A PS vote appears to have been a vote against the party of the most numerous class, in favor of the alternative nearest on the spectrum in the direction that the constituency's interest led it (i.e., to the left for nonproprietors in the north, to the right for voters other than agricultural or industrial workers in the south). The PS's campaign and the electorate's response appear to have led it to victory by turning it into a residual category.

The terms in which the Portuguese electorate voted in 1975 were thus well defined in accord with class and with culture. The distribution of votes was far from random and was, moreover, based on a well-developed political consciousness. There is considerable impressionistic evidence that ideological thinking is widely diffused among ordinary and relatively unsophisticated Portuguese (more in the more radical areas of the country, but present in the conservative areas as well). As an example, on September 29, 1974, the day after the aborted "Silent Majority" demonstration and the day before Spínola's resignation which it provoked, I asked an eighty-year-old retired agricultural worker in the Alentejo who was making so much trouble in Lisbon. His succinct reply: "*Os grandes capitais* [big capital]." He should know—he lived in a small village wholly owned by an agribusiness firm which owned hundreds of surrounding hectares and was landlord and employer to the whole town.

If it is legitimate to infer from Converse's argument a hypothesis about static correlations between social position and party choice, we must regard it as disconfirmed. Portuguese voters in 1975 clearly tended to choose a party (or at least a relative position on the political spectrum) appropriate to their own positions and distinct from the position of other groups, whether defined economically, culturally, or in some combination of the two. I will later address the question of whether voters identified their class interests accurately; for the present the point is that within classes they identified them homogeneously.

The 1975 constituent election was thus orderly both in process and in outcome. In the process, an extremely high turnout was coupled with an active, relatively peaceful campaign (violence diminished, rather than increased, during the actual campaign period). The outcome was orderly in demonstrating a system of well-defined parties successfully appealing to distinct segments of the electorate on the basis of their perceived interests.

Yet 1975 was not an orderly year. The entire period following April 25, 1974, was marked by disorder, confrontation, and the regime's inability to regulate political demands and maintain social control. The disorder has not only been exaggerated in the American press, but also almost inevitably been called "violence," a term which not only is inaccurate in most cases but also ignores the political content of the activity. It can better be called "political militancy," the term which I will henceforth use.

Though it may have been exaggerated, however, Portugal has been disorderly—the disorder is evident both in the *golpismo* of the military and in the direct expressions of demands by civilians. Civilian political militancy has been of three broad types: mass protest defined in explicitly political terms; economic struggles carried over into the political sphere; and violence by groups on the political fringe. Events of the first type include the mobilization of popular vigilance in defence of the Revolution (notably on September 28, 1974, and March 11, 1975) and attacks on Communist and other left-wing party headquarters. Economic protest has included strikes by urban and rural workers, occupations of latifundios, takeovers of factories, and mobilization against agrarian reform through the CAP (Confederation of Portuguese Farmers). Fringe-group activities have included internecine violence among left-wing parties, disruption of right-wing political meetings by Maoists, and armed resistance by the Spain-based right-wing ELP and MDLP.

This last category, having involved very small numbers of people, deserves the least attention despite the fact that it includes some of the most spectacular events (including the surrounding of the CDS convention in Porto in January 1975 by militants of the MRPP who posed such a threat that the German Christian Democrat, von Kassel, had to be evacuated by helicopter). Such incidents have been cited to prove that the Portuguese revolution was falling apart internally and that the country was on the brink of civil war. Mass political mobilization and economic struggles have often been categorized in the same way. But incidents of the latter two kinds are not "senseless." It is true that the Revolution was ill-defined and that its military leadership was unable to maintain either unity or public order. But the high degree of militancy can be explained as a consequence of the lack of stable representative structures through which demands could be channeled. The incidents themselves were expressions of the same political interests represented in the vote, and the forms they took can be explained by the organizational bases for collective action in the respective regions of the country where they prevail.

The rural south rapidly developed new political organizations after April 25. Agricultural workers, previously denied even the corporatist unions which industrial workers had had, were organized into an Agricultural Workers' Union; in Evora they went on strike in the summer of 1974 and won significant wage concessions.

Within a very short time events pushed the rural workers further. The radicalization of the Revolution after September 28 (and especially after March 11) and the passage of an economic sabotage law subjecting idle productive resources to expropriation assured rural workers of a favorable governmental response to a strategy of land occupations, and the refusal of many large landowners to abide by the sabotage law persuaded the workers that the requirements of national productivity necessitated the takeover of those lands.

In the south political activity did not emerge from a vacuum, but it did emerge in something of an institutional vacuum. Corporatist structures in the country were nominally, and to a large extent in fact, dismantled soon after April 25. The government lacked the capability to enforce a general land reform, even one restricted to large properties. What it did, instead, was provide an opportunity and a favorable climate for workers to undertake what appeared from outside to be wildcat occupations and expropriations. While the terms of agrarian reform underwent important modifications with the June 1975 law, the occupations had begun the previous fall and accelerated after March 11. A large but unknown number of these occupations were explicitly organized by the rural union. Others were in fact wildcat but occurred within the terms of the same law and the same favorable climate which made the occupiers expect governmental recognition.

Land occupation, then, was a deliberate strategy well organized and carried out by the existing political structures in the interests of rural workers. "Existing structures" include not only the union— a new and largely untested structure—but also the structures of consciousness and the political organization which existed under the aegis of the PCP, although they had previously been clandestine and therefore to some extent implicit. It was the hegemony of the Party in these areas that made it possible to carry out on the basis of occupations an expropriation and reorganization of latifundios without redistribution of property into small, potentially unviable units. Expropriated latifundios were "cooperativized," maintained in their original size and organized on the basis of collective labor and collective decision making.[21]

The system of gradual, wildcat takeover had some important negative consequences for the stability both of the fourth and fifth governments and of the cooperatives themselves: since the lands were not expropriated universally, uncertainty was created in the minds of other owners who felt their status as landowners threatened—a situation which, as we shall see, was to have crucial significance in the mobilization of northern peasants against the government of Vasco Gonçalves. Moreover, the cooperatives themselves were in a fairly precarious economic position, being undercapitalized and having to compete with well-capitalized, still privately owned enterprises. This problem became especially crucial when the fifth government was succeeded by the sixth, far less sympathetic to the cooperatives. The possibility of opportunist takeovers by groups who sold off the movable property of occupied farms and did not farm them effectively rendered the program vulnerable to criticism.

The cooperative system presented an opportunity for the political mobilization of productive labor which, had conditions been more auspicious, could have been important in transforming the chronically low productivity of southern agriculture. Such a transformation would doubtless have required several years. But the state of uncertainty and the low capitalization were combined with the political uncertainty of the declining days of the fifth government and the long period of formation of the sixth: the fact that labor was politically mobilized meant that it was also available for political mobilization outside the labor process to intervene in larger political events (as in the demonstrations in September 1975, when much of the Alentejo rode its tractors to Lisbon to demand the return of Vasco Gonçalves to the government). Mobilization for politics impeded the regularity of labor in the expropriated properties themselves.

Despite these qualifications, agrarian reform in the fourth and fifth governments was not a disorganized outburst of violence but a clearly political process. Agricultural workers who had seen their interests defended by the PCP before April 25 were already incorporated into it ideologically and to some extent organizationally. They took part in the occupation of lands under the inspiration— if not the control—of the same party for which they had voted, and for the same reasons.

The relation between partisanship and militancy among urban industrial workers in the south is more complex. The PCP's role in labor struggles has been ambivalent: it supported demands for increases in the minimum wage, but until the end of the fifth government its support of each of the successive governments was fairly uncritical, and to help stabilize those governments it discouraged strikes, excessive demands, and precipitous actions. But strikes, demands, and actions occurred, often out of the hands of the Party and the unions. A wave of strikes immediately after April 25 demanded wage concessions. Later, many factories were taken over to be managed by their workers, usually in response to their abandonment by their former owners or the owners' refusal to meet the new minimum wages. Such activities were often under the leadership of far-left parties or multiparty fronts; Communist-led unions often acquiesced in them after the fact but initiated and supported them in some industries.

But in the industrial sector, too, workers had seen the PCP as the defender of their interests prior to April 25. Though many of them expressed demands in excess of what the Party wanted to permit, and though many of them became disaffected and no longer saw it as the reliable leader of the working-class struggle, nevertheless the PCP received the overwhelming majority of their votes in 1975. No other party has yet persuaded them that it will represent their interests better.

Both in the urban and rural sectors, then, radicalized workers have vigorously defended their own interests both through economic demands, enforced by strikes, and through political demands for control of the workplace, enforced by occupations, by opposition to sabotage by owners, and by the demand for co-management. The political demands expressed through the vote, therefore, have largely been in defense of the same interests expressed through noninstitutional militancy. Workers in rural and urban areas have used both sets of political means consistently toward the same ends.

Unlike southerners, northerners had experienced years of effective demobilization and did not have a political context within which to engage in political activity after April 25. The Armed

Forces Movement made some efforts to activate them through its Cultural Dynamization Campaign, but reports indicate that—despite the MFA's rhetoric proclaiming itself a national liberation movement—its officers were poorly prepared to deal with rural northerners on their own terms. The dynamization teams preached anticlericalism and threatened local traditions. The reaction, not surprisingly, ranged from incomprehension to hostility.

But northerners, like southerners, have engaged in political activity, in the voting booths and in the streets, and again the two forms of behavior have represented the same political consciousness and the same demands. The most visible content of northern political behavior has been anticommunism. Electorally, the north supported the parties representing (in an ambiguous combination) the policies of the corporate state—particularly the corporate state's invocation and defense of religious values—and the expansion of dependent capitalism. Noninstitutionally, northern Portugal's response to political change has taken the form of hostile outbursts against the Communists and other left-wing parties. A wave of anticommunist violence in the summer of 1975 included uprisings in at least fifty towns and cities. Many party headquarters were burned down, many more were forced to close, and several people were killed in the accompanying violence.[22] Later, in the fall and winter of 1975 and 1976, peasants mobilized by the CAP demonstrated for the rescision of the communist-led agrarian reform.

Marx, Hobsbawm, and others have emphasized that the peasantry is unlikely to organize itself for political activity and that it is therefore likely to be active only when stimulated by outside leadership. There is evidence that anticommunist violence in Portugal has been led by agitators—the most notorious being the archbishop of Braga. Anticommunist attacks were generally precipitated by rallies sponsored by the Church or organized for market days to ensure maximum participation.

To say that violence was organized by outsiders, however, is not to deny the sincerity and spontaneity of individual participation. Political militancy in the north represents the same political aspirations that the northern vote represents, just as is the case for the south. The principal reward of peasant life is stability, and if that stability has been threatened for a long time by economic decline and the necessity to emigrate, those threats have arisen only gradually and been less perceptible than the sudden outburst of political change since April 25. The peasants attributed political change, not unreasonably, to communism, which raised for them the twin specters of loss of land and opposition to religion and was the same enemy the Church and the regime had been warning them about for so long. They reacted with the institutional and noninstitutional means at their disposal.

If the demands expressed by left-oriented workers (for better economic conditions, agrarian reform, and worker control) bear a direct relation to their class interests, it is not obvious that the anticommunism of northern peasants bears the same relation, for it aligns them with national political forces representing the interests which for decades permitted their economic decline and kept them politically demobilized so that they themselves could not act to prevent that decline. That the state has denied economic opportunity to rural small holders is evident from their lack of access to credit, the decline in small holdings in recent decades,[23] and the necessity of emigration.[24]

Northern peasants, unlike southern urban and rural workers, have entered into political activity without the previous ideological formation which might have led them to a more effective articulation of demands. The high correlation between abstentionism and the right-wing vote indicates that the latter arises in and depends on a context of depoliticization. Having no previous political organization, peasants have no clear sense of their interests or of political instrumentalities through which to express them. Their protests, therefore, like their votes, do not express the kinds of demands the fulfillment of which might reasonably be expected to advance their position.

But it is not obvious that there is any political solution, left, right, or center, which would serve their interests. Their current preservationism is oriented to a situation which, though it has considerable traditional legitimation and the safety valve of emigration, is economically unviable. An economic rationalization of northern agriculture would probably require consolidation of holdings, a reduction in the number of farmers, and capital investment. These changes would carry with them great competition within the class and its eventual destruction. As a class, the peasants are superseded.[25]

If the class is destined either to stagnation or to extinction, there is no rational political activity available to it as a class. In the absence of viable economic interests to defend, superseded classes commonly turn to status-oriented politics—politics oriented not to a group's market position but to an affirmation of the values with which it is historically identified in an assertion of the group's continuing claim to social worth in the face of its economic decline.[26]

In the absence of a viable economic strategy, the strategy of affirmation of values becomes the most reasonable one available to such classes.

The content of the symbols they use to affirm their social worth makes them available as allies to one or another of the classes engaged in structural political conflict (reinforcing peasant political weakness in the absence of outside leadership). In the case of Portugal, the symbols of religion and private property which resonate for peasants make them look for allies among the parties most actively defending traditional capitalism and national dependence—the technocratic bourgeoisie, who would benefit from that dependence by being the agents of exploiters, and the landowning bourgeoisie (through the CAP), who can use the peasants' opposition to agrarian reform to protect—and possibly in some instances to recapture—their land. E. J. Hobsbawm argues that in modern societies peasants who have no interests of their own to defend are likely to become stalking horses for a rural middle class;[27] in Portugal today the peasantry seems to have become a stalking horse for the rural high bourgeoisie, the owners of the largely abandoned and unproductive large estates which have been resistant to modern technology and intense cultivation to the detriment of Portuguese nutrition and the balance of payments.

The relation which I have argued exists between the objectives expressed in each group's electoral behavior and its political militancy contradicts some theories of the relation between political participation and political development. According to those theories, the clarity of the structure of political cleavages which, I argue, can be inferred from the election results is inconsistent with widespread militancy; rather, it should be accompanied by a highly developed civil culture. Where the relation between the political system and the social groups composing the society is so well developed, it is argued, institutional channels of political influence should be used to the exclusion of noninstitutional channels.

In this tradition, arguments on two different levels—the social structural and the individual—complement each other. At the structural level, what the Tillys call "breakdown theories"[28] argue that collective violence is a response to social breakdown, to political changes which disrupt personal lives—for example, according to these theories, urbanization is a prime cause of violence, which erupts because new urbanites are incapable of responding instrumentally to the new political opportunities available to them.

At the individual level, a very different body of theory argues that political participation develops more or less homogeneously: individuals who adopt strongly felt and coherent ideologies also develop a sense of political competence, become committed to the regime, and accept the norms of civil political behavior, so that they do not engage in militant, noninstitutional expressions of political demands.[29] In Jeffrey M. Paige's characterization, "such a theoretical perspective implies ... that the more that is known about the government the more it will be trusted."[30]

But it should be obvious that there is no inevitable association between levels of political information and ideology, on the one hand, and trust in the regime and acceptance of the norms of civil political behavior, on the other. The evidence from Portugal in 1974 and 1975, however, clearly belies such an association. It suggests, instead, that institutional (in this case, electoral) and extrainstitutional political behavior represent the same interests, are engaged in by some of the same people, and must be explained in the same terms. As the Tillys argue (in a version of what they call the "solidarity theory" of collective violence), collective violence is based on the same organizational structures as other forms of collective political action, expresses the same demands, and is a response to the institutional structures of the society which make it necessary and facilitate or repress it.[31]

Political militancy is a reflection of individuals' lack of trust in the regime.[32] Trust can be specific to the present regime, or it can be developed as a result of long experience. By either process, Portuguese citizens had no strong grounds for confidence in the revolutionary regime. The regime of the preceding five decades offered little basis for trust and thus did not build up strong positive affect even in those sectors where it did not generate opposition. The provisional governments which succeeded each other after April 25 were short-lived and of ambiguous political coloration. Even as the coloration became increasingly clear through the fifth government, those regimes did not receive automatic trust from any of the sectors which have been discussed here.[33] On the one hand, they were increasingly distrusted by anticommunists; on the other, their perilous stability and lack of organizational capability denied them the full confidence even of their supporters, who perceived that militancy was necessary to force the governments to act in the supporters' interests.

If citizens' perceptions encouraged political militancy, so did the political structure. In the absence of stable structures and calculable expectations of the gains to be achieved through institutional channels, shows of force are appropriate strategies, and threat and counterthreat are likely to escalate, even among supporters of the regime. When the regime is perceived to be under threat of either *contragolpe* or popular opposition, countermobilizations in its support can be expected—and on September 28 they were probably crucial in determining the outcome of the confrontation.

Militancy, whether in support of or in opposition to the regime, reflects and reinforces the absence of stable institutional mechanisms for the channeling of demands. It does not represent poorly developed political competence, limited horizons, or the lack of clear political consciousness. Rather, it represents a perception of a situation in a high degree of flux and a calculation of the means of influence most likely to be effective.

Between 1974 and 1976 Portugal underwent two years of hyperactive politics that were both traumatic and ebullient. But during this period it also proclaimed a new constitution and elected a parliament and a president. It appeared briefly that a new form of direct and responsive democracy was in the making in Portugal. Since then, prospects for the creation of such institutions appear to have vanished. It remains to be seen whether the institutions created since that time will adequately respond to the demands of its heterogeneous population—or whether, instead, its leaders will prove incompetent or its cleavages too profound to exchange these two years' system of confrontation, counterconfrontation, and direct expression of political demands for a more institutionalized, smoothly functioning, and responsive system.

Notes

This is a revised version of a paper presented at the conference "The Crisis in Portugal," University of Toronto, April 15–17, 1976. For making available the electoral and census data used (including some unpublished data from the 1970 census) I am grateful to Dr. José Francisco Graça Costa of the National Institute of Statistics; to Commander Luís Costa Correia, formerly technical secretary for political affairs; to their respective institutions; and to Philippe C. Schmitter. I also wish to express thanks for the advice and support of Joyce F. Riegelhaupt and the members of my study group.

1. Samuel P. Huntington, *Political Order in Changing Societies* (New Haven: Yale University Press, 1968), p. 407.

2. Douglas L. Wheeler, "Portuguese Elections and History," paper presented at the conference on Modern Portugal, Yale University, 1975, p. 2.

3. Discussions of the political role of the high bourgeoisie before and

after April 25, 1974, can be found in Robin Blackburn, "The Test in Portugal," *New Left Review* 87–88 (September–December 1974): 5–46; Harry M. Makler, "The Portuguese Industrial Elite and Its Corporative Relations," chapter 4 in this volume; and Hermínio Martins, "Portugal," in *Contemporary Europe: Class, Status and Power*, ed. Margaret Scotford Archer and Salvador Giner (London: Weidenfeld and Nicolson, 1971), pp. 60–89.

4. The radicalization of rural proletariats in areas where they are large has, contrary to some expectations, been noted elsewhere. Cf. Sidney W. Mintz, "The Rural Proletariat and the Problem of Rural Proletarian Consciousness," *Journal of Peasant Studies* 1 (April 1974): 291–325; Maurice Zeitlin, "Cuba: Revolution without a Blueprint," in *Cuban Communism*, 2d ed., ed. Irving Louis Horowitz (New Brunswick: Transaction Books, 1972), pp. 81–92.

5. E. J. Hobsbawm, "Class Consciousness in History," in *Aspects of History and Class Consciousness*, ed. Istvan Meszaros (New York: Herder and Herder, 1972), pp. 5–21; Karl Marx, *The Eighteenth Brumaire of Louis Bonaparte* (New York: International Publishers, 1963), pp. 123–131; Arthur L. Stinchcombe, "Agricultural Enterprise and Rural Class Relations," *American Journal of Sociology* 67 (September 1961): 165–176; Eric R. Wolf, "On Peasant Rebellions," in *Peasants and Peasant Societies*, ed. Teodor Shanin (Harmondsworth: Penguin, 1971), pp. 264–274.

6. E. J. Hobsbawm, "Peasants and Politics," *Journal of Peasant Studies* 1 (October 1973): 13; idem, "Class Consciousness in History," p. 12.

7. Hermínio Martins, "Portugal," in *European Fascism*, ed. S. J. Woolf (London: Weidenfeld and Nicolson, 1968), p. 330.

8. José Cutileiro, *A Portuguese Rural Society* (Oxford: Clarendon Press, 1971); Joyce F. Riegelhaupt, "Peasants and Politics in Salazar's Portugal," chapter 5 in this volume.

9. Makler, "The Portuguese Industrial Elite," table 4-1.

10. Martins, "Portugal," in *Contemporary Europe*, pp. 81–82.

11. Maria Antonia Palla, "As Eleições foram uma Festa," *Vida Mundial*, May 1, 1975. p. 53.

12. Philip E. Converse, "Of Time and Partisan Stability," *Comparative Political Studies* 2 (July 1969): 139–171; cf. Angus Campbell et al., *Elections and the Political Order* (New York: John Wiley and Sons, 1966); William McPhee et al., *Public Opinion and Congressional Elections* (New York: Free Press, 1962).

13. Preliminary analysis of the 1976 legislative election results, however, indicates a high continuity despite the strong shift to the right.

14. W. Phillips Shively, "Party Identification, Party Choice and Voting Stability: The Weimar Case," *American Political Science Review* 66 (December 1972): 1203–1225.

15. The implicit assumption is that the inactive population is proportionately distributed among *concelhos* and sectors; this assumption is plainly false and is perhaps responsible for some of the anomalies in Table 8-2.

16. *Concelhos* have been defined as urban according to the INE definition (containing a district capital or a city of ten thousand or more). The south includes the Algarve, the Alentejo, the urban *concelhos* of Lisbon

district, and the agrarian reform *concelhos* of Lisbon, Castelo Branco, and Santarém districts (as defined by Decree-Law 236-B/76 of April 5, 1976).

17. Jorge Gaspar and Nuno Vitorino, *As Eleições de 25 de Abril: Geografia e Imagem dos Partidos* (Lisbon: Livros Horizonte, 1976), p. 48.

18. Ibid., pp. 48–49.

19. Fernando Belo, "Da Geografia eleitoral á Geografia socio-económica," *Expresso*, May 10, 1975, p. 17; Gaspar and Vitorino, *As Eleições*, pp. 182–183.

20. As I mentioned previously, I am inferring from sectoral divisions to class divisions, on the assumption of a close correspondence between them.

21. To be sure, the collectivity of that decision making was open to some doubt, and the structure of work remained generally similar to the former structure.

22. Precise knowledge of the actual participants is unavailable. To my knowledge, no imprisonments occurred and no charges have been pressed against participants in anticommunist violence. Its location, however, strongly suggests that the greatest number of participants were peasants. The incidents tended not to be in the smallest rural towns but in the *concelho* capitals, most of which are nevertheless very small; and they generally occurred on market days when the towns were filled with people from the surrounding farm villages.

23. "Sobre a Questão Agrária," *Arma Crítica*, no. 5 (March 1976), pp. 5, 38.

24. Granted, emigration permits a tangible improvement in the material position of many, both while abroad and after their return to Portugal. But it is nevertheless evidence of and buttress to their dispossession within the Portuguese class structure.

25. I am not predicting that the peasants will disappear. Small holdings did in fact decline between 1952 and 1968, but the resistance of the peasantry may well remain strong and the regimes likely to be in power in the near future may need to let agriculture suffer for the sake of maintaining the peasants' political loyalty.

26. Joseph R. Gusfield, *Symbolic Crusade: Status Politics and the American Temperance Movement* (Urbana: University of Illinois Press, 1963); Richard Hofstadter, *The Age of Reform* (New York: Vintage Books, 1955); Max Weber, "Class, Status and Party," in *From Max Weber: Essays in Sociology* (New York: Oxford University Press, 1958), pp. 180–195.

27. Hobsbawm, "Class Consciousness in History," p. 19.

28. Charles Tilly, Louise Tilly, and Richard Tilly, *The Rebellious Century, 1830–1930* (Cambridge, Mass.: Harvard University Press, 1975), p. 4.

29. Gabriel A. Almond and Sidney Verba, *The Civic Culture: Political Attitudes and Democracy in Five Nations* (Boston: Little, Brown and Company, 1965), esp. pp. 188–207; Philip E. Converse, "The Nature of Belief Systems in Mass Publics," in *Ideology and Discontent*, ed. David E. Apter (New York: Free Press, 1964), pp. 206–261; Campbell et al., *The American Voter*.

30. Jeffrey M. Paige, "Political Orientation and Riot Participation," *American Sociological Review* 36 (October 1971): 811.

31. Tilly et al., *The Rebellious Century*, pp. 6–11.

32. William A. Gamson, *Power and Discontent* (Homewood: Dorsey Press, 1968); Paige, "Political Orientation."

33. I have not discussed militancy by the urban middle class because (with the exceptions of participation by some of its members in the vigilance of September 28 and March 11 and the activities of the far left) there has hardly been any. Provisionally, I believe that this can be explained by the better representation of middle-class interests—even of those in opposition—under both the old and the postrevolution regimes.

9. Emigration and Its Implications for the Revolution in Northern Portugal

CAROLINE B. BRETTELL

As the days and months after the April 25 coup have unfolded, the divisions within Portuguese society have become increasingly clear. Among the people, the split follows a geographical boundary which divides north from south and rural from urban. This "dualism" is not new to Portugal, but has, perhaps, been enhanced by postrevolution politics. The results of two major elections, held a year and two years to the day after the 1974 coup, clearly follow the lines of geographical fission. As Hammond has illustrated in his case study of the 1975 election, the north votes PPD; the south, socialist and communist.

The major focus of this article is upon the northern, rural sector of Portugal. The aim is modest—to try to outline some of the problems which have so far been ignored by the makers and assessors of the Portuguese revolution, problems which must be considered if the north is not to find itself still further behind in Portugal's march toward economic and social development.

I will begin my discussion by contrasting what I call the "revolutionary potentials" of the rural sectors of northern and southern Portugal. From there I will turn to a consideration of the political attitude and activity—or nonactivity—of the rural people of northern Portugal, basing my discussion upon conversations I had in 1974 and 1975 with emigrants from the north in Paris and with villagers in Portugal.[1] I do this primarily to present some of the major opinions held by these people about the process of revolution. Finally, I will turn to a discussion of two factors which have deep historical and traditional roots in the *modus vivendi* of northern Portugal— the Church and emigration—and will attempt to show how these two factors hinder in some ways the florescence of the spring buds of the April 25 revolution.

Revolutionary Potential—the North versus the South

My decision to discuss the "revolutionary potentials" of northern and southern Portugal, however briefly, is prompted by a series of inquiries and a jarring incident. While I was working at the village level, I received several letters from outsiders asking about peasant mobilization and the organization of cooperatives. In all cases, I was forced to respond negatively—that I had seen nothing,[2] except of course to read about the massive pro-Church demonstrations in the provincial towns of Aveiro, Lamego, and Braga (farther south than I was) and the attacks on communist headquarters in Famalicão (closer to home) and Ponte de Lima (only a few miles away).[3] But not only was the activity of revolution blatantly absent, so too was the rhetoric. This was made most clear to me on a brief trip through the Alentejo in mid-December 1975. We had stopped to visit the hilltop castle at Monetemor, off the road between Lisbon and Evora. As we left, several barefooted children in tattered clothes gathered around and sent us on our way with a chorus of, "Fascista! Fascista! Fascista!" In the north one must draw that word out of people and, even then, they will say that they hardly know what it means.

Included here are data (Tables 9-1–9-4) which help to summarize those economic contrasts between northern and southern Portugal which are crucial to an explanation of a revolutionary south and a nonrevolutionary north. The statistics show two clear distinctions: the contrast between latifundia and minifundia, and the high-

TABLE 9–1

Percentage of Proprietors in the Active Agricultural Population

District	%	District	%
Aveiro	48	Leiria	39
Beja	8	Lisbon	23
Braga	33	Portalegre	7
Bragança	38	Porto	23
Castelo Branco	21	Santarém	24
Coimbra	41	Setúbal	13
Evora	6	Viana do Castelo	50
Faró	32	Vila Real	34
Guarda	34	Viseu	38

Source: Eugenio Castro Caldas and Manuel de Santos Loureiro, Niveis de Desenvolvimento Agrícola no Continente Portuguesa (Lisbon: Gulbenkian, 1963).

TABLE 9–2

Percentage of Family Enterprises in the Active Agricultural Population

District	%	District	%
Aveiro	46	Leiria	32
Beja	12	Lisbon	19
Braga	43	Portalegre	8
Bragança	35	Porto	40
Castelo Branco	21	Santarém	19
Coimbra	38	Setúbal	12
Evora	6	Viana do Castelo	64
Faró	30	Vila Real	32
Guarda	36	Viseu	42

Source: Caldas and Santos Loureiro, Niveis de Desenvolvimento Agrícola.

TABLE 9–3

Percentage of Individual Farming Enterprises with More
Than Six Parcels of Land

District	%	District	%
Aveiro	40	Leiria	42
Beja	10	Lisbon	15
Braga	19	Portalegre	11
Bragança	63	Porto	18
Castelo Branco	27	Santarém	24
Coimbra	42	Setúbal	2
Evora	8	Viana do Castelo	45
Faró	24	Vila Real	48
Guarda	35	Viseu	41

Source: Caldas and Santos Loureiro, Niveis de Desenvolvimento Agrícola.
The figures in Estatísticas Agrícolas (Lisbon: Instituto Nacional de
Estatística) for 1975 are based on the Inquérito as Explorações Agrícolas
do Continente (Lisbon: Instituto Nacional de Estatística, 1968) and show
no marked changes in the agricultural structure of Portugal as it is represented in Tables 9–1, 9–2, and 9–3.

er population of salaried laborers (jornaleiros) in the agricultural
system of the north.[4] Tables 9-5 and 9-6 provide figures on emigration and demonstrate a clear divergence between north and south
for over a century.[5] Emigration from the Algarve has also been historically important, but emigration from the Alentejo, particularly
in recent years, has been directed largely to Lisbon. This is an ex-

TABLE 9–4

Salaried Rural Laborers by District

District	No.	%	District	No.	%
Aveiro	24,291	37	Leiria	45,119	56
Beja	66,727	86	Lisbon	56,059	73
Braga	30,448	36	Portalegre	43,408	89
Bragança	30,840	50	Porto	31,097	43
Castelo Branco	45,338	70	Santarém	73,237	77
Coimbra	44,358	57	Setúbal	39,434	86
Evora	49,164	92	Viana do Castelo	12,310	21
Faró	38,691	61	Vila Real	45,162	52
Guarda	38,847	60	Viseu	55,917	48
			Continental Portugal	770,447	59

Source: Carlos Almeida and António Barreto, *Capitalismo e Emigração em Portugal*, 2d ed., Cadernos de Hoje, no. 10 (Lisbon: Prelo Editera, 1974).

TABLE 9–5

Emigration from Continental Portugal According to District, 1890–1967

District	Emigrants (in thousands)	Emigration (% of total)
Aveiro	234.6	9.5%
Beja	12.6	0.5
Braga	154.6	6.3
Bragança	135.9	5.5
Castelo Branco	50.6	2.1
Coimbra	166.3	6.7
Evora	4.7	0.2
Faró	58.9	2.4
Guarda	158.9	6.4
Leiria	139.4	5.7
Lisbon	96.8	3.9
Portalegre	6.3	0.3
Porto	271.9	11.0
Santarém	47.4	1.9
Setúbal	11.9	0.5
Viana do Castelo	102.6	4.2
Vila Real	155.1	6.3
Viseu	259.8	10.5

Source: Almeida and Barreto, *Capitalismo e Emigração*.

TABLE 9–6

Emigrants from the Continent According to Destination
(*percentage of total*)

Destination	1901–30	1931–50	1951–60	1961–67
Argentina	2.1%	5.9%	3.7%	0.4%
Brazil	69.5	74.5	65.7	9.9
Canada			4.5	5.8
Holland				0.4
South Africa		0.4	1.9	2.4
USA	15.7	5.6	5.8	6.8
Venezuela		2.3	10.4	4.8
Others	12.7	10.8	3.0	3.0

Source: Almeida and Barreto, *Capitalismo e Emigração*.

tremely important point. Whereas in the south the *jornaleiros* have tended to move into the urban proletariat class of Portugal itself, the peasants from the north have moved into the proletariat of foreign countries and—as I will show later—because of the international, rather than intranational, character of emigration and urbanization, emigrants from the north are, in fact, only minimally "part of" a proletariat and therefore are not exposed in any significant way to the "politicization" which "proletarianization" tends to imply. Emigration, by removing individuals from both national and foreign proletariats, reduces the tendency to class solidification and the development of class consciousness. So too does a minifundia system of land tenure. Such a system tends to create minute scales of difference among rural peoples, enhancing competition at the expense of intraclass cooperation and interclass conflict. "A full peasant class-consciousness is conceivable in so far as differentiation within the peasantry is secondary to the common characteristics of all peasantry and their common interests against other groups and insofar as the distinction between them and other groups is sufficiently clear."[6]

Essentially, the point I wish to emphasize here is that for a variety of reasons, based upon different systems of land tenure (though naturally not explained completely by this difference), there has always been more "revolutionary potential" (even the possibility of the establishment of cooperatives) in southern Portugal. One of the best comparisons to be made is with Mexico. In a recent article on the Mexican revolution, Ronald Waterbury has noted a regional variation in peasant involvement in the 1910 revolution. He contrasts the states of Morelos and Oaxaca. Morelos was where the Revolution started. The peasants of the state of Oaxaca, on the other hand, remained relatively uninvolved if not outrightly reactionary. "The peasants of Morelos fought and died for change albeit a change back to a traditional community-oriented agrarian way of life. The peasants of Oaxaca for the most part remained passive or joined the fight to defend the status quo."[7]

Waterbury bases much of his argument upon the land tenure systems and the political status accorded to the peasants or the "rural proletarians" as a result of these systems.[8] Morelos was dominated by the hacienda (latifundia) system (43.9% of all landholding units) and was characterized by capitalistic farming and incipient industrialization. Oaxaca had a higher population, had little industrialization, and was dominated by peasant landowners (only 13.8% of all landholding units were haciendas). The few haciendas in Oaxaca were smaller, were poorer, and occupied less land surface (8.1% in Oaxaca vs. 40% in Morelos). The state of Oaxaca with its predominantly peasant form of exploitation experienced what Waterbury calls "indirect exploitation," that is, the appropriation of the *products* of peasant labor rather than the labor itself. A direct exploitation of labor was more characteristic of the state of Morelos. The implications of this distinction between direct and indirect forms of exploitation are enormous for the development of the kind of "class consciousness" necessary for revolution as it is described by Hobsbawm (quoted above).

The parallels between Mexico and Portugal are self-evident and sufficient to give one general explanation for northern conservatism. But, as I will show later, the individualism and independence which are implied in a system of small proprietorships and "peasant" exploitation are compounded by emigration and the fruits that emigration brings.

Political Attitudes of Northern Peasants
and Emigrants from the North

Although I by no means concentrated upon political issues during my brief stay in Portugal and my year in Paris, I was able to ask a few informants about the new politics in Portugal and especially about the changes they saw as a result of the revolution of the twenty-fifth of April. In Portugal, I spent four months in one village. This village might be considered representative, not necessarily of the north as a whole,[9] but certainly of the district of Viana do Castelo, which itself makes up a good portion of the northwestern province of Minho.

The village of Santa Eulalia is situated in the Lima River Valley in the *concelho* of Viana do Castelo.[10] It is by no means the most isolated of Portuguese villages but a rather large village (a *freguesia* rather than an *aldeia*) with a population of 2,295 in 394 households, according to a village census of 1973.[11] A fifth to a third of the population is away during the year, most of them in France, but some also in Germany, Brazil, Africa, the United States, and Canada. The land is very parcelized, although there are several large quintas (comparatively speaking) within the territorial limits of the village.[12] Polyculture predominates, with an emphasis on the cultivation of corn, potatoes, beans, grape vines, and other vegetables, especially the long-stemmed cabbage known as *couve gallego*. The agricultural work is carried out primarily by women (probably a result of high-level, continuous male emigration). Most of the village people over fifty, especially women, are illiterate or barely literate. In the 1975 elections there were 1,048 registered voters. Of these, over 50 percent voted for the Popular Democratic Party (PPD). Approximately 18 percent voted for the Social Democratic Center (CDS) and the Socialist Party (PS). Only 2 percent voted for the Communist Party (PCP). These figures follow the trend for the *concelho* as a whole, although the overall percentages are higher for the right-wing parties and lower for the left-wing parties. The number of emigrants living in France who actually voted in this election is too insignificant to be worthy of consideration.

A year and a half after the April coup, villagers and emigrants had gained a certain degree of perspective, and a great deal of criticism was brewing. It is by now nothing new to note the strong anticommunist sentiments which prevail in northern Portugal.[13] Santa Eulalians were no different in their views. In fact, "*Não quero o comunismo*" (I do not want communism) was the most frequent, if not the only "political" statement heard. One man commented that he thought the best solution would be to let the Communists into the government palace to run the country for a month and then to burn the palace down with them inside! This was the most extreme criticism I ever heard. Others quite simply said they did not want communism because communism meant to them that they would no longer have control over the small plots of land which had been in their families for generations.

"I voted for the PPD," one illiterate seventy-five–year–old woman said, "because 'they' say it is the party of the Church." Indeed, anticommunist ideas are still nourished in the Church as are general antirevolutionary sentiments. In Santa Eulalia, these sentiments are also nourished in the village school, which is under the direction of the village priest. One day, the priest complained to me that the national education programs are now all "communist oriented."[14] He mistrusted the recent coup, pointed to the impending economic crisis, likening it to the pre-Salazar period of the 1920s, and supported a Protestant work-ethic approach to life. "We cannot all be equal," he told a classroom full of pre-adolescents one morning. "Those who work more and save will be better off. I work for myself and you work for yourselves. It is the people who do not want to work who are poor."

But it is not only the Church which engenders these strong anticommunist, antirevolutionary, and pro-work-ethic sentiments. The life goals of the northern peasants and the basic motives for which they emigrate stand in sharp contrast to what they believe to be the major tenets of communism. In emigrating, they have found a means of self-improvement. They work hard, in a foreign country, scrimping and saving at every corner in order to buy a house or a bigger and better plot of land. Communism is a threat to this "capitalistic" spirit of self-improvement and acquisition. One of the greatest fears among emigrants in France is that their new houses, built with the French francs they have spent years accumulating, will be taken over by the Communists or inhabited by Angolan refugees.[15] The very idea of taking over someone else's property is abhorrent to them. I asked a girl one day what she and others thought about some of the wealthier quinta-owning families in the village. "No one resents them for what they have," she insisted. "It is their property and they are entitled to it." In fact, those individuals who have been successful abroad, accumulating what appear to villagers to be vast resources of wealth, are looked upon with respect. They are the stimuli for others to leave as well. The wealth and lifestyle of the enobled and the *nouveau riche* are to be emulated, not criticized or challenged.

Although fear of communism is the political opinion expressed, there are a few other common attitudes worth mentioning. Many villagers and emigrants believed that there was too much freedom (*muito liberdade*) in Portugal. They believed that they were not ready for the freedom that the Revolution had bestowed upon them. They accused one another of not knowing how to behave. One rather intelligent emigrant, returned for the summer, phrased it this way: "People in the villages cannot rule themselves. People from outside must come in to help but they also have trouble because they are strangers. The *lavrador* is ignorant. *Operários* are more informed and much better able to take stands and lead the people. People who work the land do not know what to do with this new liberty." A teenage girl noted that people think the new liberty means they can do whatever they want or feel like doing. This "excess" of liberty led her to regret the downfall of Salazarism. She was a serious student and went on that afternoon to tell me about the new "regime" which had been imposed in the school because of the disciplinary problems which were developing as a result of this "misunderstood" liberty. No smoking, no talking, no interrupting the teacher, no *"namoradoing"* (going steady). The parents of the village had given the priest *carte blanche* to institute this new "regime" and she was glad of it.

The freedom of speech was welcomed but not at the expense of peace. Another man commented: "It was true that before we could not say anything bad about the government or we would be in prison, but at least then we lived in peace. I would rather be poor but live in peace than rich and live in war. And in Portugal now, *'é a guerra!'*" The loss of peace was lamented as was the loss of respect for authority. "No one respects policemen anymore," one man noted. "Everyone thinks they can all be equal. But there always have to be rich and poor."

Some even went so far as to question what freedom they did have. One man, working in Montreal now, though he had previously spent ten years in France, wondered if he really was free when his wife had trouble taking the money he earned out of their own bank account.[16] If things became worse and communism gained force, he told me, he would immediately call his wife and four children to Canada to join him.

At the time of my conversations with the villagers, one of the most widespread beliefs was that politics was for the people of Lisbon and that the Revolution was Lisbon's revolution. *"Não percebo nada de política"* is the common response to many politically framed questions. "Politics never meant anything to me before," they said. "Why should I start now?"[17] On the contrary, their lives had improved despite Salazarism, and through the grace of emigration. This improvement disguised the ills of the old regime, covering them with all the delightful trimmings which an emigrant salary could buy. The Revolution was a threat to a continued good standard of living or to further advancement because prices were rising and their hard-earned francs were buying less.

Emigration has provided a way out for the northern peasant, a way out which, through the quirks of history and historical tradition, has not been available to southern laborers.[18] Can we call these northern peasants "resistant to change and innovation, fatalistic and politically apathetic," as those who hold a traditional view of "the peasantry" would tend to do? Resistance to changes of one kind may be counteracted by full-fledged adoption of other changes. Political apathy does not necessarily imply total apathy. Apathy itself implies indifference and a lack of emotional involvement. The people of Santa Eulalia and the Portuguese immigrants in France were not indifferent to the changes that were occurring in their country. But they perceived these changes in a distinct way. Their concerns were economic rather than political. They were raised to find solutions to their economic problems not through political pressuring and collective action but through individual initiative and emigration. In terminating this section, I quote from a letter written by a Portuguese immigrant in France to the editors of the publication *Presença Portuguesa*: "I was in Portugal in August of last year. It seemed to me that we were freer but what use is freedom if there is no work and no bread to eat. What I ask for Portugal is peace, work, and harmony.—April, 1975."[19]

The Church and Emigration—Opposing Forces

I have already mentioned briefly some of the ways in which the Church and emigration might be considered as two major forces in the northern Portuguese countryside which act in opposition to the general thrust of the Revolution of the twenty-fifth of April. I would like to elaborate here.

In Santa Eulalia, the priest speaks from the pulpit to village adults, in the classroom to village children, and through the monthly newspaper to villagers abroad.[20] Like *Presença Portuguesa*, a magazine published for Portuguese immigrants in France, the *Voz de Santa Eulalia* has assumed a political role since the twenty-fifth of April—essentially a role as interpreter of political events and party positions. Although national newspapers are available in small supply in the village, only a few villagers buy or read them. The major source of information is the village paper.[21]

The information contained in this paper has been fairly objective with regard to the process of revolution, but the voice of the Church is always present, as if it were "in the running" as well. In the pre-election issue (March–April 1975) several pages were devoted to the electoral process (including simple information on how to vote) and to the respective party platforms. The summary of these platforms was quite noncommittal, although the LCI, PUP, UDP, and FEC were criticized for the "violent means" by which they proposed to attain their political objectives. The emphasis was upon peace, and the article terminated with a quote from Pius XII: "Salvation and justice are not found in revolution but in well-directed evolution. Violence always destroys, never builds; it excites rather than calms passions; it stimulates hate and ruin not fraternity and reconciliation."

In several issues there were small articles on "*a liberdade,*" including an excerpt from the *Diário do Minho* of September 1974.[22] In the July 1975 issue (about the time the Church began to feel itself under strong criticism from Communists and leftists) there was a piece entitled "Sou reaccionário" (I am reactionary)—a defense of the Church and religion. In the October–November 1975 issue there was an article entitled "Qué revolução é esta?" (What kind of a revolution is it?). The answer is contained quite forcefully in the text: "The majority of Portuguese people are subjected to the dictums of 'progressive' Lisbon and 'her' revolution. There they lay down the 'revolutionary laws'; there they organize large street demonstrations to support this or that government; there they play with an entire people; there they carry out the most incredible purges (always in the name of the so-called revolutionary process); there they make demagogic speeches; there are the organs of social communication which massacre daily the norms of living and the conscience of the Portuguese people."

The article concludes with a call for cooperation and mutual understanding within the Christian perspective prescribed by the Gospel and Christ. This polarization of city and country, of infidels and faithful is, of course, nothing new and underscores many of the political ideas and opinions expressed by the people of the northern countryside themselves (anticommunism, desire for peace, suspicion of *liberdade,* and Lisbon's revolution).

In addition to its role as political interpreter, the Church has another role to play. It fights for its survival, and one of the best means of doing so is by remaining in contact with village emigrants who have the monetary means to support it. The newspaper is the primary mechanism for keeping villagers abroad in touch with the activities and life of the village. The annual *festa*, which takes place during the summer when many, if not most, of the emigrants return home, is another. These *festas*—in Santa Eulalia and elsewhere—have been popularly rechristened *"festas dos emigrantes."* The emigrants give their money freely, if not extravagantly, to the operation of the village *festa*. The prestige accorded to them through these donations is enormous. The sons or daughters of emigrants—in their rich costumes and carrying their abundant *tabuleiros*—are immediately recognized.[23] The church in Santa Eulalia was completely renovated with the money that emigrants gave and the newspaper itself survives largely through their contributions.[24] This interaction between the Church and the emigrants keeps the emigrants within the religious fold. But the phenomenon of emigration on its own works in many ways to keep emigrants essentially nonpolitical and relatively conservative.

Emigration has made an essentially closed society open to northern villagers. It has, as noted earlier, always provided a channel for social mobility within Portugal (within the village) through external means. This social mobility does not involve either occupational or educational mobility (necessary for social mobility within the nation as a whole) but is achieved simply through the acquisition of wealth (which for national social mobility may be nothing) by whatever means. Martins has noted the political implications of this "openness": "The calculus of social and political action is altered . . . Emigration provides a functional equivalent to openness which, however contrary to fact, mitigates class feeling."[25]

Emigration, he suggests, has made these people into "potential nonmembers of the society or class or both,"[26] even if they have not yet emigrated. They may still be physically present in the village, but their ambitions, their future plans, their imaginations are elsewhere. It is this factor of "socialization for emigration" which explains the conservativeness of village youth. I talked to several young men about their prospects and plans for the future and they all told me that if nothing turned up in Portugal itself they would "just emigrate." They gave no thought to involving themselves in forms of political action which might bring them employment within Portugal itself. Furthermore, the fruits of emigration have raised their standard of living and created a rather serious disjunction between expectations and possibilities. They do not want factory jobs in Portugal although they would readily take such jobs in France. Many of the young men in Santa Eulalia are unemployed at the moment. Their major interests are clothes and soccer. The older generation accuses them of laziness. "They simply live on the well-warmed wallets of their emigrant fathers," one lady remarked. These village young people have few sympathies with the plight of agricultural workers in the north—the life is hard, dirty, and only worth leaving. But they have even fewer sympathies with the urban proletariat who often live in poorer conditions than they do.

Those who have already been in France—young and old—also have little contact with the French proletariat and with French unions and therefore are hardly exposed to the politically heightened atmosphere which union participation suggests.[27] The low level of immigrant participation in French unions is partially the result of an abdication of responsibilities by union organizers and an animosity directed toward foreign workers by native workers.[28] It is precisely this "union problem" to which Stephen Castles and Godula Kosack direct their attention in their book on immigrant workers in Western Europe.[29] In their final proposals they go so far as to suggest the establishment of separate trade unions for immigrants. Although the immigrants may still be part of the working class (nominally perhaps), they form a distinct stratum within that class. That immigrants form a "distinct stratum" is explained by the reasons for which they emigrate in the first place and by a general lack of knowledge about union activities and political behavior. The life of their place of work is of little interest to them. Some of them may be sympathetic to union demands but they are constantly unsure of their status with regard to direct participation.

Many male emigrants, especially those working in Renault and Citroen factories, belong to the union—they have their card—but they rarely, if ever, attend union meetings. One man said his boss had informed him once that unions were for men who cannot help themselves. "I decided right then," he said, "that the union was not for me."

In short, very few of the Portuguese emigrants are gaining any kind of political experience in France which they might then transport back to rural Portugal. They express no desire to affiliate themselves with the urban working class. John Goldthorpe's comments on the English working class are quite applicable: "They see their membership of the industrial labor force as being only a transitional phase in a movement of social ascent which will ultimately bring them at least *petit bourgeois* status. Thus, while greatly concerned with the economic returns from their work, they tend not to adopt the solidaristic class conscious orientation of the established working class. They retain the more individualistic and basically conservative values of their original culture, and are reluctant to define their social position by reference to their present work situation. They are, in other words, *in* the working class, but not *of* it."[30]

This "embourgeoisement" is then realized in Portugal itself. The emigrant is a *travailleur* in France to be *petit bourgeois* in Portugal. Embourgeoisement and the suburbanization of the Portuguese countryside are strong counterrevolutionary forces. The people I talked with in Santa Eulalia insisted that their lives had improved tremendously during the last ten years. "If it were not for France," sighed one girl, "poor Portugal, where would she be."

The three types of situations which Henry Landsberger[31] cites as stimuli to peasant discontent—status inconsistency, deprivation relative to some other comparable group, and deprivation relative to one's own past status or one's expected future status—are all conspicuously absent sentiments in northern Portugal. This absence is largely the result of emigration and the economic advantages and improvements it has brought to the lives of many individuals in northern Portugal.

Conclusion

The revolution of the twenty-fifth of April had an initial impact throughout Portugal. It uprooted a deep-rooted past. But two years later, much of the northern countryside was essentially where it was prior to the twenty-fifth of April 1974. Yet this is not to claim that changes will never occur. They are inevitable, but they will take time. Perhaps without the Revolution the seeds of political change might never have been planted. Emigration brought and brings changes but changes of a superficial or partial kind. At the moment, the north of Portugal looks like a rather unsuccessful hybrid of the nineteenth and twentieth centuries with new grafted onto old in haphazard and incomplete fashion. Emigration is a problem that must be tackled by the makers of the twenty-fifth of April—whether by expanding local industry or by lending respectability to agricultural work and developing it, for, if not, "the village will never achieve its own prosperity, however many smart new bicycles and wristwatches glitter on its streets. It remains condemned to send its sons away on contract labor."[32]

Notes

I would like to thank the Canada Council and the Social Science Research Council for making it possible to conduct the research on which this article is based.

1. Neither the Revolution nor political attitudes in general were the focus of my research. "Political" statements were made off-hand and I pursued them when they came, but I did not expressly seek them out.

2. Even Silva Martins, in a recent article on agrarian reforms in Portugal, focuses most of his discussion on southern Portugal, although he does refer to the laws of the *baldios* (public land) and *arrendamento* (rent) to protect northern peasants. See J. Silva Martins, "Reforma Agrária em Portugal," *Seará Nova*, no. 1563 (January 1976), pp. 33–36.

3. As far as my contacts extended in the village, no one had participated in the events in Ponte de Lima and few talked about it. The building still stands as a symbolic shell and was pointed out to me several times by various people.

4. Note particularly the figures for the district of Viana do Castelo, where most of the research upon which this article is based was conducted.

5. A high level of emigration is not unusual in areas with parcelized land and a system of partible inheritance. The high level of emigration from Ireland in the nineteenth century cannot be explained only by the potato famine although this indeed had a strong impact. It must also be explained by a sudden switch from a partible to an impartible system of property inheritance. See Conrad Arensberg, *Family and Community in Ireland* (Cambridge, Mass.: Harvard University Press, 1940).

6. E. J. Hobsbawm, "Peasants and Politics," *Journal of Peasant Studies* 1, no. 1 (1973): 7.

7. Ronald Waterbury, "Non Revolutionary Peasants: Oaxaca Compared to Morelos in the Mexican Revolution," *Comparative Studies in Society and History* 17, no. 4 (1975): 411.

8. The conceptual distinction between "peasant" and "rural proletarian" is itself indicative of an important difference in potential rural response to revolution. For discussion of the "rural proletariat," see Sidney W. Mintz, "The Folk Urban Continuum and the Rural Proletarian Community," *American Journal of Sociology* 59 (1953): 136–143; and idem, "The Rural Proletariat and the Problem of Rural Proletarian Communities," *Journal of Peasant Studies* 1, no. 3 (1974): 291–325.

9. To contrast "the north" with "the south" is of course acceptable only to a certain extent. More detailed analysis reveals internal differences of major importance. Thus one finds traces of "communal villages" in the mountainous areas of Tras os Montes but not in the littoral north.

10. In accordance with anthropological practice, I have disguised the name of the village although all the figures are themselves accurate.

11. The official census figures of 1970 are at variance with these later village figures. A high level of emigration, which is frequently clandestine and transitory, complicates population figures enormously. A census taken in December, as the official census was, would find many people in the village who might not be there three months later. According to the files

of the village priest, there were 173 individuals or families away at the time the research was conducted. Of these, 97 were families, 45 single men, 22 single women, 8 single men, and 1 couple.

12. One quinta is 81,284 m². A piece of this (5,232 m²) has been rented since 1972 by a French emigrant. Another quinta is 27,953 m².

13. During the month of August there were numerous forest fires throughout the north of Portugal, including one on the *serra* not far from Santa Eulalia. The rumor was that the fires had been set by Communists. The preceding spring had been unusually dry—perhaps a more satisfactory explanation.

14. For children ages ten to thirteen, roughly, much of their education is transmitted over national television. The programs (in languages, science, mathematics, history, and social studies) last about twenty minutes and are then reviewed and discussed in the classroom with a teacher.

15. In the August 30, 1975, issue of *Vida Rural*, a magazine on agrarian reform, there was an article in response to an inquiry made by a reader on the rights of others to cultivate the lands of emigrants. It comes out in favor of cultivating all good land. Emigrants should rent out their lands rather than leave them uncultivated. In Santa Eulalia much of the land owned by emigrant families was tended by members of the extended family who remained in the village.

16. The *Financial Times* of London, December 18, 1975, began an article on Portugal by referring to an advertising campaign by one of the state-owned banks. The ad portrays a wad of money stuffed under a mattress threatened by inflation, thieves, rats, and fire, and the caption reads, "You know your money is safer with us at nine and a half percent." The banks have large-scale campaigns to keep the deposits coming and like to keep the money there for use. A notice I picked up in the branch of Banco Português do Atlantico in Viana do Castelo at Christmas time 1975 warned emigrants returned for the holidays to beware of speculators and false currencies. "Do your dealings with us" was the overall message.

17. An inquiry into the attitudes of Portuguese emigrants toward French politics published two years ago in *Seará Nova* noted a similar reaction. Emigrants felt uninformed and had no understanding of how political demands might improve their lot. See "A Vida Política Francesa Vista Pelos Immigrantes Portugueses," *Seará Nova*, no. 1537 (October 1973), pp. 9–10.

18. It should be noted that to emigrate requires a certain amount of initial capital. Such capital is more accessible to small landholding peasants who can always sell some land to raise money. Penniless day laborers have nothing to sell.

19. *Presença Portuguesa* is a monthly magazine published by the interdiocesan council (SITI) of the Region Parisienne expressly for Portuguese immigrants.

20. Rocha Trindade notes a similar role for the priest of the village of Queiriga in the district of Viseu. See Maria Beatriz Rocha Trindade, *Immigrés Portugais* (Lisbon: Instituto Superior de Ciências Sociais e Política Ultramarina, 1973).

21. There are several televisions in the village and most households have radios. But most often I heard music or, on Sundays, morning masses coming from the radios. Movies and variety shows were the most popular pro-

grams to watch on the television in the café, but with the general café noise level, one could barely hear anything so that those who watched political speeches missed most of what was said. I was with a family on Sunday, the eleventh of November 1975, the day of one of the important mass demonstrations in Lisbon. The television was on but little attention was paid to it and the favored topic of discussion was to decide whether Sá Carneiro, the head of the PPD, or Mário Soares, the head of the Socialist Party, was handsomer!

22. The article was entitled "A liberdade que não queremos" and suggested that Portugal did not want such liberties as ridiculing religious beliefs, lying, threatening the life and property of others, exploiting others, prostitution, and pornography. It concludes, "Não queremos esta liberdade porque isto não é liberdade. E antes, libertinagem e abuso da liberdade" (We do not want this kind of freedom because it is not freedom. It is, above all, libertinism and abuse of freedom).

23. A *tabuleiro* is an offering of food and wine given for auction to raise money for the church. Some of the girls carry this food in decorated baskets and others in tiered structures which they support on their heads. The principle is for the father or boyfriend of the girl to buy it back for her—thus a father may provide not only food but also money, which sometimes rose to three and four contos ($120–$160 in 1975) in the auction.

24. Every issue of the village paper contained a list of names, place of residence (Santa Eulalia or elsewhere—i.e., France, Germany, Africa, etc.), and the sum that had been given. Emigrant contributions were significantly greater than village contributions.

25. Hermínio Martins, "Portugal," in *Contemporary Europe: Class, Status and Power*, ed. M. Archer and S. Giner (London: Weidenfeld and Nicolson, 1971), pp. 85–86.

26. Ibid., p. 85.

27. Theodore Zeldin (*France, 1848–1945: Ambition, Love, and Politics*, vol. 1 [Oxford: Oxford University Press, 1973], pp. 265–266) cites a study by a doctor in the Tarn region. Peasants there had moved into factories or mines but often kept a piece of land on which to grow their food. "Far from reducing their hours of work by going into the mines they now worked much longer because before or after their shift underground, they would carry out about half a peasant's day of labor on their plots. Friction inevitably arose between them and those who had lost contact with the land, because they, growing a lot of food themselves, could afford to work less. The full proletarianization of these peasants was a slow process." Zeldin then cites another study carried out in the 1950s which shows that workers of agricultural origin remained more optimistic about the possibilities of moving up in the world than unskilled workers of urban origin. "They talked politics far less than other workers; they did not see society as ruled by class antagonisms. The very fact that they themselves had escaped from the land showed, as they believed, that individual effort could overcome social obstacles."

28. Jacqueline Minces, *Les Travailleurs étrangers en France* (Paris: Editions Seuil, 1973), p. 325, cites the following attitudes: "The national workers only see the migrant workers as strike breakers. In their eyes, they are people who do not need to be defended because they are better off

here than at home anyway; because they profit from all the social advantages that France offers; and because they come to eat the bread of the French and to spend French money in their own countries."

29. Stephen Castles and Godula Kosack, *Immigrant Workers and Class Structure in Western Europe* (London: Oxford University Press, 1973).

30. John H. Goldthorpe et al., *The Affluent Worker in the Class Structure* (Cambridge: At the University Press, 1969), p. 12.

31. Henry A. Landsberger, *Rural Protests* (London: Macmillan, 1974).

32. Neal Acherson, "Room at the Bottom," *New York Review of Books*, February 5, 1976, p. 23.

10. Analysis and Projection of Macroeconomic Conditions in Portugal

RUDIGER DORNBUSCH, RICHARD S. ECKAUS, AND
LANCE TAYLOR

There seems to be virtually unanimous opinion in Portugal that there was a catastrophic decline in economic activity in the last half of 1974 and during 1975. Appraisals include phrases like "verge of chaos" and "brink of disaster." In the face of such gloom, it may be regarded as unwarranted optimism to maintain that, although the situation was quite tenuous, at the beginning of 1976 the Portuguese economy was surprisingly sound. While there was dangerous potentiality for further real declines in output and income, more unemployment and inflation, there was also the potentiality for strong recovery. However, it should be emphasized that the optimism expressed here is conditional, at best. The problems are profound and righting them will be a different operation. Yet, it is possible to reduce the further economic traumas which will have to be suffered by Portugal and to place the economy on a stable footing in the medium run.

Enormous economic and social changes have occurred in Portugal since April 25, 1974. Important parts of the system of production and finance have been nationalized and reorganized. The participation of labor in decision making has increased as has labor's share of the national product via large, though somewhat uneven, increases in wages. Price inflation, though beginning to accelerate even before April 1974, has become an important fact of everyday life. And all of this has been accompanied by surging processes of political change.

Besides the adjustments within Portugal, there have also been international changes so profound as to provoke talk of a "new international order." Any economic diagnosis and prescription for Portugal must take these international developments into account. The Portuguese revolution coincided with an almost world-wide depresssion which had a particularly strong impact on Portugal's major trading partners. That and the independence of its former African colonies contributed to a sharp reduction in Portugal's exports. The depression in Western Europe, by increasing unemployment and reducing the incomes of emigrant workers, also reduced the flow of remittances. In previous years these were large enough to convert an unfavorable import-export trade deficit to a current account surplus in the Portuguese balance of payments.

Increases in oil and other fuel and commodity prices caused the same sharp deterioration in the Portuguese terms of trade that afflicted other Western European countries which are large importers of primary products and exporters of manufactures. The relative openness of the Portuguese economy made this a substantial loss of real income. These international changes have also been important contributors to internal inflation in Portugal, as in the rest of the world.

Although the depressions in Western Europe and the Western Hemisphere have a variety of sources, they may be viewed in part as a response to the balance of payments pressures created by the unfavorable change in their international terms of trade. The economies have been depressed, creating unemployment and reductions in consumption and investment, in order to reduce imports and pass on international price increases to domestic prices.

To an outside observer reading only the national statistical tables and not a word about social revolution, the record during this period in Portugal would not appear so different from that of the rest of Europe, with some puzzling discrepancies. While the economy was depressed, personal consumption increased and, as noted, labor's share of the national income did also. But the major trends of reduced production and investment, balance of payments deficits, and inflation would all look quite familiar and even in some respects less serious for Portugal than in some of the other countries of Western Europe.

The appearance of some statistical similarities in the developments in 1974 and 1975 in the Portuguese economy and those of some other European nations is both suggestive and potentially misleading. Thus, it is essential to have a clear diagnosis of the sources of the current difficulties of the Portuguese economy before attempting to make policy prescriptions. If the problem is really "chaos" and disruption of the organization of production and management in enterprises, then, in effect, there are "supply bottlenecks" which must somehow be overcome before a reasonable semblance of prosperity can be restored and the conditions for future growth created. If the problems are partly the result of loss of foreign markets due to international concern over the ability of Portuguese suppliers to meet delivery schedules because of labor unrest, then again there is a kind of supply bottleneck which has its origins in the economic and political uncertainties within the country. On the other hand, suppose that the problems mainly originate abroad in losses of export markets and emigrant remittances due to foreign recessions. Then the remedies must be essentially of the aggregate demand stimulation type, with special concern for the direction of new investment to create new sources of foreign exchange earnings. And, if the problems have multiple sources of these and other types, then an appropriate mixed strategy must be developed.

It would be difficult to trace causes and effects and assign relative weights to the various influences in the best of circumstances, with timely and reasonably comprehensive and reliable data and a backlog of studies of export and import elasticities, productivity, capacity utilization, and so on. There is no point in repeating the customary complaints about the inadequacies of Portuguese economic statistics, though they surely contribute to the high degree of uncertainty which is associated with any diagnosis and risk connected with any projection. These qualifications should be kept in mind while reading this report.

Macroeconomic Conditions in 1975

For a country experiencing thorough social reform, a major change in its foreign trade position, and six revolutionary governments in nineteen months, Portugal enjoys unexpectedly good economic health. While real output clearly dropped in 1975, the decline was not precipitous; the best estimate is a 3 percent decrease in gross domestic product (GDP). By comparison with other OECD countries, the Portuguese experience does not appear to be much worse than average; in fact the economy's performance has been quite robust when the political uncertainties of 1975 are taken into account. By comparison, GDP decline in 1975 for the United States was about 3 percent; in West Germany, close to 4 percent; and in Italy, almost 4.5 percent.

TABLE 10–1

National Accounts for 1975 (*Millions of contos of 1974*)

	Consumption	Investment	Government	Exports	Less Imports	Total
Agriculture, forestry, fishing	66.9			6.4	–13.6	59.7
Manufacturing	100.4	32.1	15.3	36.4	–79.4	104.8
Construction		11.6				11.6
Services	105.5		30.7	16.5	–13.1	139.6
Indirect taxes less subsidies	31.3					31.3
Public transfers						
Total	304.1	43.7	46.0	59.3	–106.1	347.0

Note: A conto is 1,000 escudos.

TABLE 10–2

National Accounts for 1974 (*Millions of contos of 1974*)

	Consumption	Investment	Government	Exports	Less Imports	Total
Agriculture, forestry, fishing	62.0	2.0		8.3	–16.5	55.8
Manufacturing	101.8	51.6	15.3	49.2	–96.8	121.1
Construction		19.3				19.3
Services	97.3		30.7	23.6	–20.2	131.4
Indirect taxes less subsidies	31.3					31.3
Public transfers				11.2	–13.1	–1.9
Total	292.4	72.9	46.0	92.3	–146.6	357.0

ESTIMATES OF AGGREGATE REAL INCOME IN 1975

To provide a basis for analyzing the current economic situation, a crude set of estimates for the national income accounts in 1975 has been prepared. As explained in the Appendix, the technique for constructing the accounts was to gather informed assessments of current trends in sectoral outputs and aggregate demand patterns, and exploit the identities of the accounting system to force these disparate numbers into a coherent pattern. The exercise would have been impossible without collaboration of economists in the Bank of Portugal and the Ministry of Finance, who provided many insights into the Portuguese economy.[1]

Table 10-1 presents estimates for 1975, and Tables 10-2 and 10-3 present national income statistics for 1973 and 1974 on the same disaggregated basis. Associated with Tables 10-1 and 10-2 are the percentage changes from 1974 to 1975 in the sources and uses of national output, as shown in Table 10-4. As just indicated, estimates of many of these percentages along with the levels of economic aggregates in 1974 provided the basis for the first step in making the 1975 estimates. The picture which emerges from these numbers is that of an economy whose overall level of activity was maintained by buoyant consumer demand. Because of income redistribution under the Revolution, personal consumption rose from 73 percent of national product in 1973 to 82 percent in 1974 and continued to increase in real terms in 1975. On the other hand, investment in fixed capital (and possibly in inventories) declined sharply, and with it activity in construction and industries manufacturing building products. Exports have stagnated, from loss of markets both in the former colonies and in the recession-plagued Common Market. But due to lagging activity in manufacturing, which uses many imported intermediate inputs, imports declined as well, and the deficit on trade account actually fell from something like 54 million contos in 1974 to 51 million in 1975 (in current prices of each year).

The upshot of all these movements was an estimated decrease in real gross domestic product between 1974 and 1975 of 2.8 percent, a significant output loss but less alarming than some other estimates have made it. Changes in sectoral production levels, the decline in manufacturing especially, agree quantitatively with independent assessments as of late 1975. There is scattered evidence that the slowdown in economic activity may have worsened in the latter part of 1975.[2]

TABLE 10–3

National Accounts for 1973 (*Millions of contos of 1973*)

	Consumption	Investment	Government	Exports	Less Imports	Total
Agriculture, forestry, fishing	42.7	1.3		6.4	−9.3	41.1
Manufacturing	65.4	39.0	12.7	38.4	−63.9	91.6
Construction		16.3				16.3
Services	71.8		25.5	22.3	−10.5	109.1
Indirect taxes less subsidies	26.9					26.9
Public transfers				9.1	−11.0	−1.9
Total	206.8	56.6	38.2	76.2	−94.7	283.1

TABLE 10–4

Percentage Changes in Important Economic Aggregates, 1975/1974

Levels of Value Added		Aggregate Demand by Type	
Agriculture	+7.0%	Consumption	+4.0%
Manufacturing	−13.5	Investment	−40.0
Construction	−40.0	Exports	−35.7
Services	+6.2	Imports	−27.6
Gross domestic product	−2.8	Trade deficit	−13.8

PRICE AND WAGE CHANGES IN 1975

A good guess at the increase in a generalized price index, such as the GDP deflator, might be 20 percent. Such a magnitude is consistent with the outmoded Lisbon consumer price index, scattered information on increases in labor and import costs, and money velocity considerations.[3]

Wages also increased substantially during the year. Table 10-5 presents the available price and wage index data. While skepticism with respect to the numbers is warranted, the relatively larger increase in wages than prices which is shown does appear to be valid.

THE GOVERNMENT SECTOR IN 1975

Turning to fiscal issues, it is estimated that the cash deficit of the consolidated government sector ran to something like 33 million contos in 1975, even with an abnormally low public investment expenditure of 13 million contos. A deficit of such magnitude was inevitable, even though it was without precedent in Portugal. The fundamental rationale for the observed increase in government expenditure with respect to tax receipts is nothing other than the

TABLE 10–5

Indices of Recent Wage and Price Levels in Portugal
(*1970 = 100*)

	Average Wholesale Prices of Domestic Production	Wages in Industry and Transportation (Lisbon)
1973/I	118	128.77
II	119	134.35
III	122	140.17
IV	131	144.33
1974/I	148	154.26
II	152	177.25
III	154	194.33
IV	160	198.58
1975/I	162	204.31
II	164	n.a.

Source: National Institute of Statistics, *Monthly Statistical Bulletin*, Bank of Portugal.

TABLE 10–6

Monetary Data (*Millions of contos*)

	1973				1974				1975				
	I	II	III	IV	I	II	III	IV	I	II	III	Nov.	Dec.
Currency	35	36	39	38	39	51	59	70	76	85	100ᴾ	103ᴾ	112ᴾ
M_1 = Currency + Demand Deposits	126	131	141	166	156	158	162	183	177	186	204*	209*	226*
M_2 = M_1 + Time Deposits	244	256	272	301	301	307	320	342	342	351	362*	366*	386*
Foreign assets, net	72	73	76	78	73	69	69	63	58	55	45*	39*	37*
of which: Bank of Portugal	67	67	70	72	68	65	63	56	51	48	38ᴾ	33ᴾ	32ᴾ
Monetary Base	62	65	69	71	68	72	81	95	89	95	111ᴾ	116ᴾ	130ᴾ

* Estimate.   ᴾ Provisional.

Note: The figures for currency are obtained from the numbers of currency and coin outstanding less bank vault cash. For November 1975, bank vault cash is assumed equal to 3 billion escudos; for December 1975, it is assumed equal to 4.7 billion escudos. The estimates of M_1 and M_2 figures for September 1975 are obtained from a sample of eight banks and the Caixa Geral de Depositos, and those for November and December 1975, from a sample of four banks and the CGD. Net foreign assets include gold valued at the "offical" price.

TABLE 10–7

Money Multipliers, 1973–1975

	1973				1974				1975				
	I	II	III	IV	I	II	III	IV	I	II	III	Nov.	Dec.
Currency/Base	.56	.55	.57	.53	.57	.71	.73	.74	.85	.89	.90	.89	.86
M_1/Base	2.03	2.01	2.04	2.33	2.29	2.19	2.00	1.92	1.99	1.96	1.84	1.80	1.74
M_2/Base	3.94	3.94	3.94	4.24	4.43	4.26	3.95	3.60	3.84	3.69	3.26	3.16	2.97

economy's shift into a current account deficit position in its balance of payments.

In the past, Portugal was able to run current account surpluses, making it possible for the government accounts to be in balance without having a major depressing effect on the economy. However, in the new circumstances of reduced exports and remittances and higher import prices, there is a chronic current account deficit. Such an excess of foreign exchange payments over receipts diverts purchasing power abroad and cuts back effective demand *within* the country. The loss in demand can be offset in various ways, but an excess of government spending over revenues is by far the most effective on a large scale. Had there not been a government deficit in 1975, the private sector would have had to adjust to the trade deficit by cutting investment and consumption with consequent reductions in imports. There *were* substantial, though undesired, reductions in investment. However, Portuguese authorities wisely supported personal consumption by *not* following "balanced budget" policies.

MONEY AND FINANCE IN 1975

The changing balance of payments situation also led to fundamental modifications in the money supply process in Portugal. Putting the matter briefly, the source of domestic money creation is no longer a balance of payments surplus and has become domestic credit creation instead. Table 10-6 gives the details in the form of quarterly data on the principal monetary aggregates. The last two lines show the increasing divergence between the monetary base and the net external assets of the Bank of Portugal, with international reserves falling while the monetary base (reserves plus domestic credit) increases.

The decline in the Bank of Portugal's net foreign assets is the financial counterpart of the current account deficit, the real causes of which have already been discussed. One important point to note is that the quarterly loss in reserves has stayed roughly constant in nominal terms since mid-1974. With an inflation rate of 20 percent, the real deficit is actually declining. This is another piece of evidence supporting the conjecture that the recession in Portugal is deepening—real demand for foreign resources is dropping off as the level of economic activity declines.

The monetary data in Table 10-6 show a rising stock of currency in the hands of the public throughout 1974 and 1975. The stock of currency has been rising absolutely and relative to both M_1 and M_2. This is borne out by Table 10-7, which shows an increase from 1973 to 1975 in the ratio of currency to monetary base and a decline in the M_1 base and M_2 base ratios. Previous commentators have noted as two important explanations the redistribution of income toward labor and the preference for currency that arises because of the nationalization of banks and political events that appear to render bank deposits more vulnerable to state control and supervision. While this rising trend for currency continued through November 1975, there is some evidence that since that time some stabilization of the behavior of currency has taken effect.

The large increase in the currency-to-money ratio since 1973 should be of no concern to policy makers. The argument that the large stock of currency outstanding could lead to sudden and uncontrollable dishoarding or to a reflow into the banking system resulting in a credit explosion is of little substance. First, dishoarding can be financed as much by deposits as it can by currency so that there is no presumption that the stock of currency is a measure of likely changes in the velocity of circulation (the ratio of money to income). Second, a reflow of currency into the banking system, if it took place, would make the banks more liquid. Whether it would lead to a credit explosion is entirely a matter of credit demand and monetary policy. As a matter of monetary policy it is very easy to offset increased bank liquidity by reduced discounts or increased reserve requirements so that from this perspective also there is no need for concern. Perhaps, even more importantly, the current investment climate is assuredly not one where a credit explosion is to be feared.

The next question concerns the growth rate of monetary aggregates M_1 and M_2 in 1975 and the issue whether monetary growth was sufficient or perhaps even excessive. Table 10-6 shows that monetary growth from the third quarter of 1974 to the third quarter of 1975 was 26 percent for M_1 and 13 percent for M_2. The increase in M_1 relative to M_2 reflects primarily the fast growth of currency that accounts for about 50 percent of M_1 and only about 28 percent of M_2. Using end-of-year monetary estimates, the growth rate of monetary aggregates for the fourth quarter of 1975 relative to the fourth quarter of 1974 is 23 percent for M_1 and 13 percent for M_2.

It is safe, therefore, to infer that monetary growth during 1975 was of the order of 25 percent, certainly not falling short of 20 percent and certainly not in excess of 30 percent. This contrasts with a growth of M_1 in the preceding year of only 10 percent. The adequacy of this monetary growth has to be judged relative to the essentially exogeneous increases in wages and prices. Given a rate of price increase of around 20 percent, the monetary growth was about adequate to finance a constant level of real income with allowance for some decline in velocity. In fact there is a presumption that velocity should have declined because of the effect of income redistribution on money demand. If this additional factor is taken into account, then monetary growth in the 1974/75 period was, if anything, rather modest and the monetary situation was tight.

To judge the extent of the tightness, it is necessary to form a judgment about the effect of income redistribution on money demand. A rough, and rough indeed, idea of the magnitudes involved was obtained by first dividing money holders into two groups that, respectively, will be identified with earners of labor incomes and earners of income from capital and other sources. The recipients of labor income will increase their demand for money by an amount equal to their income elasticity of demand for money times initial money holdings times the percentage change in their incomes. Similarly, the recipients of other types of income will reduce their money demand by their income elasticity times initial money holdings times the percentage change in the income. Total demand for money will increase because the income elasticity of money demand is significantly higher for low-income groups as compared to high-income groups.

The magnitude of the increase in money demand will depend on three factors: (a) the difference in income elasticities, (b) the initial distribution of money holdings, and (c) the magnitude of the income redistribution. To obtain an estimate of this increase in demand for money, the following assumptions are made: (a) labor's share in income has risen, as a consequence of the redistribution of income, from 45 percent to 65 percent income; (b) initially, wage earners held 60 percent of the stock of M_1; and (c) finally, labor has an income elasticity of demand for money of unity as compared to 0.5 for recipients of other incomes. These assumptions yield an increase in total money demand of 24 percent. An alternative and very conservative estimate would assume an initial income distribution and money holding distribution for each group of 50 percent and income elasticities of unity and 0.5, respectively. This leads to an increase in money demand of 7.5 percent. If, in addition, it is recognized that the refugee inflow raised population and, therefore, money demand by 3 percent to 4 percent, it is safe to assume that these factors in combination contributed to an increase in mon-

TABLE 10-8

Money, Income, and Velocity, 1970–1975

	1970	1971	1972	1973	1974	1975
Income (GDP)	179	200	233	283	357	421
M_1	93	105	122	166	183	226
Velocity (Income) (M_1)	1.92	1.90	1.91	1.70	1.95	1.86
M_2	156	189	235	301	342	386
Velocity (Income) (M_2)	1.15	1.06	.99	.94	1.04	1.09

ey demand of at least 10 percent and perhaps as much as 25 percent over the period since the second quarter of 1974. Although the exact number is obviously quite uncertain, it is nevertheless safe to conclude that a significant increase in money demand results from these sources.

While the income redistribution served to increase money demand at each level of income, an opposing force derives from the effect of inflationary expectations. The anticipation of inflation continuing at the level experienced in 1975 would cause substitution from money to real assets, such as consumer durables. Households will attempt to evade the depreciation of the purchasing power of their wealth by holding real assets. The empirical magnitude of this factor is hard to assess. It is not reasonable, however, to assume that the doubling of the inflation rate in 1974/75 as compared to the 1970/73 period should have contributed to a reduction in money demand by 10 to 20 percent at each level of income.

On balance, therefore, we would expect some reduction in velocity, perhaps of the order of 5 to 10 percent. This is, in fact, borne out in a rough manner by Table 10-8, which shows money, income, and velocity figures for the 1970–1975 period.

The implication of the preceding analysis is that monetary policy was about right and perhaps even somewhat tight considering the low money growth in 1974. The analysis lends support to the view that the estimate for 1975 of a nominal income growth of about 16 percent (20% inflation and a 3% decline in real activity) is a reasonable approximation of events. If the inflation had been significantly higher, that would imply an unreasonably high number for velocity. Conversely, if there had been a significantly larger decline in real activity, that would imply too much of a fall in velocity relative to what can be rationalized from the effects of income redistribution.

SUPPLY CONSTRAINTS

Although this diagnosis of the factors determining the economic conditions of 1975 has, so far, stressed influences on the demand side, "supply constraints" arising from labor unrest and management difficulties were also significant. Unfortunately, the evidence on these matters consists largely of anecdotes and newspaper stories which owe at least some of their wide acceptance to repetition. It is also possible that the labor and management problems of relatively large enterprises in the Lisbon region have colored the entire outlook. There is no adequate quantitative information about the degree and sources of disorganization in productive establishments. The new legal constraints on release of workers would make it difficult to use labor productivity data for this purpose in any case. Since demand and production have certainly fallen, while virtually a full complement of workers have been retained, as a matter of arithmetic, productivity has fallen.

A brief but rather wide-ranging discussion with public and private management officials gave the impression that the stories of disruption in production may have been exaggerated. There have certainly been labor unrest, an increase in absenteeism, a reduction in the effectiveness of supervision at the shop level, and a slowdown in work speeds in some cases. Other situations were mentioned in which there was no decline in productivity. Where slowdowns have been observed, they were related to reduced backlogs so that workers were only extending the visible work load over a longer period. It was felt that an increase in orders would be accompanied by increases in productivity. Interestingly, there were general reports of recent reductions in worker militancy which had interfered with production.

It is difficult to draw general lessons from fragmentary and anecdotal evidence. However, some conclusions appear warranted from all the information available. (a) Productivity has fallen, but at least part of the decrease is due to lack of demand and the inability of management, both private and public, to discharge workers. (b) Labor is more active than under the *ancien regime*, both in wage demands and in pressing a variety of pent-up grievances. Because this is a novelty in Portugal it would, in itself, tend to create a climate of labor militancy in which the appearance is less than the reality, which might be no more difficult than in most other Western European countries. (c) There have been substantial wage increases but these have been uneven in their spread and, therefore, inequitable to those groups which have been left behind in the inflationary process.

Prospects for 1976

The economic situation in 1976 and the years following will be affected strongly by the rate of recovery from recession of those economies which have been the major markets for Portugal's exports. Even more importantly, the economic situation over the next year will depend crucially on internal events: the outcome of farm production as affected by weather and agricultural reorganization and the effectiveness of government domestic policies to stimulate and direct economic activity.

AGGREGATE REAL DEVELOPMENTS

In such circumstances, economic forecasts are unusually risky. Because of this, two alternative projections are made, based on different assumptions with respect to export trends and agricultural production. In making the projections for 1976, the procedure has been to postulate a plausible set of goals for the economy and then develop their implications for overall growth and the role of the government, using the alternative assumptions about exports and agriculture. The conditional nature of the projections should be emphasized since both may seem somewhat optimistic, though in different respects.

A major difference in the two projections is in the assumptions which they embody with respect to domestic agricultural output in 1976 and in export performance. Agricultural production in 1976 in the first projection is assumed to return to the levels achieved in 1974. In addition, exports in the first projection are assumed to grow in 1976 above their 1975 levels, but by only 3 percent, which would still leave them well below their 1974 levels. The first projection is somewhat optimistic both with respect to the domestic investment targets which could be achieved and with respect to the success of domestic policies in modulating the growth of imports and consumption.

In the second projection, agricultural output in 1976 is assumed to be less than that of 1975 by only 2 percent. Exports are assumed to grow at a rate of 15 percent, which, if continued and augmented somewhat, would mean a recovery to 1974 levels by 1977. Investment in the second projection is less buoyant than in the first, as-

TABLE 10–9

Aggregate Demand Levels in 1975
in 1975 Prices (*Millions of contos*)

Consumption	364.9
Investment	52.4
Government	55.2
Exports	65.2
Less imports	−116.7
GDP	421.0

suming only that the real levels of 1974 will be reached but not exceeded.

It is assumed in both projections that the expansion of the economy will not be constrained in order to reduce substantially the trade deficit which should be expected to accompany that expansion or the government deficit. The objective of this government deficit is not to finance immediate additional increments in consumption, but to generate new investment. This would create capacity and improve productivity in order to regain export markets and increase domestic income.

The first step in making the 1976 forecasts was to convert the 1975 real GDP estimates of Table 10-1 from 1974 to 1975 prices. This was done utilizing rough indications supplied by the Lisbon cost of living index and approximations to changes in international prices. The results are shown in Table 10-9. The real national product estimates of the first projection are shown in level terms in Table 10-10 and in growth rate form in Table 10-11. The latter shows that 5.6 percent real GDP growth is projected for 1976, if the rather ambitious targets regarding consumption and investment increases are in fact met.

The national product figures for Projection II generated by these assumptions are shown in Table 10-12 and, in summary form, with associated growth rates from 1975 levels in Table 10-13. The real rate of growth implied in Projection II is even higher than that for Projection I and is the result of the assumed higher agricultural production and export achievements offset to only a limited degree by the lower investment projections.

Projections I and II embody relatively optimistic assumptions, although with respect to somewhat different components of national demand and output. It should be emphasized again, however, that the optimism is conditional: skillful and forceful government action

TABLE 10–10

Projection I: National Accounts for 1976 (*Millions of contos of 1975*)

	Consumption	Investment	Government	Exports	Less Imports	Total
Agriculture, forestry, fishing	82.7	2.5		6.4	−24.6	67.0
Manufacturing	124.0	65.7	20.0	41.2	−107.0	143.9
Construction		24.6				24.6
Services	129.1		40.0	18.7	−18.7	169.1
Indirect taxes less subsidies	40.0					40.0
Public transfers						40.0
Total	375.8	92.8	60.0	66.3	−150.3	444.6

Note: In detail, the assumptions for the first projection are (*a*) Real consumption will continue to increase in the aggregate. Per capita consumption will not be permitted to fall in spite of the economic difficulties which Portugal faces, but will rise slightly as a result of continued adherence to an incomes policy and push for distributional equity. Taking population growth into account, the projected rate of growth for consumption was set at 3%. It was estimated that 22% of consumption expenditures would go to agriculture and 33% to manufactures. (*b*) Real investment will regain its long-term growth path by increasing to a level equal to two years' growth at 3% from the 1974 level. This represents an increase in investment demand of 77% over 1975 and is the most optimistic of the assumptions embodied in the projection. (*c*) Because of some disruption in land reform and depletion of capital, agricultural output falls back to its 1974 level in real terms. (*d*) Government consumption rises 8.7% in real terms, to 60 million contos, a number frequently cited in discussions. (*e*) Agricultural exports remain at their 1975 level in real terms, while manufactured and service exports rise 3%. (*f*) Manufactured imports are estimated by assuming that the direct-and-indirect import content of manufactures for consumption, government, and export demands is 40% and is 50% for investment goods. Service imports are held down to a level just sufficient to offset service exports. (*g*) Indirect taxes (including 4.5 million paid to local authorities) are assumed to be 40 million contos, an increase of 6.5% over 1975.

TABLE 10–11

Aggregate Demand Levels Estimated for 1975 Compared with
Projection I for 1976 and Implied Growth Rates in 1975 Prices
(*Millions of contos*)

	1975	1976	Growth Rates
Consumption	364.9	375.8	3.0%
Investment	52.4	92.8	77.1
Government	55.2	60.0	8.7
Exports	65.2	66.3	1.7
Less imports	−116.7	−150.3	28.8
Gross domestic product	421.0	444.6	5.6

would be required within the framework of foreign and domestic
constraints which shape the projections.

Table 10-14 contains the estimates of the savings-investment
flows for 1973, 1974, 1975, and 1976, according to the two projections. Private saving is derived as a residual for 1973–75, and government current surplus as the residual in 1976.[1] The major point
to be noted is the steady swing of the current account deeper into
deficit in recent years. To repeat a point already made, adverse shifts
in the terms of trade, lagging exports, and the strong import dependence of its production structure have made it impossible for
Portugal to cover its visible trade deficit by remittance flows from
its workers "exported" to the Common Market and the New World.
Because Projection II assumes higher exports, it embodies a lower
current deficit than Projection I, but in both projections the trade
deficit for 1976 is much larger than in previous years. In Projection I, there is no anticipated decline in the government deficit.
Projection II does embody a reduced government deficit. In both
projections the deficit is neither more nor less than the domestic
counterpoise to a large foreign exchange gap. The details of the
government accounts estimated for 1975 appear in Table 10-15.

From Table 10-14, the current expenditure deficit of the government in 1976, according to Projection I, is 17.6 million contos.
When 25 million contos of investment expenditure are added to
this, the cash deficit becomes 42.6 million contos, or 9.6 percent
of GDP. Details of the consolidated government budget associated
with Projection I are shown in Table 10.16.

Although Portugal has traditionally been a country in which the
government has not run a deficit, this situation probably changed
permanently in 1975. The cash deficit for that year estimated here
amounts to 7.8 percent of GDP. By the standards of most countries,

TABLE 10–12

Projection II: National Accounts for 1976 (*Millions of contos of 1975*)

	Consumption	Investment	Government	Exports	Less Imports	Total
Agriculture, forestry, fishing	82.7	1.5		7.0	−20.3	70.9
Manufacturing	124.0	61.9	20.0	46.0	−107.0	144.9
Construction		23.1				23.1
Services	129.1		40.0	20.8	−18.2	171.7
Indirect taxes less subsidies	40.0					40.0
Public transfers				3.8	−2.2	1.6
Total	375.8	86.5	60.0	77.6	147.7	452.2

Note: The detailed differences in the bases for the second projection as compared to the first are (*a*) Real investment will reach but not exceed the levels of 1974. (*b*) Agricultural output falls by only 2% in 1976 as compared to 1975. (*c*) Agricultural exports remain at their 1975 levels but industrial and service exports each increase by 15%. (*d*) Manufacturing and service imports remain virtually unchanged from the levels of Projection I. (*e*) Some small gains are made in international transfers.

TABLE 10–13

Aggregate Demand Levels Estimated for 1975 Compared with
Projection II for 1976 and Implied Growth Rates in 1975 Prices
(*Millions of contos*)

	1975	1976	Growth Rates
Consumption	364.9	375.8	3.0%
Investment	52.4	86.5	65.1
Government	55.2	60.0	8.7
Exports	65.2	77.6	19.0
Less imports	−116.7	−147.7	26.6
Gross domestic product	421.0	452.2	7.4

TABLE 10–14

Savings-Investment Balances, 1973–1976
(*Millions of contos of each year*)

	1973	1974	1975	Projection I 1976*	Projection II 1976*
Private saving	57.5	50.9	44.5	50.0	50.0
Government saving	7.6	−4.1	−20.0	−17.6	−10.0
Total investment	56.6	72.9	52.4	92.8	86.5
Current account surplus	8.5	−26.1	−27.9	−60.4	−46.5
Exports less imports	−18.5	−54.3	−51.5	−84.0	−70.1
Remittances	27.0	28.2	23.6	23.6	23.6
Total	65.1	46.8	24.5	32.4	40.0

* 1976 estimates are expressed in millions of contos of 1975.

particularly when they are in recession, this is not astounding. But when one considers that the deficit in 1974—the year of the Revolution—was only 1.1 percent of GDP, the change looms large. Few countries have managed almost one year of revolutionary government with essentially a balanced budget!

Table 10-17 contains the government budget implied by Projection II. In this table, government investment is maintained at the same level as shown in Table 10-16 for Projection I, but transfers are reduced to reflect the smaller government deficit of 35.0 contos or 7.8 percent of GDP.

BALANCE OF PAYMENTS POLICY

The economy is a seamless web, and actions aimed at influencing one part of it ultimately impinge on the rest. Nonetheless, it is

TABLE 10–15

Government Receipts and Expenditures, 1975
(*Millions of contos of 1975*)

Receipts		Expenditures	
Direct taxes	45.0	Transfers	57.7
Social Security	25.0	Social Security	30.0
Other central government	16.5	Other	27.7
Other local government	3.5		
		Government consumption	55.2
Indirect taxes	37.6		
Central government	33.5	Government investment	13.0
Local government	4.1		
Miscellaneous revenues	10.3		
Cash deficit	33.0		
Total receipts	125.9	Total expenditures	125.9

TABLE 10–16

Projection I: Government Receipts and Expenditures, 1976
(*Millions of contos of 1975*)

Receipts		Expenditures	
Direct taxes	46.5	Transfers	53.1
Social Security	25.0	Social Security	30.0
Other central government	18.0	Other	23.1
Other local government	3.5		
		Government consumption	60.0
Indirect taxes	40.0		
Central government	35.5	Government investment	25.0
Local government	4.5		
Miscellaneous revenues	9.0		
Cash deficit	42.6		
Total receipts	138.1	Total expenditures	138.1

useful to start policy analysis at some point of extreme tension, such as the balance of payments in Portugal's case. As just mentioned, if investment recovers and there is health growth in real output, the current account deficit might rise to about 60 million contos as in Projection I, or 46.5 million contos in Projection II (see Table 10-18). If suppliers' credits for a substantial fraction of capital goods imports (33 million contos in total in Projection I,

TABLE 10–17

Projection II: Government Receipts and Expenditures, 1976
(*Millions of contos of 1975*)

Receipts		Expenditures	
Direct taxes	46.5	Transfers	45.5
Social Security	25.0	Social Security	28.0
Other central government	18.0	Other	17.5
Other local government	3.5	Government consumption	60.0
Indirect taxes	40.0	Government investment	25.0
Central government	35.5		
Local government	4.5		
Miscellaneous revenues	9.0		
Cash deficit	35.0		
Total receipts	130.5	Total expenditures	130.5

TABLE 10–18

Alternative Projects of Requirements for Balance of Payments Financing

Projection I: Financing the 1976 Trade Deficit (*Millions of 1975 contos*)	
Trade deficit (imports less exports)	84.0
Less emigrant remittances	−23.6
	60.4
Less suppliers' credits for capital goods Imports (one-half of such imports)	−16.4
	44.0
Projection II: Financing the 1976 Trade Deficit (*Millions of 1975 contos*)	
Trade deficit (imports less exports)	70.1
Less emigrant remittances	−23.6
	46.5
Less suppliers' credits for capital goods Imports (one-half of such imports)	−15.5
	31.0

and 31 million contos in Projection II) are obtained, the balance of payments deficit might be around 40 million contos in Projection I or 30 million contos in Projection II. Such deficits could be financed by some combination of gold sales and foreign debt. In a small country, deficits of such magnitude cannot persist indefinitely and steps must be taken to eliminate them. But in the short run the trade gap is unavoidable, and estimates discussed below indicate that, if worse comes to worst, it could in principle be financed by long-term borrowing on gold or outright sales for perhaps two years.

The essential problem is that of the relative competitive power in international trade of Portugal's industries. Increases in wages and import costs in Portugal have been substantial, and as economists of all persuasions have recognized, including socialist economists from Marx on down through Sraffa and Kalecki, money cost increases inevitably get passed along in prices. With costs and prices rising more rapidly for the moment at home than abroad, Portuguese exports are losing competitiveness; new policies are called for. There are various alternative mechanisms to be considered, ranging from increasing the subsidies to firms now being given through the banking system to exchange rate adjustments. In choosing among alternatives, the potential advantages must be considered by providing explicit market signals to the segments of the economy remaining under private control.[5]

The importance of foreign exchange earnings to medium-term development in Portugal suggests that particular attention should be given to export-stimulation policies. Possibilities include (a) generous use of tax drawbacks in favor of export industries—a policy followed with success by South Korea and Brazil; (b) establishment of subrosa export quotas for major firms, another policy followed by those countries; (c) protection of exporters against exchange risk via the Bank of Portugal selling them foreign currency futures at discount; (d) not permitting export industries to be so heavily penalized by wage increases. In the particular case of tourism, Portugal still appears to be price competitive, but a special exchange rate might bolster the confidence of travelers made apprehensive by recent political events.

On the import side, the first thing to recognize is that over one-half of Portugal's imports are intermediate goods, required to maintain production. Another fifth or so are investment goods, which also should not be cut back. Among the remaining imports, the case for high tariffs or quantitative restrictions against cars, consumer durables, their components, and their fuels is clearcut. The quantitative restrictions cut more cleanly, can be rescinded easily in response to manufacturers' sales of Portuguese-made components to branches abroad, and are perhaps to be preferred. In any case, the share of imports affected by such measures will be small, say 5 or 10 percent of the total. This is not an argument against restricting luxury imports, but only an observation that their reduction will not conjure away the balance of payments problem.

Some reductions are also possible in imports of agricultural and food products, especially maize for animal feeding. The value of maize imports was substantial in 1975, in part because of high world prices which are now falling. However, maize is also a luxury good, since it is ultimately used to satisfy a taste for grain-fed beef which is apparently growing in Portugal as in the rest of Western Europe. Scant social harm will result from cutting imports by postponing for some little time the country's acquisition of an unsalubrious taste for cholesterol and protein. Restricting meat demand by letting prices for choice cuts go up while maintaining prices for lower quality beef might be the appropriate policy device.

There is no case at all for reducing staple food imports. Even if agriculture performs badly next year, the volume of staple purchases abroad will not be great, and there is some chance of obtaining special terms from suppliers like the United States or France. Any restriction in staple supplies will lead to sharp price increases in either legal or parallel markets because consumers almost always bid up prices for scarce basic foods as they attempt to avoid doing without. Import restriction would save little foreign exchange, rekindle inflation, and penalize the poor, who would be forced out of staple food markets by price increases much more rapidly than affluent segments of the population.

In the medium term, in order to reduce balance of payments problems, investment should be directed toward export-creating and import-substituting industries. Possible new exports might be ascertained by close study of the trade patterns of Spain or Greece at Portugal's per capita income level and with roughly analogous resource endowments. Choice of import substitution alternatives should be made on the basis of relative costs and benefits. In such projects, measuring returns in terms of foreign exchange benefits *net* of associated foreign exchange costs for intermediate inputs and capital goods is often convenient. Pushing exports rather than import substitutes may be less risky from the point of view of society at large, since if a new export industry cannot compete effectively in foreign markets it is likely to fail. Inefficient import substitution industries can always be kept alive by high enough tariffs and an enterprise once in operation usually comprises enough vested interests, ranging from petty merchants selling to the lowest-paid employees up to the board of directors and local provincial authorities, to call projection forth.

Finally, if it chooses, Portugal should be able to borrow easily because it has a relatively small amount of foreign debt. With political stability, the country will become a more attractive credit risk, for either bankers or direct investors. Regardless of what attitudes the government may finally adopt toward foreign borrowing, steps taken now to establish contacts will create rapport with lenders should Portuguese authorities choose to utilize their services.

FISCAL POLICY

It has already been noted that barring unforeseen revisions downward of food and fuel prices and an extremely rapid European recovery, which would stimulate both Portuguese exports of goods and services and emigrant remittances, the country will have to contend with a large payments deficit. Further, it has been argued that, since the payments deficit is equivalent to a substantial loss of purchasing power within Portugal, the government should run a deficit to create enough demand to maintain a high level of economic activity. The operational questions are how the deficit should be implemented fiscally and the sectors of the economy it should benefit.

The choice of the policy instrument made by government for expansion of the economy is of great importance. Money should be spent sensibly in all ways possible. For example, an obvious area of interest is civil construction. A vastly increased program of civil works will stimulate a lagging sector, create demand for products of state-owned industries, and add very little to the balance of payments deficit. The program might take the form of public works (e.g., acceleration of construction of the Lisbon subway and the irrigation project), investments directed to saving foreign exchange (e.g., renovating the Portuguese fishing fleet), or an attempt to reestablish private housing demand. For housing purchasers, an increase in the terms of mortgages they can obtain or a reduction in down-payment requirements would probably do more to stimulate demand than feasible adjustments in interest rates.

If the government deficit is generated through stimulation of consumption directly via food subsidies or indirectly through wage increases to public employees, the effect on the balance of payments deficit would be larger. Moreover, no new capacity to produce goods and services would be created.

As pointed out above, the deficit actually required to maintain aggregate demand will depend crucially on what happens to exports. Export prospects in turn depend on the rate of recovery in Portugal's major markets. If European recovery is rapid, some increase in taxes might then become appropriate. Plans for this contingency could include stipulation of the foreign trade signals that could trigger a tax increase. In order to improve the Portuguese trade position in the medium term, modernization of existing export industries and investment in new ones will be required.

A *realistic* appraisal of the country's export prospects is an immediate priority area of government activity. This will necessarily bring government functionaries into areas of the economy about which they are relatively uninformed and in which they can learn the myriad details of industrial operation only from people who have long experience in production, marketing, and finance. To put the matter bluntly, the direction of government expenditure in Portugal will require information and expertise which must be acquired as rapidly as possible.

WAGE AND PRICE POLICY

Most of the points which are relevant to wage and price interventions have already been made and are simply summarized here.

1. The two key policy requirements are wise management of government deficit spending and establishment of some sort of control over the wage escalation. In the short, and even medium, term there are all kinds of maneuvers, ranging from crawling peg devaluation to bond indexization which can be used to blunt the impact of inflation. But in the long run, Portugal's economic position will become intolerable if its inflation continues to accelerate or even establishes a trend rate far in excess of that of its trading partners.

When inflation is well established, monetary policy is virtually useless as an instrument of control, as experience in countless Latin American stabilization attempts has shown. Monetary restriction invariably acts first on real output, creating unemployment and harming the poor, while prices continue to surge upward. In these conditions, the only way that the inflation rate can be stabilized is to cut back money wage increases to a steady rate of growth, since import costs must rise domestically in the medium run as the local currency is devalued to retain trade competitiveness and recipients of most nonwage incomes, including the government, sooner or later find ways to retain their real earnings intact.

Under such circumstances, a politically acceptable structure of wage payments growing around the trend rate of inflation must be established. Those wage increases of 1975 which departed most drastically from the average will have to be dissipated by price increases, and undoubtedly some other segments of the labor force will have to be compensated for real income losses. Under these circumstances, establishment of a trend rate of inflation may be impossible, but it is a goal which must be kept in mind.

2. Specific recommendations about wage control require political as well as economic judgments. However, it may be noted that in some cases government spending on things like housing projects for workers, local medical and recreational facilities, and so on can be substituted for money wage increases. Since such spending will *not* be "inflationary" in the usual sense of creating excess aggregate demand, it should be utilized whenever possible. Similarly, emphasis on such fringe benefits as institutionalization of grievance procedures and better pensions may reduce the inflationary impact of 1976 wage settlements.

3. The potential role of price controls in regulating inflation in the Portuguese economy remains obscure, as it does in most places. Rent controls have apparently been effective, and if they are continued some means must be found to replace housing construction activity undertaken by prospective landlords in the past. With strictly controlled rents, such small capitalist investors will simply disappear, perhaps to be replaced by real estate operators who speculate on future inflation and building depreciation. Other controlled prices, for example those of transport services, will probably have to be released sooner or later. The role of price control, if it can actually be applied, should probably be to moderate price fluctuations for staple foods and other necessities, and to permit reasonable price increases or keep government-controlled industries solvent. Widespread, active intervention would tax the capacity of the bureaucracy and divert it from efforts to increase economic productivity in the medium run.

4. Finally, one should not forget that there are surely groups in Portugal, perhaps politically important ones, whose real incomes are going down because of inflation. While it was impossible to

find enough data about the personal distribution of income to make any assessment of this problem, its political and ethical importance means that it should not long be ignored.

FINANCIAL POLICIES

Financial policy should be deployed to support the real economic targets already laid out. Specifically, monetary control should not be used to fight inflation, a task better left to wage and incomes policy. Rather, the objective of the monetary authorities should be to create enough money to support the expansion in nominal income. Assuming that wage increases can be contained, an increase in prices at the rate of 15 to 20 percent combined with real growth of 5 to 7 percent will imply a growth in nominal income in the range of, say, 20 to 27 percent. Accordingly, if money demand remains unchanged relative to income, a corresponding growth in M_1, currency and demand deposits, of the order of magnitude of 25 percent is called for.

Monetary growth at this rate may be difficult to achieve, strange as it may seem. The ordinary source of money creation is in the government budget deficits. But most of the growth in the base will have to derive from domestic credit creation in the form of retirement of public debt, to the extent that this can be significant, and primarily from increased discounting of commercial bank claims. If there is no significant change in the behavior of currency, the required increase in commercial bank liabilities to the central bank will have to be of the order of 25 million contos, representing a dramatic change in the money supply process. The commercial banking system in turn will have to support the money expansion by credit expansion, both to the private sector and nationalized industries. The planned increase in investment spending therefore finds its counterpart on the financial side in bank credit and money expansion.

The fact that monetary expansion will increasingly derive from domestic credit expansion has already been noted. Table 10-6 shows that since March 1974 the source of domestic money creation has no longer been monetization of reserve gains but rather domestic credit creation to finance budget deficits and credit to the domestic private sector and nationalized industries. The world oil price increase, the world recession, the redistribution of income, and the proposed expansionary programs will all be reflected in continued reserve losses on the part of the central bank. While historically of little precedent, this is to be viewed as perfectly normal for a country in Portugal's position.

A question arises whether Portugal will be able to provide the external finance for an expansionary macroeconomic policy of the kind proposed above via a balance of payments deficit and continued reserve losses. For that purpose it is important to recognize that the reserve item in Table 10-6 is primarily made up of gold valued at $40 an ounce. In spite of the recent decline, the actual market price of gold is much higher. Therefore, the book value of the gold reserves seriously understates the resources actually available. While it is unquestionably true that the gold reserves are somewhat illiquid because substantial sales would cause the world price to decline, it can be safely assumed that the reserves are amply sufficient to finance the large balance of payments deficits associated with expansionary programs envisaged in either Projection I or Projection II. It is this particular fact that strongly supports an expansionary policy for now and a disregard for external financing constraints.[6]

The external financing of the trade deficit has relied to a large extent on remittances. It would appear that a policy of the Bank of Portugal which consists of offering exchange rate guarantees on future remittances would prove very fruitful in restoring the confidence necessary to encourage remittances. While such a policy may lead to some capital losses, there is no doubt that it will exert a major effect in terms of confidence and may well prove a source of net foreign exchange savings.

The continuing high rates of inflation make it desirable to make available to savers some form of financial asset that enjoys protection against the depreciation of purchasing power. Here it would seem appropriate to create some form of indexed time deposit, again on a personalized quota basis, that allows an amount of escudos to be held with the benefit of an interest rate at least equal to the actual rate of inflation. Since this savings vehicle is primarily designed for the protection of lower-income groups, the personal allowance needs only to be small and perhaps equal to three months' income. We note that indexation of saving deposits is another of the policies that can be traded off for reduced wage bargains and thus becomes a potentially important part of the macroeconomic policy package.

In the medium term the economic prospects of Portugal depend to a significant extent on its ability to expand the export sector, and in particular those sectors where its mix of wage costs and skill levels compares favorably with those of major competitors, such as the light-manufacturing industries. Therefore, considerable attention should be given to the financial facilities that can be created for these industries, in particular the credit terms for investment in plant and equipment and the export credit terms that these firms can offer. It would appear useful to create an institution, perhaps within the central bank, that is charged specifically with the financial concerns of the export sector.

From a longer term perspective, it becomes important to reshape the financial structure and institutions of Portugal to match the changes in ownership and property structure. Among the questions to be addressed are the relationships between the central bank and the nationalized banking sector. From a viewpoint of monetary policy, the maximum integration is desirable. The efficiency of credit allocation, on the contrary, may call for a maximum of decentralization and discretion at the individual bank level. Since the objectives of monetary policy can reasonably well be implemented by reserve requirements and discounting, it would seem that a fair amount of decentralization will prove desirable. More important is the question of the creation of broader financial markets for debt and equity instruments. A satisfactory savings performance is enhanced by the availability of attractive savings vehicles. The case for some indexed saving deposits has already been noted. The financing of governing deficits by debt creation has, in turn, the side benefit of making monetary policy via open market operation more feasible.

Appendix

In this appendix, the methods used to develop the preceding quantitative assessments of the current Portuguese economic situation are sketched briefly. The main reason for going into some detail here about the calculations is to lay bare the assumptions, heroic and otherwise, which had to be made in our attempt to force Portugal's inadequate statistics into a national accounting balance sheet. Particularly when others with better knowledge of Portugal may be in a position to improve on the guesses made, candor is a virtue. Knowledgeable persons can easily use the techniques, which essentially rely on shameless exploitation of national accounting identities, to come up with more reliable assessments of 1975 and 1976.

The real descriptions of the economy are essentially contained in Tables 10-1, 10-2, and 10-3, giving sets of national accounts for 1973 through 1975. The accounts for the first two of these years are in principle "known." The estimates appearing in the October 1975 IMF report on Portugal were relied upon but these refer only to aggregate GDP and similar concepts. However, a good deal of what is going on in the Portuguese economy at present has differential sectoral impacts: for example, investment demand is low, which hits the construction industry especially hard; agricultural output in 1975 was high; and so on. Therefore, some disaggregation to specific sectors seemed worthwhile.

Basically, the numbers in Tables 10-2 and 10-3 were inferred by using the national accounts estimates of value added at factor cost in each sector as exact reference points. These are given in the far right-hand column headed "Total" in the tables. Reading to the left, tabulated data on imports and exports permit the breakdown of foreign trade by sectors, on a series of assumptions regarding the relationship between the customs categories and our aggregation scheme.[7] Government consumption expenditure was assumed to be divided one-third into manufactured products and two-thirds into services, which are typical shares in most countries, and the major part of investment expenditure not going directly into value added in construction was assumed to be directed toward manufacturing industry. Given these estimates, sectoral consumption levels in the far left-hand column were derived as residuals, as indeed is the aggregate consumption estimate in the official accounts. All indirect taxes were assumed in the final analysis to enter into consumption expenditure, a not unreasonable first-order approximation.[8] To obtain the Table 10-1 estimates of the economic situation in 1975, the following assumptions were made about the economic situation in that year vis-à-vis 1974:

1. Total consumption rose 4 percent in real terms, to account for population increase plus some apparent improvement in real living standards; 22 percent of consumption expenditure went to agriculture, and 33 percent to manufactures.

2. Investment demand fell off by 40 percent, with investment in agriculture going to zero, construction demand falling by 40 percent, and the rest of the decrease affecting manufacturing. Capital goods imports appear to have fallen by 30 to 35 percent in 1975, which is consistent with the 37 percent decrease in investment demand for manufactures.

3. Industrial imports fell by 18 percent overall, while agricultural

and manufactures exports fell by 23 percent and 26 percent respectively. Exports and imports of services (mainly tourism) fell by 30 percent and 35 percent respectively.

4. Agricultural output in a good crop year increased by 7 percent over 1974.

5. Government consumption expenditure and indirect tax receipts stayed constant in real terms.

Using these assumptions, and the accounting identities which must hold down columns and across rows in our tables, a preliminary assessment of the economic situation in 1975 was derived.

Notes

This report is an outcome of an OECD-sponsored mission to Portugal in December 1975 and presented to Dr. José Da Silva Lopes, president of the Banco de Portugal. Neither the OECD nor the Banco de Portugal has any responsibility for its content; that rests entirely with the authors.

1. The many people who provided information are of course not responsible for the use made of it. Also, the estimation methods have been set out in detail in the Appendix, so that people who take exception to our projections can determine the consequences of their own revisions for the overall set of numbers.

2. For example, electricity production in the third quarter was 18 percent below its 1974 level, and showed an apparently more-than-seasonal decrease in relation to the second quarter. Capacity utilization in both consumer and nonconsumer goods manufacturing seems to have fallen since March 1975, according to preliminary results of the *Inquérito de Conjuntura*.

3. On the cost side, the shares of imports, wages, and payments to other factors are about 20, 50, and 30 percent, respectively. Nominal increases of 13 percent in import costs (world price increases plus the tariff surcharge) and 40 percent in wages together with no change in nominal payments to "capital" give a cost inflation estimate of 23 percent. Some of this has no doubt been contained by price controls.

4. Private savings are estimated at 11.1 percent of GDP in 1976, or 5.8 percent of emigrant remittances. Both shares are about one-half percent higher than the corresponding values in 1975, but well below their pre-revolutionary 1973 levels of 28 and 15 percent, respectively. The decline in overall savings effort reflects income redistribution since the Revolution and, in fact, helps offset some of the deflationary impact of foreign saving flowing into Portugal via the balance of payments deficit.

5. A little-noted aspect of the now-subsided 1975 wave of nationalizations is that it largely affected sectors responding to *derived* demands; i.e., industries producing intermediate goods but not final products were nationalized. Such sectors as consumer goods and exports which actually give rise

to intermediate demand were largely left in private hands. Paradoxically, in a highly socialized economy (a conservative estimate would put 50% of economic activity under some sort of state control) the government must still resort to incentives to the private sector to generate demand for the industries it manages. Further, since the leading export sectors—textiles and metallurgical industries—are in highly competitive world markets, the issue of price incentives becomes more crucial still. For the medium term, key sectors in the Portuguese economy are likely to remain capitalist. The government has little choice but to play the price-dominated capitalist game with their owners.

6. The adjustment of the escudo exchange rate and the composition of the foreign exchange and gold reserve portfolio held by Portugal are important issues which require a separate study.

7. The most important assumptions were that 75 percent of "food" imports were agricultural products, while 25 percent of such exports come directly from Portuguese agriculture.

8. The shares of the different sectors in total consumption show reassuring stability in the two years:

Shares in Total Consumption

Sectors	1973	1974
Agriculture	0.2065	0.2120
Manufactures	0.3162	0.3482
Services	0.3472	0.3328
Indirect taxes	0.1301	0.1070

11. The Present Economic Situation: Its Origins and Prospects

MÁRIO MURTEIRA

In order to understand the present "crisis" in Portugal it is necessary to analyze the economic situation. However, an analysis of the present situation makes no sense without looking to the recent past, to the period before the April 25, 1974, MFA coup d'état and what occurred immediately afterward. Just as necessary is an evaluation, no matter how tentative, of the major alternatives for the near future. It is also equally important to make certain methodological qualifications. The economic "crisis" in Portugal is not a mere fluctuation in the level of employment and income, as can be observed in the development of mature capitalism.

During 1974 and for several months into 1975 we witnessed in Portugal increasing class struggle which led to the creation of a "prerevolutionary situation." While that situation changed, after the events at the end of 1975, we are still quite far from a relatively stable society, with an established institutional framework where economic and political activities follow certain fixed rules, even very broad ones. The present rules of the economic and political game in Portugal are still very loose and the "crisis" is, in fact, a tumultuous process of transition and adjustment, developing through a sort of trial-and-error approach. In that context, an orthodox economic analysis of the Portuguese situation would be completely misleading. The economic dimension of the social process has to be understood in terms of a global interaction of different factors, some of them external or exogenous to Portuguese society.

Considering the complexity of the matter, it is rather difficult to attempt a synthesis in a few pages. Instead of attempting a comprehensive, global approach to the subject, I will concentrate on certain economic key questions, those which are in my judgment the most decisive for understanding the Portuguese economic "crisis." Accordingly, I will consider briefly the following topics:

1. The model of economic growth before the April revolution
2. Qualitative changes of the Portuguese economy in 1974/75
3. External dependence and fundamental problems in the present economic situation
4. Alternative possible responses to the present "crisis"

Portuguese Economic Growth over the Last Quarter Century

During the last quarter century, the Portuguese economy underwent the most rapid growth in its history and the process was in almost regular acceleration until the general economic crisis of capitalism began in 1974. Roughly speaking, we can consider two phases in that period, the first covering the fifties and the second, the sixties—following a short period of trouble at the beginning of the decade when the colonial wars started in the Portuguese territories in Africa, and Portugal signed the Stockholm convention that instituted the European Free Trade Association (EFTA). The main difference between the two periods is the much greater openness to and dependence on international capitalism in the second phase.

Around 1950, Portugal had an annual per capita income of under two hundred dollars; 47 percent of the labor force was employed in agriculture; and cork, wolfram, wine, wood, and canned fish accounted for about 70 percent of exports. By the early seventies, per capita income had risen to nearly nine hundred dollars; only one-third of the country's total manpower was employed in agriculture; and more than 60 percent of exports were manufactured goods.

What were the principal factors determining this structural change in the Portuguese economy during these two decades? Obviously, the deeper roots of change lay in the general trends of European capitalism. Portuguese economic growth was not a result of endogenous forces—of either state interventionism or private capitalist development—but mainly a consequence of economic growth in the more advanced European capitalist countries. This is not to say that the state had no role in economic growth or that Portuguese capitalism had no internal capacity for adaptation and development. I wish only to stress the fact that the main changes in the Portuguese economy and society were determined by forces acting from outside its frontiers which shaped the country's internal transformation.

TABLE 11-1

Sectoral Activity Expressed in Terms of
Percentage of GNP (1) and Employment (2)

Sector	1950		1960		1970	
	(1)	(2)	(1)	(2)	(1)	(2)
Primary	28	48	24	44	17	32
Secondary	38	25	34	29	45	33
Tertiary	34	27	42	27	38	35

Source: Planning Ministry (Portugal).

In the early sixties a policy of relative economic autarchy was no longer possible—even in the enlarged context of the Portuguese colonial empire, which was later to be referred to as an integral part of a common regime and, more diplomatically, as a single common Portuguese market. Salazar was first convinced of the necessity of adhering to EFTA in 1960; afterward, in the middle sixties, he was also forced to adopt a more liberal policy in relation to foreign investment. In fact, direct investment came to play an increasing role in the Portuguese economy in the second half of the sixties and the beginning of the seventies.

The conditions of external dependence that acted most vigorously in the Portuguese economy were the following: First, exports and imports grew more rapidly than the national product; this was especially true of imports. Second, the flow of trade with foreign countries also increased more than trade with the colonies. Third, the government tried, simultaneously, to participate in the general movement toward European economic integration and to promote economic and political integration in the escudo area, that is, inside the colonial empire or the "Portuguese common market." In practice, what happened was more a process of economic disintegration, both within Portugal and in the overseas territories. In what sense can we speak of economic disintegration in Portugal?

The economic growth of the country in the sixties was mainly growth in the secondary sector—manufacturing industries and construction. While this growth also had some effect on tertiary activities, it did not induce any positive changes in agriculture. In Table 11-1 we can see the reduction of the primary sector's share in GNP and employment.

At first glance this evolution seems normal and in accord with the historical experience of economic growth in various countries. But, in Portugal this meant the absolute stagnation of agricultural production, with two important consequences: increasing dependence on food imports (in 1973, for instance, imports in grains, fish, and meat counted for about 13% of total imports) and massive exodus from rural areas throughout most of the country.

Industry is restricted to a few limited areas of Portugal, mainly the Lisbon-Setúbal region in the south and the Aveiro-Porto-Braga region in the north. Agriculture is still the principal economic activity in most of Portuguese territory. The archaism of production relationships in agriculture was never seriously attacked by either Salazar's or Caetano's regime.

Massive migration to European countries (not to the colonies or Brazil, as in former periods of Portuguese history) was also a major factor promoting structural change. Between 1960 and 1970 annual emigration underwent a fivefold increase; in fact total population declined during the last of the sixties. One result of this was a relative shortage of labor in Portugal and a certain increase in real wages (although at a rate inferior to that observed in most of the developed European countries).[1] Another consequence was the increasing importance of worker's remittances from abroad as a source of financing the balance of payments.

This process of economic growth can be considered part of the process of *underdevelopment* in the sense that it increased the economy's dependence on factors external to Portugal and implied a growing disadjustment among patterns of production and resource exploitation, monetary demand, and the basic needs of the majority of the population. As income distribution was very unequal—in fact, labor's share of national income was reduced to about 48 percent in 1973—economic growth in Portugal was in practice a limited development, according to a West European pattern of consumption, accessible only to a minority of the population. This situation made possible a favorable balance of payments in which huge reserves of gold and foreign currency equivalent to almost two years of imports were accumulated by the end of 1973.[2] Emigrant remittances, receipts from tourism, foreign currency surpluses from the colonies, and a net increase in direct foreign investment were more than sufficient to finance substantial imports of consumer goods. The fact that foreign trade deficits increased fourfold between 1964 and 1973 consequently posed no serious problems to the general equilibrium of the balance of payments.

In this process of economic growth and social underdevelopment, the weak link was the continuation of the colonial war and the total incapacity of the Caetano regime to find a political solution for it. This single fact explains the thinking behind the desire of others to find a political solution; it alone accounts for the rationale of the MFA coup in April 1974.

Qualitative Changes
in the Portuguese Economy in 1974/75

Between the fall of Caetano's regime and parliamentary elections in April 1976, Portugal had six provisory governments. Each of them was the result of certain precarious relationships between civilian and military political forces and, with the possible exception of the sixth government, all were weak executive bodies, filled with internal tensions and contradictions. What is important here are not the various economic policies pursued by these governments,[3] but rather the main qualitative changes which occurred during those two years.

The first important change has been, obviously, the destruction of a repressive political regime, the principal raison d'être of which was the avoidance of any organized pressure from the workers. It should not be necessary to dwell on this to remember the role of the secret police, or the absence of labor and union rights. The consequence of this change has been a completely new situation in the labor market and the emergence of acute class struggle. Not only has there been strong pressure for higher wages, but also different power relations have emerged at factory, enterprise, and branch levels.

In such a context it is easy to understand that the emergence of new class relations in Portugal led to increasing pressure for nationalization and land reform. In fact, at present, it is in those two areas that the most important structural changes have taken place.

It has been estimated that the public sector of the economy now counts for 25 percent of value added, 24 percent of employment, and 45 percent of investment. Before 1974, the size of the public sector was about 12 percent of value added, 18 percent of employment, and 18 percent of investment. In terms of its contribution to national product and investment, the public sector's share of the economy more than doubled. Nevertheless, this share is still comparable to that of several European capitalist countries, for instance, France and Austria. On the whole, about two hundred firms were nationalized and the holdings of the largest private groups that controlled the essential economic activities in banking, finance, and industry are now in the state's hands.

TABLE 11–2

Distribution of Portugal's Foreign Trade by World Areas

	1964		1973		1974		1975*	
	Imp.	Exp.	Imp.	Exp.	Imp.	Exp.	Imp.	Exp.
OECD countries	72.7	64.1	76.7	78.9	72.2	79.0	69.8	79.7
EEC and EFTA	*54.2*	*45.9*	*56.5*	*62.5*	*53.5*	*62.8*	*48.4*	*65.5*
Other	*18.5*	*18.2*	*20.2*	*16.4*	*18.7*	*16.2*	*21.4*	*14.2*
Ex-colonies	14.9	25.1	10.1	14.8	10.5	11.0	5.3	8.8
Eastern Europe	1.3	1.3	1.4	0.6	1.3	0.9	2.3	2.2
Oil-producing countries†	4.9	0.4	2.5	0.2	6.3	0.2	11.7	0.3
Other	6.2	9.1	9.3	5.5	9.7	8.9	10.9	9.0
Total	100	100	100	100	100	100	100	100

Source: Planning Ministry (Portugal).
* January–November.
† Saudi Arabia, Bahren, Iran, and Iraq.

As far as land reform is concerned, the large latifundia in the south of the country were occupied by the workers. Some 1,300 large landowners have had their property expropriated, *de facto* if not *de jure*, and one million hectares are now being exploited in collective units. These changes in traditional productive relations have involved, more or less directly, 250,000 workers. Nevertheless, agriculture in the center and north of Portugal has remained practically unchanged.

In short, we can regard the principal qualitative changes in the Portuguese economy since 1974 as the result of a *mass movement against the major centers of private economic power*, mainly monopolies and latifundia, that emerged from the destruction of the old repressive political and social regime.

The above-mentioned structural changes in the Portuguese economy—changes that we cannot consider as definitive, since they depend on the future political evolution of the country—signified, in practice, the destruction of a certain economic order. Considering the political instability and the continuing struggle for power, it is not surprising that few if any steps have been taken to set up a *new* economic system. During these two uncertain years, two attempts were made to elaborate a medium-term economic plan, but both failed, due to the absence of a necessary minimum of political consensus.

In Table 11-2 we can observe the geographic structure of Portugal's foreign trade (in percentage terms). The great majority of this trade is concentrated in the OECD area, yet the part played by central planning economies in that trade is very small. The net decrease of Portuguese exports and imports to its former colonies is, at the moment, the most important change in the structure of the country's external trade. What the picture in Table 11-2 shows is an increasing trade dependence of Portugal relative to the capitalist countries, above all the European industrialized nations. Development of trade relations with Third World countries will depend on, among other things, the stabilization of Portugal's new political relations with the young nations that have emerged from the long liberation wars in Portuguese Africa.

One major point that deserves special mention in discussing recent structural changes in Portugal is the employment situation. The trend of decreasing population, mentioned before, has been completely reversed, not only because of a reduction of emigration to Europe, but chiefly because of the return of more than 350,000 people from Africa, most of them from Angola. The general employment situation over the last decade was one in which there was a relative shortage of labor, and economic growth was accompanied by a reduction in the size of the economically active population. It is hard to imagine a situation of this kind in the years to come.

External Dependence and Fundamental Problems in the Economic Situation

The complexity and gravity of the present economic "crisis" are easy to understand if we think of the different sorts of disturbing factors that have converged upon the "normal" functioning of the Portuguese economy: world economic crisis, disintegration of a repressive political and social regime lasting almost forty years, increasing class struggles, incapacity of the new political structure to rebuild the economic system, and chaotic decolonization of Angola.

Production decreased 3 percent in 1975, mainly in capital goods industries and consumption. Obviously, private investment has practically ceased, and public investment cannot compensate for this decline. Unemployment is about 10 percent of the resident active population, not including 70,000 unemployed people recently returned from Angola; the total number of unemployed workers is now probably above 400,000.

After a substantial reduction in the inflation rate during 1975, the cost of living is again increasing very fast, despite the austerity measures decided on by the government of Mário Soares. During 1976 the rate of inflation probably reached the same order of magnitude (an almost 40% increase per year) registered in the first months of 1974, before the Revolution, when Portugal experienced at the time one of the highest rates of inflation in Europe.

As for the balance of payments, Portugal lost in 1974 and 1975 about 40 billion escudos of its reserves, and according to trends at the time of writing, the exhaustion of the gold owned by the Bank of Portugal will occur during 1978, even assuming a rather optimistic set of hypotheses. Imports are now about twice the value of exports, and the prospects for increasing either emigrant remittances or tourism receipts are not enough to compensate for the huge deficit in the trade balance.

It is clear that the Portuguese economic "crisis" is much deeper than a short-term recession in a capitalist society, given a stable institutional framework. The economic structure of the country is obviously in transition, but it is not easy to capture the ultimate direction of that transition. Transition toward socialism? The word *socialism* has far too many different meanings, particularly in Portugal. It is perhaps worth mentioning the fact that all but one of the four dominant political parties in the country present themselves as defenders of the best way to a socialist development of the Portuguese economy and society.

In fact, it is perhaps useful to separate two sets of factors acting on economic structure. On the one hand, we have the important qualitative changes mentioned above, resulting from the workers' fight against private economic power. On the other hand, there are the changes in the external involvement of the Portuguese economy in the world economy, resulting from decolonization and the international economic crisis of capitalism, not to mention the consequences of the internal transformation of Portuguese society itself.

There are two major structural problems in the present economic situation, one being unemployment and the other, the balance of payments' deficit. The disadjustment of the traditional economic growth model, in relation to these two problems, is quite obvious. It took almost a quarter of a century to create in the secondary sector of the economy the number of jobs equivalent to the present number of unemployed resident workers. That sort of growth model is not employment generating, and it must be completely changed if massive emigration is no longer possible and a reduction in the actual rate of unemployment is considered to be the first priority of the country's economic policy strategy.

With respect to the balance of payments, import substitution and export promotion do not seem practicable over the short run, at least in the necessary magnitude and speed considering the time limits set for the exhaustion of the country's gold reserves. Change in the actual levels and patterns of consumption seems feasible only in a process of revolutionary transition to socialism that is now out of the question. Much more probable is a situation of increasing dependence on foreign economic and financial support, with a corresponding reduction of internal freedom of choice for Portuguese policy makers.[4]

Possible Alternative Responses to the Economic "Crisis"

After five centuries of world expansion and more or less romantic adventures and misadventures in different continents, Portugal seems definitively condemned to finding a place in Europe, even if in South America and Africa new Portuguese-speaking nations are in a position to play an increasing role in world affairs. The transition problem for Portugal, even in economic terms, must be transition toward Europe. However, even if we accept this view, it is obvious not only that Europe is capitalist but also that it too is in the midst of a difficult process of transition.

For several months during 1974 and 1975, it seemed possible that Portugal would assume a certain autonomous role in the current process of social change in Europe. As has happened before, what has since become more plausible is the domination of the Portuguese process by forces acting from the outside. The present political situation in the country, where the leading parties are clearly pro-Western and nonrevolutionary, confirms that view. The great question would seem to be the possibility of overcoming a *structural economic crisis*, the dimensions of which I have tried to describe, with a political structure of a Western European type.

If that possibility should be foreclosed, it remains to be seen what course the country will take, given the real strength of the mass movement which has emerged from the April "revolution." However, even if the romantic populism of certain MFA leaders, now apparently out of the political game, is discredited and harmless, it is difficult to imagine in this country, in the near future, a reactionary military regime, as we can find in some Latin American countries.

A more distinct possibility is continuation of the (now) convergent process of learning and adjustment between civilian and military political forces, searching for some equilibrium point in class relations in Portugal, in order to find finally a more truly "representative" political structure and a stable system of power, distinct from that created by Salazar in the thirties—a system that is no longer possible.

Whatever occurs, the economic situation will be *more determining rather than determined* relative to the political process in Portugal, because there is not yet a stable system of power with a corresponding basis of support.

In a recent article about Portugal, Paul Sweezy has written: "Engels somewhere remarked that it was a sure thing that on the day after the revolution the entire opposition would be solidly united under the banner of pure democracy."[5] In Portugal, after the revolutionary situation of 1975, such "democratic unity" turned out to be the first stage of counterrevolution. With the increasing strength of conservative forces, we have reason to fear that the movement of the pendulum from left to right will reach some steady position not even remotely "democratic."

It is also worth mentioning, in this context, the reflections of a British economist, Dudley Seers, who, on facing the situation of an underdeveloped dependent economy, suffering from inflation, unemployment, and external disequilibrium, raised the following question: "Could structural problems be drastically resolved by adopting central planning and comprehensive controls, including extensive nationalization, higher taxation, wage mobilization, mobilizing youth for work in the countryside, and by breaking away politically from the United States—what one can conveniently summarize as the 'Cuban solution'?"[6]

Among the different conditions making such an alternative possible, Seers saw the following as most important: "It is hard to imagine a Cuban system without a political organization permeating the bureaucracy, to ensure that controls are operated without corruption and to induce the public to accept the sacrifices required. An organization of this type and on this scale emerges gradually during an armed struggle with both nationalist and social objectives, involving a large section of the population, judging from historical experience (e.g., Soviet Union and China, as well as Cuba) and *only during such a struggle*."[7]

The MFA facilitated the liberation of Portugal's ex-colonies. It brought down a political regime in Portugal. But today the idea of the MFA as a national liberation movement is no more than an illusion of the past.

Notes

1. This was also a consequence of the increasing size of the armed forces, owing to the colonial war.

2. The gold reserves' value at market prices.

3. For a discussion of the economic policies of these provisory governments, see Mário Murteira, "Política económica dos governos provisórios," *Economia e Socialismo* (Lisbon), April 1976.

4. For a discussion of alternative economic strategies in Portugal, see Mário Murteira, "Portugal: O problema da independência económica," *Análise Social* (Lisbon), no. 44 (1975).

5. Paul Sweezy, "Class Struggles in Portugal," *Monthly Review*, September 1975, p. 13 n. To this he adds: "One appreciates the profundity of the observation when one reads day after day in the *New York Times* and other loyal apologists of capitalism and imperialism about the dread-

ful violations of democracy (and socialism too, no less!) perpetrated by the wicked Portuguese militarists. And if someone says to me that I malign the Portuguese Socialist Party by calling it bourgeois and tries to drive home the point with the assertion that it is no more bourgeois than most of the other European socialist parties, I answer: Exactly so—neither more nor less."

6. Dudley Seers, "A Step towards a Political Economy of Development," in *Third World Employment*, ed. Richard Jolly et al. (Baltimore: Penguin Education Books, 1973), p. 409.

7. Ibid., p. 410.

Epilogue

STANLEY G. PAYNE

If, less than a decade ago, studies on contemporary Portugal in the social sciences seemed almost nonexistent, the present volume indicates that substantial progress has been made in recent years. This is, of course, no more than a beginning, but it can help point the way to the kind of research that is needed if we are to gain a deeper and fuller understanding of twentieth-century Portugal commensurate even with the level of knowledge about contemporary Spain.

It is a commonplace that until very recently Portugal was largely ignored because the country seemed small, backward, and insignificant. Size, however, is a function not merely of the dimensions of an individual case under study but also of the range, spectrum, or category of political and social developments in which a country is involved. The problems of transformation and modernization of Portugal can now be seen as in no way isolated phenomena, but typical of a broad spectrum of south European and Luso-Hispanic countries. Similarly, the backwardness of Portugal refers primarily to its slow rate of technological and industrial development. The cultural norms of its elites, the social norms of many of its inhabitants, the precocious alterations of its political superstructures, and its active colonial expansion in modern times have not been very backward at all, but in some aspects remarkably swift and rapid adjustments to new political, cultural, and international trends. The significance of modern Portugal is directly related to these considerations and to the broader place of the Portuguese world in global affairs, down to the apparent stabilization of the Portuguese revolution in 1976.

Portugal can probably be considered the oldest unaltered nation-state in the world. The historic identity of the national state, together with Portugal's complete cultural identification with the philosophical, juridical, and civic norms of Western Europe, encouraged an unusually early transition to the formal structure of elite, or "censitary," liberalism in the 1820s.[1] There was perhaps little remarkable in this, since the entire Luso-Hispanic world in the Americas began to adopt the formal constitutional systems of parliamentary liberalism while failing almost completely to achieve a functioning operation thereof. In Portugal, the challenge of the reactionary neotraditionalist right was faced and overcome earlier (by 1833) than in any other country, and Portugal was the first polity in the south European and Luso-Hispanic worlds to develop a stable and functioning censitary liberal system (by the 1850s). Such nominal civic precocity during the first half of the nineteenth century may perhaps be attributed not merely to the factors listed above but also to the relative size and relative homogeneity (or limited diversity) of the country and, inversely, to the lack of urbanization and new socioeconomic foci or centrifugal pressures that made Portugal rather easier to govern than many contemporary states in that period.

The course of Portuguese civic development, and its limitations, may be scrutinized with reference to the "crisis-sequence" theory developed by the Social Science Research Council's Committee on Political Change in 1967–70. This theory posits a normal five-phase or five-crisis sequence of political problems in the modern nation-state polity, concluding that the failure to surmount any one of the crises at a later stage of development unravels the system and resurrects the problems associated with the earlier phases. The crisis sequences are, in order, identity, legitimacy, participation, penetration (and access), and finally distribution.[2]

As suggested above, national identity has never been at issue in modern Portugal, at least in the most formal sense, and this made it easier to move at an early date to resolution of the legitimacy of the modern liberal polity. The problem of participation in the political system was soon resolved in its preliminary phase by the stabilization of a censitary, politically dualist regime. Yet the greater problem of participation, so much at issue for most states by the end of the nineteenth century, proved very hard to resolve in Portugal. Formal concession of universal male suffrage, adopted elsewhere in southern Europe between 1890 and 1913, was never introduced at any time in Portugal until complete universal suffrage finally went into practice in 1975. The direct problem of civic participation thus remained much more at issue in Portugal than in any other polity at a similar approximate level of development in the early twentieth century. This protracted restrictiveness, or elitism, has, among other things, induced a certain school of interpretation, led by Howard Wiarda, to posit the inherit "corporatism," for want of a better term, of Portuguese institutions.

The breakdown of the liberal constitutional monarchy in 1910 was not due exclusively to a crisis of participation that revived the question of the legitimacy of the regime. It was due also to broader problems of access and penetration in the structural modernization of the country, and in its ambiguous, uncertain role within the general framework of Western imperialism. It was the curious fate of the First Republic (1910–1926) to fail to resolve either of these problems, though in various ways a fresh start was made with both. The First Republic was not a democratic system, due to continuing censitary restrictions on illiterate peasants and also to a general domination of the political/electoral machinery much of the time by the Democratic Party. Its sixteen years were the most politically chaotic of any single European (and probably also Luso-Hispanic) state in the twentieth century. The fragmentation of the political system was the more impressive given its restrictive nature, though the resulting problems of personalism, factionalism, and status rivalry have commonly been encountered at approximately the same level in Latin American polities that also experience circular political processes which fail to achieve a more complex threshold of organization.

The absence of mobilization had clearly become a salient characteristic of Portuguese political society by the 1920s, and this was true compared even with other economically backward societies in the eastern part of southern Europe. In the Balkans, the clash with foreign imperialism and the stimulus of intense, pugnacious nationalism to some extent served as catalysts for a greater degree of mobilization than general social conditions might otherwise have permitted. The historic identity of Portugal, together with its unique colonial role, discouraged the emergence of any sort of active twentieth-century nationalist movement in Portugal, where specific frustrations and conflict over foreign affairs and colonial policy instead took the more limited form of elite and semi-elite controversies over policy access. Thus, in terms of the limited circularity of political conflict under the First Republic, the final breakdown in 1926 was the conclusion of a process in some respects more similar to contemporary breakdowns in Chile, Argentina, and also Greece than to the more common patterns of breakdown that occurred between 1922 and 1936 in other south European countries.

At the same time, the broader dimensions of slowly expanding social conflict—and the crisis of distribution, to use the language of the sequence theory previously employed—should not be ignored. Revolutionary syndicalism and socialism or communism, while never attaining the scope that would seem to threaten the entire system as did their analogues in Italy and Spain, nonetheless contributed to the overloading of the First Republic. Despite the low overall mobilization of the polity, such sociopolitical pressures potentially foreshadowed a more radical type of twentieth-century European conflict.

As the protracted political struggles over participation and access, together with the hesitant emergence of new problems of distribution, finally destroyed the parliamentary regime, the basic question of institutionalization was reopened once more. What was at first surprising and initially almost unique was that the military overthrow of the liberal system in 1926 proved definitive for half a century, eventually producing the second institutionalized new authoritarian system in southern Europe. Alone among south European and Luso-Hispanic countries, Italy had moved directly from the abrogation of parliamentarianism to a continuously institutionalized regime without the false starts and circular convolutions of nearly all the other dictatorships of the 1920s, but Portugal followed course only a few years later.

To what was the early "success" of Salazarism due? Proponents of the thesis that the Estado Novo merely codified a more explicitly authoritarian brand of "Portuguese corporatism" must themselves bear the burden of proof, for prior to the 1920s there was virtually no corporative theory extant in Portuguese politics, and what little there was had been translated fairly directly from Catholic and right-wing theorists in other lands. Drastic systemic changes depend above all else on leadership, and the emergence of Salazar, Carmona, and a few other key figures of their circle was no doubt indispensable to the process. Conversely, the circumstances of "historical conjuncture" can explain little, for at the very same time Spain's first modern venture in authoritarian government broke down completely (1930–1931). The fact that Portugal, unlike Spain, had still not entered the era of mass politics had something to do with it, for a still largely unmobilized society was easier to regiment and repress. Similarly, Salazar did not have to develop (or confront) any radical new mass movement of revolutionary nationalism, such as fascism, national socialism, or the Romanian Iron Guard.

The term "fascism" has been used with tedious frequency in recent years both inside and outside Portugal to refer to the Salazarean system, but of course there was never any Portuguese equivalent of the original Italian fascist movement. The Estado Novo was of a different and much more common type: the syncretic and semipluralistic right authoritarian systems that dominated nearly all of eastern and southern Europe as well as much of Latin America in the years before World War II. Indeed this was the most common and distinctive new regime type of the first half of the twentieth century, and somewhat similar systems continue to emerge in parts of the Third World during the 1970s. Such regimes had little to do with fascism, and Salazar drew a clear distinction between the erstwhile principles of the rightist Estado Novo as distinct from revolutionary fascist or leftist movements, on the one hand, and more aggressive, radical new nationalist regimes like that of Italy or Germany, on the other.

If the Estado Novo was not so anomalous a regime as it appeared at first glance in the post-1945 context of Western Europe, its politics and elite structure were more complicated than has generally been supposed, and Schmitter's study helps to erase the simplistic shibboleths about the rule of the "landed oligarchy," the "*comprador* bourgeoisie," and other such phrases. The identity and bases of the leadership elements in non-Marxist authoritarian regimes must be studied empirically and on their own terms rather than by means of theoretical abstractions and ideological preconceptions. What Schmitter has done so well for the first years of the Salazar regime ought now to be extended across the whole range of the Estado Novo to gain a clearer understanding of the continuities and changes in elite leadership and recruitment, particularly in the quarter-century after 1945.

The same holds to an even greater extent for the long history of Portuguese pretorianism, which has now been seriously examined almost for the first time by the studies in this volume and the very recent books by Douglas Wheeler and Douglas Porch. Nothing comparable to the treatment of pretorianism in Spain, Greece, or Latin America exists in the case of Portugal, even though the record of Portuguese pretorianism is one of the longest in the world, going back to 1817 and thus second only by a few years to that of Spain. The "rich" history of Portuguese pretorianism has spanned the three classic phases of pretorianism in the Mediterranean and Latin American worlds, namely, the liberal pretorianism of the nineteenth century (one of whose last major expressions was the Portuguese revolt of 1910), the right authoritarian pretorianism of the first half of the twentieth century (one of whose first manifes-

tations occurred in Portugal in 1915), and the radical transforma-
tional/modernizing pretorianism of the second half of the twentieth
century, whose only exemplar in Europe has been exactly the Portuguese case.

The politics of the Portuguese military has never represented a
single political sector but rather has spanned the entire larger spectrum of Portuguese political society. That was as true in 1825 as
in 1975. A major achievement of Wheeler's work in this volume
is to expound systematically the variety and extent of military resentment and revolt against the Estado Novo, even in its presumed
heyday.

Nonetheless, the Portuguese military coup of 1974 has seemed
unique because it constituted the only occasion in which the army
of a significant European colonial power rebelled against the home
imperial regime in the midst of a major conflict to retain colonial
sovereignty. Some interpreted this to mean that Portugal either was
no longer or never had been a "Western" country due to its limited
economic development, but the downfall of the Estado Novo and
the onset of the Portuguese revolution did not entirely deviate from
earlier European patterns, given the drastic changes in context that
had developed by the 1970s. With the single exception of post-Franco
Spain, all previously institutionalized modern European authoritarian systems since the time of Napoleon I have fallen primarily
through external rather than internal pressure—concretely through
defeat in war (France, 1815 and 1870; Italy, 1943; Germany, 1945;
the East European dictatorships, 1939 to 1945). The Portuguese
military revolt occurred only after a large sector of the officer corps
had concluded that the regime had either been defeated in Africa
or was engaged in an unwinnable war due to drastic changes in
the international context. In this, as in so many other ways, the
unique or seemingly odd features of Portuguese institutions and
politics differ less severely from general European norms than seems
the case at first glance.

Even so, only the merest beginning has been made in the study
of modern Portugal, either at home or abroad, and the range of further questions posed by the research in the present volume is very
extensive. They begin, of course, with history in the most basic
sense, for, despite the valiant efforts of Oliveira Marques, Wheeler,
and a number of Portuguese historians, the basic history of modern
Portugal is still to a large degree unexplored. We do not even have
complete narratives of many of the most important episodes, much
less systematic investigation of social, economic, or institutional

history. Much of the nineteenth century in Portugal still remains a somewhat generalized blur. The two scholars just mentioned have done much to clarify our understanding of the First Republic, but monographic work on the major groups or problems of early-twentieth-century Portuguese affairs is almost totally lacking. As usual, somewhat more attention has been devoted to the left than to other groups by scholars and writers, but even there most topics have been treated in only fragmentary fashion.

As the Estado Novo recedes into history, an increasing amount of material will become available to students. There, too, almost everything is yet to be done, in terms of both the "inner history" of the regime (if indeed that ever becomes possible) and its institutional functions. Comparative study with the other right authoritarian systems of southern Europe also deserves careful attention. Lucena and Wiarda have particularly focused on the limited and abortive reforms of the *caetanato*. This crucial transition period will merit considerable study, as will the major phases of the struggle in Africa and the traumatic decolonization of 1974–75. It is obviously premature to speak of the history of the Portuguese revolution since as of the date of writing it has still not completely come to an end. This is obviously a grand topic that will attract a great deal of interest in the future.

The merest beginning has been made in the study of Portuguese society both as a whole and with respect to its principal sectors, particularly concerning their relationship to politics and broader economic issues. Perhaps the predominant theme in this volume, in one sense or another, has been the sociology of political change, and in that regard, most of the papers raise at least as many questions as they answer. Major investigation of the institutional and political sociology of the military, along the lines of the studies of Busquets for Spain and Stepan for Brazil, are badly needed. Although we have learned something about the historical geography of certain elites and of the capacity of the main parties during the Revolution to mobilize among certain social groups and in certain geographic areas, most aspects of the interconnections between society and the new parties (or the old institutions or the old opposition) are yet to be examined. While a beginning has been made in the anthropological study of peasant society, this should encourage extension into the realms of economics and sociology.

We have only begun to get beyond the obvious cliché of the underdevelopment of the Portuguese economy to a more precise examination of its institutions and functioning. Major differences and imbalances emerged in the course of this underdevelopment, yet they are mostly understood in a general and haphazard way. The distinctions between "growth" and "development" during the second half of the Estado Novo have been mentioned by several commentators but require more complete analysis. Finally, the new Portuguese economic system, whose outlines are now only vaguely descried, will apparently represent a bolder venture into a partially socialistic variant of social democracy than anything yet seen in northern Europe. Its future course will attract worldwide attention. The short-term effects of all drastic revolutions are destructive not constructive, and in the two years from 1974 to 1976 the Revolution lived in part off capital reserves accumulated by the Estado Novo. The achievement of a new level of full production will be extremely difficult, but if it can be done the Portuguese model will become a much more attractive paradigm than, for example, the "Yugoslav path to socialism." The present historical conjuncture is obviously an extremely difficult one that will handicap such a process, but the Portuguese case may turn out to have predictive potential as a forerunner rather than a delayed-development model. As Spain returns to pluralist democracy, so-called Eurocommunism gains strength in Italy, and the French left bids to take over the government of the Fifth Republic, a new advance in social democracy under political freedom could serve as an example for the transformation of southwestern Europe. The problems involved—for Portugal, as for other "Latin" countries—are so staggering that it is altogether premature to predict any lasting success, but Portugal has finally earned a chance for the last to become first.

Notes

1. The term "censitary liberalism" refers to the original form of liberal government in Western Europe which restricted the suffrage to a limited body of the wealthier citizenry according to the census of income and tax ratings.
2. Leonard Binder et al., *Crises and Sequences in Political Development* (Princeton, N.J.: Princeton University Press, 1971), p. viii.

Appendix

First Meeting: University of New Hampshire, October 10–14, 1973

FIRST SESSION: GENERAL BACKGROUND
ON MODERN PORTUGAL

Co-Chairpersons: Joyce F. Riegelhaupt (Anthropology, Sarah Lawrence College), Douglas L. Wheeler (History, University of New Hampshire)

Papers: Hermínio Martins (Sociology, St. Anthony's College, Oxford)

Joel Serrão, (History, Technical University, Lisbon), "Decadence and Regeneration in Contemporary Portugal"

PROBLEMS AND PROSPECTS FOR
RESEARCH TODAY IN PORTUGAL

Discussants: Henry H. Keith (History, University of Brasilia, Brazil), Joyce F. Riegelhaupt, Douglas L. Wheeler, Susan Schneider (History, University of Massachusetts, Boston)

SECOND SESSION: THE FIRST PORTUGUESE
REPUBLIC, 1910–1926

Chairperson: Stanley G. Payne (History, University of Wisconsin)

Papers: Douglas L. Wheeler, "Situation Obscure—the 28th of May Movement and the Fall of the Parliamentary Republic"

Richard A. Robinson (History, University of Birmingham, England), "The Religious Question and the Catholic Revival in Portugal, circa 1900–1930"

Discussants: John Vincent-Smith (History, Britannia Royal Naval College, Dartmouth, England), Thomas C. Bruneau (Political Science, University of Montreal)

THIRD SESSION: EDUCATION AND THE ECONOMY IN MODERN PORTUGAL

Chairperson: Thomas C. Bruneau

Papers: Henry H. Keith, "Point, Counterpoint in Reforming Portuguese Education: 1950–1973"

Francisco Pereira de Moura (Economics, Technical University, Lisbon), "The Development of the Portuguese Economy: 1945–1973"

Discussants: Carlos Picado Horta (Business School, Columbia University; on leave from the Secretariado Técnico, Lisbon), G. Mars (Sociology, University of Pittsburgh)

FOURTH SESSION: OPEN DISCUSSION OF PROBLEMS OF PORTUGUESE IMMIGRATION

Chairperson: Hermínio Martins

FIFTH SESSION: PORTUGUESE CORPORATISM

Chairperson: Lawrence S. Graham (Government, University of Texas, Austin)

Papers: Philippe C. Schmitter (Political Science, University of Chicago), "Corporatist Interest Representation and Public Policy Making in Portugal"

Howard J. Wiarda (Political Science, University of Massachusetts, Amherst), "The Portuguese

Corporative System: Basic Structures and Current Functions"

Discussant: Douglas Chalmers (Public Law and Government, Columbia University)

SIXTH SESSION: THE MODERN PORTUGUESE STATE

Chairperson: Douglas L. Wheeler

Papers: Harry M. Makler (Sociology, University of Toronto), "Political Men among the Portuguese Industrial Elite"

Lawrence S. Graham, "Portugal: The Bureaucracy of Empire"

Peter McDonough (Institute for Social Research, University of Michigan), "Intra-Elite/Mass Study Designs"

Discussant: Juan J. Linz (Political Science and Sociology, Yale University)

SEVENTH SESSION: CONTEMPORARY RURAL PORTUGAL

Chairperson: Michael Kenny (Anthropology, Catholic University of America)

Papers: Twig Johnson (Anthropology, Columbia University), "Ethnography of Work in a Portuguese Fishing Village"

Joyce F. Riegelhaupt, "Peasants and Politics in Portugal: The Corporate State and Village 'Nonpolitics'"

Discussant: Patricia Goldey (Anthropology, London School of Economics)

EIGHTH SESSION: OPEN DISCUSSION OF RESEARCH DESIGNS, PROBLEMS, AND PROPOSALS ON PORTUGAL

Chairperson: Juan J. Linz

Second meeting: Yale University, March 28–29, 1975

FIRST SESSION: JUAN J. LINZ,
"INTRODUCTORY REMARKS"

Papers: Philippe C. Schmitter, "Retrospective and Prospective Thoughts about the Liberation of Portugal"

Peter McDonough, "Structural Factors in the Decline and Fall of Portuguese Corporatism"

SECOND SESSION

Papers: Rhona M. Fields (Sociology, Clark University), "The MFA and the Non-State Nations of Portuguese Africa: Symbiotic Revolutions"

Eusebio Mujal (Political Science, Massachusetts Institute of Technology), "Communist Parties in Spain and Portugal"

Frank L. Casale and Kenneth M. Coleman (Political Science, University of Kentucky), "On Predicting the Electorate Appeal of Political Parties in Portugal: Social Structure and Partisanship in a Post-Corporatist Latin Political Culture"

THIRD SESSION

Paper: Harry M. Makler, "The Portuguese Industrial Elite and Its Corporative Relations: A Study of Compartmentalization in an Authoritarian Regime"

FOURTH SESSION: OPEN DISCUSSION OF PORTUGUESE SOCIAL STRUCTURE AND ELECTORATE SURVEY

Chairperson: Juan J. Linz

Participants: Thomas C. Bruneau, Frank L. Casale, Kenneth M. Coleman, John L. Hammond (Sociology, Columbia University), John Logan (Sociology,

State University of New York at Stony Brook),
Peter McDonough, Harry M. Makler, Joyce F.
Riegelhaupt, Philippe C. Schmitter, Douglas L.
Wheeler, Howard J. Wiarda

Third Meeting: University of Toronto, April 16–17, 1976

FIRST SESSION: THE SALAZAR/CAETANO
REGIME AND ITS BREAKDOWN

Chairperson: David L. Raby (History, University of Toronto)

Papers: Philippe C. Schmitter, "Social Origins, Economic Bases and Political Imperatives of Authoritarian Rule in Portugal"

Mário Murteira (Economics, Universidade Técnica de Lisboa), "The Origins and Characteristics of the Portuguese Economic Crisis"

Discussants: Harry M. Makler, César Oliveira (Gabinete de Investigações Sociais, Universidade de Lisboa), Stanley G. Payne

SECOND SESSION: THE ORIGINS AND
FUNCTIONING OF THE MFA

Chairperson: Thomas C. Bruneau

Papers: Douglas L. Wheeler, "The Military and the Portuguese Dictatorship, 1926–1974: The Honor of the Army"

Lawrence S. Graham, "The Military and the Revolution in Portugal: The Politicization of the Armed Forces"

Rhona M. Fields, "The Political Intervention of the MFA from April 1974 to March 1975"

Discussants: Robert Jackson (Political Science, Carlton University, Ottawa), António R. Bandeira (York University and Ciência Política, Universidade Técnica de Lisboa), Florestan Fernandes (São Paulo)

THIRD SESSION: THE CULTURAL RESPONSE

Chairperson: Ivana Versiani (Hispanic Studies, University of Toronto)

Paper: Alexandrino Severino (Spanish and Portuguese, Vanderbilt University), "Literary Trends since the Revolution"

Comments: Fernando Martinho (Portuguese Literature, University of California, Santa Barbara)

Paper: Caroline Brettell (Anthropology, Brown University), "Emigration and Its Implications for the Revolution in Northern Portugal"

Discussants: Joyce F. Riegelhaupt, David Gregory (Anthropology, Dartmouth College)

FOURTH SESSION: CIVIL SOCIETY: POLITICAL PARTIES, THE LABOR MOVEMENT, AND THE CHURCH

Chairperson: J. H. Galloway (Geography, University of Toronto)

Papers: Thomas C. Bruneau, "The Role of the Catholic Church in Portuguese Politics"

César Oliveira, "The Labor Movement and the Political Parties before and after the 25th of April"

John L. Hammond, "The Elections of April 1975 and the Popular Political Movements"

Discussants: Twig Johnson (Anthropology, University of Maine), Howard J. Wiarda, Grant Amyont (Political Studies, Queen's University)

FIFTH SESSION: PORTUGAL AND
THE AFRICAN CONNECTION

Chairperson: R. Cranford Pratt (Political Economy, University of Toronto)

Papers: John Saul (Political Science, York University), "Decolonization in Portuguese Africa and Its Impact on Portugal"

René Pélissier (The Sorbonne, Paris), "Notes on the Second Angolan War"

Fernando Martinho, "The Meaning of Hope: An Approach to African Poetry in Portuguese"

Discussants: Gerald J. Bender (Political Science, University of California at Los Angeles), Jonathan Barker (Political Economy, University of Toronto)

SIXTH SESSION: THE INTERNATIONAL PROJECTION OF THE REVOLUTION AND THE FUTURE PROSPECTS FOR PORTUGAL

Papers: Gabriel Fischer (Political Science, Acadia University), "Portugal and the Western Press, 1974 –1976"

António R. Bandeira, "Recent Developments in the MFA"

Discussants: Mário Murteira, Douglas L. Wheeler